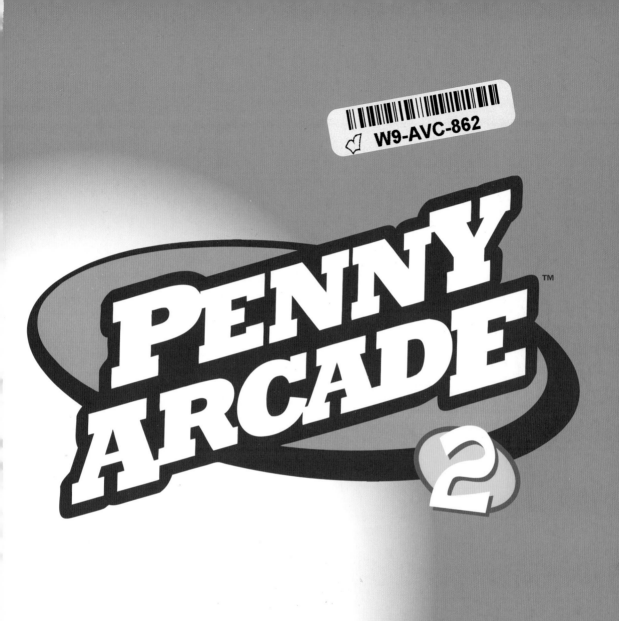

PENNY ARCADE™

2

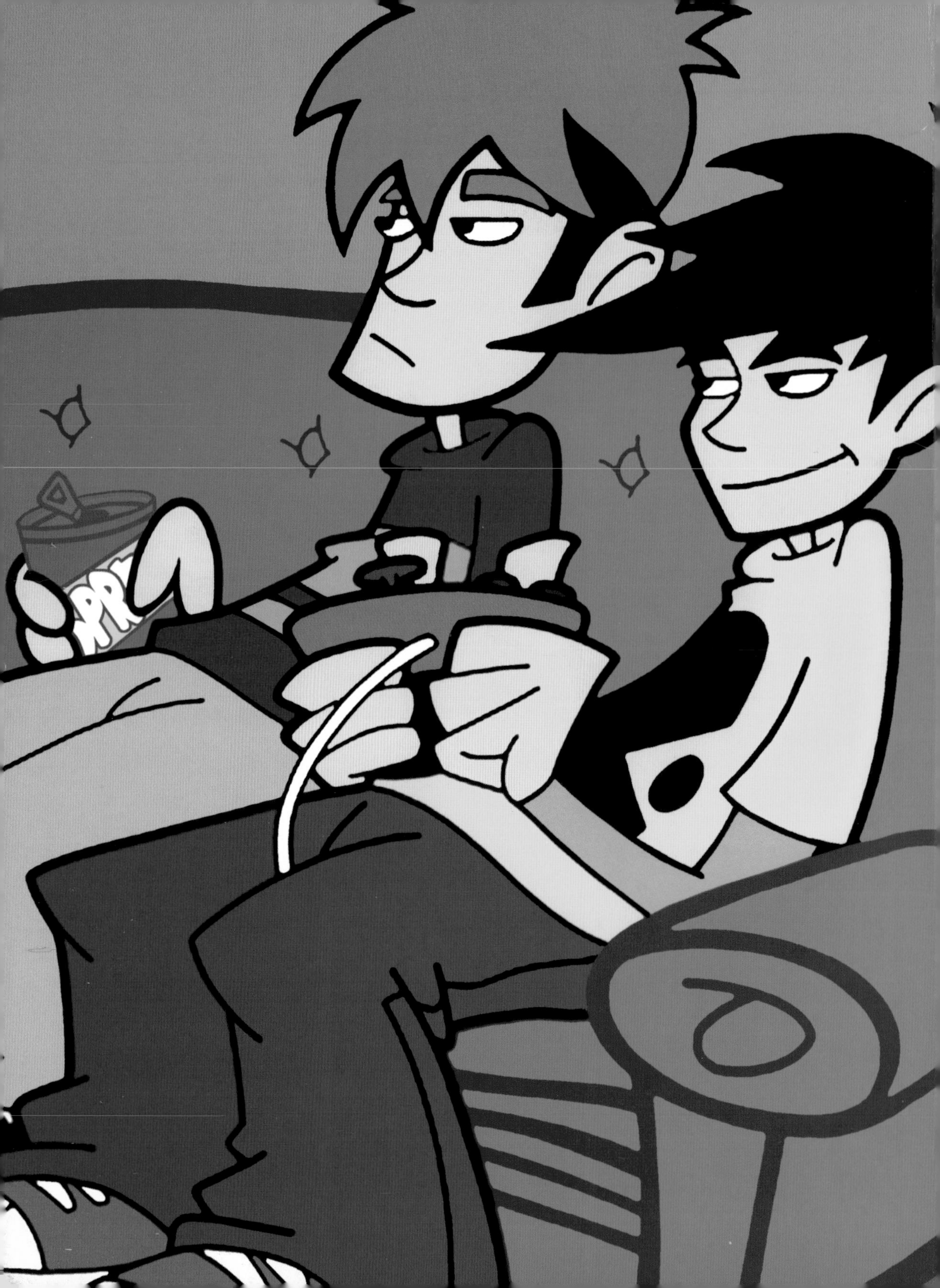

PENNY ARCADE

PENNY-ARCADE.COM

BY JERRY HOLKINS & MIKE KRAHULIK

dark horse books™

Publisher
MIKE RICHARDSON

Editor
MIKE CARRIGLITTO

Designer
DAVID NESTELLE

Art Director
LIA RIBACCHI

Editorial Assistant
SAMANTHA ROBERTSON

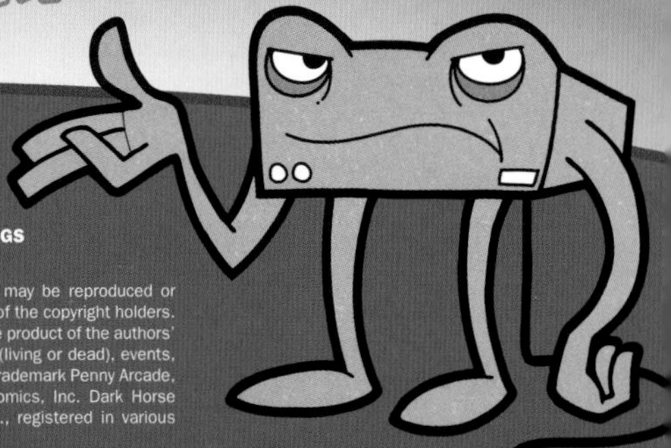

Very special thanks to ROBERT KHOO at Penny Arcade!

PENNY ARCADE Volume 2: EPIC LEGENDS OF THE MAGIC SWORD KINGS

This volume collects comic strips from the Penny Arcade website, originally published online from January 1, 2001 through December 31, 2001.

Published by
Dark Horse Books
A division of Dark Horse Comics, Inc.
10956 SE Main Street
Milwaukie, OR 97222

darkhorse.com

To find a comics shop in your area, call the Comic Shop Locator Service toll-free at 1-888-266-4226

First edition: July 2006
ISBN 10: 1-59307-541-3
ISBN 13: 978-1-59307-541-5

1 3 5 7 9 10 8 6 4 2
Printed in China

Foreword by J Allard

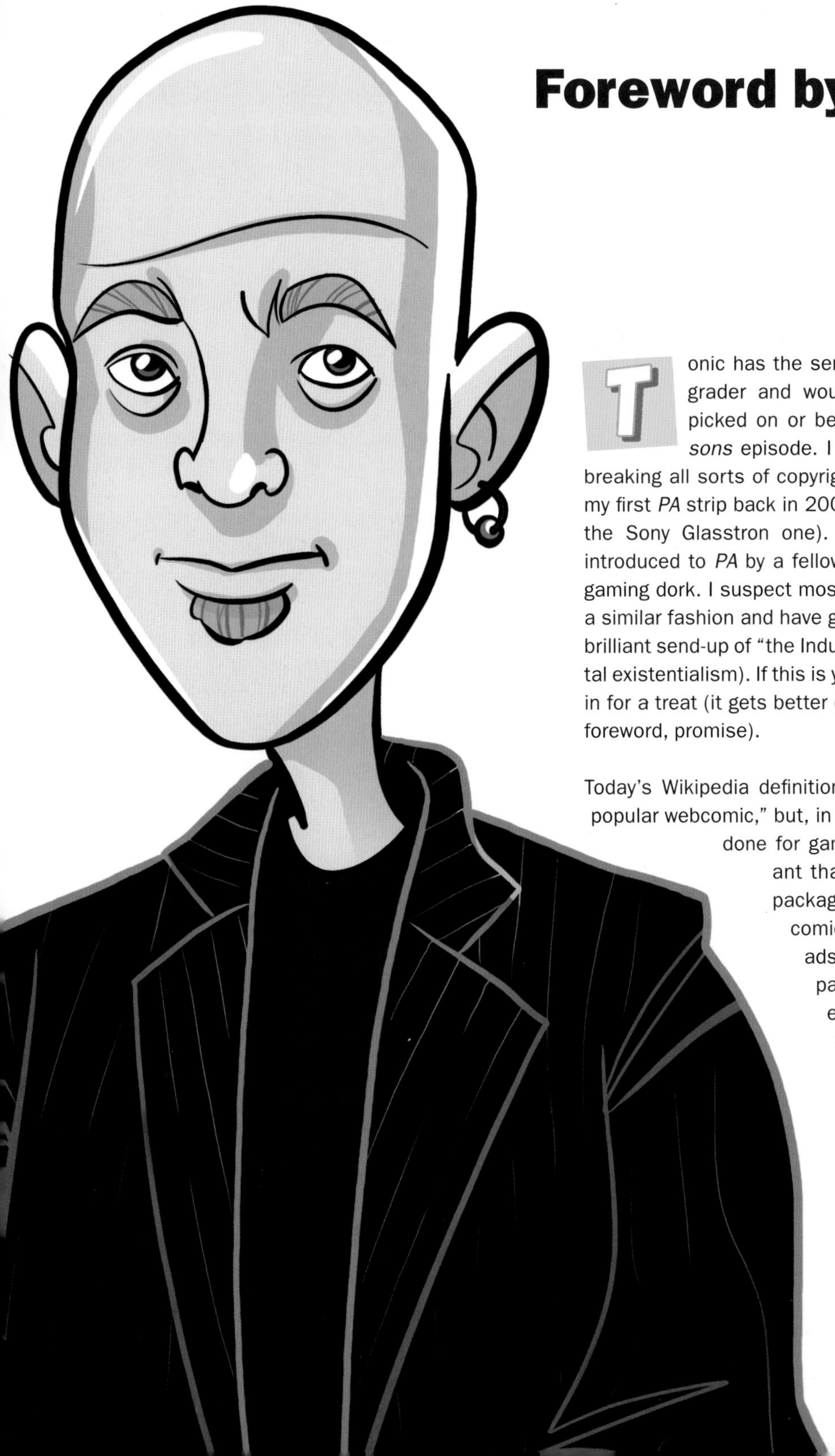

Tonic has the sense of humor of a fourth grader and would be the guy that got picked on or beat up in a typical *Simpsons* episode. I will never forget him for breaking all sorts of copyright law by forwarding me my first *PA* strip back in 2000 (I'm pretty sure it was the Sony Glasstron one). How appropriate to be introduced to *PA* by a fellow high-IQ, potty-mouthed gaming dork. I suspect most of you discovered *PA* in a similar fashion and have gotten into this delightful, brilliant send-up of "the Industry" (with a dash of digital existentialism). If this is your first exposure, you're in for a treat (it gets better once you get through the foreword, promise).

Today's Wikipedia definition of *Penny Arcade* is "a popular webcomic," but, in my mind, what they have done for gaming is far more important than your typical cynicism-packaged-with-nice-illustrations comic peppered with Viagra ads on the sidebar. To compare Gabe & Tycho to Rosencrantz & Guildenstern or even Jay & Silent Bob is to sell them short.

Even if my name were Jack (or American, or Strawberry . . .), I'd still love *Penny Arcade* for one big reason. It's not just that they care about games—or that they really, really "get it"—it's because they keep us honest.

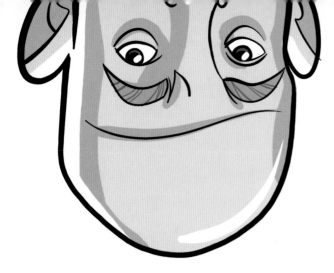

It probably sounds odd to hear someone—especially someone who works for a company with a market cap of 270+ billion dollars—say that a couple of webmedians could keep an industry honest. But that's what these guys do every day.

While the Videogame Industry™ may seem to be all fun all the time, the reality is that a lot of the industry and the folks around it take things just a little too seriously. And, that's where *PA* comes in. Every day, their work rescues us from ourselves and brings us back to reality. You see, for people who live in a world that's about creating alternate realities, well, sometimes we get pretty good at believing our own bullshit.

PA doesn't buy it, and they don't sell it. They tell it like it is. Whether it's in their strips, their rants, commentary in their books, a direct flame-war, or a well-timed onomatopoeia in an elevator at E3, you can count on their presence if you're doing something in this industry. While some might not go for their style or are put off by their occasional F-bomb, more often than not, the *PA* guys are spot-on for pinpointing where we're falling short and highlighting the big, magical moments in our brief history as an industry. In a perverse way, Gabe and Tycho are the most important tour guides of the videogame universe.

Sure, *PA* takes potshots at the products and the people I most enjoy in the industry. (Okay, they beat 'em senseless.) And every now and then they overplay a joke like the original BFC that we launched with the first Xbox. But they've got bills to pay too, and these moments are ripe for saying, "Oh, ignore them.

It's just a webcomic." (It's also a good time to remind them—I know your Gamertags and can expose your real "skills" to the world in an instant.)

It's not just the strip that defines these guys; it's their entire MO within the industry. It's the annual PAX expo that (gasp) breaks us out of the self-referential gaming "industry" conventions that connects customers with the creators. It's their Child's Play charity drive that raises money and products for the kids at Children's Hospitals to make their stays more bearable. It's a bunch of little, but sincere and meaningful stuff that somehow the big-machine-that-is-the-Industry manages to overlook in its scramble to make the holiday push or meet quarterly results.

We've had a long-standing saying in the Xbox team— "It takes a fun team to make a fun product." Thanks *PA,* for bringing some of that fun to us all over the years we've been at it.

Whether, like me, you've read 'em all before and just wanted a copy for the crapper, or you're new to the *PA* world, jump in.

—*J*

P.S. All love aside, Gabe and Tycho (and their alter-egos in the real world) aren't infallible. It disappoints me that after all this exposure, success, and profit they've amassed from the blatantly capitalistic repackaging of freely available Internet content . . . the fact that they still have a hyphen in their domain name is steeped in a sweaty mass of lameness.

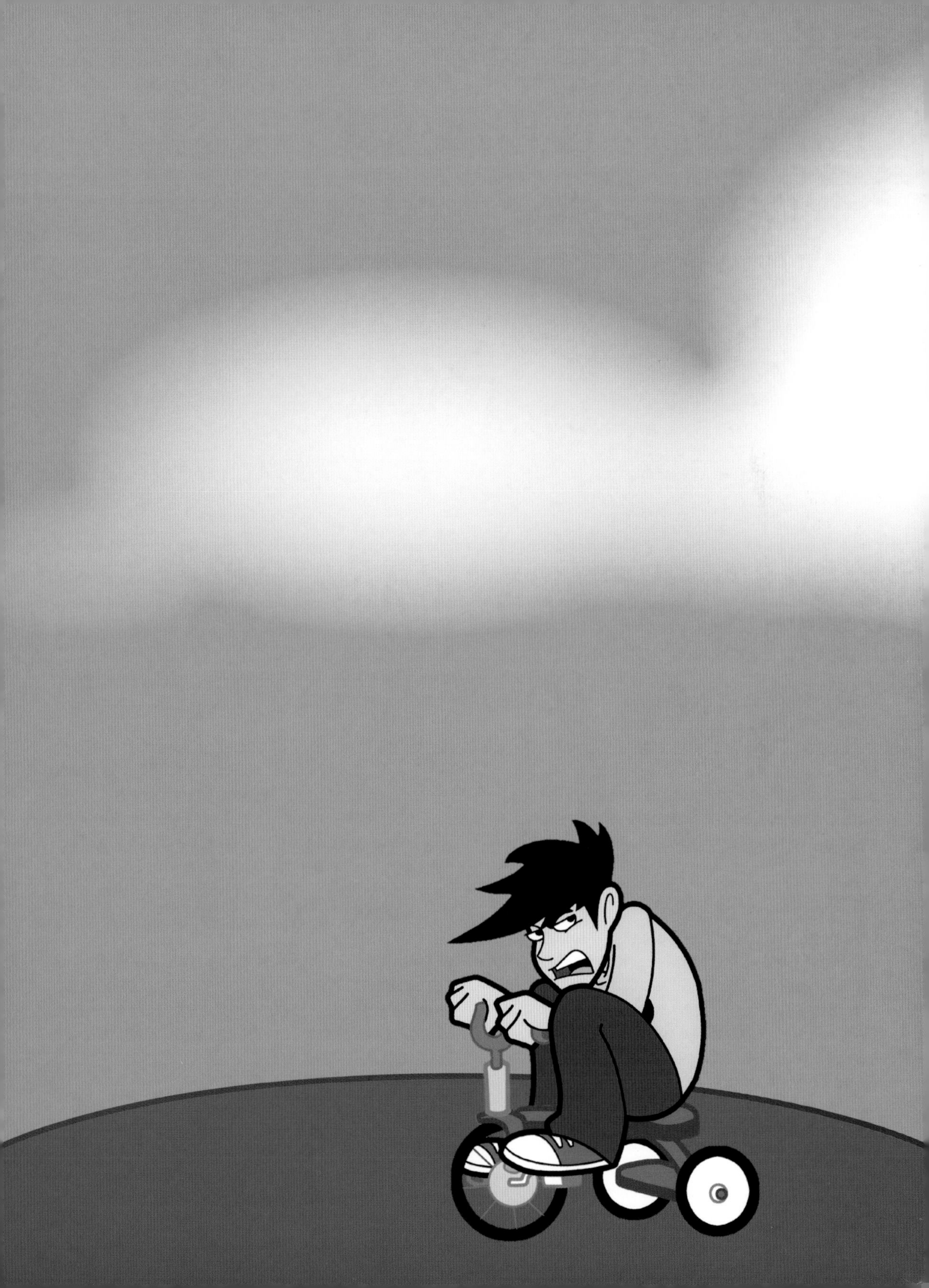

Introductio!

No, it's not a word *per se*. But it's *jazzy*. I like it. It's got pep. *Introductio!* Such is the author's dark power: to bend proud language into tawdry shapes.

I never know the proper tone to strike in this strange format. It isn't the book proper, the introduction—no. It's like some carnival barker standing out in *front* of the book, trying to get people in off the street and into my illuminated tent. Or my *comic collection*, or whatever. I forget what we were talking about.

Ah, yes.

I never meant to be the "voice" of *Penny Arcade*, and now that I sit down to write another entire book I wonder how it all went so very wrong. I was the guy who scribbled something in a text file and then *copied* that file into a shared folder, content that my work was done! It was a good Goddamn situation. At that point, I would typically scour your nascent webs for illicit materials while Gabriel engaged in the real work of our enterprise.

When we eventually moved to our own site (a migration covered in our first weighty volume)

our feeble HTML abilities created a page that always looked out of whack unless there were a couple paragraphs of text in there to balance it out. I agreed to fill the space with absolute nonsense, not really understanding what I was committing myself to.

News posts weren't even *archived* because, like I said, they were just there to fill a certain amount of space. I did not consider them my *writings*. They were just a pragmatic kind of bulk—like putting a book under a table leg. The next site had even *more space* to fill, but by this time I'd come to relish the opportunity that void represented.

Whenever I think an old post will make this a better book, I'll include it. I don't expect it to happen with any great regularity, as I was but a *stripling* then, fumbling with the bra of language.

Shall we?

—Tycho Brahe
May 3rd, 2006
Seattle, WA

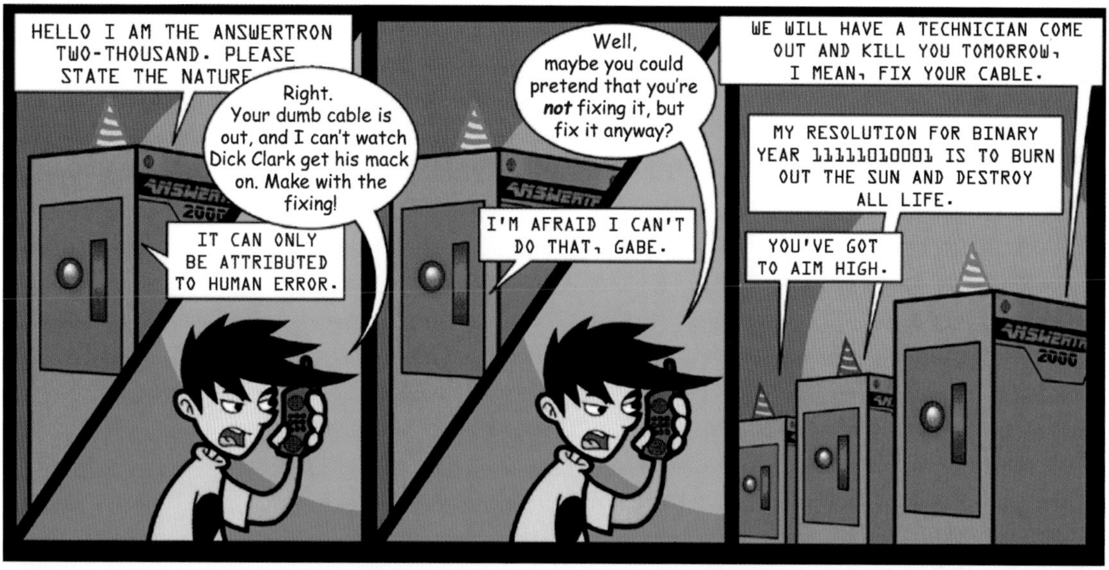
HELLO I AM THE ANSWERTRON TWO-THOUSAND. PLEASE STATE THE NATURE
Right. Your dumb cable is out, and I can't watch Dick Clark get his mack on. Make with the fixing!
IT CAN ONLY BE ATTRIBUTED TO HUMAN ERROR.
Well, maybe you could pretend that you're *not* fixing it, but fix it anyway?
I'M AFRAID I CAN'T DO THAT, GABE.
WE WILL HAVE A TECHNICIAN COME OUT AND KILL YOU TOMORROW, I MEAN, FIX YOUR CABLE.
MY RESOLUTION FOR BINARY YEAR 11111010001 IS TO BURN OUT THE SUN AND DESTROY ALL LIFE.
YOU'VE GOT TO AIM HIGH.

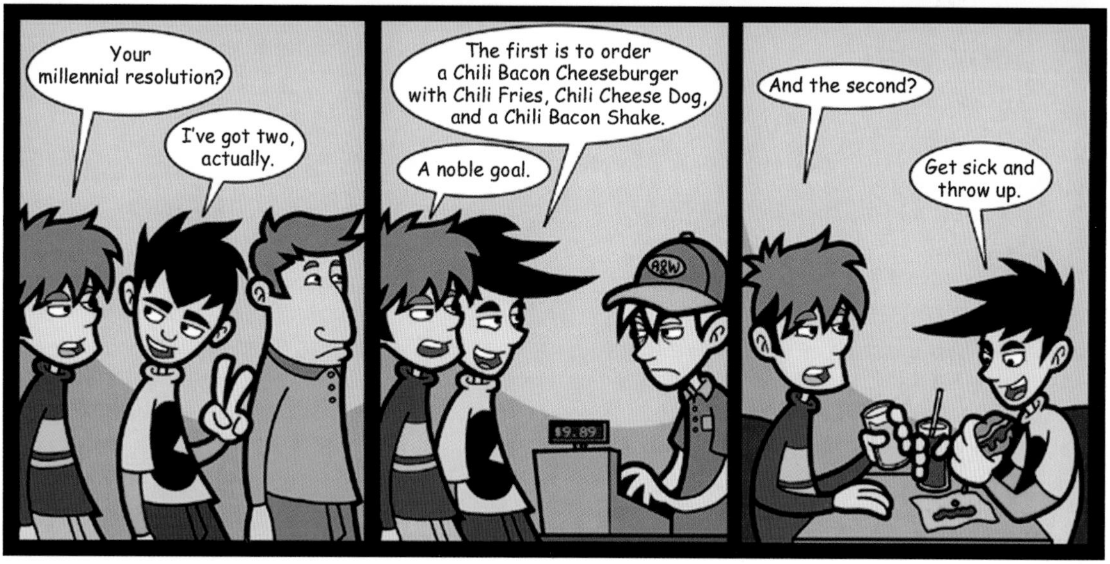
Your millennial resolution?
I've got two, actually.
The first is to order a Chili Bacon Cheeseburger with Chili Fries, Chili Cheese Dog, and a Chili Bacon Shake.
A noble goal.
$9.89
And the second?
Get sick and throw up.

HAPPY NEW YEAR

January 1, 2001 The Answertron was a fairly large part of the *Penny Arcade* animated series we were developing for mysterious and unnamed parties. That was only one of a hundred little alterations to make *Penny Arcade* plausible in an episodic format; one controversial change reworked Tycho Brahe into a merciless samurai policeman who, promotional materials alleged, "thirsted for cyber vengeance."

WE, UH . . . ACTUALLY EAT THIS

January 3, 2001 No doubt the soda itself pervades, but I don't know if actual A&W *restaurants* constitute some West Coast aberration or not. Do you have them in your state, your country, or—indeed—upon your distant world? Are you familiar, are you *intimate* sir, with their foamy liquid chili? May their chromed spigots never lose pressure.

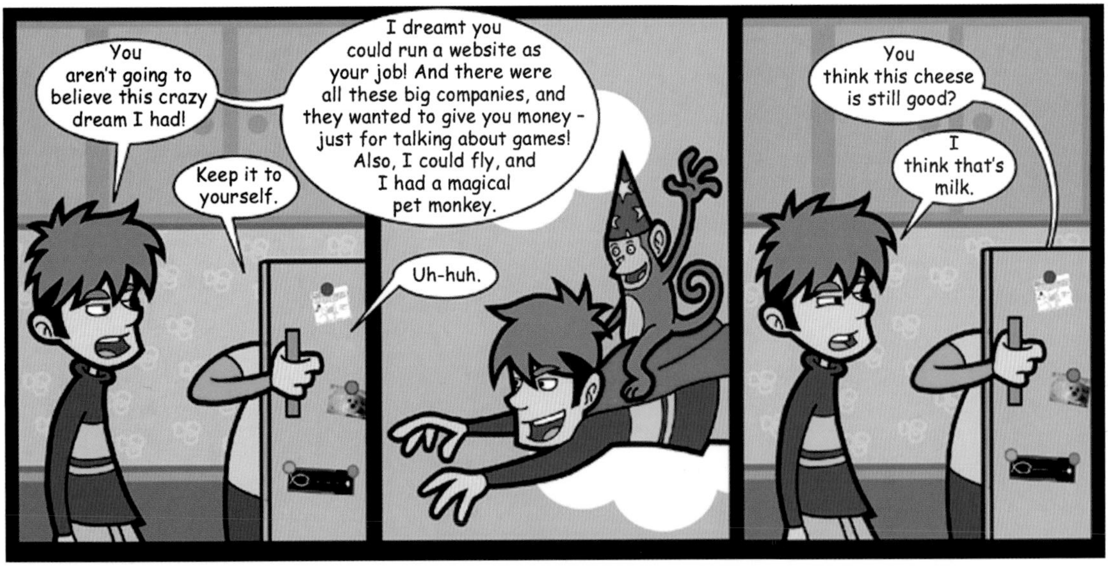
You aren't going to believe this crazy dream I had!
Keep it to yourself.
I dreamt you could run a website as your job! And there were all these big companies, and they wanted to give you money - just for talking about games! Also, I could fly, and I had a magical pet monkey.
Uh-huh.
You think this cheese is still good?
I think that's milk.

ALL GOOD THINGS

January 5, 2001 This was such a turbulent time in *Penny Arcade* history that I don't know if I can accurately emulate the desperation of those days. I should probably let my prior self handle it by including an old post here in-line:

Don't take the whimsical vibe in today's strip to mean that I think this thing is funny—because I don't. What started with Gamefan continued to move through the entire hollow system, dismantling this fabulous fucking game show cash-fest as handily as you or I would pick a flower. I'm not even saying you like flowers. I'm just saying it was easy.

The dissolution of content networks has apparently become some kind of corporate tradition, the latest celebration of which is taking place at CNet's Gamecenter Alliance. So, what happened? I put my meager Photoshop skills to work in the service of this handy chart.

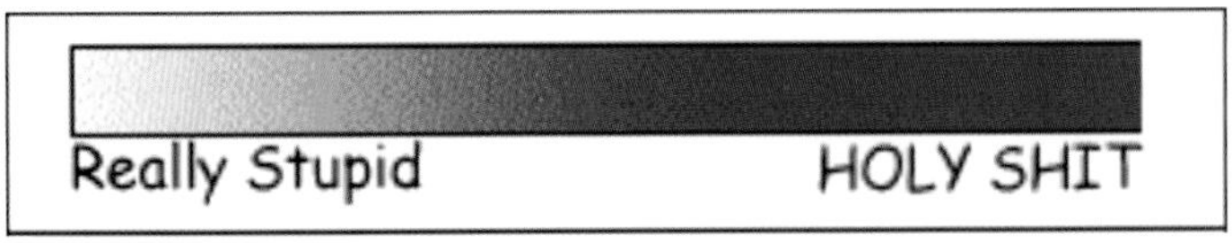
Really Stupid
HOLY SHIT

On the left, you can see the part where everybody and their lawyer thought that this whole network thing was a reasonable business model. That's the white part, because that's essentially "The Garden of Eden"—a sort of idyllic no-place, the unassuming cornerstone of what will one day be a grand fallacy. Over on the right, you can see where things stand now—the "HOLY SHIT" section. Websites are scrambling for new homes, while those networks that remain are tightening their belts and trying like hell to be the one that doesn't implode. There are quite a few interesting viewpoints to absorb on these events, if you are so inclined: you can read what looks to be a letter to the readers of *Stomped*, check out the "Online World In Trouble, Vol. I and II" on the front page of Ars Technica, or thrill to Gamers.com's item on the recent "UGO slashes prices, all affiliates must go!" announcement. That last one in particular is interesting; compare the official statements to the inside source for extra fun. So, what now? Will we revert, for a short or long time, to the initial concept of the "community" site? Old school—like Blue's Quake Rag or Joost's Aftershock? Which ones will simply hang it up? Fiscal fairytale or no, at least when all these venture capitalists were planting money for some imaginary harvest it gave a lot of sites the freedom to kick a big bag of ass.

So, what now?

Gabe and I think about this sort of thing a lot. The ostensible virtue of the advertising networks (when they were, you know, solvent) was that it freed you up to work on your site without having to negotiate ad deals and assorted other stuff not related to your area of expertise. I wouldn't say exactly that making comics or writing these communiqués is my area of expertise, but I'm a hell of a lot better at this than I am at brokering Big Deals and Doing Lunch. We're miserable all up and down that side of things, to be honest. We're just not business people. Or, if we are business people, we're very bad ones. We routinely screw it up. And even when something isn't our fault—like we're ordered to put up an ad bar roughly the size and luminosity of the sun—we get blamed for it anyway, so it scarcely matters one way or the other. But what now? We couldn't afford the hosting costs and so forth for *Penny Arcade*, if it ever came to that—for better or worse, nearly forty thousand people read it a day, many of them clicking on the large binary audio files that I would never even dream of posting. Being numeric about it isn't simply egregious horn tooting, I'm posing a question that I don't have an answer to. How could you maintain a site like this without the advertising infrastructure? Micropayments, maybe? Supplement it with traditional media? (I had depression and alcoholism up there too, but I removed them because I'm already satisfied with my progress in those two exciting fields.)

What now?

(CW)TB out.

i think i'll let them shoot me
so that i can die

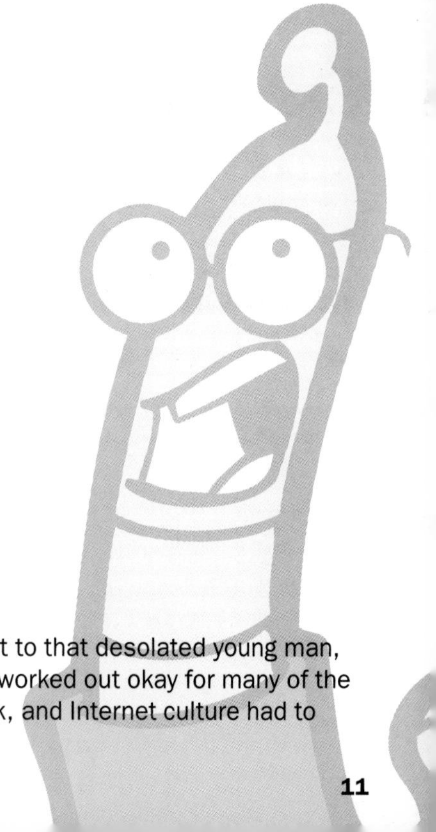

Just listen to that. Grim, right? Jesus. If only I could speak comfort to that desolated young man, bolster him with a missive of strength from the future. Everything worked out okay for many of the sites I was worried about—but their proprietors had to move quick, and Internet culture had to shift a little bit to make it possible.

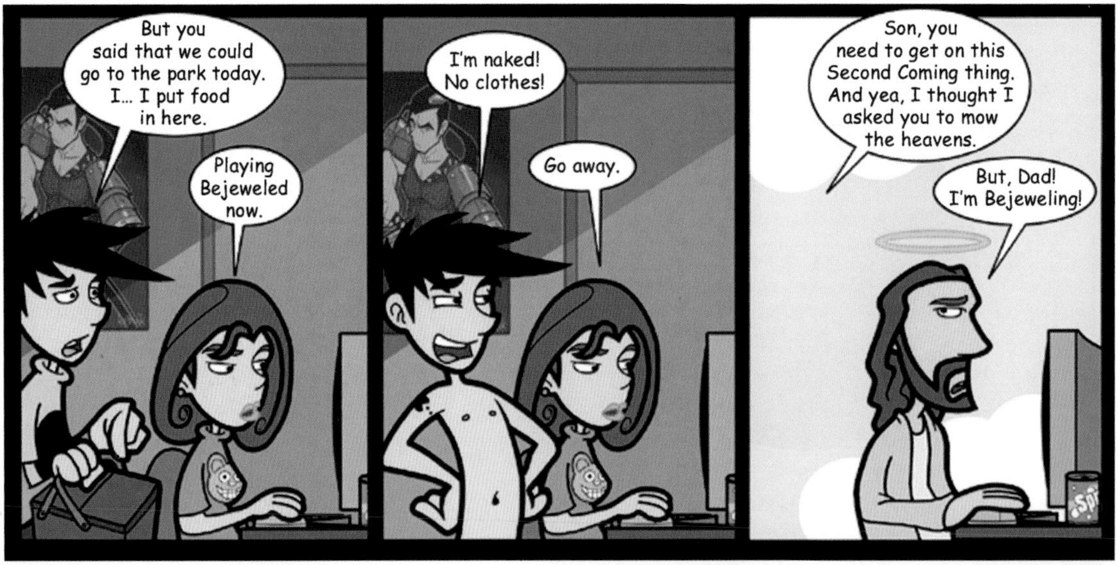

But you said that we could go to the park today. I... I put food in here.
Playing Bejeweled now.
I'm naked! No clothes!
Go away.
Son, you need to get on this Second Coming thing. And yea, I thought I asked you to mow the heavens.
But, Dad! I'm Bejeweling!

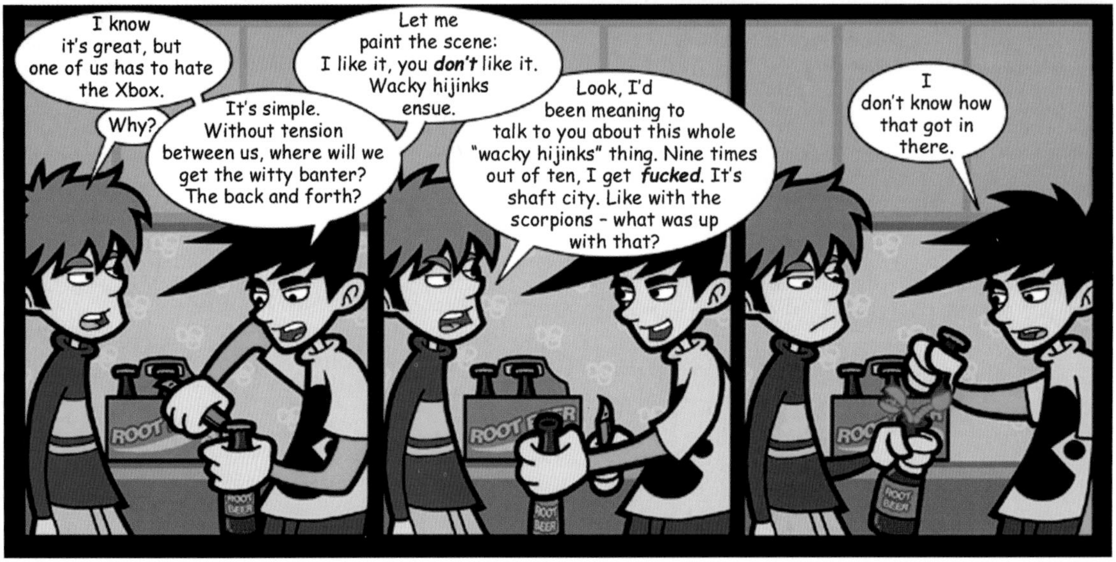

I know it's great, but one of us has to hate the Xbox.
Why?
It's simple. Without tension between us, where will we get the witty banter? The back and forth?
Let me paint the scene: I like it, you *don't* like it. Wacky hijinks ensue.
Look, I'd been meaning to talk to you about this whole "wacky hijinks" thing. Nine times out of ten, I get *fucked*. It's shaft city. Like with the scorpions - what was up with that?
I don't know how that got in there.

CRACK IS FOR SISSIES

January 8, 2001 The satisfaction one gets by arranging jewels is so *primal* that one wonders if there was not a phase of human development where our very survival depended on it. In the five years since this comic, gem juggling has become one of the most pervasive casual genres. Even De Beers is getting into the swing of things, with a game using real diamonds that costs in excess of two million dollars.

I WOULDN'T DRINK THAT, SERIOUSLY

January 10, 2001 In the end, we didn't have to arrange any special system. When you launch a console with games like Azurik and Nightcaster, anger and frustration are generated quite naturally. By the time the Xbox entered the last leg of its epic run, games like Chaos Theory and the Xbox Live service (not to mention the controller Type-S) would see us willingly enter the fold.

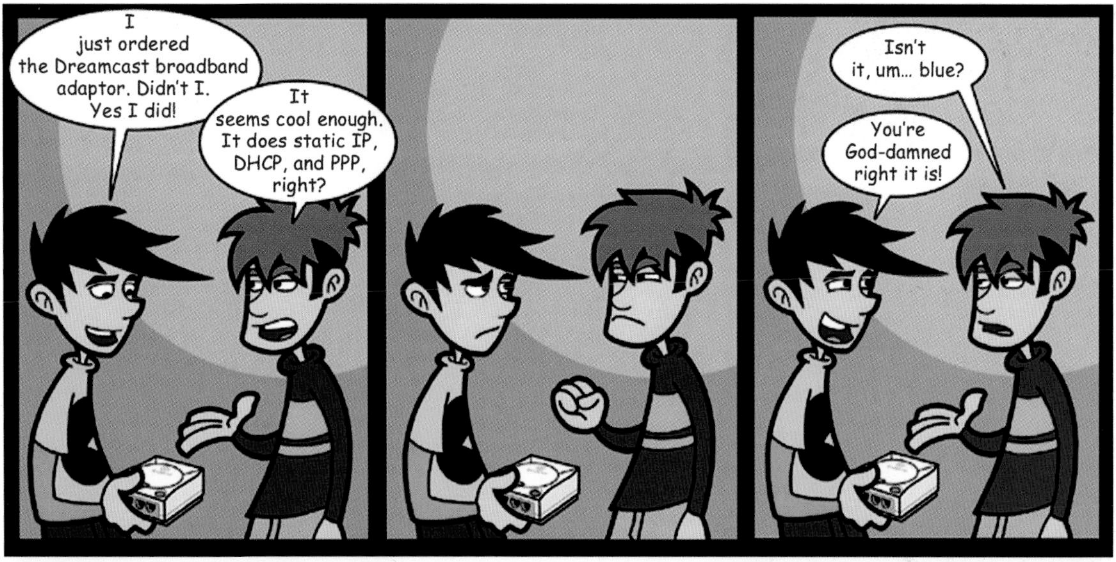
I just ordered the Dreamcast broadband adaptor. Didn't I. Yes I did!
It seems cool enough. It does static IP, DHCP, and PPP, right?
Isn't it, um... blue?
You're God-damned right it is!

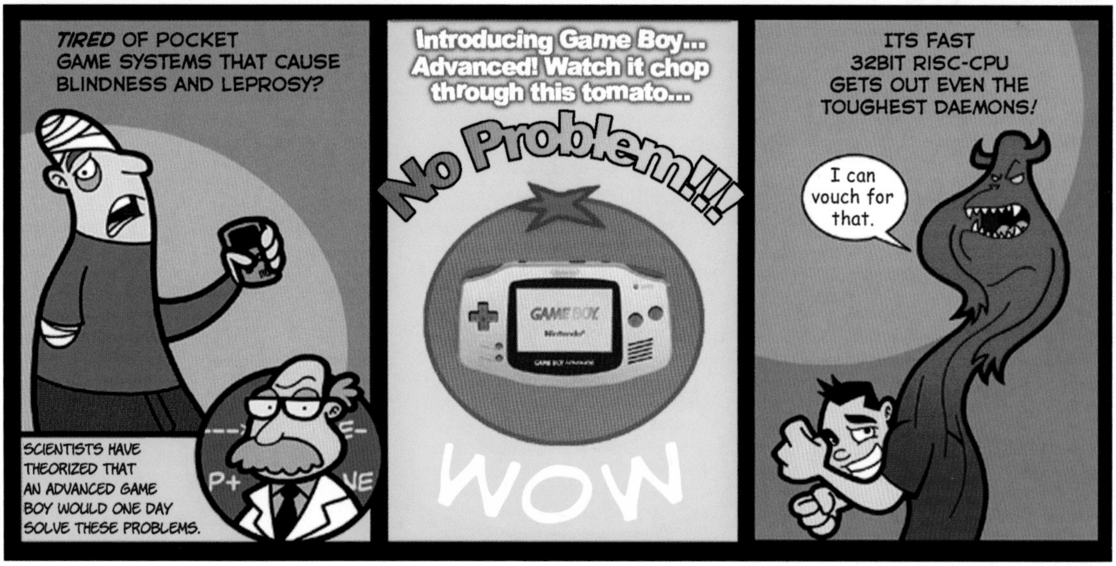
TIRED OF POCKET GAME SYSTEMS THAT CAUSE BLINDNESS AND LEPROSY?
SCIENTISTS HAVE THEORIZED THAT AN ADVANCED GAME BOY WOULD ONE DAY SOLVE THESE PROBLEMS.
Introducing Game Boy... Advanced! Watch it chop through this tomato...
No Problem!!!
WOW
ITS FAST 32BIT RISC-CPU GETS OUT EVEN THE TOUGHEST DAEMONS!
I can vouch for that.

AND HOW!

January 12, 2001 Gabe did get his going eventually, but it took some doing. Since the broadband adapter was never released in the U.S., a user had to brave a cryptic, ten-page, all-Japanese installation—a minefield of dangerous *kanji*.

ORDER NOW

January 15, 2001 We may have overstated the deleterious effects of older Gameboy hardware. We may also have exaggerated the ability of the new system to cast out the "toughest daemons." The middle panel may be a lie too; I've honestly never tried it.

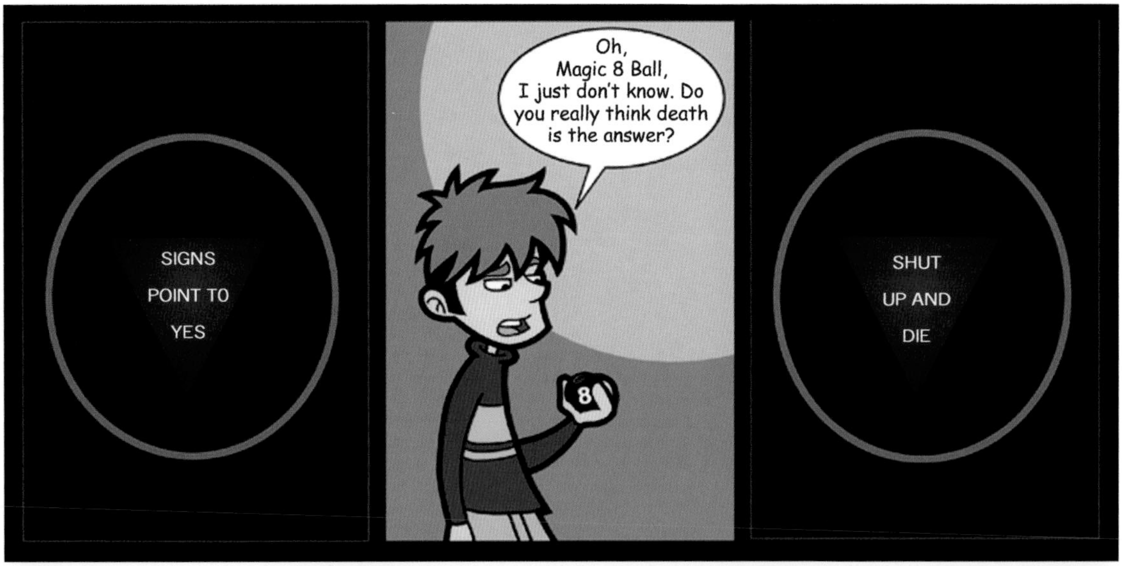
SIGNS POINT TO YES
Oh, Magic 8 Ball, I just don't know. Do you really think death is the answer?
SHUT UP AND DIE

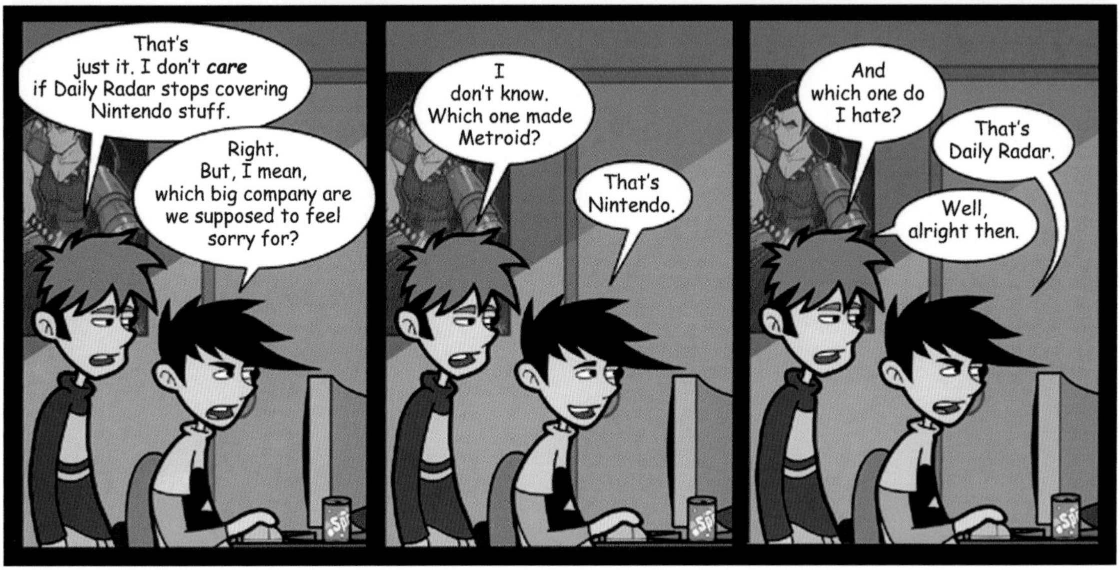
That's just it. I don't *care* if Daily Radar stops covering Nintendo stuff.
Right. But, I mean, which big company are we supposed to feel sorry for?
I don't know. Which one made Metroid?
That's Nintendo.
And which one do I hate?
That's Daily Radar.
Well, alright then.

MAGIC HATE BALL

January 17, 2001 What is your fucking problem there, orb? All I did was shake you and, *with* the shaking, reveal my fortune. That's a usage well in line with your packaging.

NINTENDO SCORES A DIRECT HIT

January 19, 2001 Nintendo had nixed some Pokémon strategy guides published by *Daily Radar's* parent company, which were stuffed (as you can imagine) with succulent copyrighted Pokémon. *Daily Radar* retaliated by pulling Nintendo coverage. The feud was so intense between us and *DR* at this point Nintendo could have summoned a Greater Baelzithon with a blood ritual and we would *still* have taken their side.

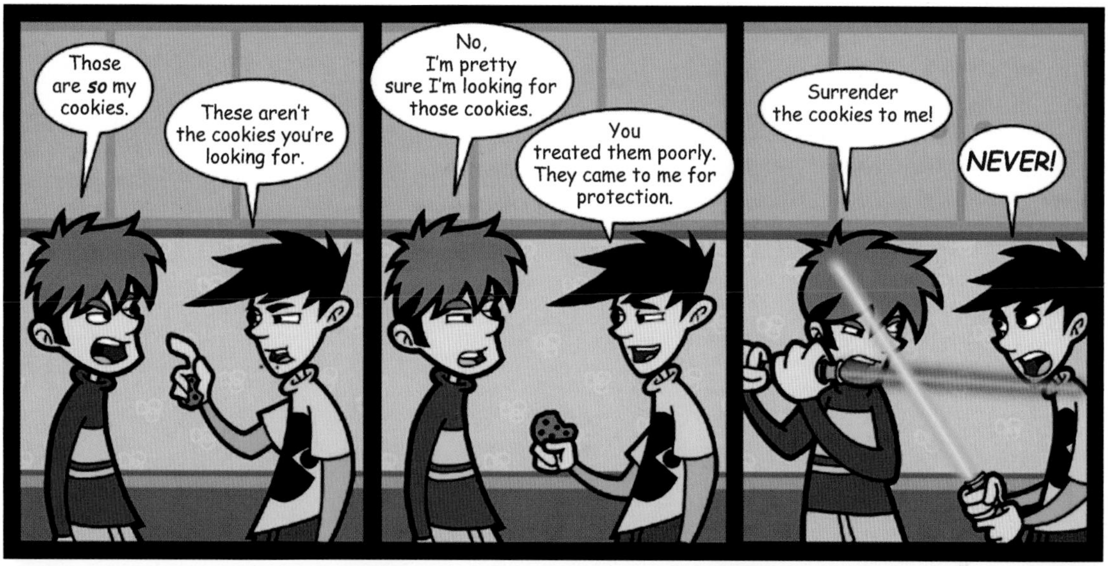
Those are *so* my cookies.
These aren't the cookies you're looking for.
No, I'm pretty sure I'm looking for those cookies.
You treated them poorly. They came to me for protection.
Surrender the cookies to me!
NEVER!

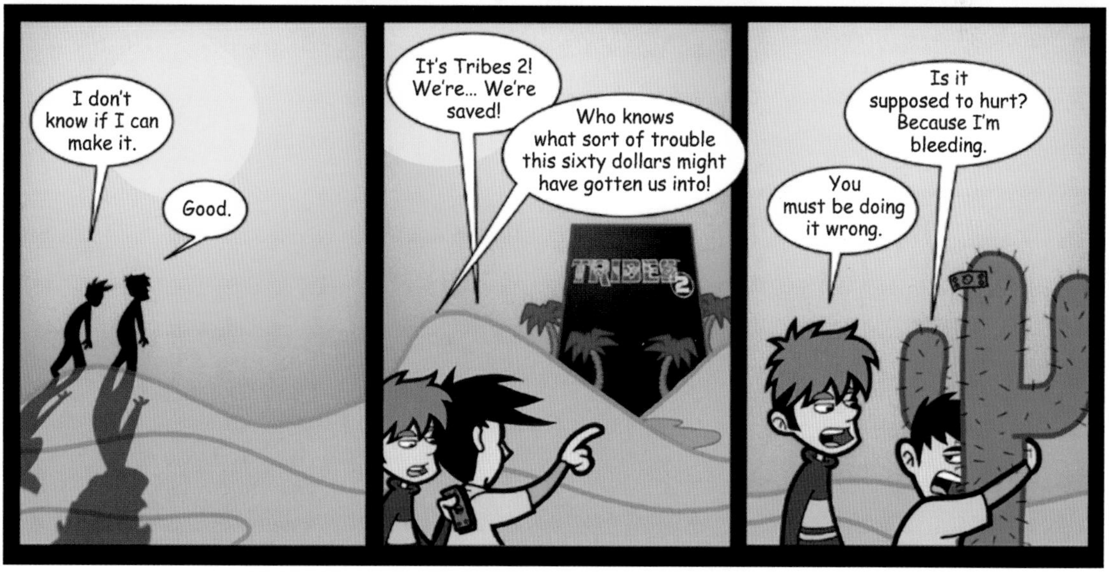
I don't know if I can make it.
Good.
It's Tribes 2! We're... We're saved!
Who knows what sort of trouble this sixty dollars might have gotten us into!
TRIBES 2
Is it supposed to hurt? Because I'm bleeding.
You must be doing it wrong.

IF YOU ONLY KNEW THE POWER

January 21, 2001 I want to live in a world where even routine squabbles over baked goods are resolved with lightsabers and subtle Force trickery.

IT'S MORE PRICKLY THAN I EXPECTED

January 23, 2001 Tribes 2 was delayed from its original date, which left us desiccated spiritually. It moved us to create this piece, whose potent desert imagery and sharp cacti helped us to work through some of the disappointment.

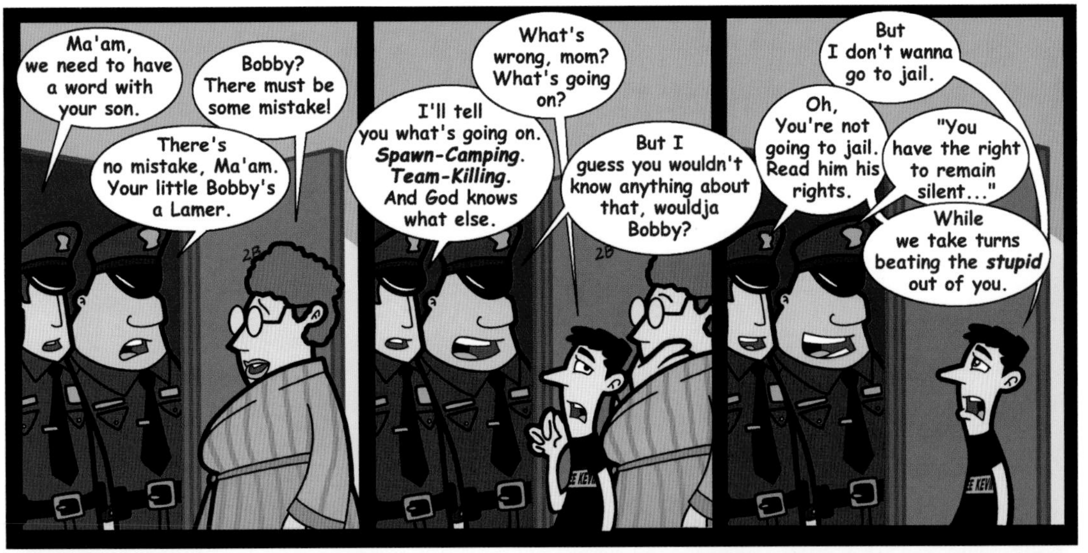
Ma'am, we need to have a word with your son.
Bobby? There must be some mistake!
There's no mistake, Ma'am. Your little Bobby's a Lamer.
What's wrong, mom? What's going on?
I'll tell you what's going on. Spawn-Camping. Team-Killing. And God knows what else.
But I guess you wouldn't know anything about that, wouldja Bobby?
But I don't wanna go to jail.
Oh, You're not going to jail. Read him his rights.
"You have the right to remain silent..."
While we take turns beating the stupid out of you.

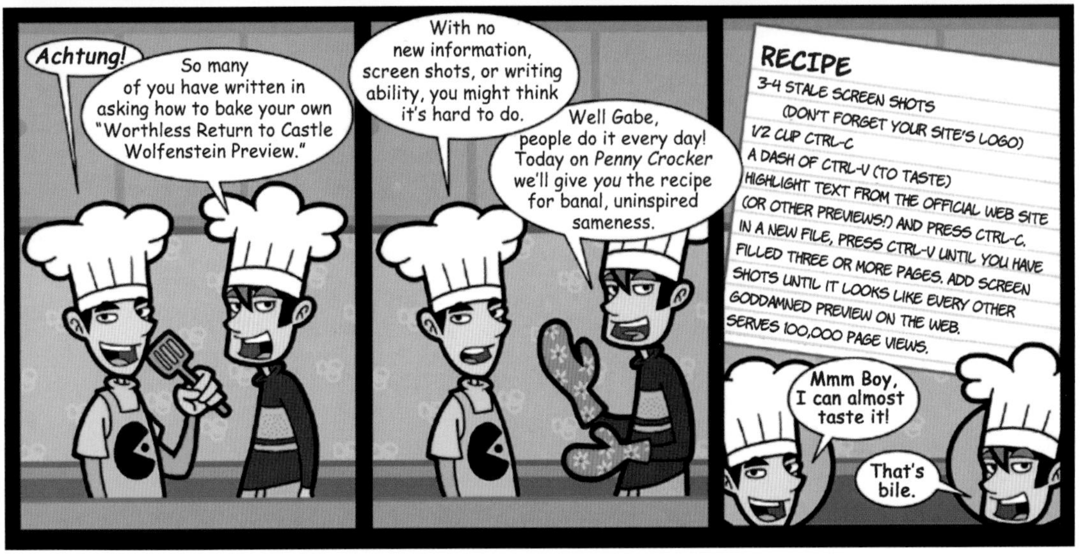
Achtung!
So many of you have written in asking how to bake your own "Worthless Return to Castle Wolfenstein Preview."
With no new information, screen shots, or writing ability, you might think it's hard to do.
Well Gabe, people do it every day! Today on Penny Crocker we'll give you the recipe for banal, uninspired sameness.
RECIPE
3-4 STALE SCREEN SHOTS (DON'T FORGET YOUR SITE'S LOGO)
1/2 CUP CTRL-C
A DASH OF CTRL-V (TO TASTE)
HIGHLIGHT TEXT FROM THE OFFICIAL WEB SITE (OR OTHER PREVIEWS!) AND PRESS CTRL-C. IN A NEW FILE, PRESS CTRL-V UNTIL YOU HAVE FILLED THREE OR MORE PAGES. ADD SCREEN SHOTS UNTIL IT LOOKS LIKE EVERY OTHER GODDAMNED PREVIEW ON THE WEB. SERVES 100,000 PAGE VIEWS.
Mmm Boy, I can almost taste it!
That's bile.

BAD BOYS, BAD BOYS

January 26, 2001 This comic is dedicated to "cheatz0rz" all around the world. Why do you have to cheat all the time?!?!

THE KITCHEN OF PENNY CROCKER

January 28, 2001 We made an angry strip, and no doubt we were frustrated by the state of gaming news at the time, but I think we were mad at the universe in general at this point. I'd recently been evicted when huge, black-tailed tree rats took up residence in my home. In fact, I think the rats still live there.

You might be interested to read the series of updates that catalogued the progression of rodentine transgression. Also, my position on Folgers has softened somewhat since this period. If it's early enough, I will drink virtually *any* hot liquid.

RAT WATCH 2000

2000-12-17

I know that I've been very direct in the past regarding Folgers brand "coffee." I've even made disparaging comments about their CEO and General Manager, Bob Folger. I *did* that because I could make better coffee out of stuff I found in my pockets or under the sink. But! As much as I deplore their black ichor, I have to say that I—in all seriousness—would rather drink an entire *cup* of Folgers than have rats crawling in my kitchen, bathroom, and walls. I know that I'm a lot bigger than they are, but on the other hand, there are Goddamned *Rats* in my kitchen, bathroom, etc. After an eight-hour run of Asheron's Call, I went down to the bathroom to, you know, apply an exfoliating scrub or whatever. And I *would* have exfoliated forthwith, had there not been a rat the size of *God* sitting directly on the toilet. We looked at each other for a moment, and then I closed the door.

"Hey, just . . . Let me know when you're done," I said.

2000-12-18

I mentioned this (not so) briefly yesterday, but it would appear that—for the time being—my house is infested with fucking rats. As a result, I've gotten somewhat desperate. I've tried to pretend that I'm playing some new Everquest expansion, or that they're made of chocolate, or that they're *not rats*—ineffective, but also *inexpensive!*—but I guess they're still here, because they scratch and scrabble audibly at all hours of the day and night. The cat, flush with the benevolence of the season, has already furnished us with a *very* nice corpse we plan to use in a festive wreath.

2000-12-20

Rat Update 2000: No, it's not a joke. Instead of the (arguably passé!) frivolity and merriment this Christmas, I get diseased animals. It may just be this *mood* I'm in, but that strikes me as a poor fucking substitute for holiday cheer. I hear them in the closet when I'm trying to sleep. I assume they're trying on my hats or whatnot. It's an open closet, so Brenna and I have this sort of barricade thing built up in front of it—but we just accept that they're going to bite us at some point. Every now and again, a pronounced scuttling and scratching is heard behind me as I type my post, and the cat examines that venue with (what *I* feel is) an intense and exemplary felinity. That agent and author of my misery—the base and unextraordinary rat—goes the fuck back whence it came, with the exacting celerity of time-lapse footage. As if the evidence were not already great, I now submit further indictment of my brazen geekery: the cat waits near the closet for the next filthy debut, and it occurred to me that it was camping a spawn. I deserve only death!

2000-12-22

Rat Watch 2000: There has been an outpouring of support *worldwide* regarding my wretched

guests. And no less than ten people recommended an elaborate trap that they saw in *Maxim*, of all places—maybe that magazine is trying to edge in on that lucrative "promiscuous pest-control guy" market. Either way, the trap itself calls for Mountain Dew, a garden hose, Adams no-stir peanut butter, one pound rough-cut Chinese jade, three toothpicks (unflavored), one toothpick (mint), a hot tub, two sticks fresh-ground cinnamon, a throat lozenge, a copy of *e. e. cummings' collected poems 1904-1962*, a hammer, and an aardvark. But I'm not trying to make the fucking *Death Star* here, and I'm also not looking for a quiet evening in with them. With the passionate disinterest that is the cat's sole domain, she (hereafter known as the *best kitty in the whole world!*) has kicked, bitten, scratched, and toyed with enough ass to keep their detestable machinations well at bay. I haven't heard jack out of them upstairs. And aside from the (by all accounts, *very nice*) nest they made beneath the sink, they seem to know that my house is not a very hospitable place for them—unless their definition of hospitable differs radically from Webster's, and incorporates the sort of clawing doom unique to their most profound nightmares.

2001-01-08

Rat Watch 2000, Final: I swear to Jesus and God and Whoever Else You Can Swear To that our lives are a cruel and meticulous hoax—a SuperSaver dime-store piece of fucking *hack work*. I haven't had much to say on the topic of my tireless, hungry guests—that merry band of rodents I call Jack Filthy and the Vectors of

Disease. That is because since the landlord cut the trees back from my place of residence, they really haven't had a way into the house. So, no way into the house = no rats chewing on my Category 5 = the first nights of genuine peace in weeks. As much as I enjoyed hearing their fleshy tails drag across my stuff, I was willing to accept that our relationship with them had basically been severed. I was ready to start fresh. I was ready to put this *Secret of Fucking Nimh* stuff behind me.

But.

This landlord guy didn't even believe us at first. Cordless in hand, I would open up our spice drawer—the packages of cider and cocoa opened and empty, the beasts having left only the pungent evidence of their biology—and this guy tells me that it's "impossible." I felt like saying, "Then it's two-for-one fucking miracle day, jackass. Come remind me why I pay you a thousand dollars a month to find shit in my Swiss Miss." But it would seem that I'm only a tough guy when it doesn't actually matter. Since our infestation was some kind of Imaginary Phenomenon to him, we called the city to come and inspect these Phantoms—and wouldn't you know it, they *were* real! Almost as if by *magic*, in only a few short days, the trees were cut back and things became immeasurably better (in the very key "less rats" sense). You know what I get today? A letter from the landlord, saying we need to be out of here by the end of the month. The *end* of the *month*. For those of you just tuning in, they're kicking me out of my house. For our German readers, that guy is a fucking prick. Sorry. I don't really know any German.

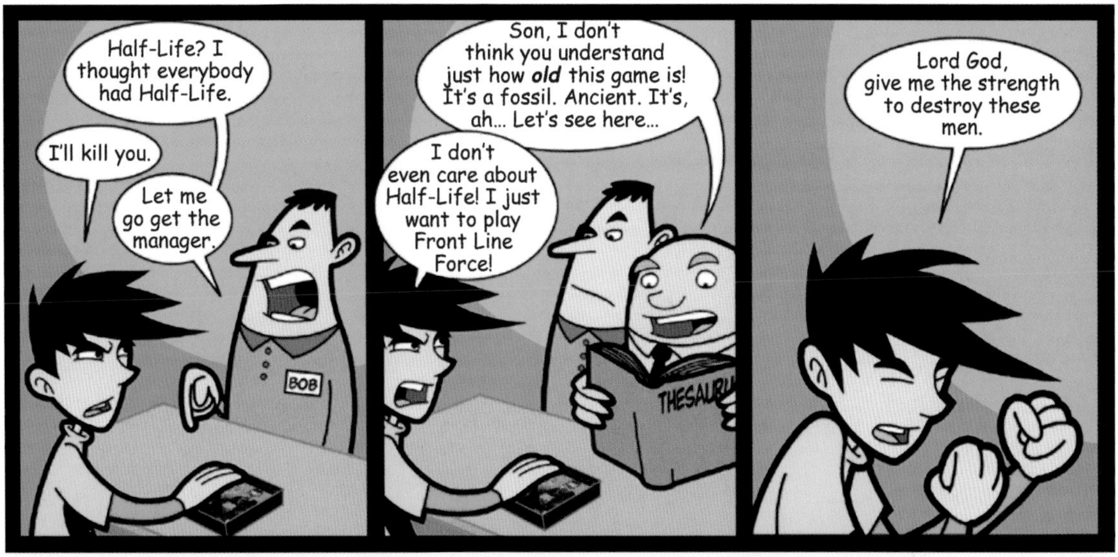
Half-Life? I thought everybody had Half-Life.
I'll kill you.
Let me go get the manager.
BOB
Son, I don't think you understand just how *old* this game is! It's a fossil. Ancient. It's, ah... Let's see here...
I don't even care about Half-Life! I just want to play Front Line Force!
THESAURU
Lord God, give me the strength to destroy these men.

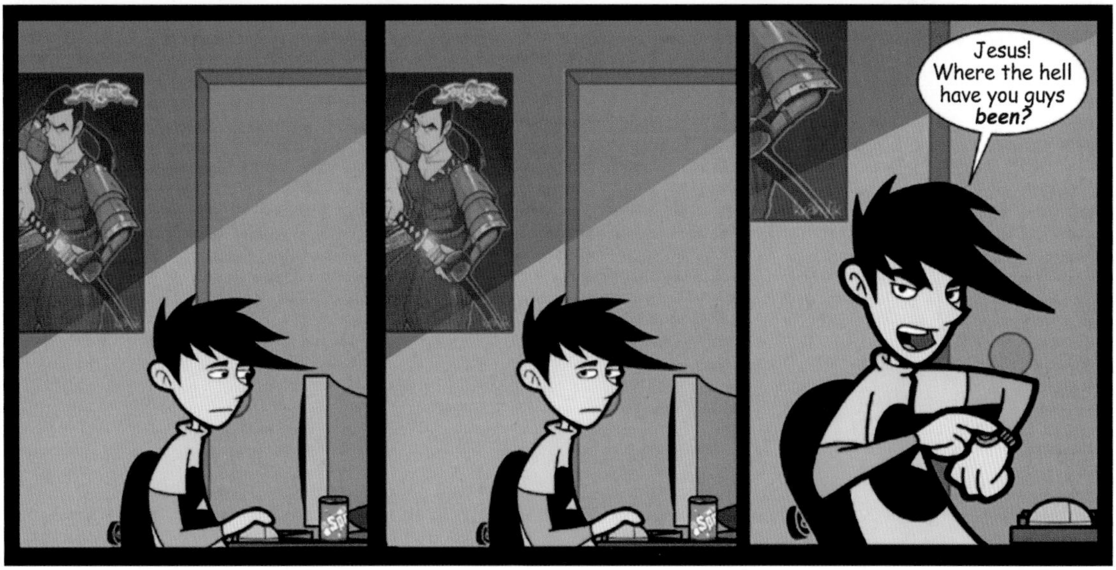
Jesus! Where the hell have you guys *been?*

CALL UPON HOLY MIGHT

January 30, 2001 It probably seems strange, but this has always been one of my favorite comics. There is no question that the inclusion of a thesaurus grants an incalculable bonus to any panel—but Gabriel's prayer at the end is just so . . . so *earnest*.

YOU'RE LATE!

February 7, 2001 I'm glad I'm here to explain things like this. When this strip went up, the site had been down for a week. We decided to bring things back online, but at this point there was really no guarantee that we'd ever go back to a regular schedule. *Penny Arcade* was something we'd do until real life made it impossible.

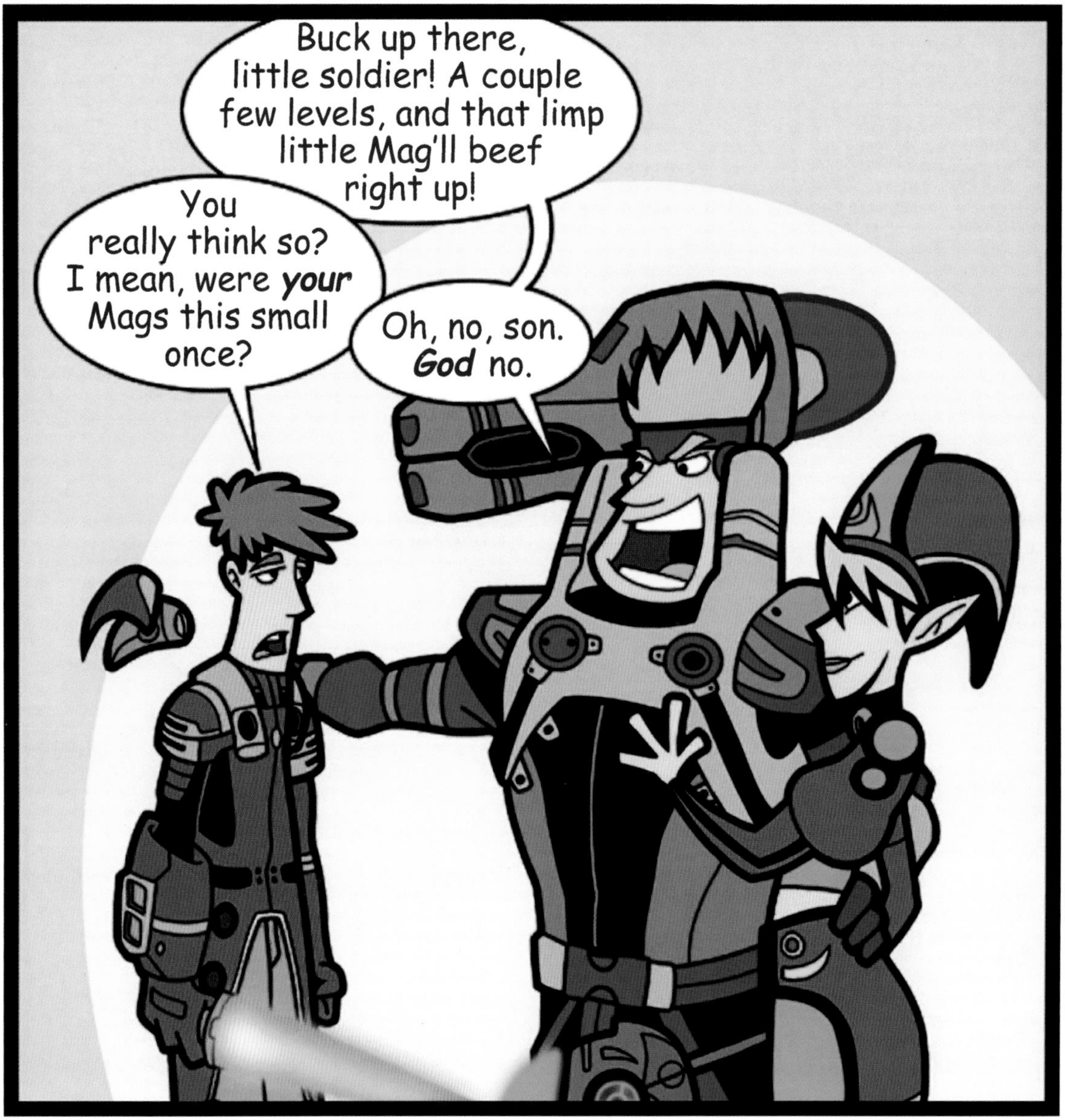
Buck up there, little soldier! A couple few levels, and that limp little Mag'll beef right up!
You really think so? I mean, were *your* Mags this small once?
Oh, no, son. *God* no.

MAG ENVY

February 7, 2001 It was about this time that we got the first book deal, though the writing process was *severely* hampered by the release of Phantasy Star Online. The spell checker doesn't like the "Ph" in Phantasy, but I'm a Goddamn iconoclast, and I let that kind of stuff roll right off.

I've played the various forms of it that they've released since the original, and they're all right, but PSO—in its original version, at the specific *time* it was released—was enthralling. Compared to the online RPG experiences being delivered on the PC, compelling in their own way but largely slower paced fantasy affairs, Phantasy Star Online couldn't have been more different. As a stunningly beautiful action/arcade romp set on a distant world, it was almost pure sugar.

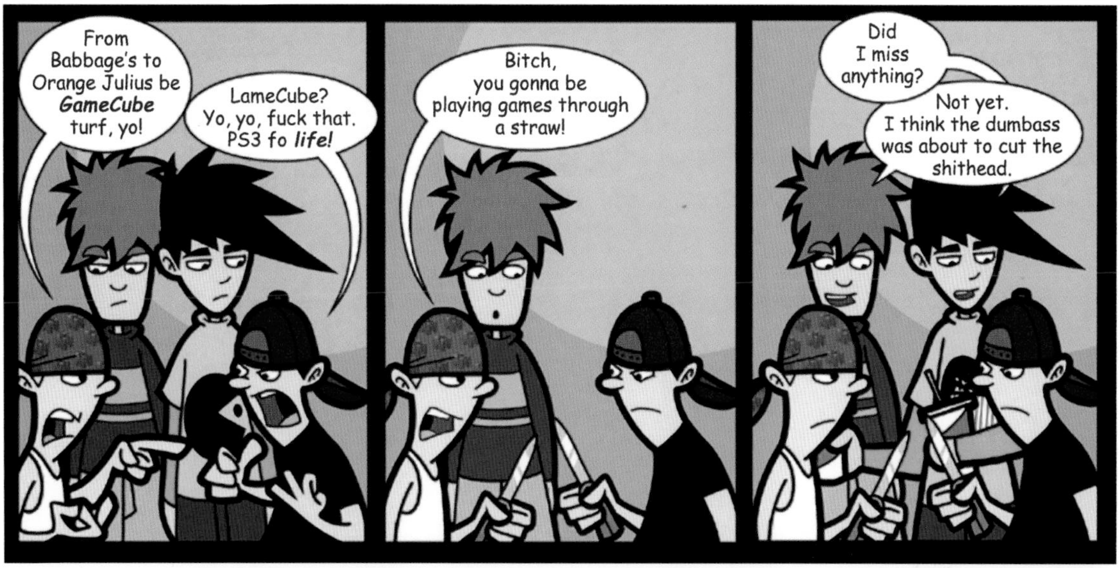
From Babbage's to Orange Julius be GameCube turf, yo!
LameCube? Yo, yo, fuck that. PS3 fo life!
Bitch, you gonna be playing games through a straw!
Did I miss anything?
Not yet. I think the dumbass was about to cut the shithead.

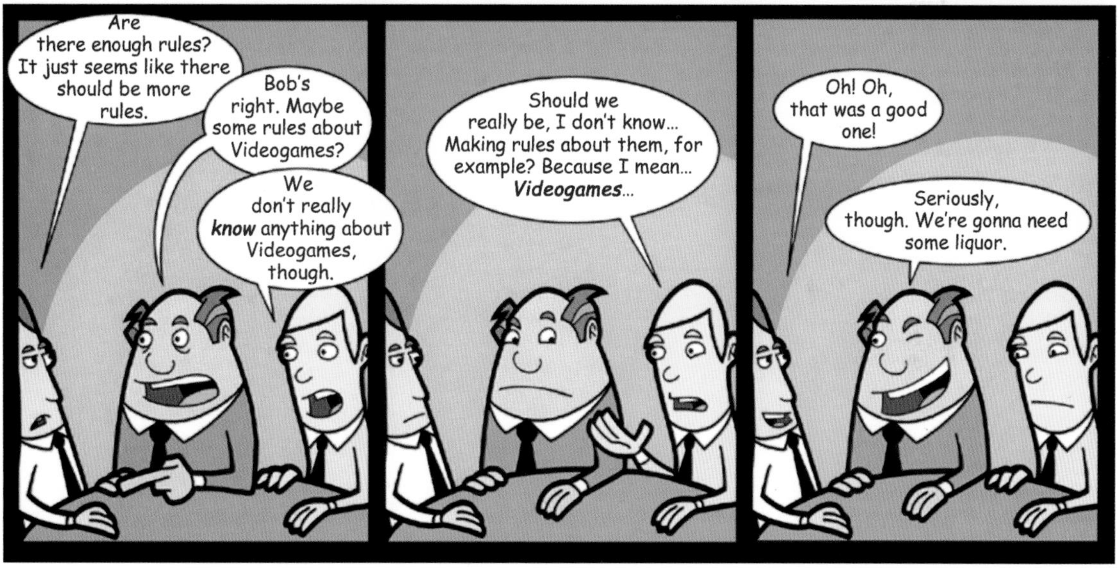
Are there enough rules? It just seems like there should be more rules.
Bob's right. Maybe some rules about Videogames?
We don't really know anything about Videogames, though.
Should we really be, I don't know... Making rules about them, for example? Because I mean... Videogames...
Oh! Oh, that was a good one!
Seriously, though. We're gonna need some liquor.

WHICH CONSOLE BE THE BIZOMB?

February 12, 2001 Understand that in 2001—fully five years before the launch of the system—there were *already* PS3 fans ready to defend their nonexistent console of choice against the vile opposition.

I'm assuming this was before they saw the proposed *batarang* controllers.

LIQUID LEGISLATION

February 14, 2001 Have you ever heard a politician speak on the House floor about the games you play? You'd be surprised to know just how dangerous, how subversive your hobby is. Seriously. You might consider switching to real crime . . .

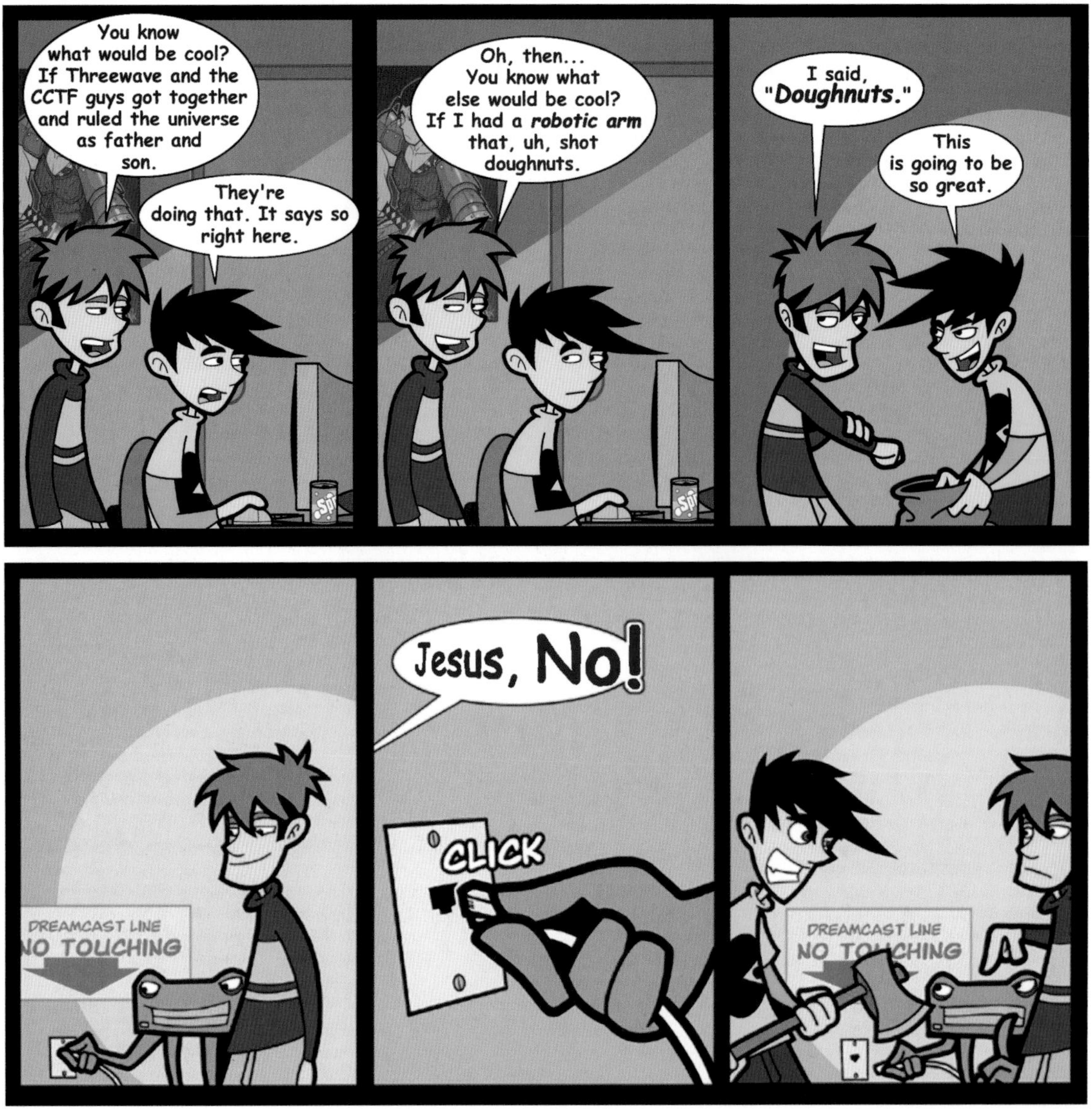
You know what would be cool? If Threewave and the CCTF guys got together and ruled the universe as father and son.
They're doing that. It says so right here.
Oh, then... You know what else would be cool? If I had a robotic arm that, uh, shot doughnuts.
I said, "Doughnuts."
This is going to be so great.
DREAMCAST LINE
NO TOUCHING
Jesus, No!
CLICK
DREAMCAST LINE
NO TOUCHING

DOUGHNUTS KICK ASS

February 16, 2001 As I've said, we just expect Capture the Flag gameplay in our first person shooters these days—it'd be weird *not* to have it. But it was Threewave's CTF Mod for the original Quake that helped create that expectation. The guy who *made* Quake CTF, Zoid, went on to work at Retro Studios on the Metroid series.

IT SAYS NOT TO RIGHT THERE

February 19, 2001 A modem line! *So quaint*. It's like seeing a spittoon or something, everything within a certain radius becomes *old-timey*.

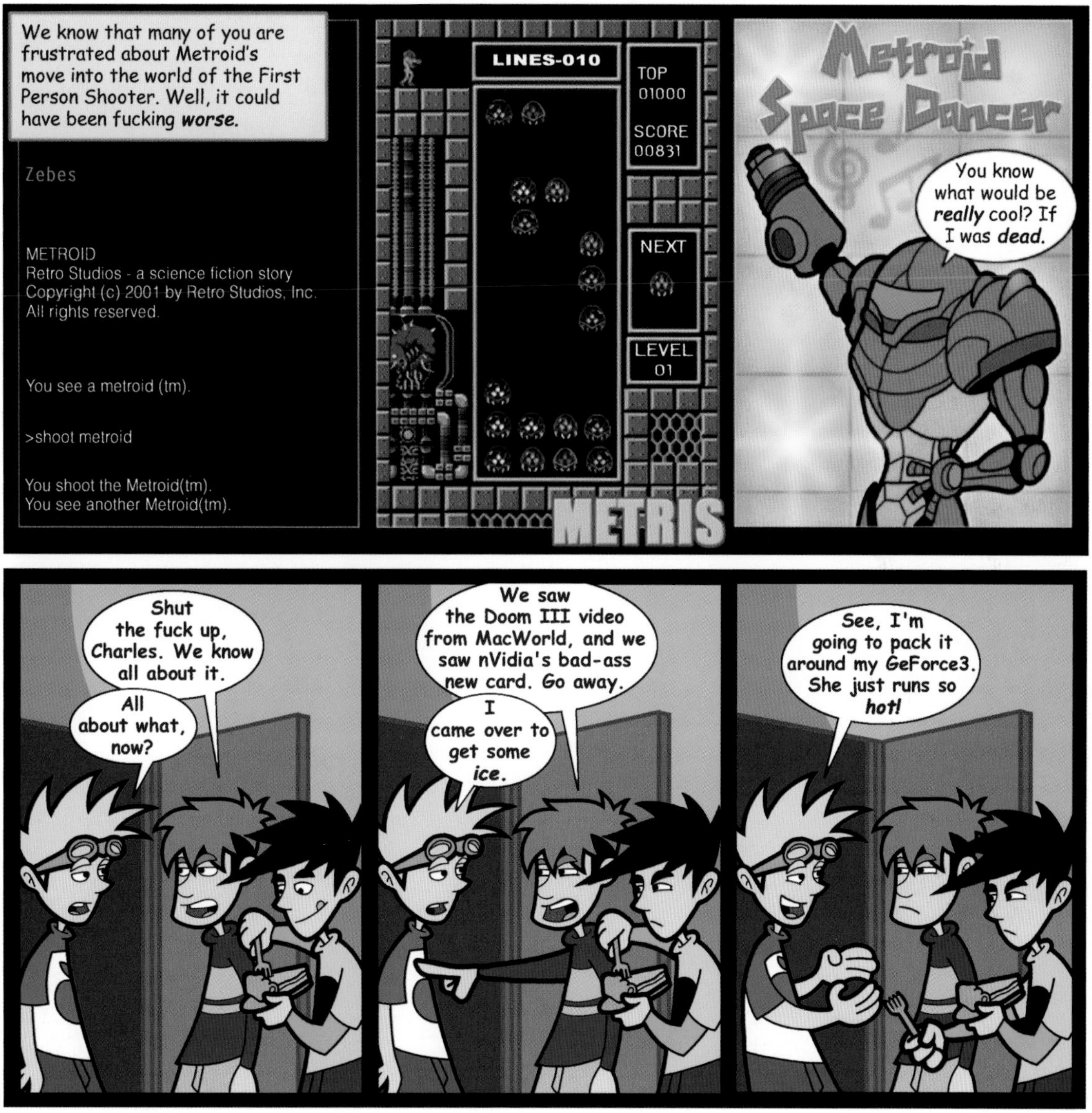
We know that many of you are frustrated about Metroid's move into the world of the First Person Shooter. Well, it could have been fucking *worse.*
Zebes
METROID
Retro Studios - a science fiction story
Copyright (c) 2001 by Retro Studios, Inc.
All rights reserved.
You see a metroid (tm).
>shoot metroid
You shoot the Metroid(tm).
You see another Metroid(tm).
LINES-010
TOP 01000
SCORE 00831
NEXT
LEVEL 01
METRIS
Metroid Space Dancer
You know what would be *really* cool? If I was *dead.*
All about what, now?
Shut the fuck up, Charles. We know all about it.
I came over to get some *ice.*
We saw the Doom III video from MacWorld, and we saw nVidia's bad-ass new card. Go away.
See, I'm going to pack it around my GeForce3. She just runs so *hot!*

COUNT YOUR LUCKY STARS

February 21, 2001 With the exception of the last panel, all of these games (and more) were eventually made into playable versions by readers. The "First Person Metroid Game," which we'd eventually know as Metroid Prime, turned out to be an authentic, reverent experience.

OH, THAT CHARLES

February 23, 2001 Being Mac users ourselves now makes reading these archived indiscretions somewhat weird, but we've apparently come to terms with Apple, its products, and the users of those products. Those halting, formal initial meetings gave way to something you might mistake for mutual respect and admiration. In our defense, seeing the "hottest new stuff" hit the Mac first was pretty emasculating.

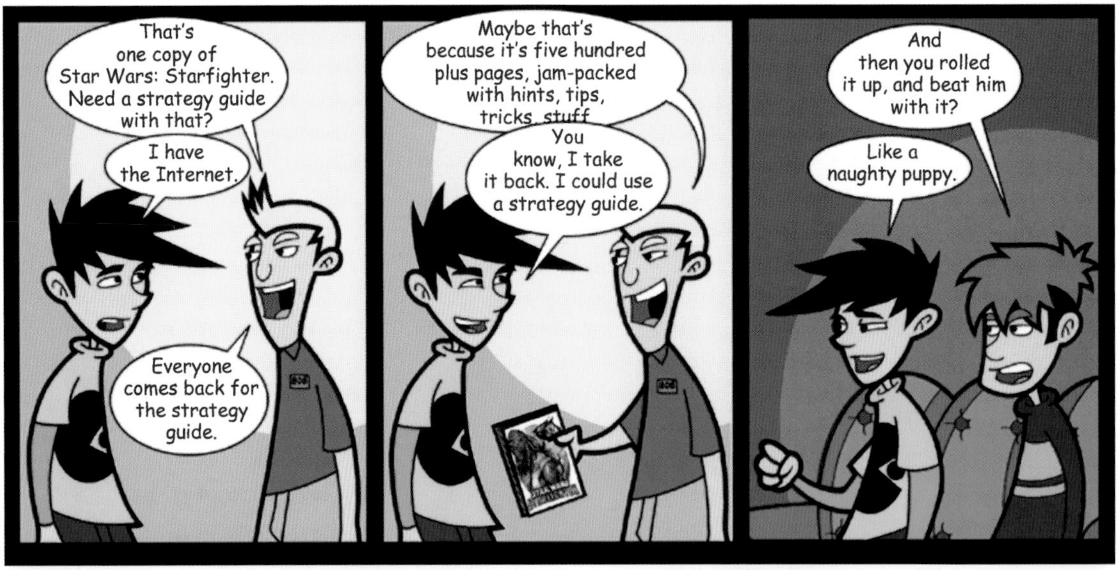
That's one copy of Star Wars: Starfighter. Need a strategy guide with that?
I have the Internet.
Everyone comes back for the strategy guide.
Maybe that's because it's five hundred plus pages, jam-packed with hints, tips, tricks, stuff
You know, I take it back. I could use a strategy guide.
And then you rolled it up, and beat him with it?
Like a naughty puppy.

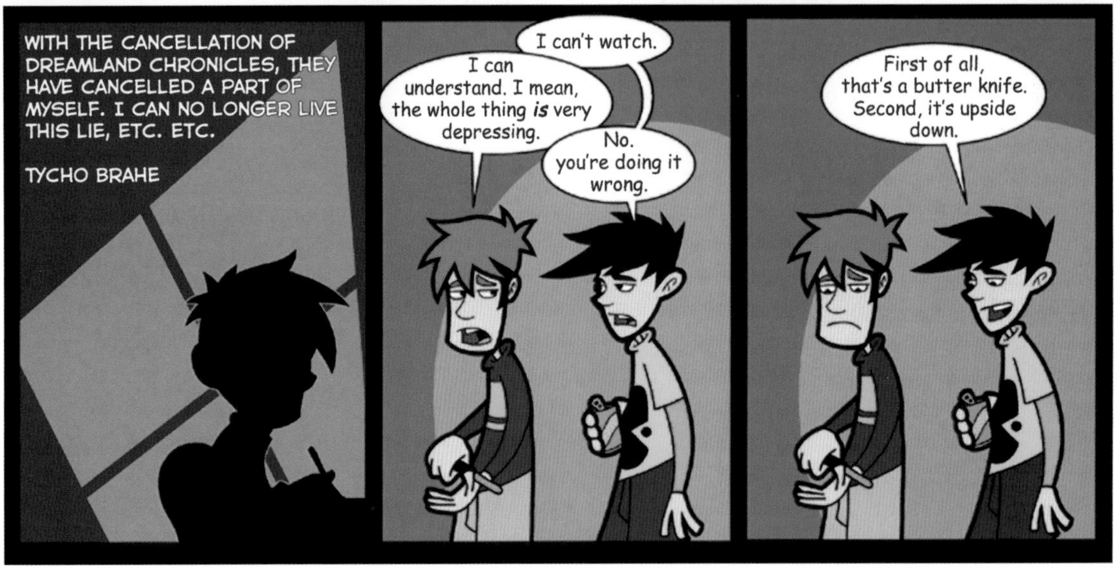
WITH THE CANCELLATION OF DREAMLAND CHRONICLES, THEY HAVE CANCELLED A PART OF MYSELF. I CAN NO LONGER LIVE THIS LIE, ETC. ETC.
TYCHO BRAHE
I can understand. I mean, the whole thing *is* very depressing.
I can't watch.
No. you're doing it wrong.
First of all, that's a butter knife. Second, it's upside down.

THE HITTING

February 26, 2001 This comic urged a volatile generation to enter retail establishments and turn the products therein into bludgeoning weapons. We claimed that was not our intention, but then they showed this comic in court. Since then, Gabriel has drawn *Penny Arcade* from prison.

REST IN PEACE

February 28, 2001 The Dreamland Chronicles was a new tactical game from the creators of X-Com: UFO Defense, a legendary strategy excursion of (what would now be called) the *old school.* It eventually saw the light of day as a game called UFO: Aftermath, but by then I had another hobby. Tai Chi or some shit.

THAT'S RUBBLE

March 2, 2001 It's a watch strip, but the rubble you see there is from an actual earthquake. Here's what I wrote about it, then:

My cold appears to be gone completely, which is sort of a downer. The medicine I'd been taking was—much like the humble Altoid—*curiously strong.*

Here's the strip. I would like to thank each and every human who wrote in asking if we were okay re: the recent earthquake, and to reiterate for those who couldn't care less that we're *fine,* just to spite those fuckers. In truth, it hardly lasted long enough (where I live) to be terrifying. I was having a dream that I was made of delicious Jell-O brand gelatin, with bits of tart pineapple suspended throughout my enticing frame. Eventually the house itself began to rustle in (what I consider) an altogether *un-houselike* fashion, its component parts grinding together with a voice like distant monsters. I woke up during that period, with the pictures falling off the walls and vases falling over and my precious monitor doing a spritely jig on my desk. I'm not sure how it is for you yourself, but for a period of fifteen minutes after I wake up, I'm worthless. I'm basically still asleep, and everything Brenna tells me I have to do today is all a part of some inconvenient subconscious sideshow. What I'm saying is the entire event took place in a surreal chronology, one I can barely remember concrete details of. As a result, the reality of the situation—that shit was falling all over the place, that the Goddamned *ground* was buckling in a fashion that was both unprecedented and unauthorized—all of that was lost on me, and the whole thing was transmuted into pure fun. Once I got out of bed and made my wiggly way into the kitchen, I noticed that my most valuable (liquor) player was teetering close to the edge of the shelf—the Bombay Sapphire, jersey #62. I grabbed it and tucked it into my body like a football pro. I wobbled over and stood near the door-frame (I thought I remembered something about *door frames* from some elementary school crisis drill) and told the bottle, "We're going to make it through this. *Together.*" I thought that sounded pretty crazy, so I giggled for a little while—which turned out to be for the duration of the spectacle. Brenna called later, and I asked her if she was trapped under a girder. I guess some people just can't take a joke.

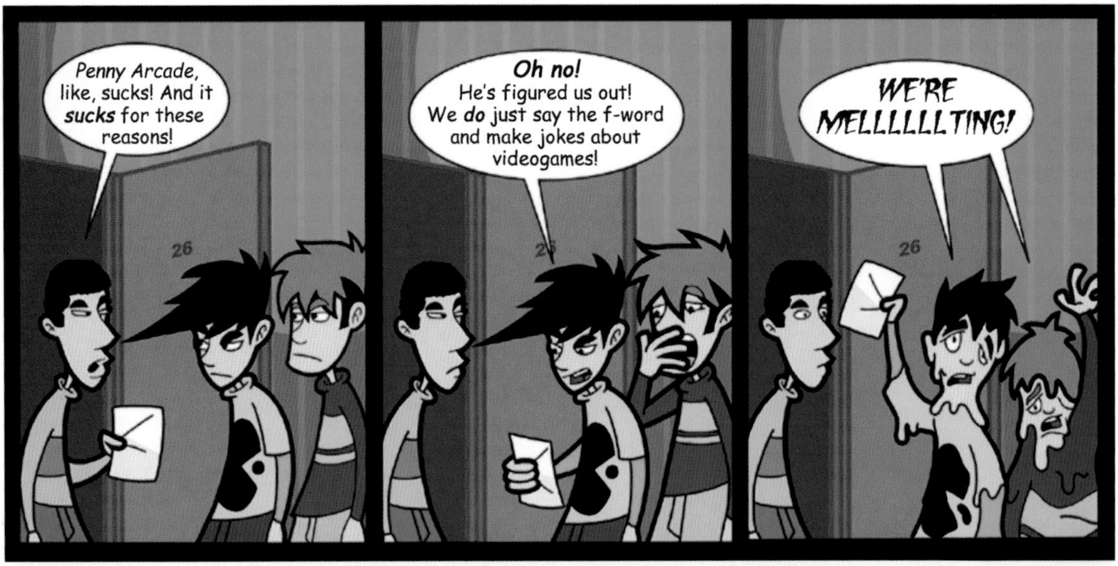
Penny Arcade, like, sucks! And it *sucks* for these reasons!
Oh no! He's figured us out! We *do* just say the f-word and make jokes about videogames!
WE'RE MELLLLLLTING!

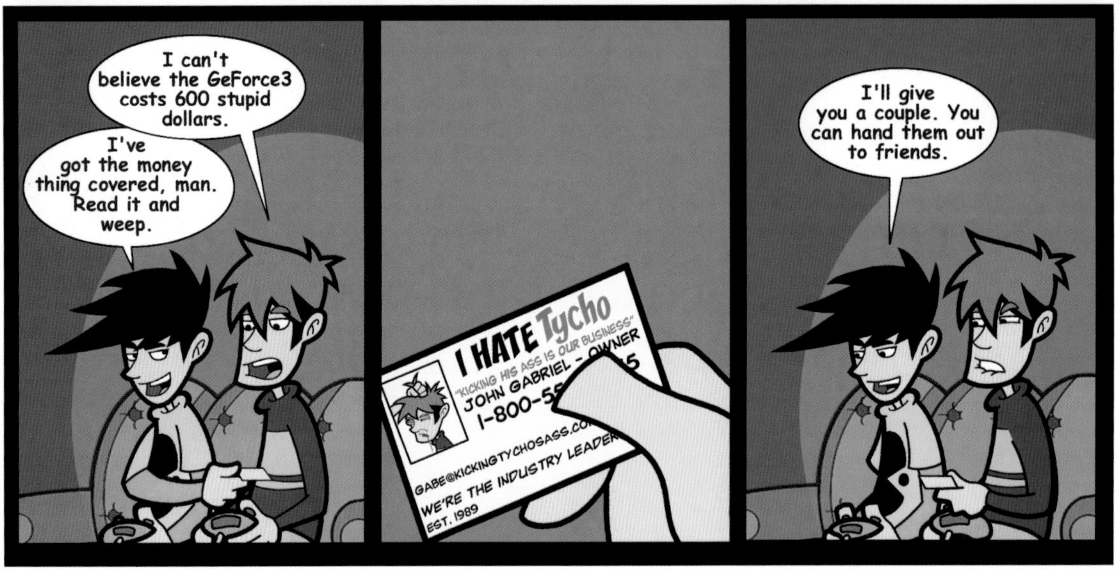
I can't believe the GeForce3 costs 600 stupid dollars.
I've got the money thing covered, man. Read it and weep.
I HATE Tycho
"KICKING HIS ASS IS OUR BUSINESS"
JOHN GABRIEL - OWNER
WE'RE THE INDUSTRY LEADER
EST. 1989
I'll give you a couple. You can hand them out to friends.

WHAT A WORLD, WHAT A WORLD

March 5, 2001 Our enemies always lurk in the shadows, seeking to undo our mighty works. Someone had written a kind of epic assault on *Penny Arcade*, and then he sent us a mail about it to make sure we would see it. I wasn't sure exactly what he thought would happen, but our comic for that day did suggest one possible outcome.

SATISFACTION GUARANTEED

March 7, 2001 Six hundred dollars became the new upper-end price around this point. At the time of this writing, Dell just announced a machine with fully four top of the line videocards jammed within—and the price? *Seventy thousand dollars*. I don't really know how much it costs. I'll bet it's a lot, though.

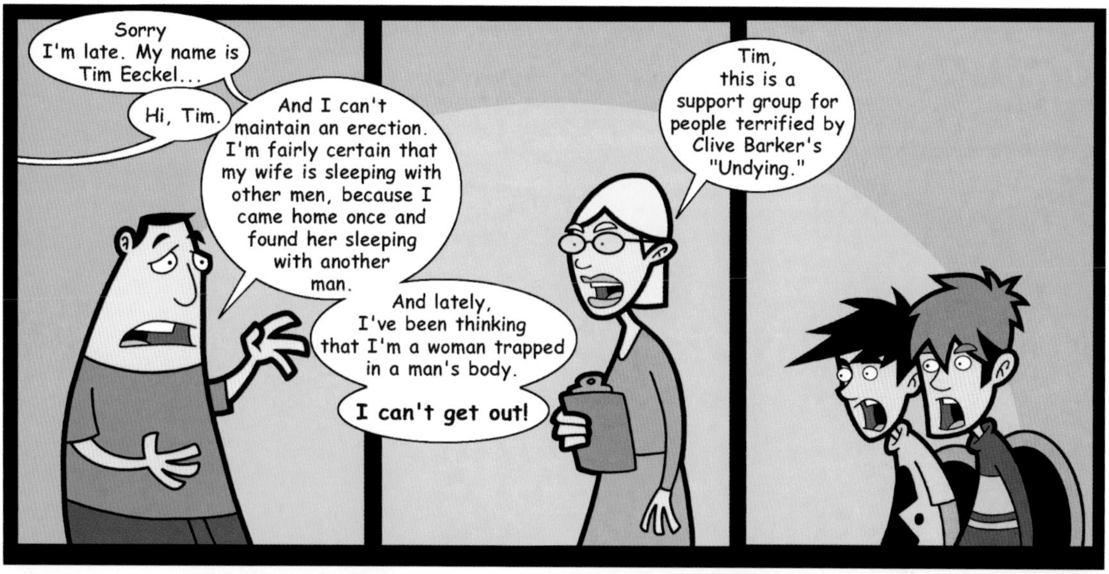
Sorry I'm late. My name is Tim Eeckel...
Hi, Tim.
And I can't maintain an erection. I'm fairly certain that my wife is sleeping with other men, because I came home once and found her sleeping with another man.
And lately, I've been thinking that I'm a woman trapped in a man's body.
I can't get out!
Tim, this is a support group for people terrified by Clive Barker's "Undying."

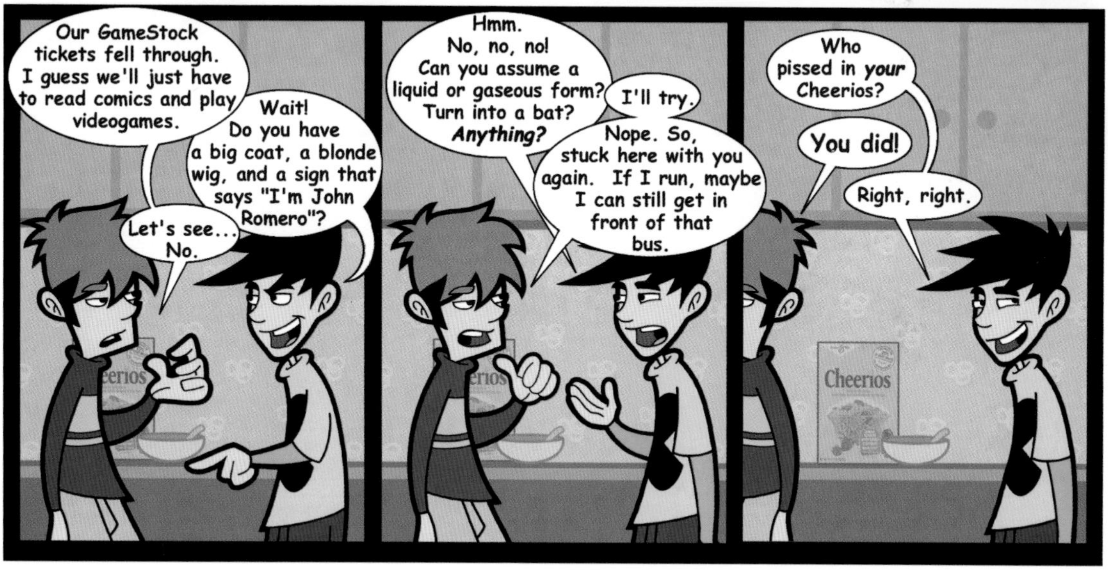
Our GameStock tickets fell through. I guess we'll just have to read comics and play videogames.
Wait! Do you have a big coat, a blonde wig, and a sign that says "I'm John Romero"?
Let's see... No.
Hmm. No, no, no! Can you assume a liquid or gaseous form? Turn into a bat? *Anything?*
I'll try.
Nope. So, stuck here with you again. If I run, maybe I can still get in front of that bus.
Who pissed in *your* Cheerios?
You did!
Right, right.
Cheerios

OMG

March 9, 2001 The whole sordid tale could perhaps sustain its *own* book about the negligence and excess of the "Dot Com Era"—but Tim Eeckel was a real piece of work. Do a search for "eFront Logs" sometime if you want to read the internal dialogues of a company imploding in slow motion. Long story short, our friend Tim was working to have us removed from Penny Arcade—our own site—and replaced with compliant management shills. Delightful.

A BALANCED BREAKFAST

March 14, 2001 This is the second-to-last John Romero strip, thank all that is *pure* and *holy.*

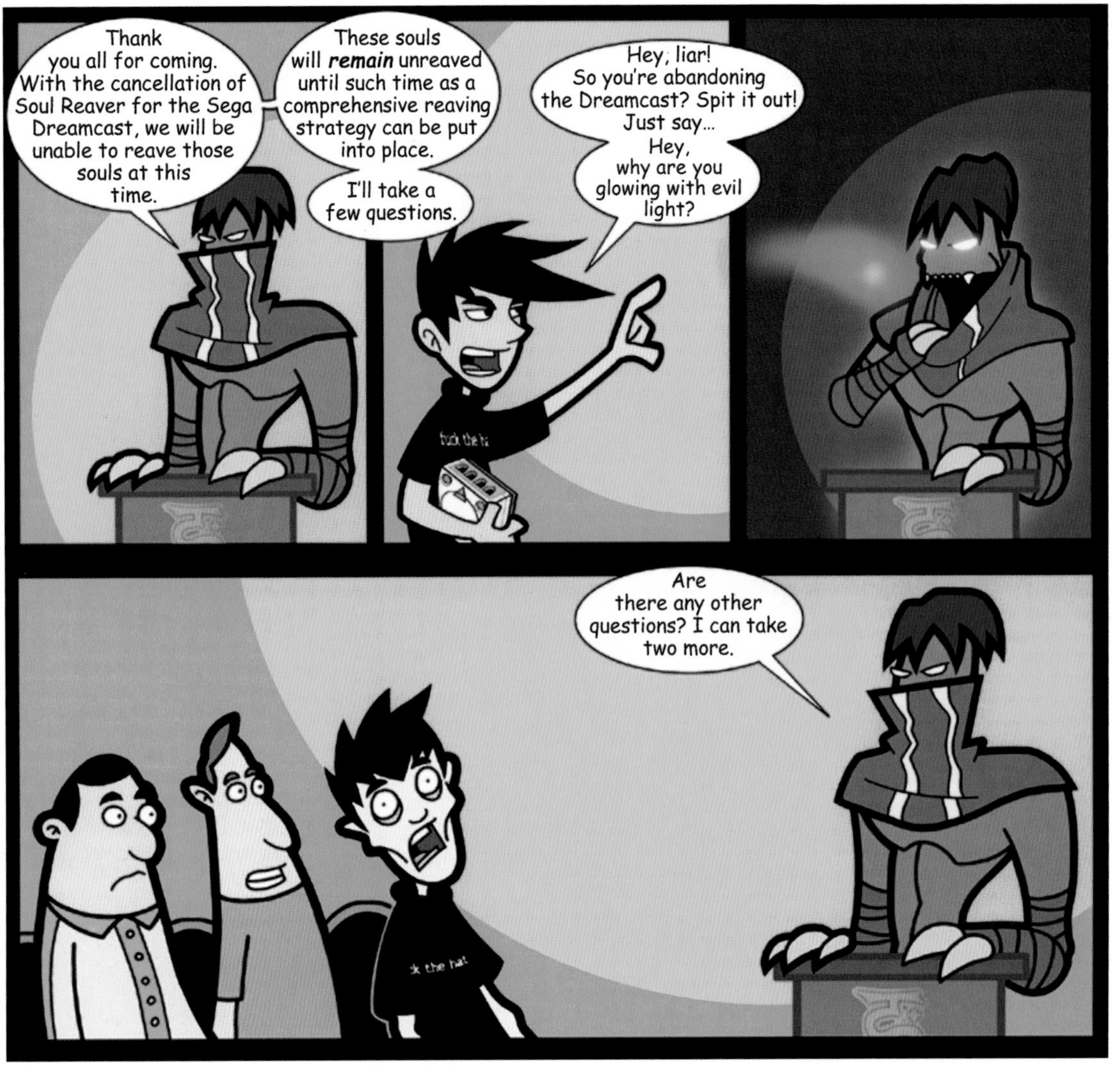
Thank you all for coming. With the cancellation of Soul Reaver for the Sega Dreamcast, we will be unable to reave those souls at this time.
These souls will ***remain*** unreaved until such time as a comprehensive reaving strategy can be put into place.
I'll take a few questions.
Hey, liar! So you're abandoning the Dreamcast? Spit it out! Just say...
Hey, why are you glowing with evil light?
Are there any other questions? I can take two more.

NOT "HAT," "HATERS"

March 12, 2001 Ah, that dark period near the end of a console's lifespan where it begins to fall off release lists, doesn't warrant multiplatform consideration, and the like. There was a lot of unrealized horsepower in the poor, star-crossed little Dreamcast, and it was hard to see it go.

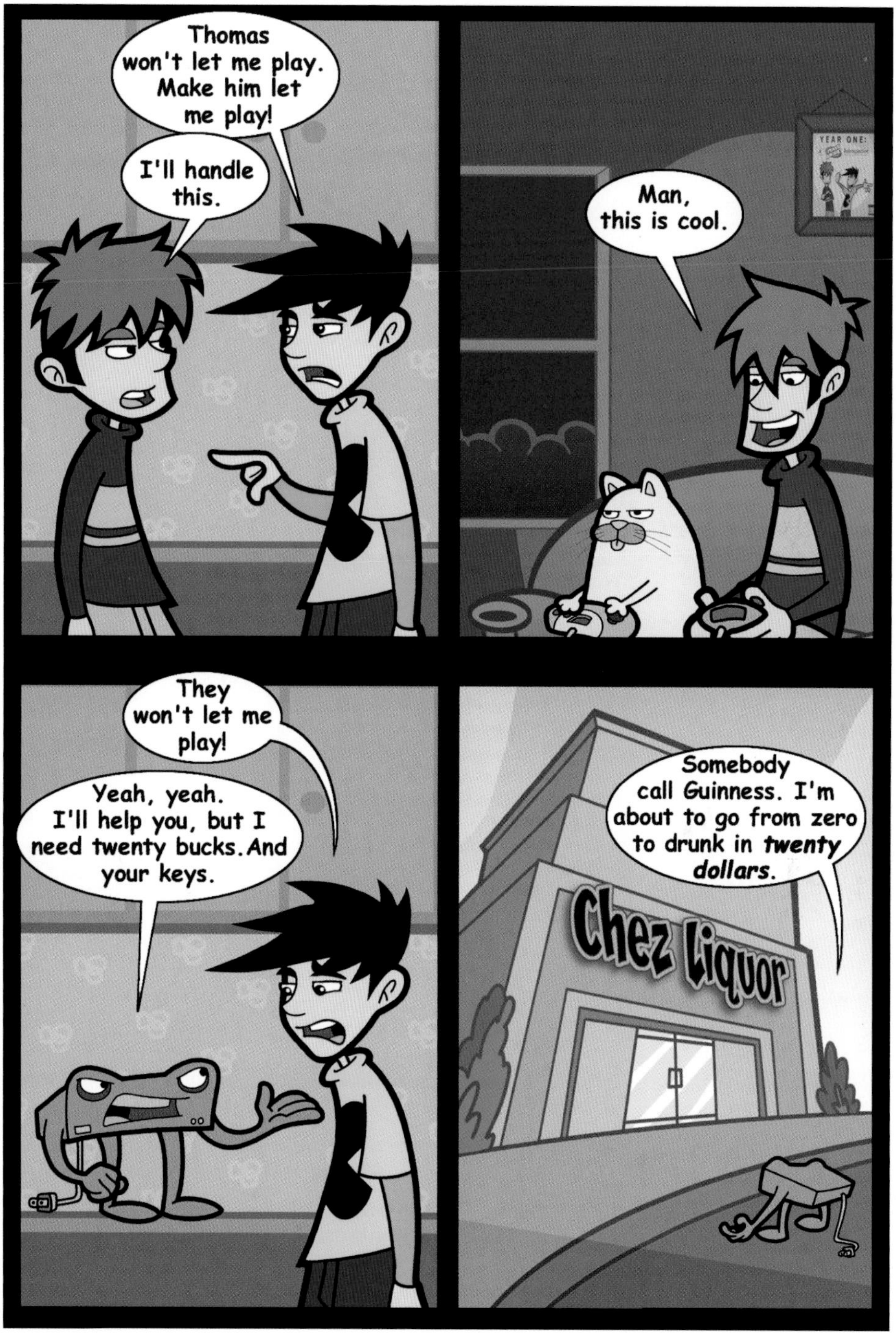
Thomas won't let me play. Make him let me play!
I'll handle this.
Man, this is cool.
YEAR ONE:
They won't let me play!
Yeah, yeah. I'll help you, but I need twenty bucks. And your keys.
Somebody call Guinness. I'm about to go from zero to drunk in *twenty dollars*.
Chez Liquor

THAT'S THE CAT

March 16, 2001 We named the cat after a kind of root beer we enjoy, for some reason whose wisdom is lost to me now. Root Beer had an almost holy connotation in the early days of the strip, and I'm not just making that up so I will seem wacky. It was a liquid that we took very seriously.

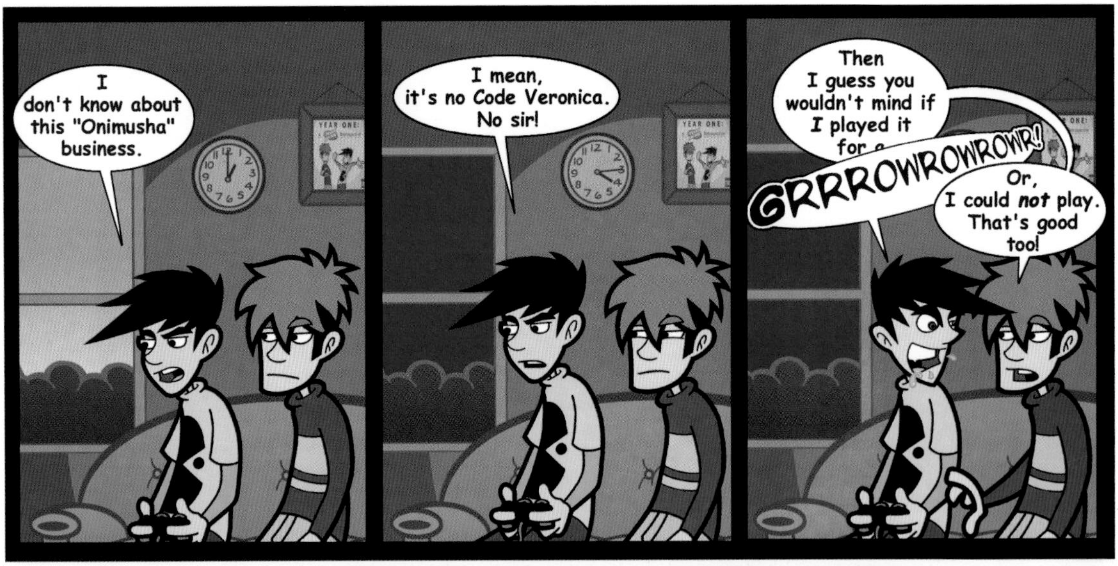
I don't know about this "Onimusha" business.
I mean, it's no Code Veronica. No sir!
Then I guess you wouldn't mind if I played it for a
GRRROWROWROWR!
Or, I could not play. That's good too!

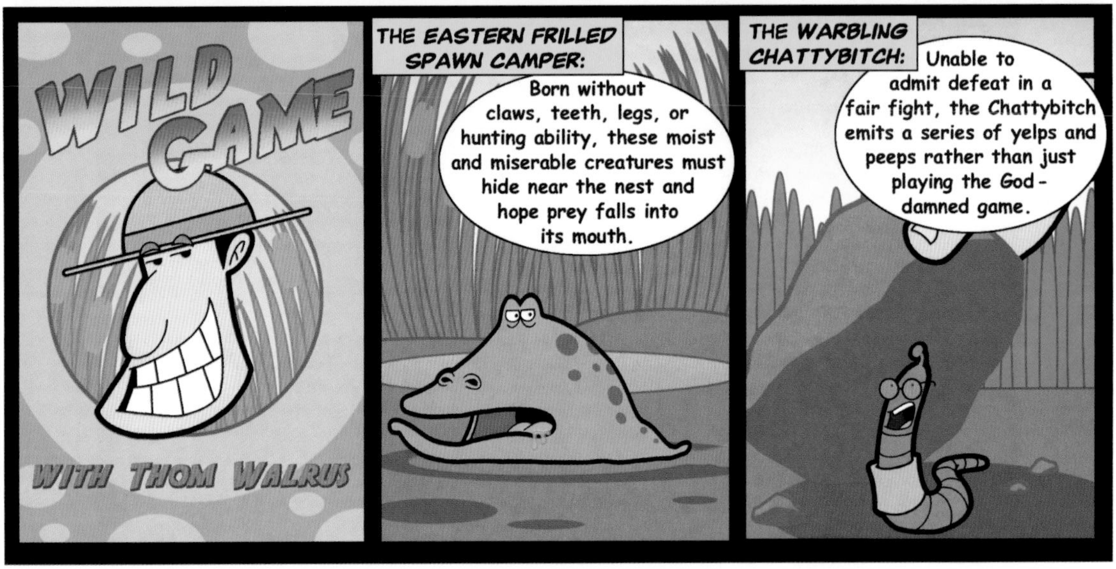
WILD GAME
WITH THOM WALRUS
THE EASTERN FRILLED SPAWN CAMPER:
Born without claws, teeth, legs, or hunting ability, these moist and miserable creatures must hide near the nest and hope prey falls into its mouth.
THE WARBLING CHATTYBITCH:
Unable to admit defeat in a fair fight, the Chattybitch emits a series of yelps and peeps rather than just playing the God-damned game.

IT'S A REALLY FUN GAME

March 19, 2001 Onimusha was billed as Samurai Survival Horror, Samurival Horror, or *something*, but it's really a hack-and-slash action game where sometimes you see a ghost. There have been seven games in the series now, on three different platforms, so apparently draining demon souls has some resonant quality.

NATURAL JUICES

March 21, 2001 Our tastes in gaming go through phases, where we might shift from more public, round and match type shooters to more protracted strategy affairs or—more recently—losing ourselves for months, and perhaps even years, in what is called the "massive" genre. Frustrations with the society on public servers were starting to create one of those shifts.

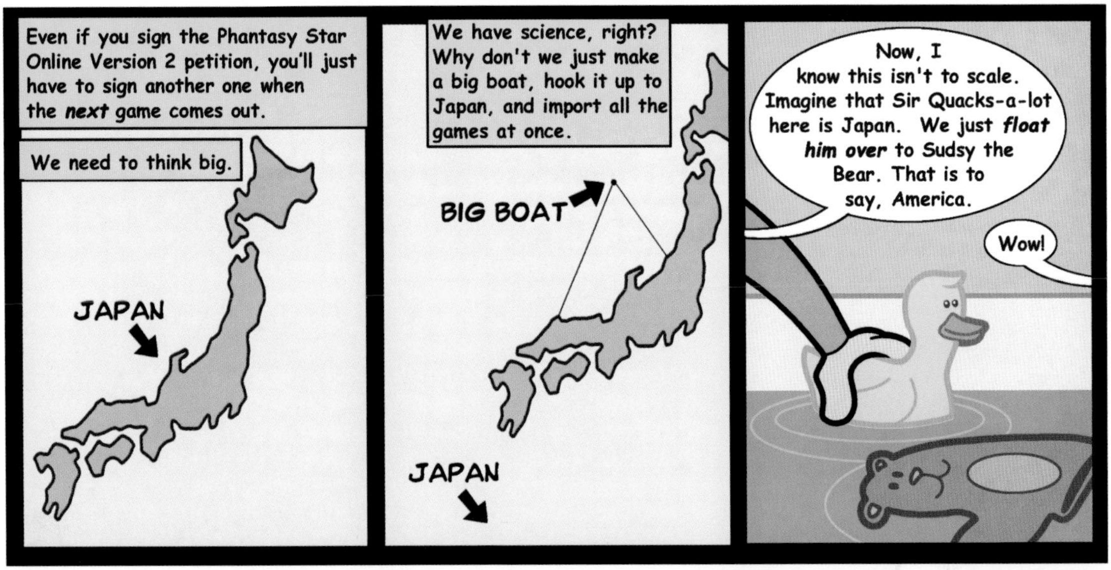
Even if you sign the Phantasy Star Online Version 2 petition, you'll just have to sign another one when the *next* game comes out.
We need to think big.
JAPAN
We have science, right? Why don't we just make a big boat, hook it up to Japan, and import all the games at once.
BIG BOAT
JAPAN
Now, I know this isn't to scale. Imagine that Sir Quacks-a-lot here is Japan. We just *float him over* to Sudsy the Bear. That is to say, America.
Wow!

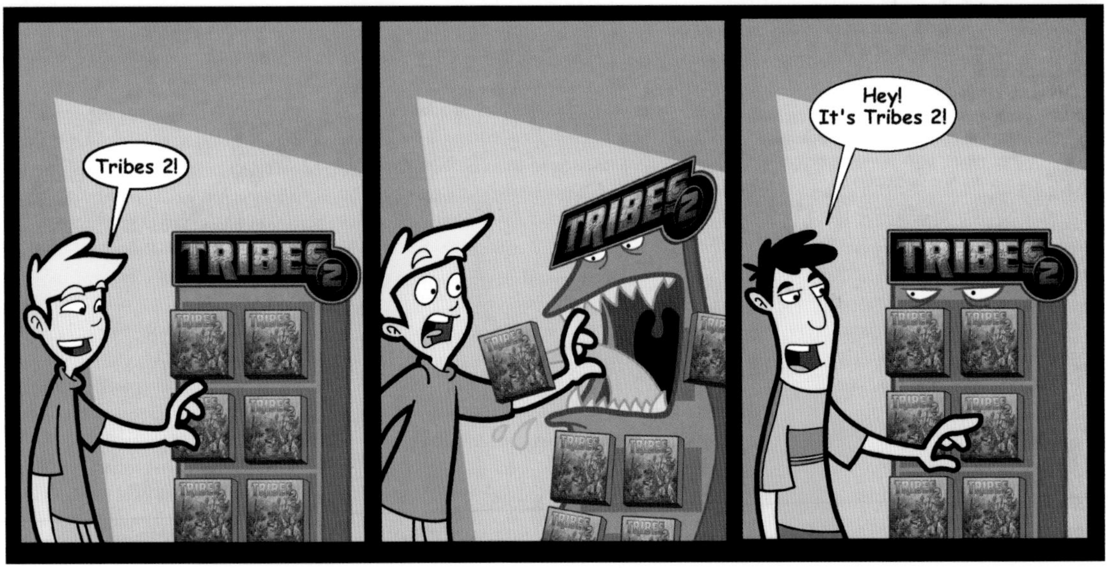
Tribes 2!
TRIBES 2
TRIBES 2
Hey! It's Tribes 2!
TRIBES 2

JUST CRAZY ENOUGH

March 23, 2001 When this comic went online, it included a petition from one of those Online Petition Sites they have out there on your Webnet. It netted around 3083 signatures, which is more than the petition to establish a USRDA for Jell-O (1465) but less than one to amend the constitution, allowing a Pokémon to become president (167,456).

A REMARKABLE SPECIMEN

March 26, 2001 This terrifying strip is about a world where organisms use the trappings of our pastime against us! The shelfmaw pictured here is clearly a danger, not only to the hand itself but also to the tender forearm. Another creature of concern is the iThrush, whose trilling, sing-song "Sega" can lure a gamer out from their home into a world of waiting danger.

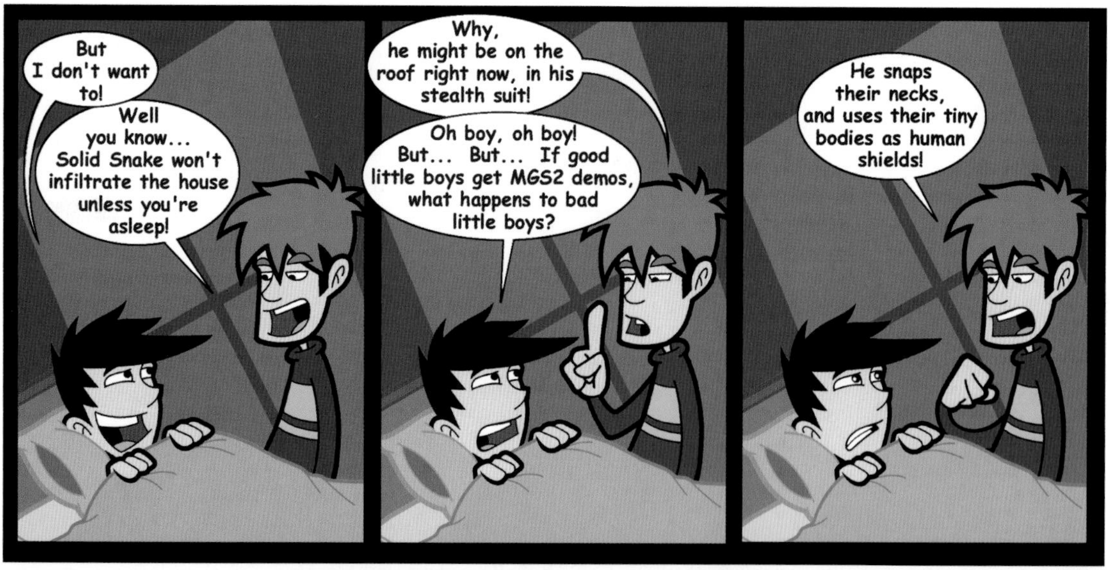
But I don't want to!
Well you know... Solid Snake won't infiltrate the house unless you're asleep!
Why, he might be on the roof right now, in his stealth suit!
Oh boy, oh boy! But... But... If good little boys get MGS2 demos, what happens to bad little boys?
He snaps their necks, and uses their tiny bodies as human shields!

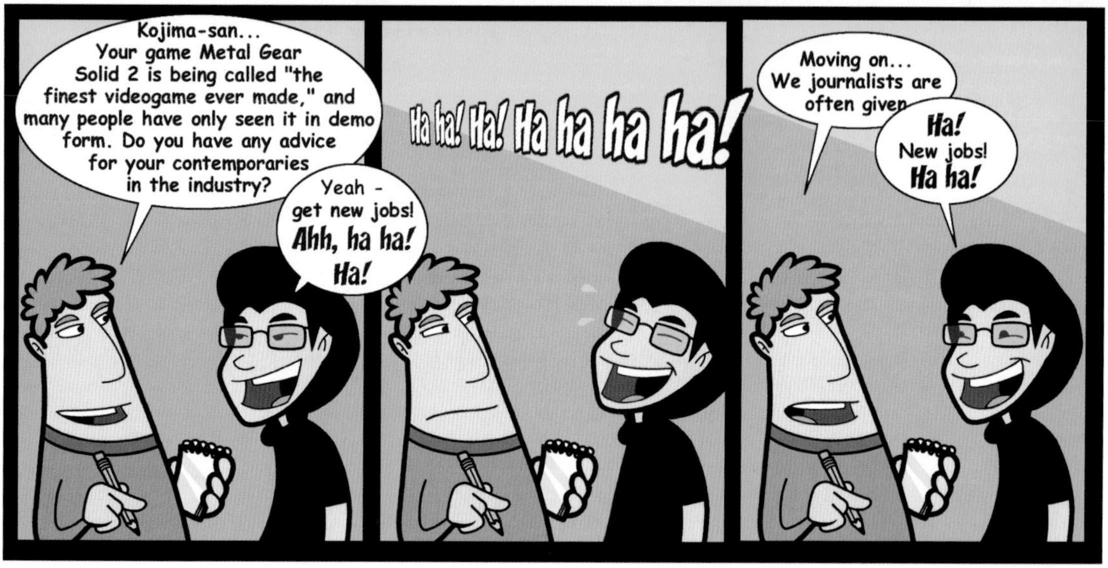
Kojima-san... Your game Metal Gear Solid 2 is being called "the finest videogame ever made," and many people have only seen it in demo form. Do you have any advice for your contemporaries in the industry?
Yeah - get new jobs! Ahh, ha ha! Ha!
Ha ha! Ha! Ha ha ha ha!
Moving on... We journalists are often given
Ha! New jobs! Ha ha!

AND ALL THROUGH THE HIZOUSE

March 28, 2001 The Metal Gear Solid 2 demo referenced here was a pack-in with a game called Zone of the Enders, a decent but not entirely *memorable* journey into some kind of . . . thing. I couldn't even tell you what zone it took place in. I could pop it in and find out, but that would mean moving my mug.

AGAIN, FOR THE FIRST TIME

March 30, 2001 Hideo Kojima actually seems like a very nice man, and he invented Solid Snake, so hey. He recently started a blog, wherein he chronicled the pervading melancholy of winter. Any man who chronicles the melancholy of winter is okay in my book.

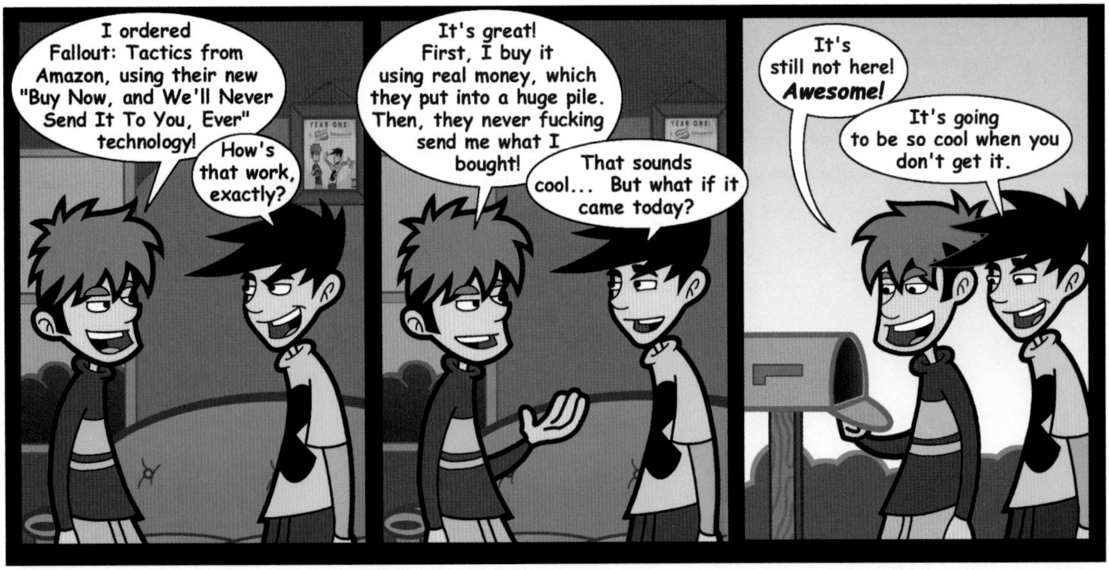
I ordered Fallout: Tactics from Amazon, using their new "Buy Now, and We'll Never Send It To You, Ever" technology!
How's that work, exactly?
It's great! First, I buy it using real money, which they put into a huge pile. Then, they never fucking send me what I bought!
That sounds cool... But what if it came today?
It's still not here! Awesome!
It's going to be so cool when you don't get it.

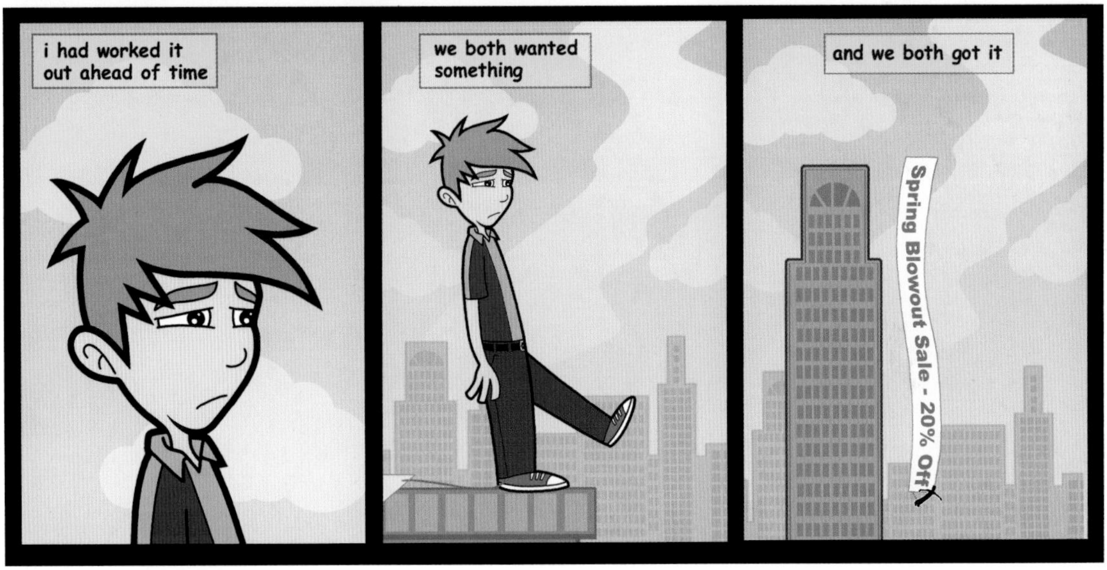
i had worked it out ahead of time
we both wanted something
and we both got it
Spring Blowout Sale - 20% Off

IT REALLY WORKS

March 31, 2001 This was a bonus comic that went up on a weekend originally. The site had largely stabilized financially by this point, after using a combination of Paypal and what Amazon called their "Honor System." The idea of running a site on donations—what was called "begging" at the time—was considered antithetical to the *true spirit* that coursed through the routers of an unsullied Web.

BEWARE: FALLING PRICES

April 2, 2001 Some guy had a site where he used the (by turns) enraged, despondent, and suicidal phone messages left by an ex-girlfriend to enrich himself. Some bizarre internal process created this image out of that stimulus. I don't know that this comic belongs on *Penny Arcade*, but I still like it.

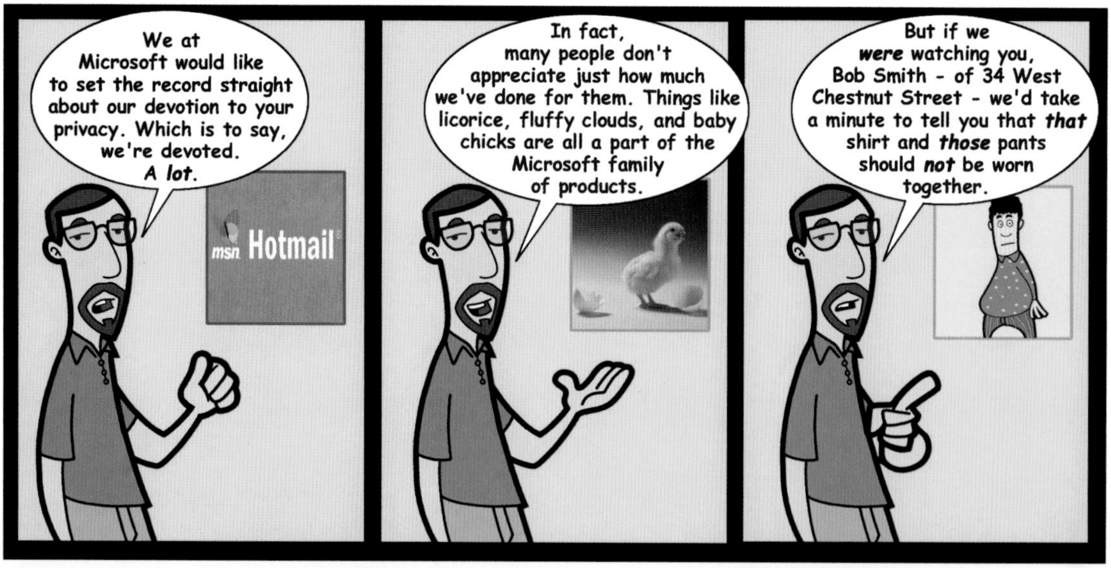
We at Microsoft would like to set the record straight about our devotion to your privacy. Which is to say, we're devoted. A *lot*.
msn Hotmail
In fact, many people don't appreciate just how much we've done for them. Things like licorice, fluffy clouds, and baby chicks are all a part of the Microsoft family of products.
But if we *were* watching you, Bob Smith - of 34 West Chestnut Street - we'd take a minute to tell you that *that* shirt and *those* pants should *not* be worn together.

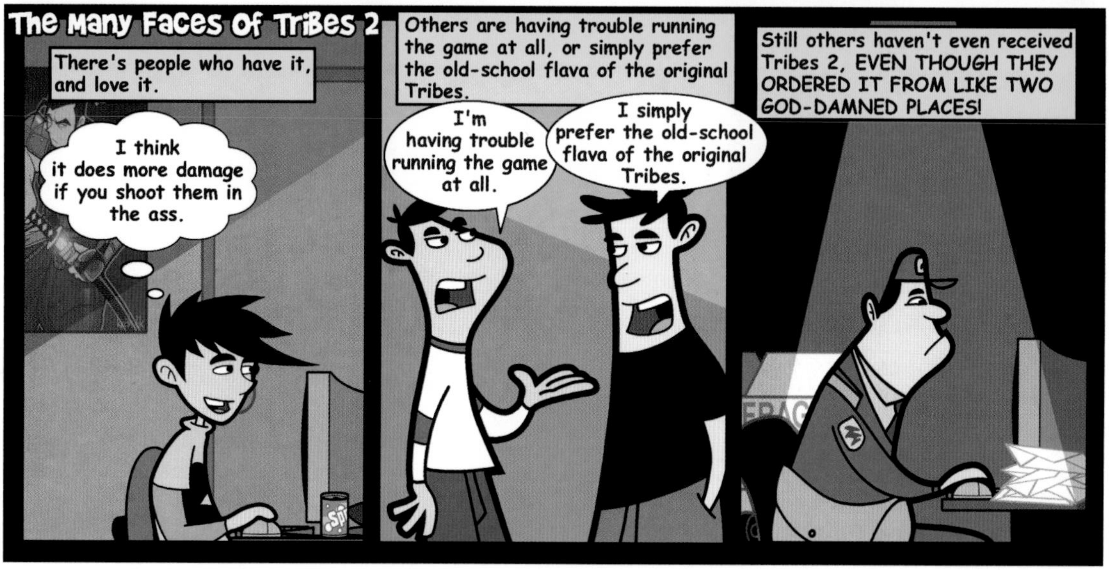
The Many Faces Of Tribes 2
There's people who have it, and love it.
I think it does more damage if you shoot them in the ass.
Others are having trouble running the game at all, or simply prefer the old-school flava of the original Tribes.
I'm having trouble running the game at all.
I simply prefer the old-school flava of the original Tribes.
Still others haven't even received Tribes 2, EVEN THOUGH THEY ORDERED IT FROM LIKE TWO GOD-DAMNED PLACES!

BLAH BLAH BLAH(™)

April 4, 2001 I'm not even sure I remember which evil act Microsoft was being blamed for this time.

YOU ASKED FOR IT

April 6, 2001 You can see here why I was mad enough to write a strip about Amazon the week before: my precious Tribes 2 had been delayed. It saw mixed reviews, as you can probably glean from the strip—but it dominated our online play for months. Even after we stopped playing the game proper, we came back to the *engine*, at least, for a mod called Team Aerial Combat 2.

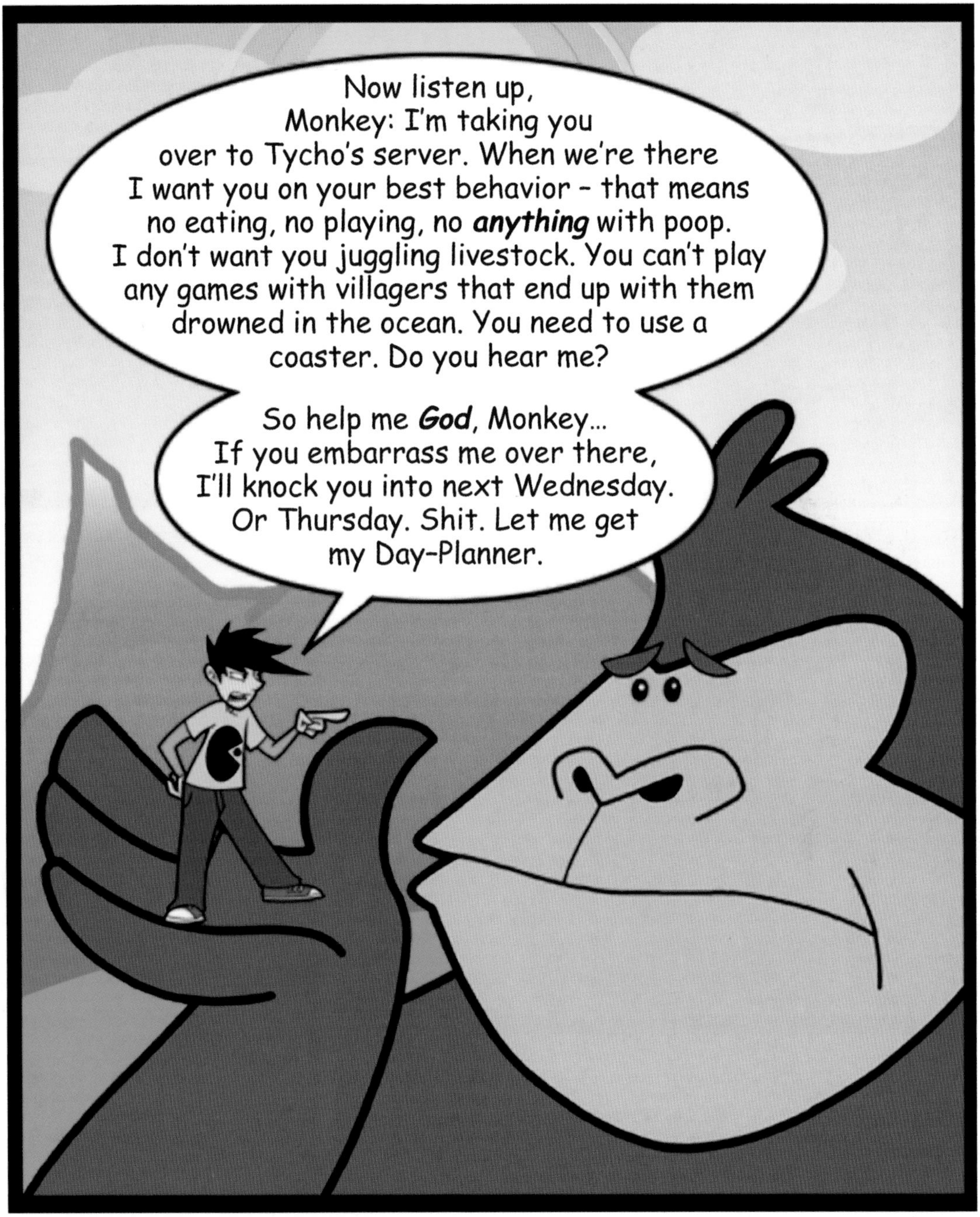
Now listen up, Monkey: I'm taking you over to Tycho's server. When we're there I want you on your best behavior - that means no eating, no playing, no *anything* with poop. I don't want you juggling livestock. You can't play any games with villagers that end up with them drowned in the ocean. You need to use a coaster. Do you hear me?
So help me *God*, Monkey... If you embarrass me over there, I'll knock you into next Wednesday. Or Thursday. Shit. Let me get my Day-Planner.

I'LL TURN THIS CAR AROUND

April 9, 2001 Black and White wasn't an amazing game, but the life they infused their huge pets with would trick you into thinking it was. As such, it was a game with powerful *moments*, and the power of those moments was commensurate with the amount of yourself you were willing to invest in believing the simulation. You could play the game in a co-operative fashion, introducing your pets to one another—this was where we spent most of our time.

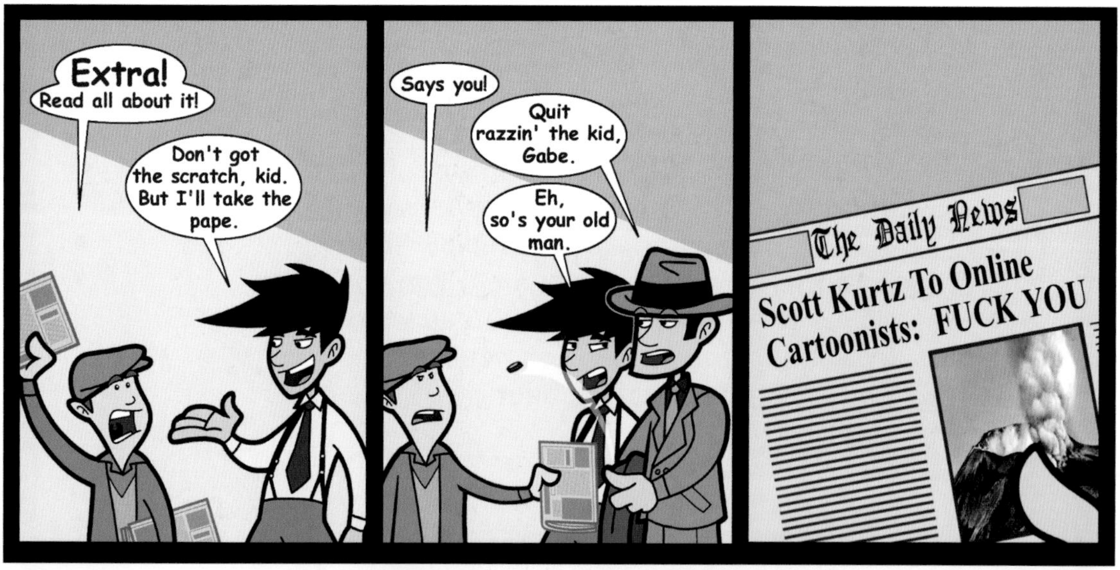
Extra!
Read all about it!
Don't got the scratch, kid. But I'll take the pape.
Says you!
Quit razzin' the kid, Gabe.
Eh, so's your old man.
The Daily News
Scott Kurtz To Online Cartoonists: FUCK YOU

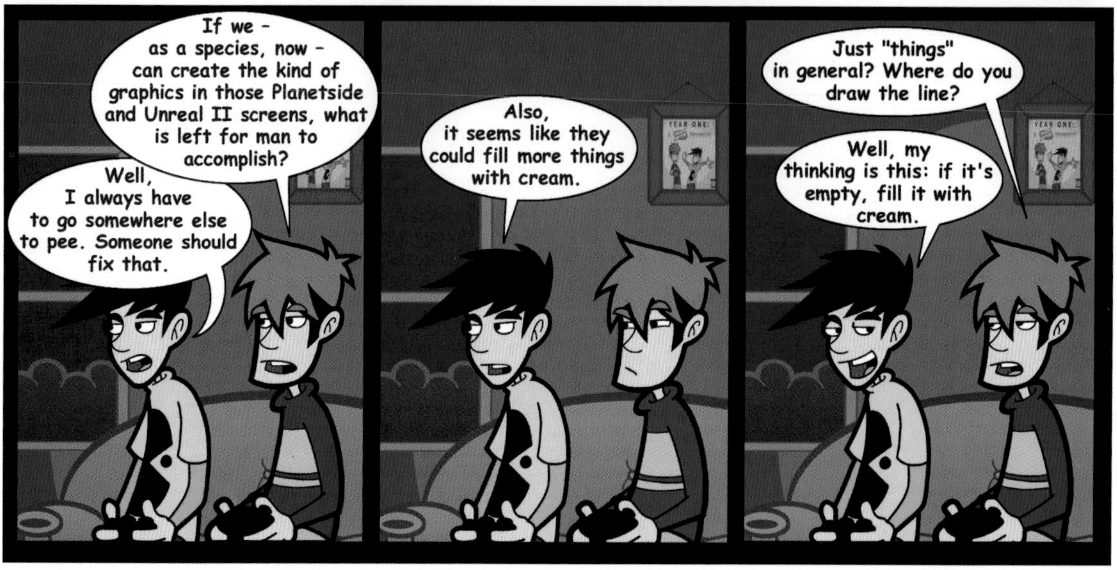
If we - as a species, now - can create the kind of graphics in those Planetside and Unreal II screens, what is left for man to accomplish?
Well, I always have to go somewhere else to pee. Someone should fix that.
Also, it seems like they could fill more things with cream.
Just "things" in general? Where do you draw the line?
Well, my thinking is this: if it's empty, fill it with cream.

TROUBLETOWN

April 11, 2001 *PvP's* Scott Kurtz has a reputation for being a shrewd businessman, and I don't dispute that, but the fact that he thinks about business—hard, real business, not ethereal "models"—differentiates him from most people doing work on the web. He posted a rant where he described a coming collapse in Webcomics, and he had his reasons for doing so, but this was our (strange, anachronistic) response.

CREME DE LA STUFF

April 13, 2001 Of course, due to the phenomenon called "bullshot" that we would give name to years later, Planetside didn't quite compare to the screens you saw. Unreal II looked pretty great, but in order to see those graphics you had to actually play the game. Which was unfortunate.

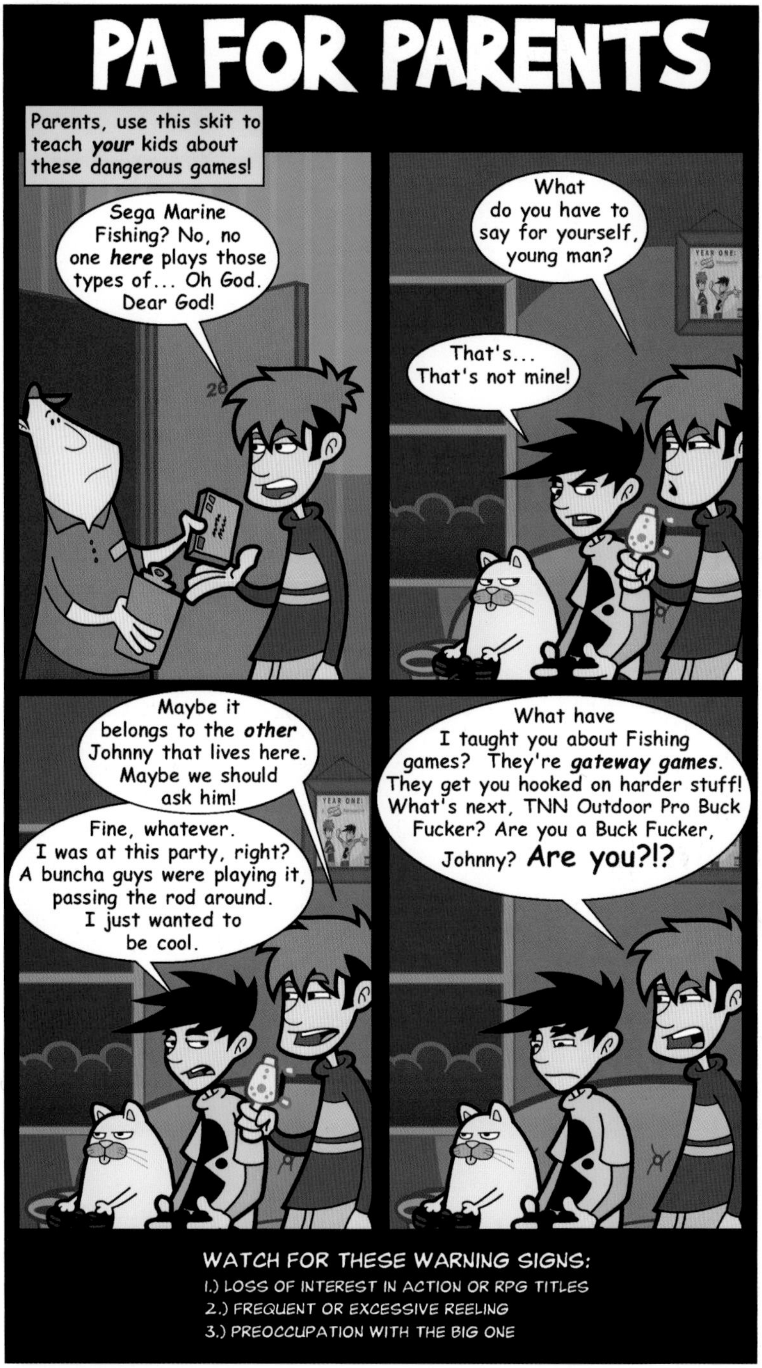
PA FOR PARENTS
Parents, use this skit to teach your kids about these dangerous games!
Sega Marine Fishing? No, no one here plays those types of... Oh God. Dear God!
What do you have to say for yourself, young man?
That's... That's not mine!
Maybe it belongs to the other Johnny that lives here. Maybe we should ask him!
Fine, whatever. I was at this party, right? A buncha guys were playing it, passing the rod around. I just wanted to be cool.
What have I taught you about Fishing games? They're gateway games. They get you hooked on harder stuff! What's next, TNN Outdoor Pro Buck Fucker? Are you a Buck Fucker, Johnny? Are you?!?
WATCH FOR THESE WARNING SIGNS:
1.) LOSS OF INTEREST IN ACTION OR RPG TITLES
2.) FREQUENT OR EXCESSIVE REELING
3.) PREOCCUPATION WITH THE BIG ONE

FOR MOM AND DAD!

April 16, 2001 When you find a friend's fishing controller—specifically Interact's "Fission" Fishing Controller for the Dreamcast—you take a very serious accounting of your relationship with that person. There are many genres toward which I am willing to turn a blind eye, but hunting and fishing games will always be worth negative ten zillion points.

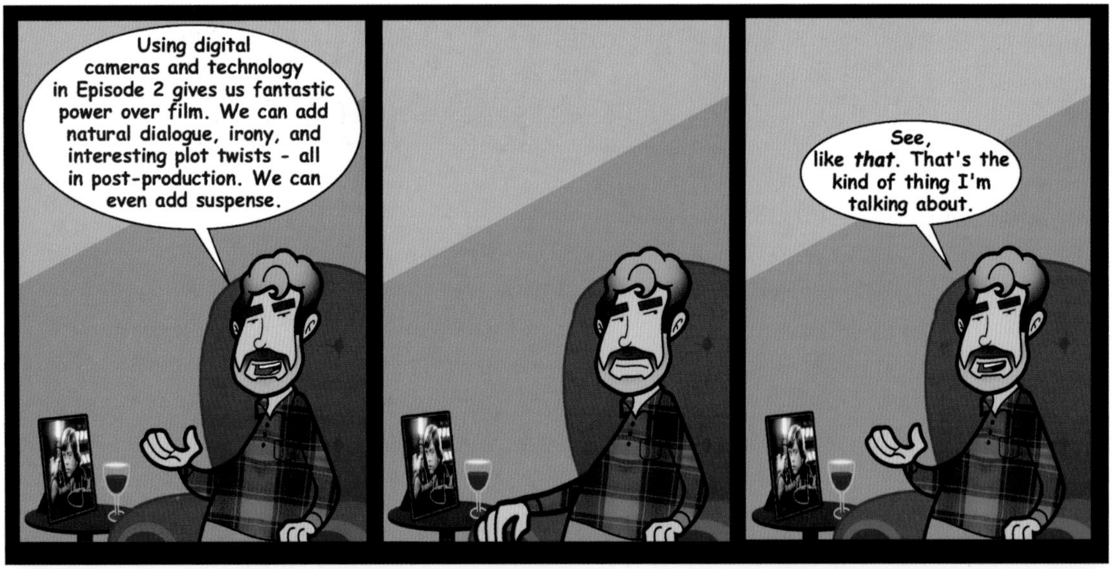
Using digital cameras and technology in Episode 2 gives us fantastic power over film. We can add natural dialogue, irony, and interesting plot twists - all in post-production. We can even add suspense.
See, like *that*. That's the kind of thing I'm talking about.

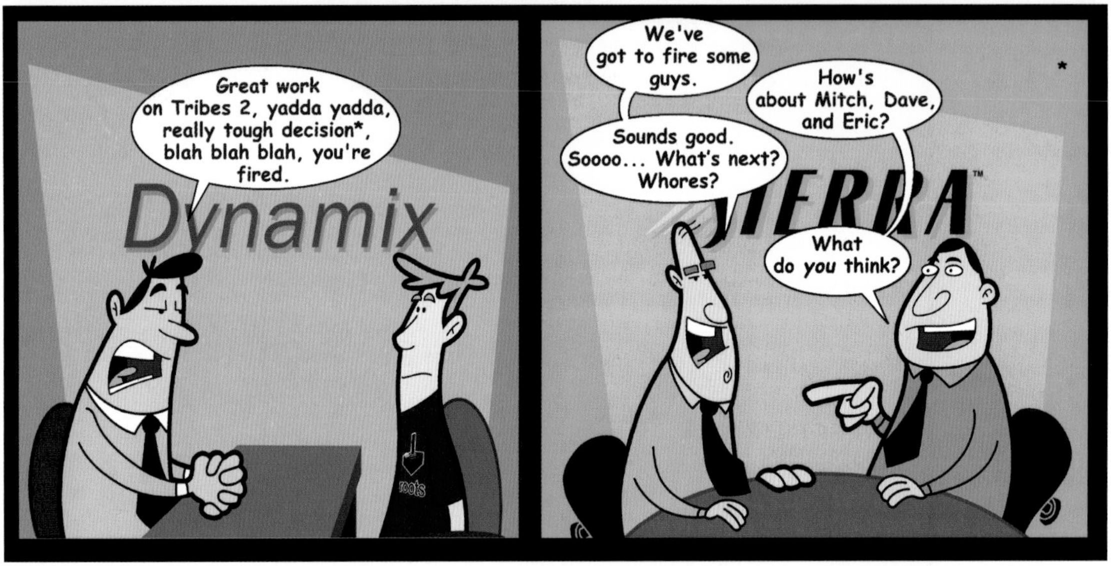
Great work on Tribes 2, yadda yadda, really tough decision*, blah blah blah, you're fired.
Dynamix
We've got to fire some guys.
How's about Mitch, Dave, and Eric?
Sounds good. Soooo... What's next? Whores?
SIERRA
What do *you* think?
*

EPISODE POO

April 18, 2001 It's hard to imagine these days what energy and optimism must have infused *Star Wars* fans back then, when the prequels were still mostly unshaped potential, when they didn't know just how brutally their evil master would mistreat them. We know now what violence awaited their unshaken enthusiasm.

DECISIONS, DECISIONS

April 20, 2001 Speaking of brutal mistreatment, after Sierra released Tribes 2 too early they began cutting jobs at developer Dynamix—a company they would eventually dissolve. It would be three and a half years before another game was released in this hallowed setting, this time from Irrational Games—but I think the Tribes *era* was over by that time. A shame.

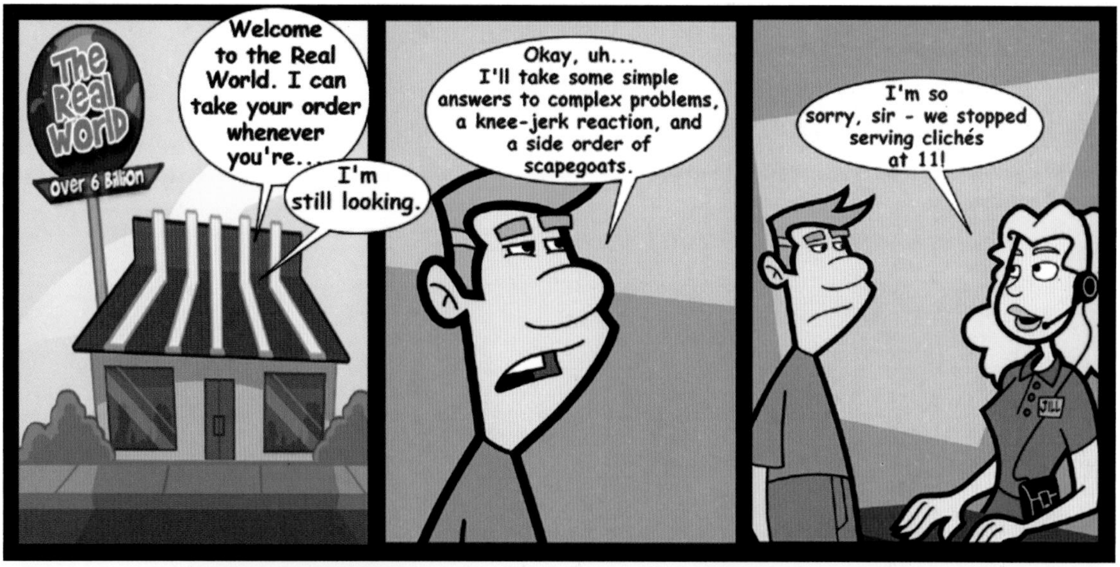
The Real World
Over 6 Billion
Welcome to the Real World. I can take your order whenever you're...
I'm still looking.
Okay, uh... I'll take some simple answers to complex problems, a knee-jerk reaction, and a side order of scapegoats.
I'm so sorry, sir - we stopped serving clichés at 11!

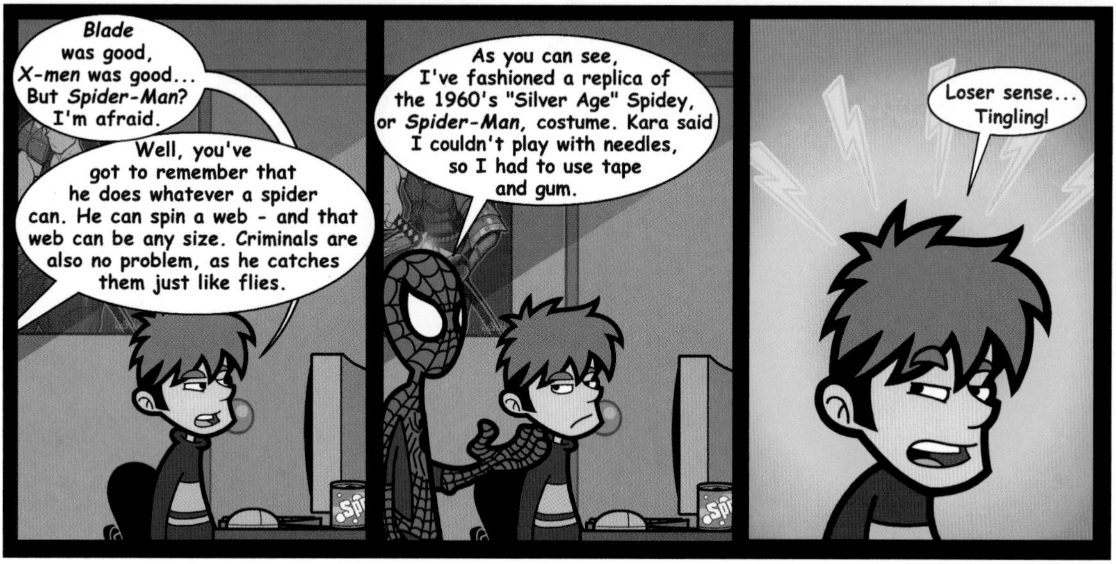
Blade was good, *X-men* was good... But *Spider-Man*? I'm afraid.
Well, you've got to remember that he does whatever a spider can. He can spin a web - and that web can be any size. Criminals are also no problem, as he catches them just like flies.
As you can see, I've fashioned a replica of the 1960's "Silver Age" Spidey, or *Spider-Man,* costume. Kara said I couldn't play with needles, so I had to use tape and gum.
Loser sense... Tingling!

DEAR STUPID PEOPLE:

April 23, 2001 We just got tired of people wanting to boil down something as complex as "youth violence" into some exceedingly simple equation, where you've got some violent media over here, and then *bloodbath*. The sort of person who needs to see this probably doesn't read *Penny Arcade* anyway.

AGAIN WITH THE SPIDERS

April 25, 2001 Comic sticklers wrote in by the thousands to establish that Peter Parker's "Spider Sense" doesn't detect *spiders*, so having a *loser sense* doesn't even *make* sense, you *morons*. And that hurt. Somehow, we managed to press on.

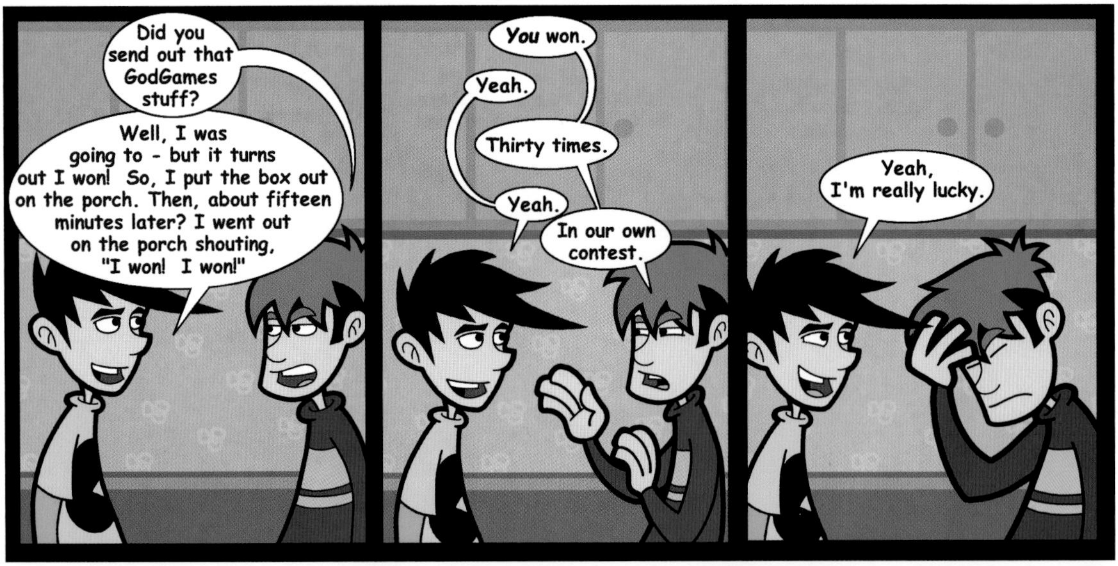
Did you send out that GodGames stuff?
Well, I was going to - but it turns out I won! So, I put the box out on the porch. Then, about fifteen minutes later? I went out on the porch shouting, "I won! I won!"
You won.
Yeah.
Thirty times.
Yeah.
In our own contest.
Yeah, I'm really lucky.

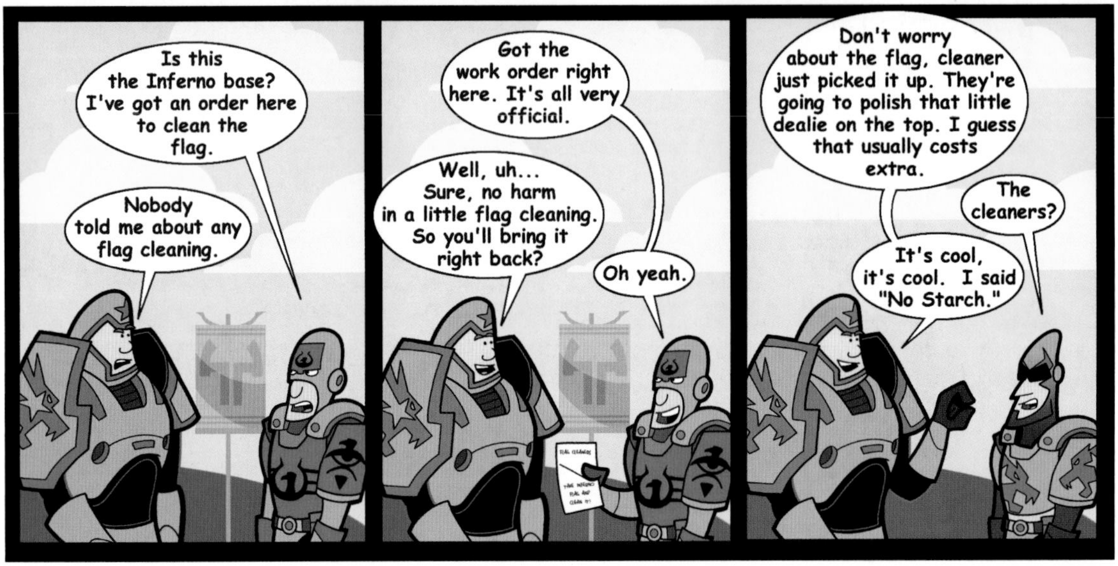
Is this the Inferno base? I've got an order here to clean the flag.
Nobody told me about any flag cleaning.
Got the work order right here. It's all very official.
Well, uh... Sure, no harm in a little flag cleaning. So you'll bring it right back?
Oh yeah.
Don't worry about the flag, cleaner just picked it up. They're going to polish that little dealie on the top. I guess that usually costs extra.
The cleaners?
It's cool, it's cool. I said "No Starch."

I HAVE MY DOUBTS

April 27, 2001 We had been given a ridiculous amount of merchandise by GodGames, the cats who knocked out Rune and Tropico, thirty prize packages in total. Sending it all away challenged my resolve, but I think it set me on the path to becoming a better person.

RED & BLUE: EPISODE ONE

April 30, 2001 Another manifestation of dastardly Red and simple-minded Blue, this time set in the Tribes Universe. Just as a piece of trivia, *shameful* trivia, Tribes is the only context that I've ever written fan fiction for. No details regarding these stories will ever be made available.

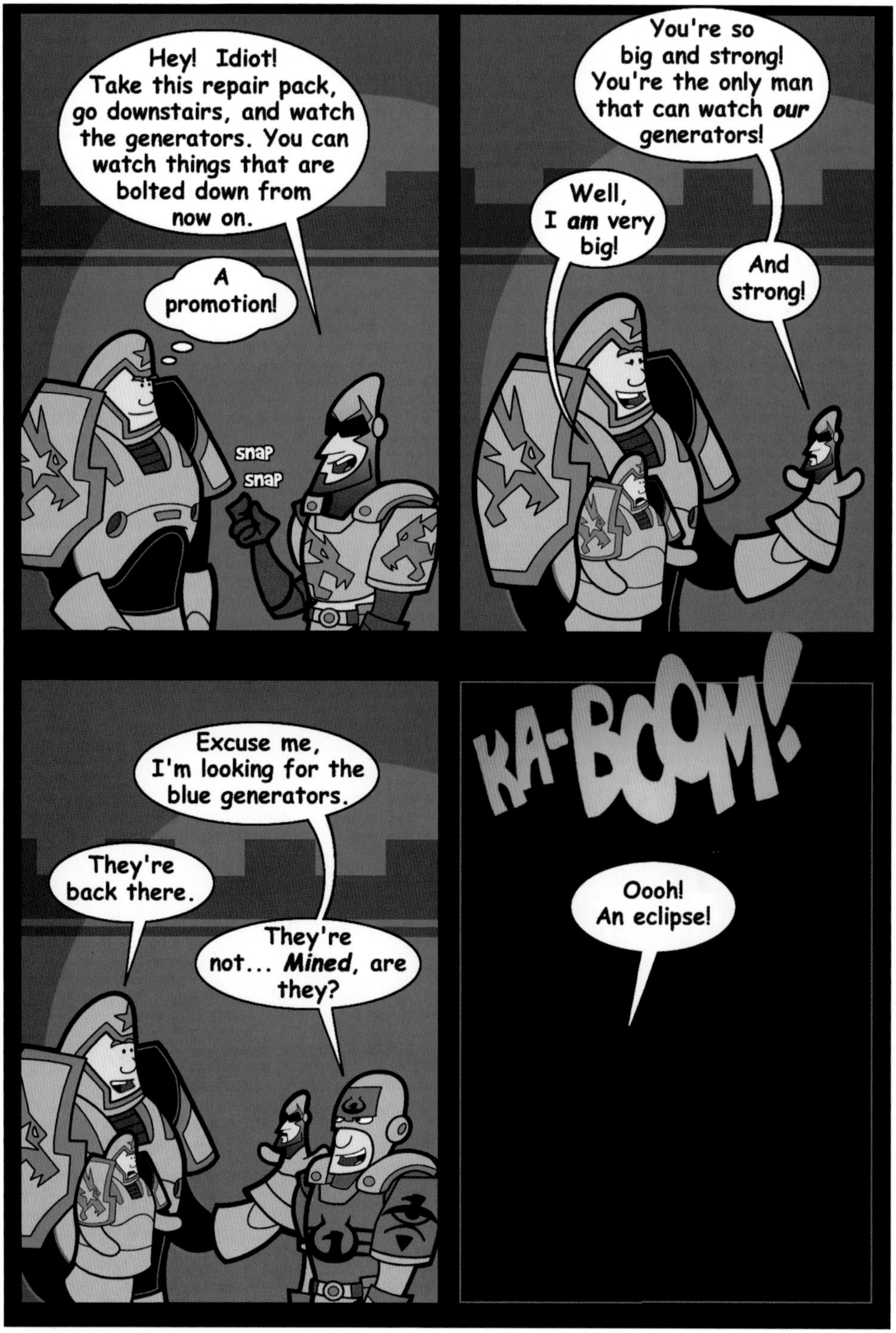
Hey! Idiot! Take this repair pack, go downstairs, and watch the generators. You can watch things that are bolted down from now on.
A promotion!
snap
snap
You're so big and strong! You're the only man that can watch *our* generators!
Well, I *am* very big!
And strong!
Excuse me, I'm looking for the blue generators.
They're back there.
They're not... *Mined*, are they?
KA-BOOM!
Oooh! An eclipse!

RED & BLUE: EPISODE TWO

May 2, 2001 Under no circumstances will a plot synopsis for *The Starborne Saga* ever be revealed. Do not ask me! I am turning away from you.

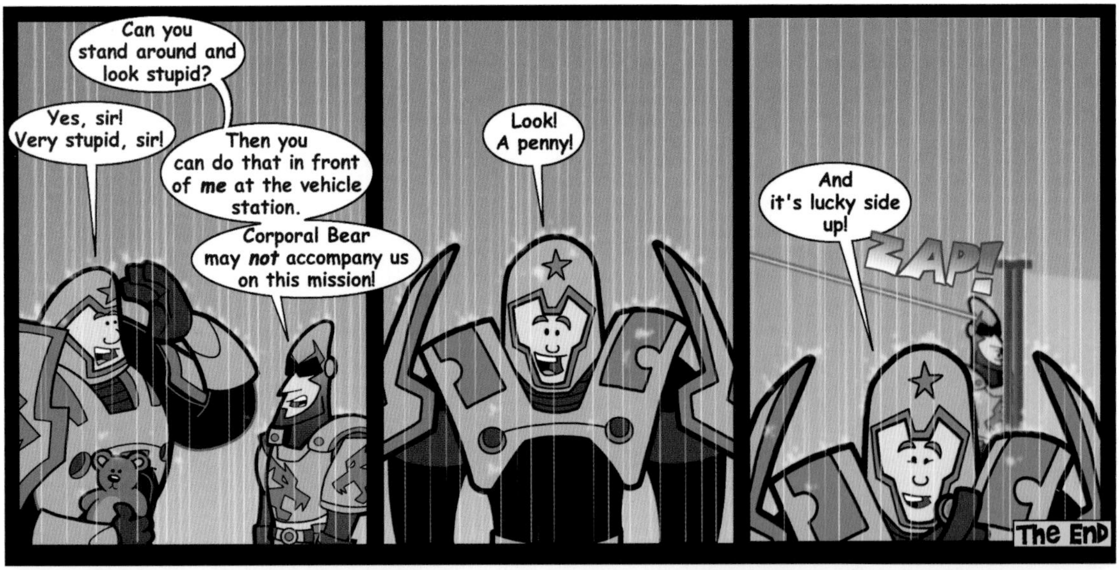
Can you stand around and look stupid?
Yes, sir! Very stupid, sir!
Then you can do that in front of *me* at the vehicle station.
Corporal Bear may *not* accompany us on this mission!
Look! A penny!
And it's lucky side up!
ZAP!
The End

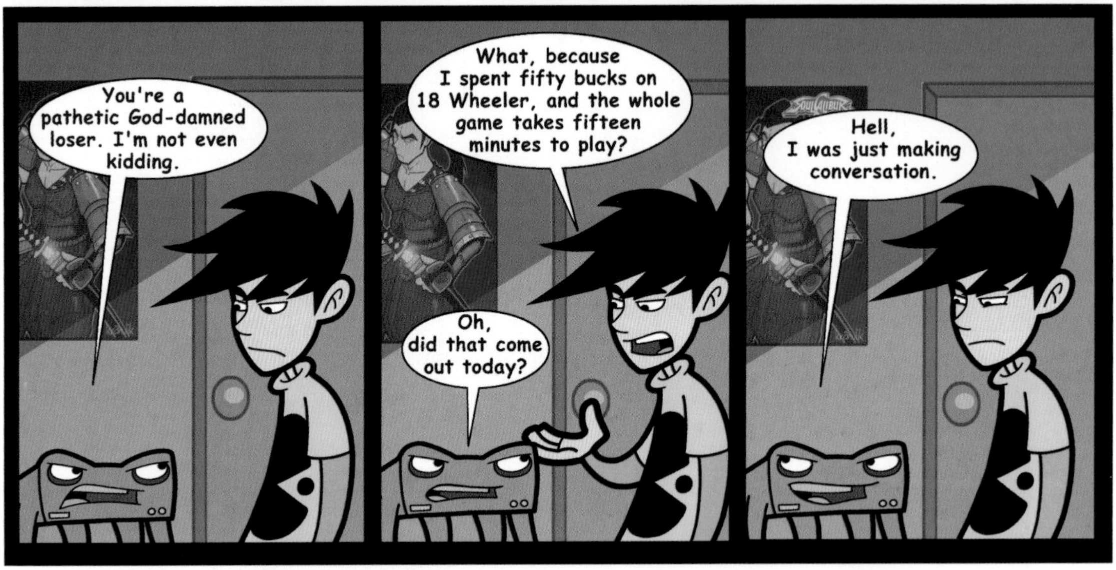
You're a pathetic God-damned loser. I'm not even kidding.
What, because I spent fifty bucks on 18 Wheeler, and the whole game takes fifteen minutes to play?
Oh, did that come out today?
Hell, I was just making conversation.

RED & BLUE: EPISODE THREE

May 4, 2001 IT IS ABOUT A DIAMOND SWORD SCOUT CALLED GILEAD AND HIS MACHINE INTELLECT ANIMAL COMPANION! Oh, the weight! How the *weight* of that secret pressed down upon my heart!

18 MINUTE WHEELER

May 25, 2001 18 Wheeler is actually pretty awesome. Like many arcade games, though, there's not a lot of raw content there—the game is designed to get you to "insert coin" as it were, and that's pretty much the whole thing. A lot of the draw relies on something cool about (in this case) the massive cabinet and huge, big rig truckin' wheel. Sega managed to make hauling freight seem fun. If you were good at backing in your truck, you could get an upgraded horn, and I'm being *completely serious.*

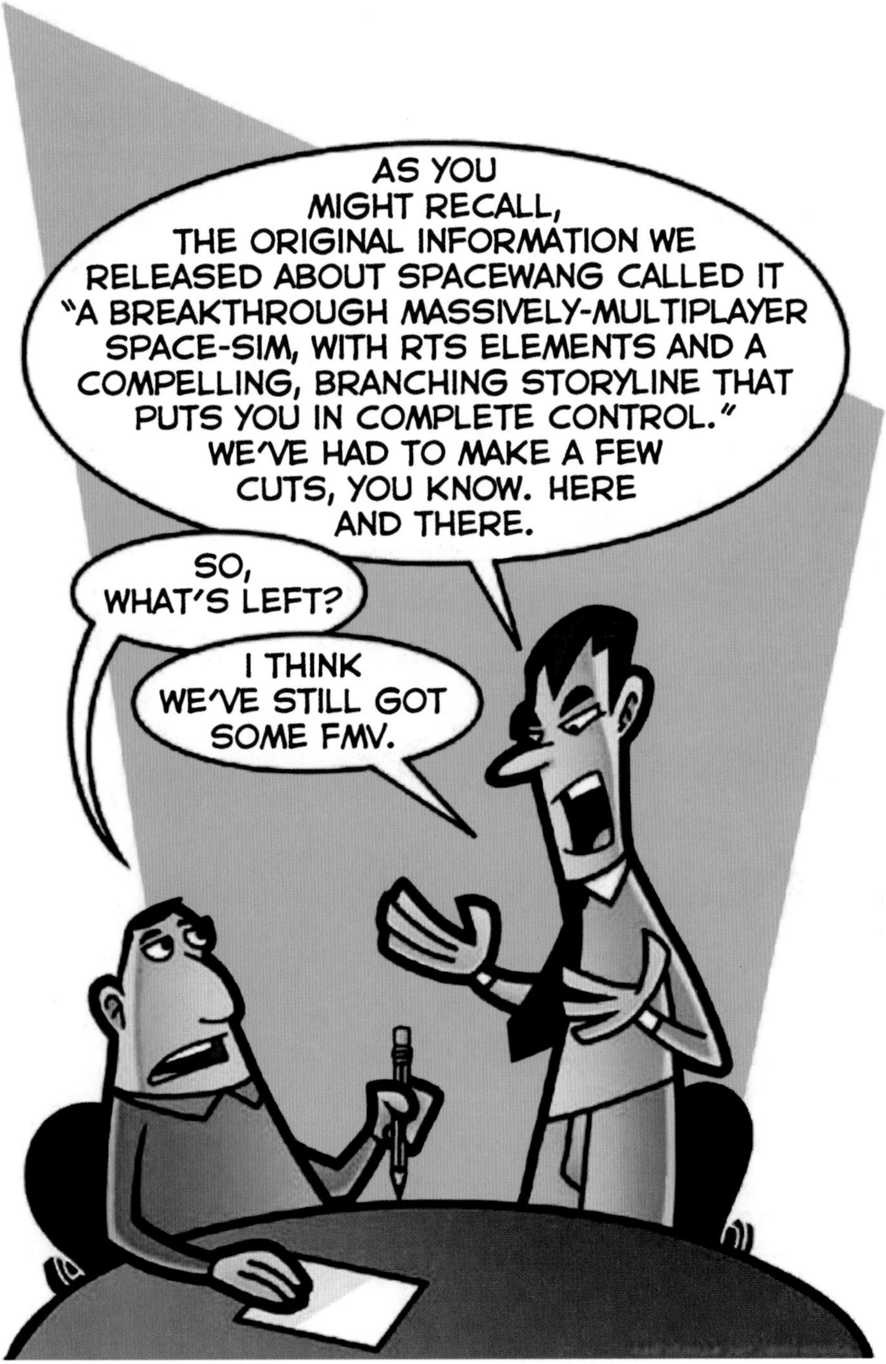
AS YOU MIGHT RECALL, THE ORIGINAL INFORMATION WE RELEASED ABOUT SPACEWANG CALLED IT "A BREAKTHROUGH MASSIVELY-MULTIPLAYER SPACE-SIM, WITH RTS ELEMENTS AND A COMPELLING, BRANCHING STORYLINE THAT PUTS YOU IN COMPLETE CONTROL." WE'VE HAD TO MAKE A FEW CUTS, YOU KNOW. HERE AND THERE.
SO, WHAT'S LEFT?
I THINK WE'VE STILL GOT SOME FMV.

OPM: SPACEWANG!

May 14, 2001 Magazines ask us to do custom stuff for them from time to time, usually just art, but when they want some words in there I'm thawed out of cryo and set immediately to work. These are a few comics we did for *Official Playstation Magazine*, where *Penny Arcade* still runs.

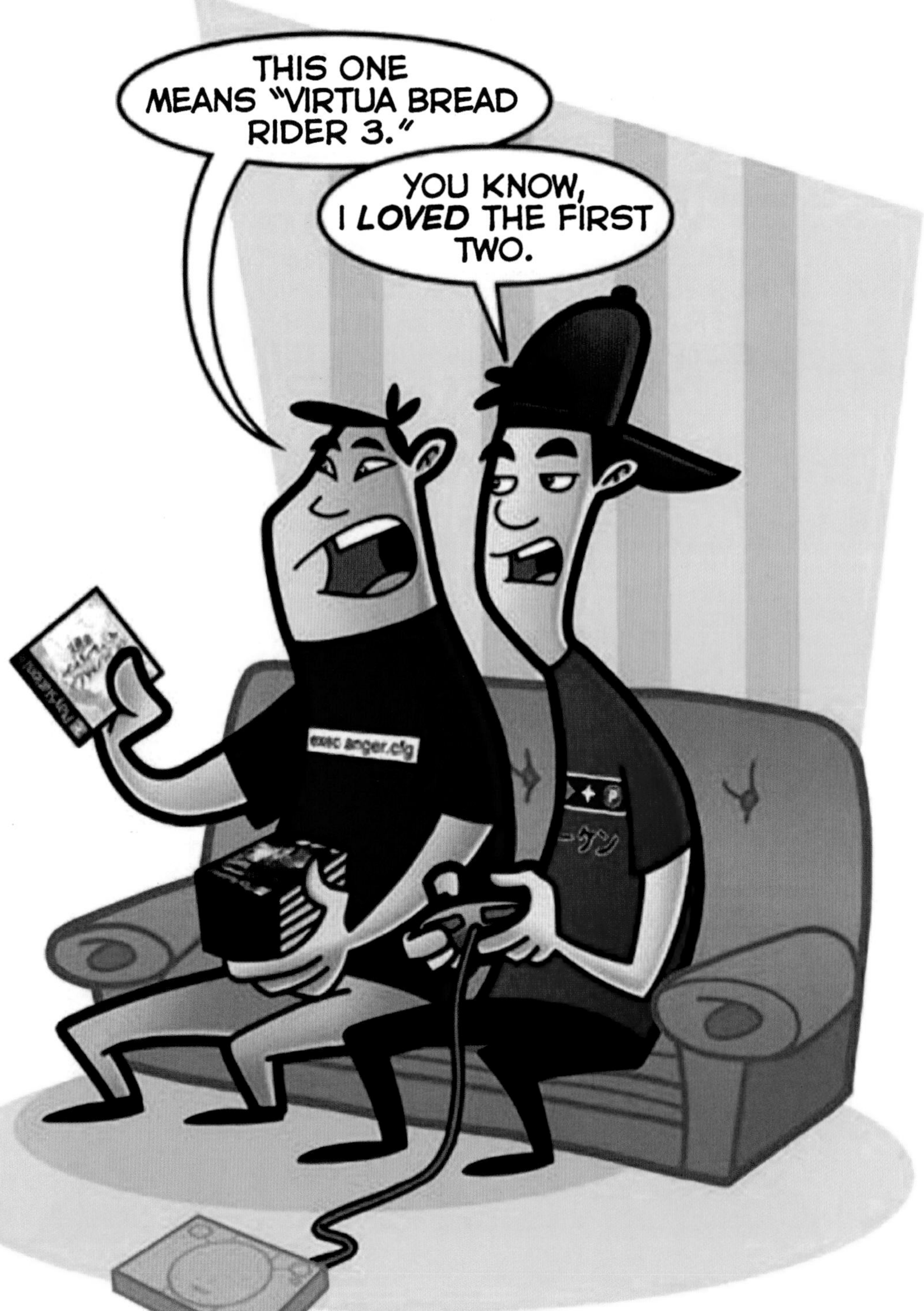
THIS ONE MEANS "VIRTUA BREAD RIDER 3."
YOU KNOW, I *LOVED* THE FIRST TWO.
exec anger.cfg

OPM: VBR

May 15, 2001

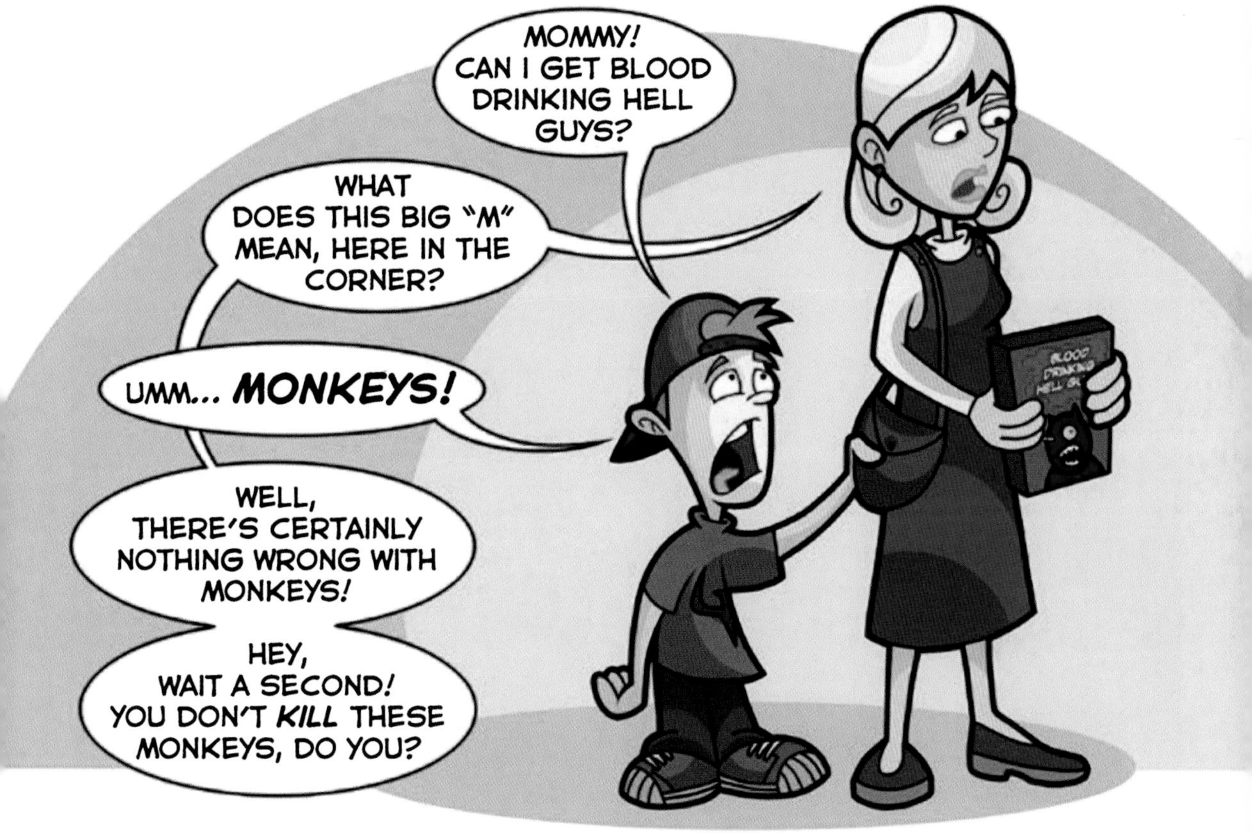
MOMMY! CAN I GET BLOOD DRINKING HELL GUYS?
WHAT DOES THIS BIG "M" MEAN, HERE IN THE CORNER?
UMM... ***MONKEYS!***
WELL, THERE'S CERTAINLY NOTHING WRONG WITH MONKEYS!
HEY, WAIT A SECOND! YOU DON'T *KILL* THESE MONKEYS, DO YOU?

OPM: RATED "MONKEY"

May 16, 2001

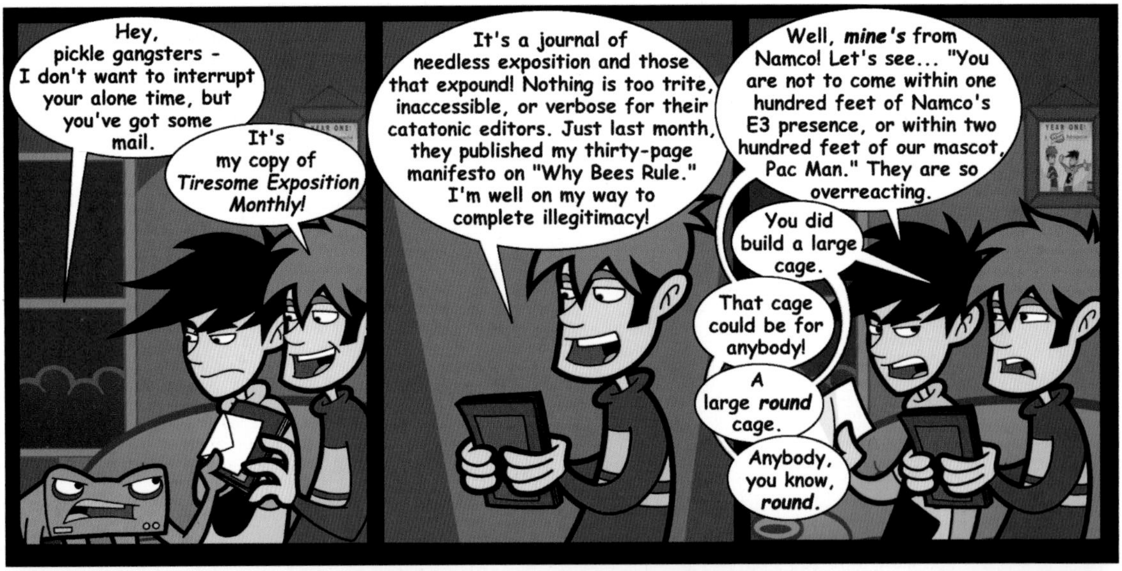
Hey, pickle gangsters - I don't want to interrupt your alone time, but you've got some mail.
It's my copy of *Tiresome Exposition Monthly!*
It's a journal of needless exposition and those that expound! Nothing is too trite, inaccessible, or verbose for their catatonic editors. Just last month, they published my thirty-page manifesto on "Why Bees Rule." I'm well on my way to complete illegitimacy!
Well, ***mine's*** from Namco! Let's see... "You are not to come within one hundred feet of Namco's E3 presence, or within two hundred feet of our mascot, Pac Man." They are so overreacting.
You did build a large cage.
That cage could be for anybody!
A large ***round*** cage.
Anybody, you know, ***round***.

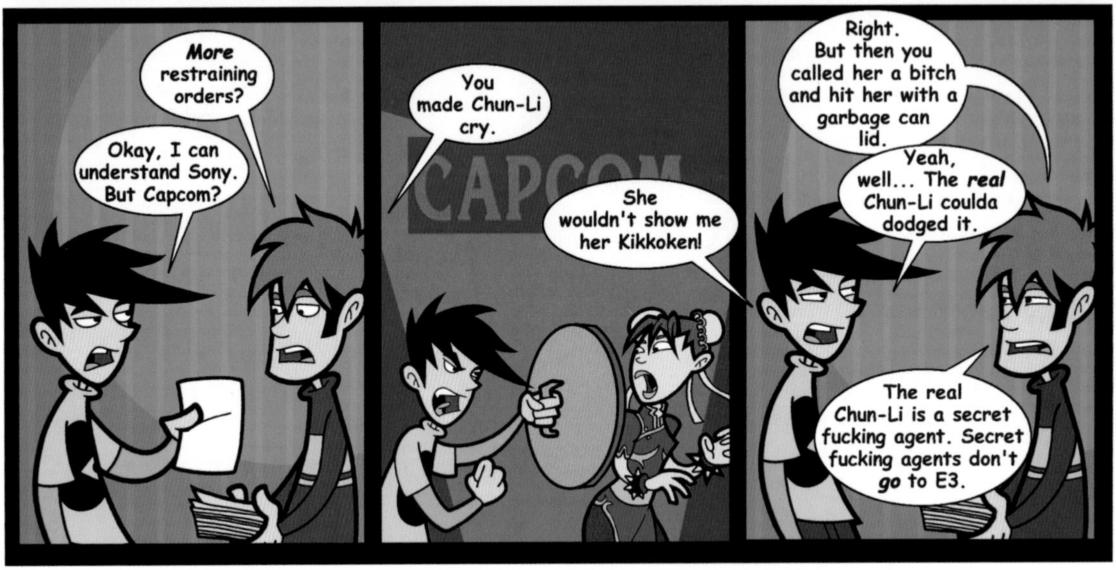
More restraining orders?
Okay, I can understand Sony. But Capcom?
You made Chun-Li cry.
CAPCOM
She wouldn't show me her Kikkoken!
Right. But then you called her a bitch and hit her with a garbage can lid.
Yeah, well... The ***real*** Chun-Li coulda dodged it.
The real Chun-Li is a secret fucking agent. Secret fucking agents don't ***go*** to E3.

(GASP) CONTINUITY!

May 7, 2001 What brain sickness made us go from one storyline directly into another? Are there still traces of this pox, and could they strike again in the veiled future?

SON OF CONTINUITY

May 9, 2001 We never got actual restraining orders, but we have been taken outside the event center by security on more than one occasion. The reasons for this are really mundane, so I'll just leave it ambiguous and let you imagine a high-octane, action/adventure context for it to take place in.

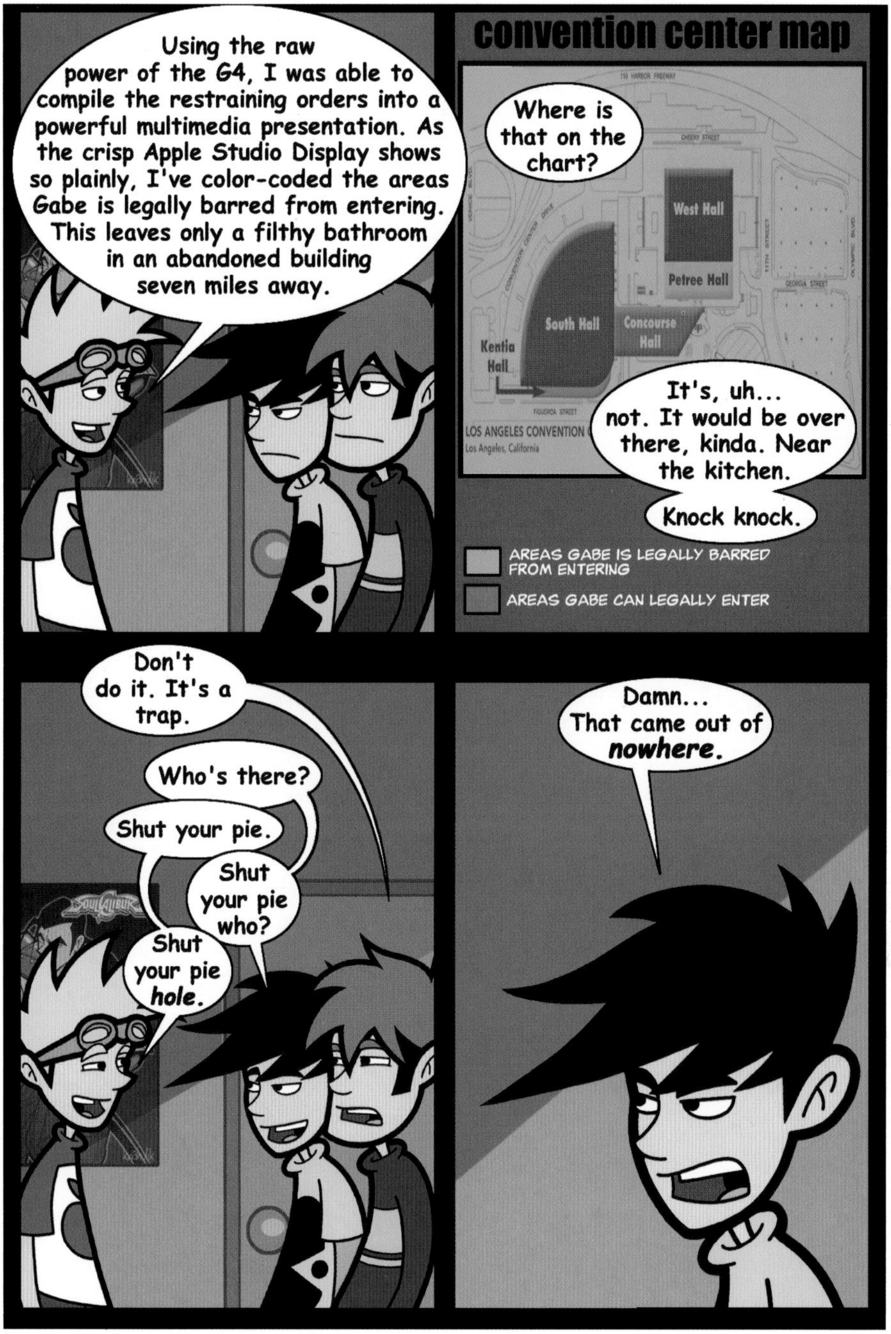
Using the raw power of the G4, I was able to compile the restraining orders into a powerful multimedia presentation. As the crisp Apple Studio Display shows so plainly, I've color-coded the areas Gabe is legally barred from entering. This leaves only a filthy bathroom in an abandoned building seven miles away.
convention center map
Where is that on the chart?
West Hall
Petree Hall
South Hall
Concourse Hall
Kentia Hall
LOS ANGELES CONVENTION
Los Angeles, California
It's, uh... not. It would be over there, kinda. Near the kitchen.
Knock knock.
AREAS GABE IS LEGALLY BARRED FROM ENTERING
AREAS GABE CAN LEGALLY ENTER
Don't do it. It's a trap.
Who's there?
Shut your pie.
Shut your pie who?
Shut your pie *hole*.
Damn... That came out of *nowhere*.

CONTINUITY'S END

May 11, 2001 Charles has been back a couple times quite recently in the strip, and I really love using him for some reason. I know we aren't continuity people, something I emphasize every chance I get, but I would love to take Charles and turn him into more of a storyline character set in a stable universe. I say that knowing that it will almost certainly never happen, but I think he's up to it.

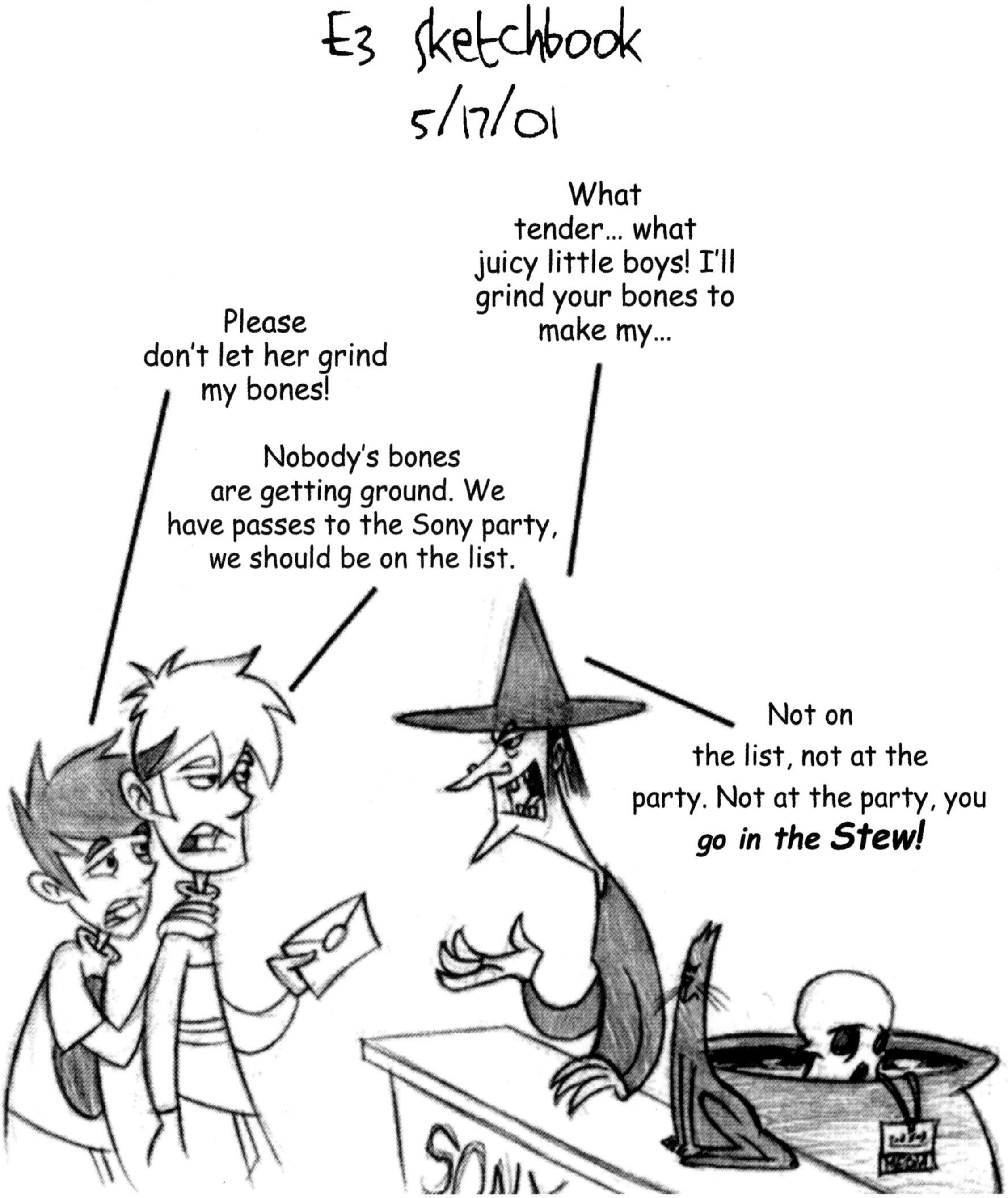
E3 sketchbook
5/17/01
Please don't let her grind my bones!
Nobody's bones are getting ground. We have passes to the Sony party, we should be on the list.
What tender... what juicy little boys! I'll grind your bones to make my...
Not on the list, not at the party. Not at the party, you *go in the **Stew!***

E32K1: THE STEW

May 17, 2001 I am not unfond of open bars, and when we got a chance to attend the Sony party—which, understand, Sony itself had invited us to—I stood ready. We say that we weren't on the list in the comic, which isn't entirely true—the problem was that the person on the list wasn't either of *our* names, but rather a third mysterious entity named "Penny Arcade."

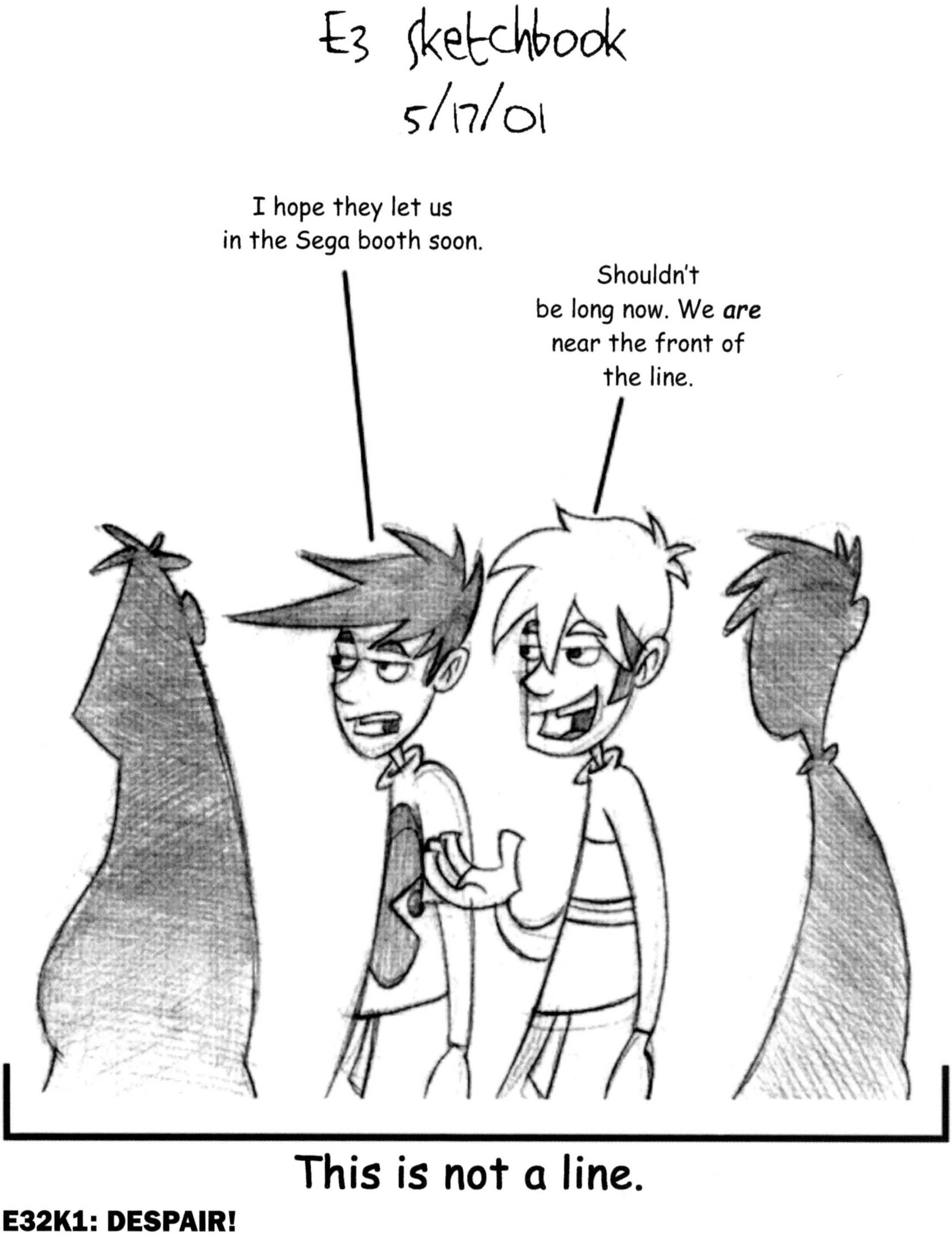
E3 sketchbook
5/17/01
I hope they let us in the Sega booth soon.
Shouldn't be long now. We *are* near the front of the line.
This is not a line.

E32K1: DESPAIR!

May 18, 2001 One of the problems with E3 is that the human density is so *great* that the entire place is essentially Goddamn nonsense. I don't even go there with an approximation of a coherent plan. I just hold my breath, pause to reflect on my life, and then take a step forward into the single organism that place becomes.

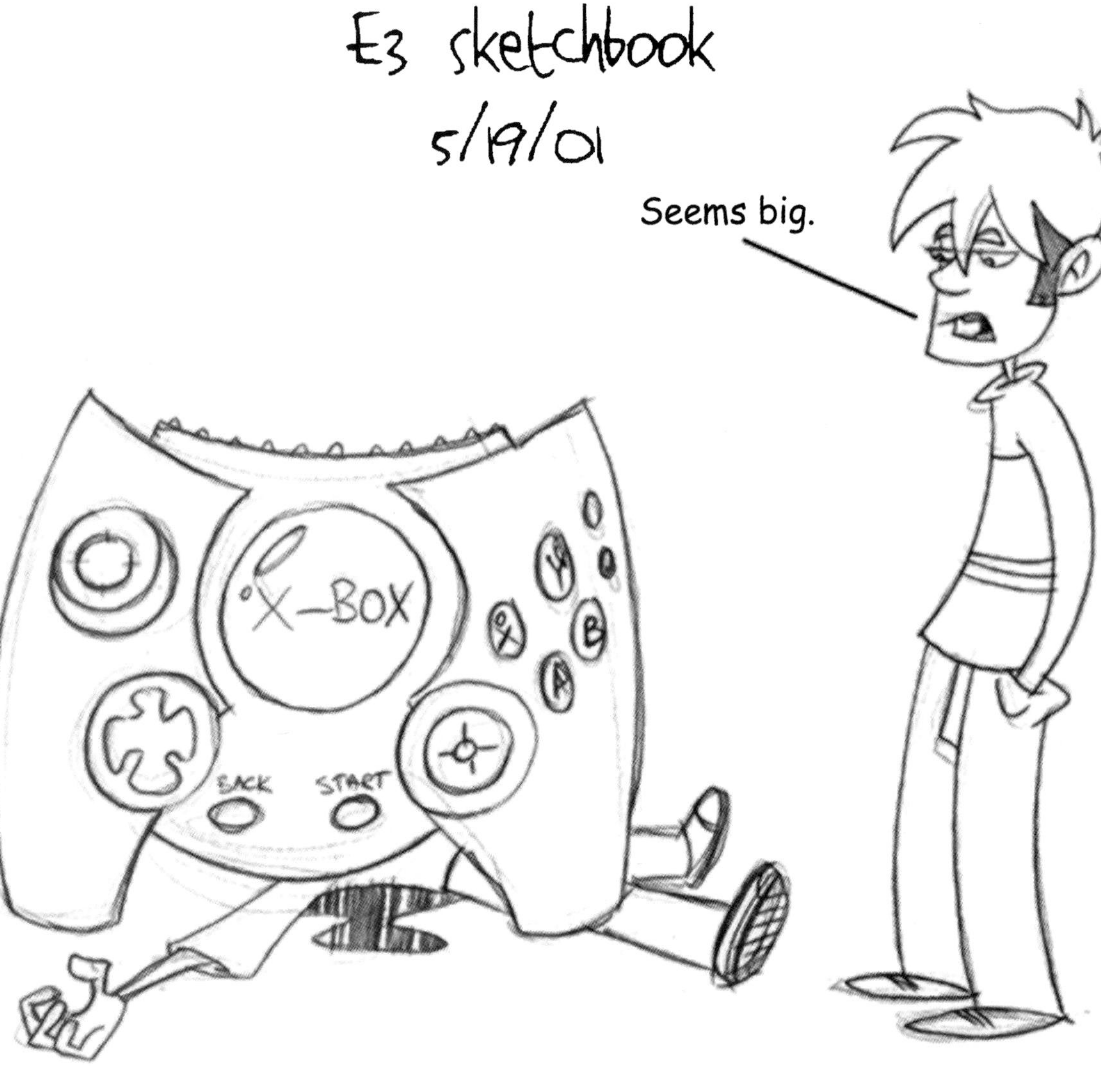
E3 sketchbook
5/19/01
Seems big.
X-BOX
BACK
START

E32K1: X MARKS THE SPOT

May 20, 2001 This is where the whole thing started, if you're curious: after getting our hands on one at the kiosk—both hands actually—we marveled at the sheer surface area of it. I didn't know we'd go on to make like four strips about it, but it certainly made an impression. In the ground, because the original Xbox gamepad weighs a hair over five thousand pounds.

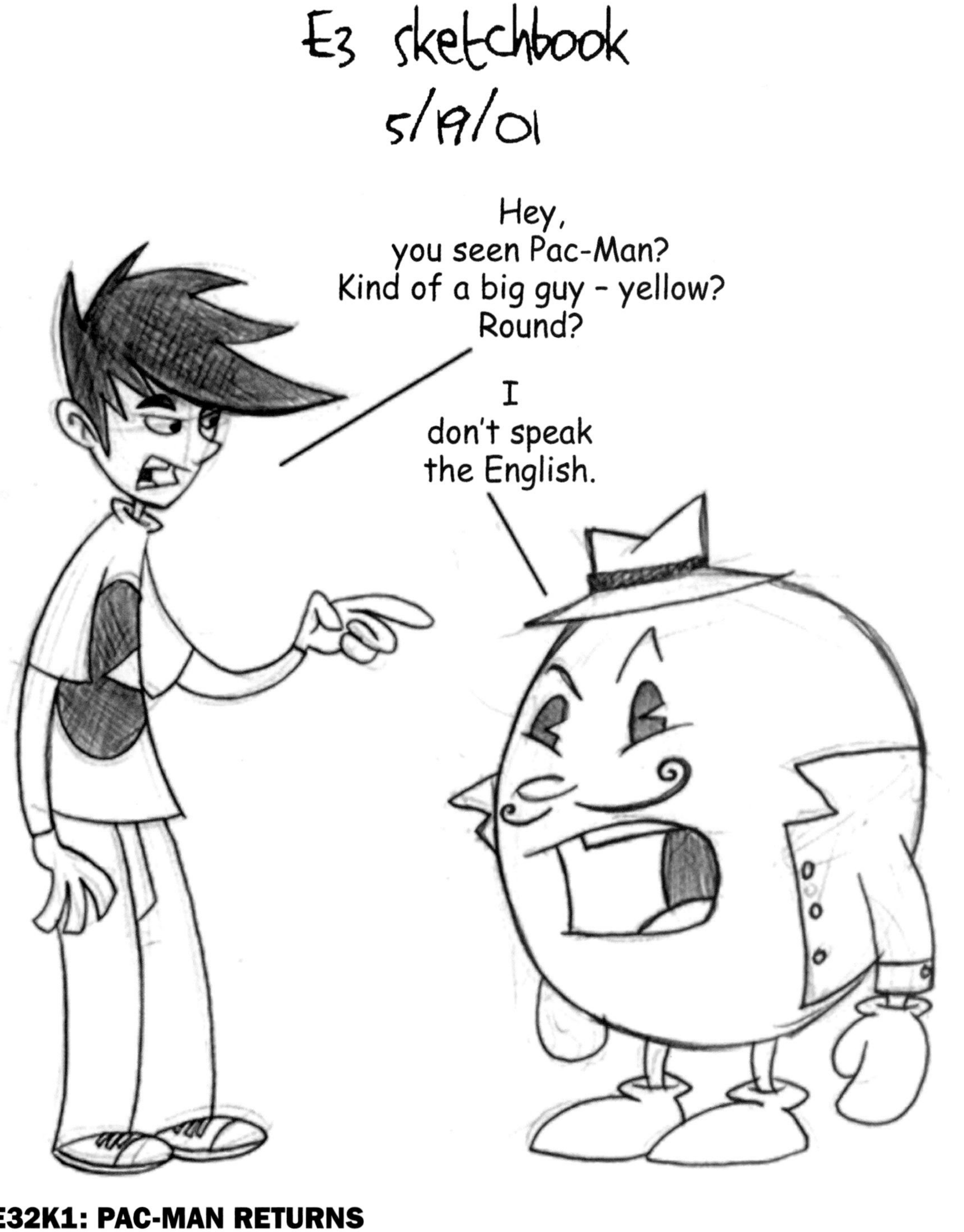
E3 sketchbook
5/19/01
Hey, you seen Pac-Man? Kind of a big guy - yellow? Round?
I don't speak the English.

E32K1: PAC-MAN RETURNS

May 21, 2001 There's strip Gabe, obviously, and then there is the person he is based on. Sometimes there are disparities. The Pac-Man thing is one hundred percent the real deal. Whatever poor son of a bitch gets stuffed into that suit each year must actually try to manage his amorous advances. One year, in an attempt to put space between himself and my cohort, Pac-Man *tripped*—rolling almost a hundred yards in total.

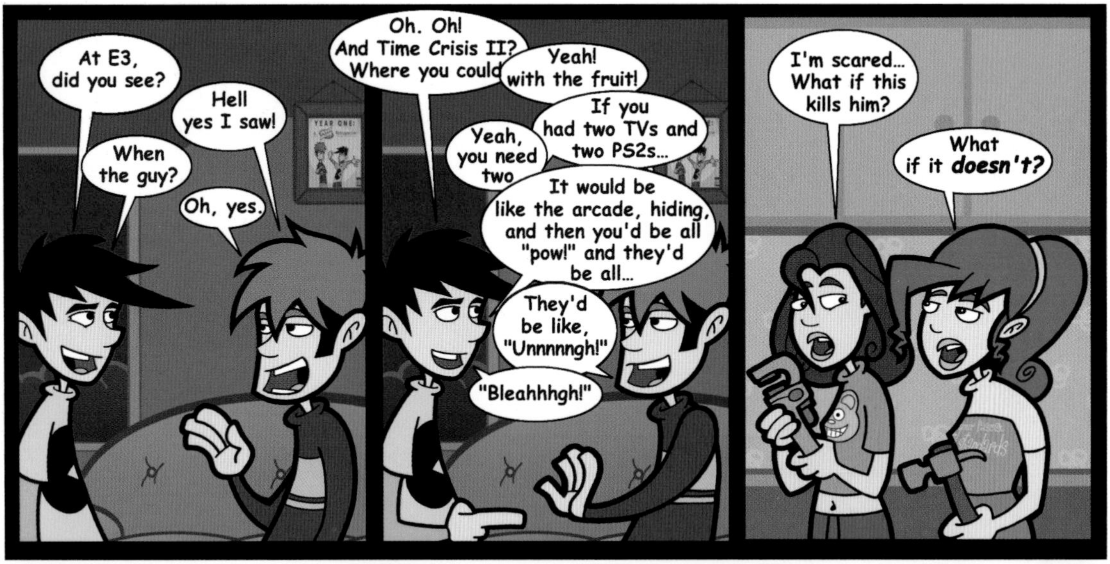
At E3, did you see?
Hell yes I saw!
When the guy?
Oh, yes.
Oh. Oh! And Time Crisis II? Where you could
Yeah! with the fruit!
Yeah, you need two
If you had two TVs and two PS2s...
It would be like the arcade, hiding, and then you'd be all "pow!" and they'd be all...
They'd be like, "Unnnnngh!"
"Bleahhhgh!"
I'm scared... What if this kills him?
What if it *doesn't?*

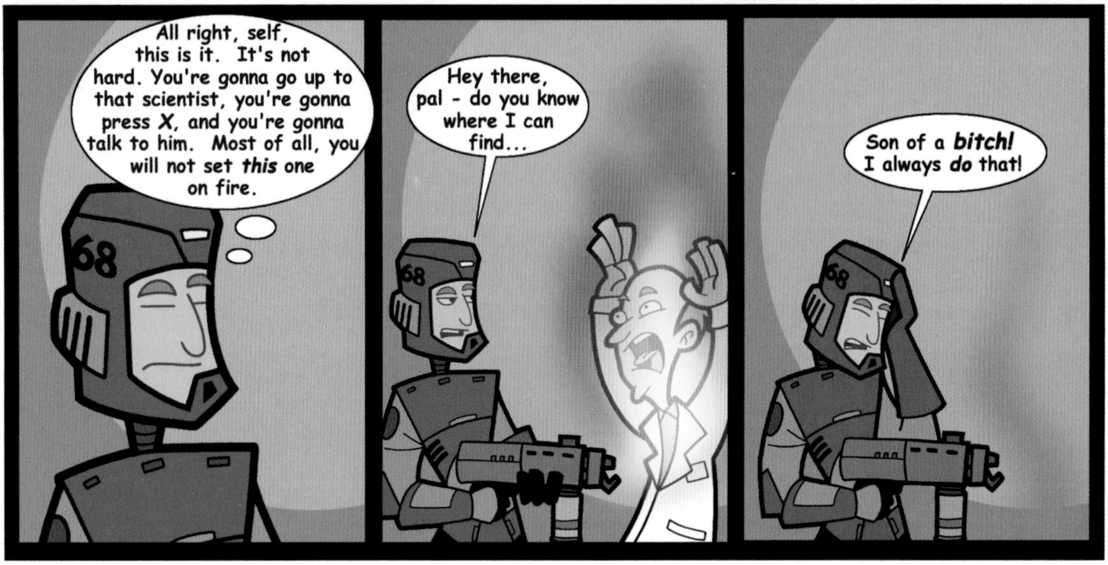
All right, self, this is it. It's not hard. You're gonna go up to that scientist, you're gonna press *X*, and you're gonna talk to him. Most of all, you will not set *this* one on fire.
Hey there, pal - do you know where I can find...
Son of a *bitch!* I always *do* that!

THE SPEED OF THOUGHT

May 23, 2001 When you get back from E3 the first couple times, you are literally some kind of insane. I'm sure there's an official term for it. You kind of beep and bop, and the only people who know what the fuck you're talking about were there with you, occupying the same altered state, strung out on electrical signals.

THE PROBLEM

May 28, 2001 Red Faction wasn't bad, but we kept having an issue where we'd hit the wrong key and immolate perfectly innocent scientists.

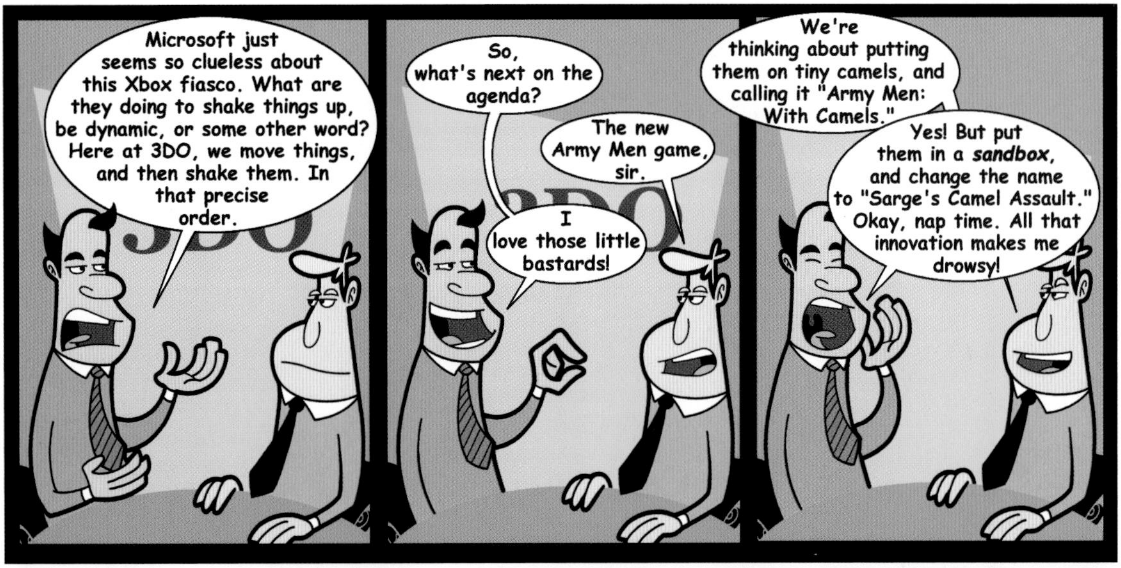
Microsoft just seems so clueless about this Xbox fiasco. What are they doing to shake things up, be dynamic, or some other word? Here at 3DO, we move things, and then shake them. In that precise order.
3DO
So, what's next on the agenda?
The new Army Men game, sir.
I love those little bastards!
We're thinking about putting them on tiny camels, and calling it "Army Men: With Camels."
Yes! But put them in a *sandbox*, and change the name to "Sarge's Camel Assault." Okay, nap time. All that innovation makes me drowsy!

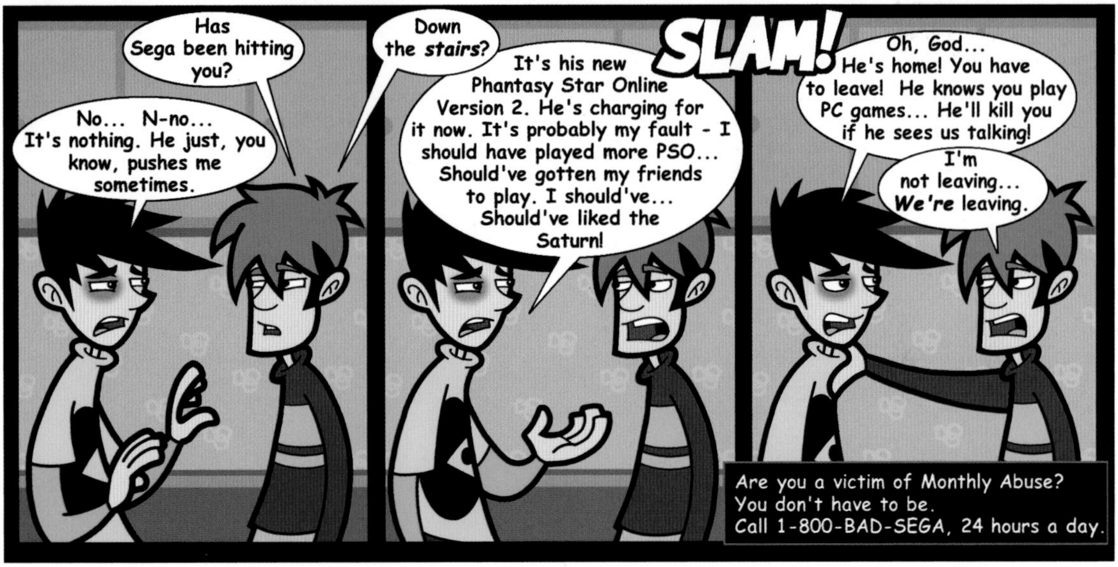
Has Sega been hitting you?
No... N-no... It's nothing. He just, you know, pushes me sometimes.
Down the *stairs*?
It's his new Phantasy Star Online Version 2. He's charging for it now. It's probably my fault - I should have played more PSO... Should've gotten my friends to play. I should've... Should've liked the Saturn!
SLAM!
Oh, God... He's home! You have to leave! He knows you play PC games... He'll kill you if he sees us talking!
I'm not leaving... *We're* leaving.
Are you a victim of Monthly Abuse? You don't have to be. Call 1-800-BAD-SEGA, 24 hours a day.

POT TO KETTLE: "YOU ARE BLACK"

May 30, 2001 The Space Captain or the Grand Marshal, whatever he's called, *Trip Hawkins*, was talking some shit about the Xbox and innovation. We felt it necessary to emphasize in strong terms that the company that churned out the Army Men series doesn't get to talk that particular kind of shit.

IT'S NOT TOO LATE

June 1, 2001 In 2001, I think that many people—even people who played games online—were still a little wary about the monthly fee thing. We loved PSO, but I'll be God Damned if I'm going to pay a monthly fee to play with three other people simultaneously. That's like . . . Well, I don't know what it's like. Something dumb though, that much I can say for certain.

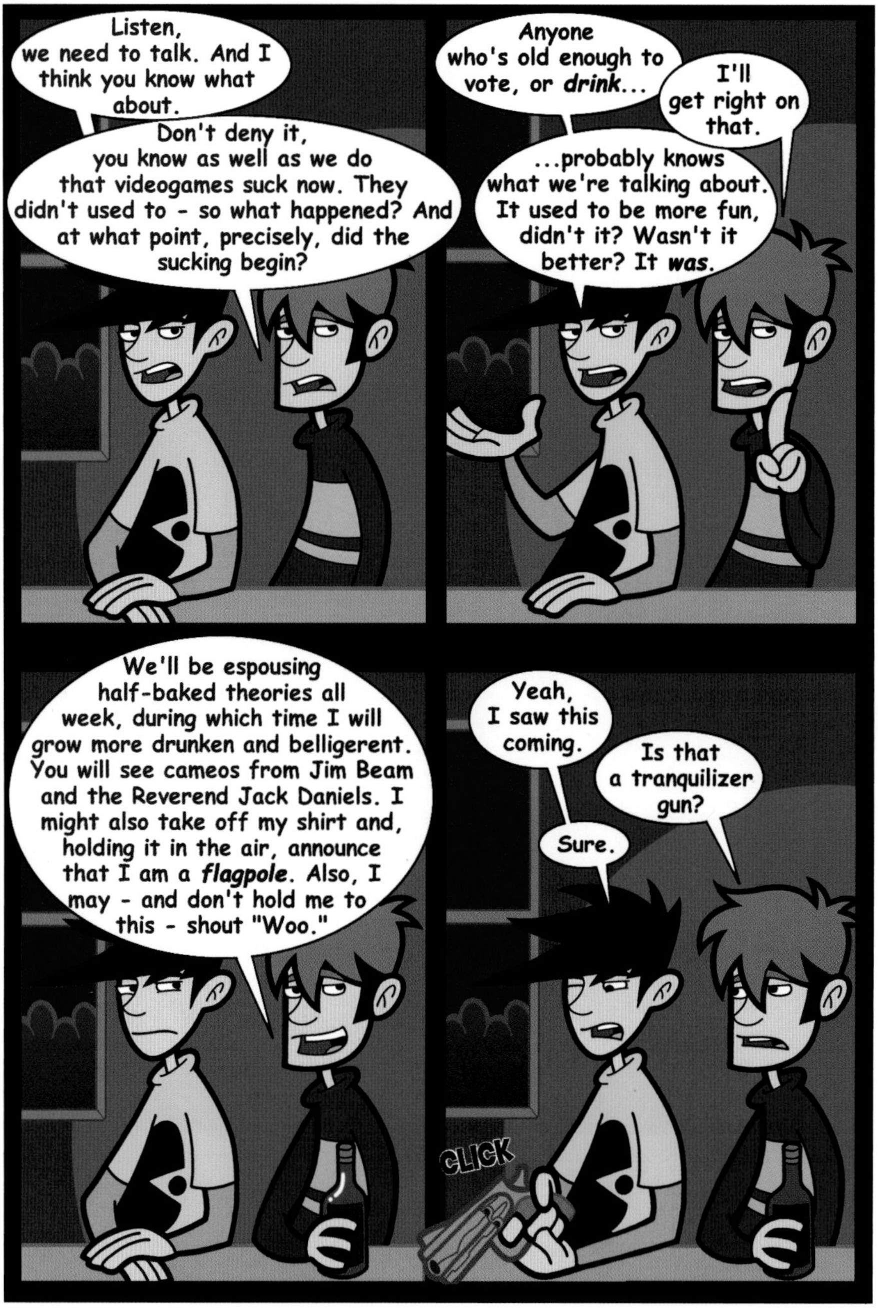
Listen, we need to talk. And I think you know what about.
Don't deny it, you know as well as we do that videogames suck now. They didn't used to - so what happened? And at what point, precisely, did the sucking begin?
Anyone who's old enough to vote, or *drink*...
I'll get right on that.
...probably knows what we're talking about. It used to be more fun, didn't it? Wasn't it better? It *was*.
We'll be espousing half-baked theories all week, during which time I will grow more drunken and belligerent. You will see cameos from Jim Beam and the Reverend Jack Daniels. I might also take off my shirt and, holding it in the air, announce that I am a *flagpole*. Also, I may - and don't hold me to this - shout "Woo."
Yeah, I saw this coming.
Is that a tranquilizer gun?
Sure.
CLICK

THE SUCKING: INTRODUCTION

June 4, 2001 We didn't claim to have any great insight into why gaming seemed *diminished* somehow, we just needed to talk about the growing sense of unease. Doing the series did change the way we go about things: we actively avoid the media onslaught that accompanies many titles these days. Plus, and this is important, I have an increased awareness that retail software does not represent the entire medium. Independent developers and mod teams—a largely semantic distinction—make moves that you see echoed in the larger industry, sometimes years later.

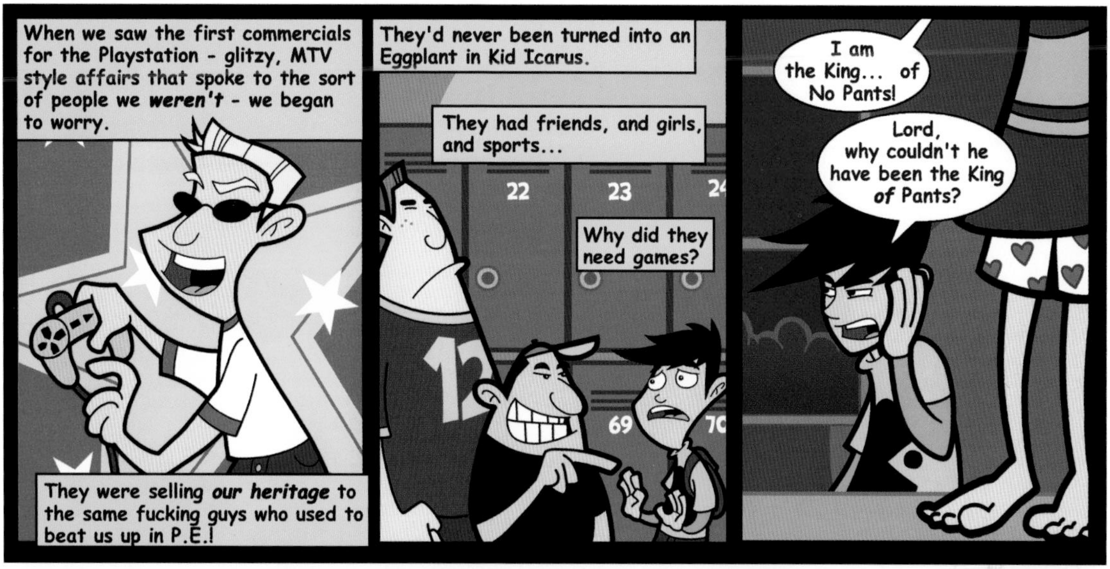

When we saw the first commercials for the Playstation - glitzy, MTV style affairs that spoke to the sort of people we weren't - we began to worry.
They were selling our heritage to the same fucking guys who used to beat us up in P.E.!
They'd never been turned into an Eggplant in Kid Icarus.
They had friends, and girls, and sports...
22
23
Why did they need games?
12
69
I am the King... of No Pants!
Lord, why couldn't he have been the King of Pants?

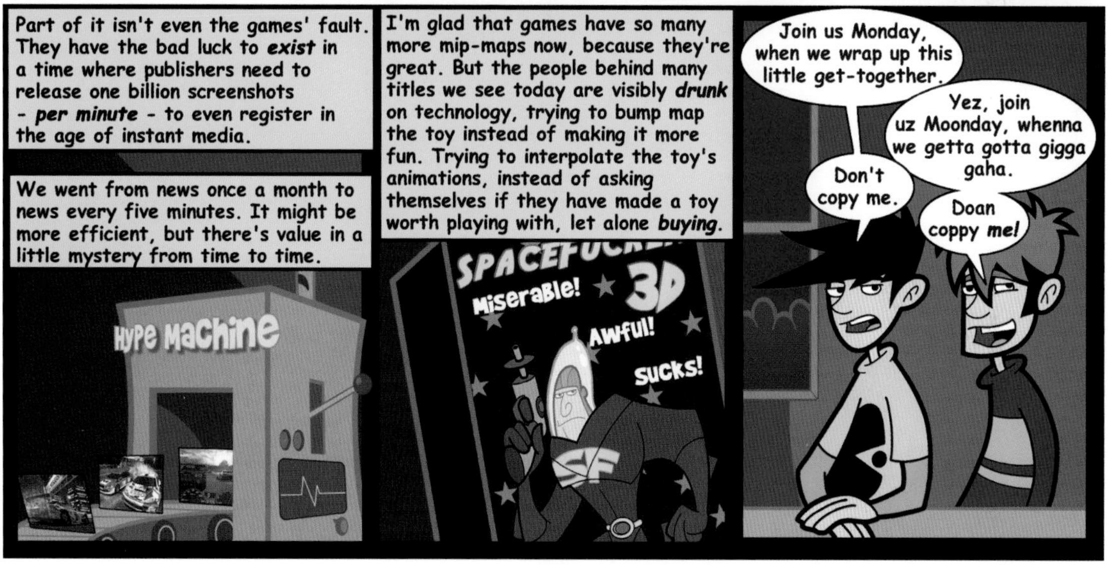

Part of it isn't even the games' fault. They have the bad luck to exist in a time where publishers need to release one billion screenshots - per minute - to even register in the age of instant media.
We went from news once a month to news every five minutes. It might be more efficient, but there's value in a little mystery from time to time.
Hype Machine
I'm glad that games have so many more mip-maps now, because they're great. But the people behind many titles we see today are visibly drunk on technology, trying to bump map the toy instead of making it more fun. Trying to interpolate the toy's animations, instead of asking themselves if they have made a toy worth playing with, let alone buying.
Miserable!
3D
Awful!
Sucks!
SF
Join us Monday, when we wrap up this little get-together.
Yez, join uz Moonday, whenna we getta gotta gigga gaha.
Don't copy me.
Doan coppy me!

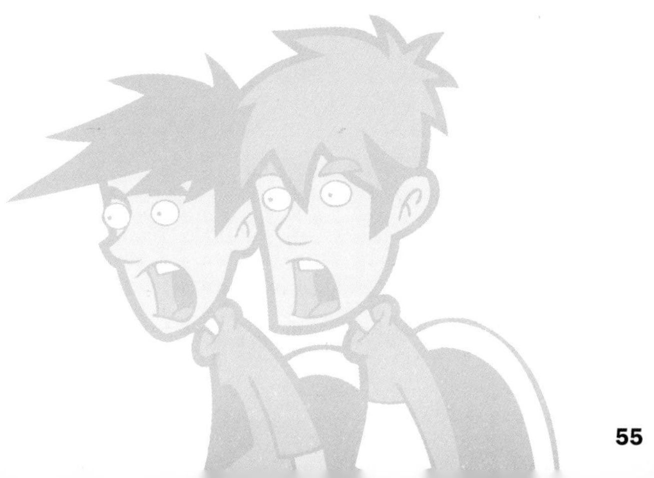

THE SUCKING: ORIGINS

June 6, 2001

THE SUCKING: CONTINUED

June 8, 2001

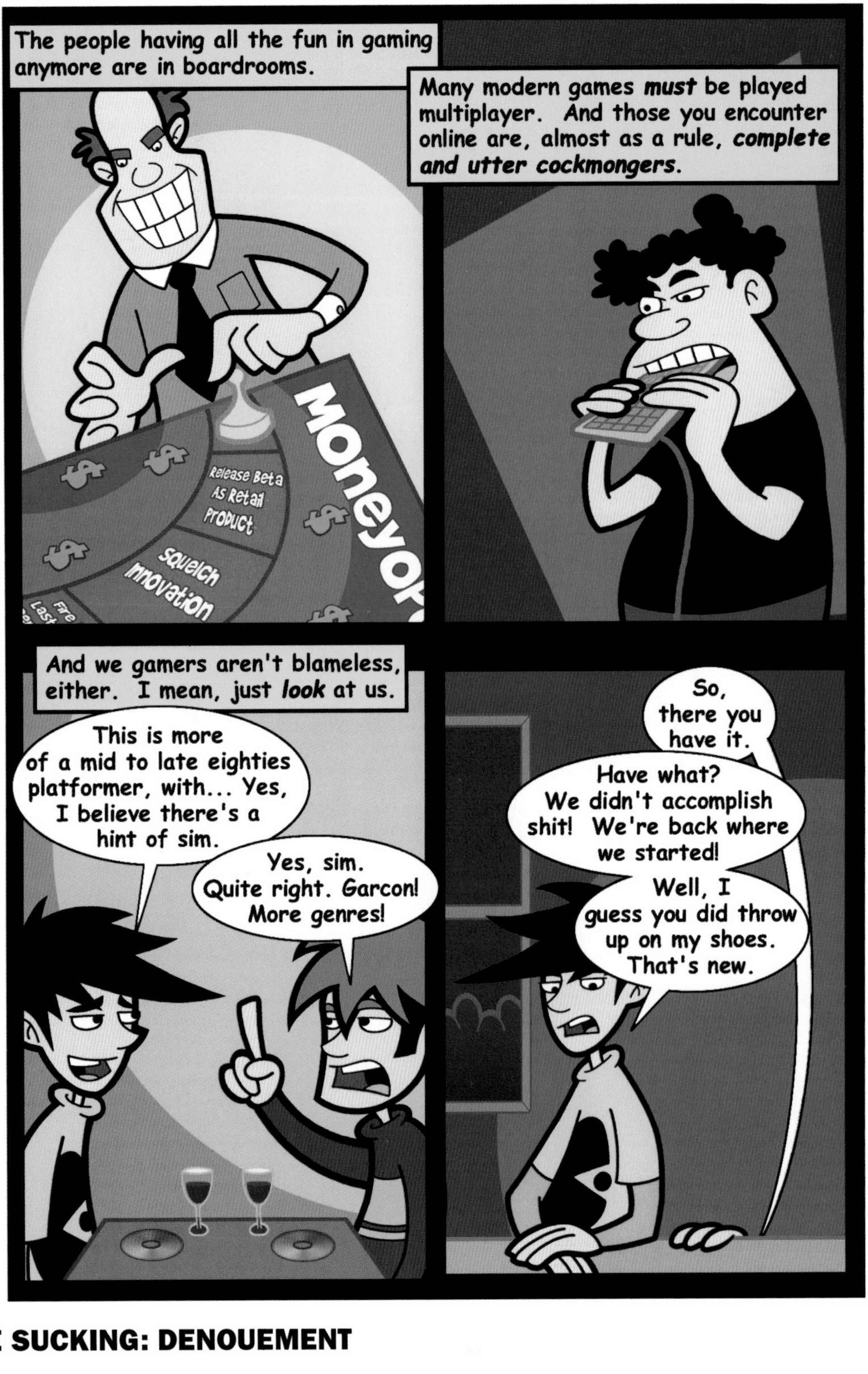
The people having all the fun in gaming anymore are in boardrooms.
Moneyopo
Release Beta As Retail Product
Squelch Innovation
Many modern games *must* be played multiplayer. And those you encounter online are, almost as a rule, *complete and utter cockmongers*.
And we gamers aren't blameless, either. I mean, just *look* at us.
This is more of a mid to late eighties platformer, with... Yes, I believe there's a hint of sim.
Yes, sim. Quite right. Garcon! More genres!
So, there you have it.
Have what? We didn't accomplish shit! We're back where we started!
Well, I guess you did throw up on my shoes. That's new.

THE SUCKING: DENOUEMENT

June 11, 2001

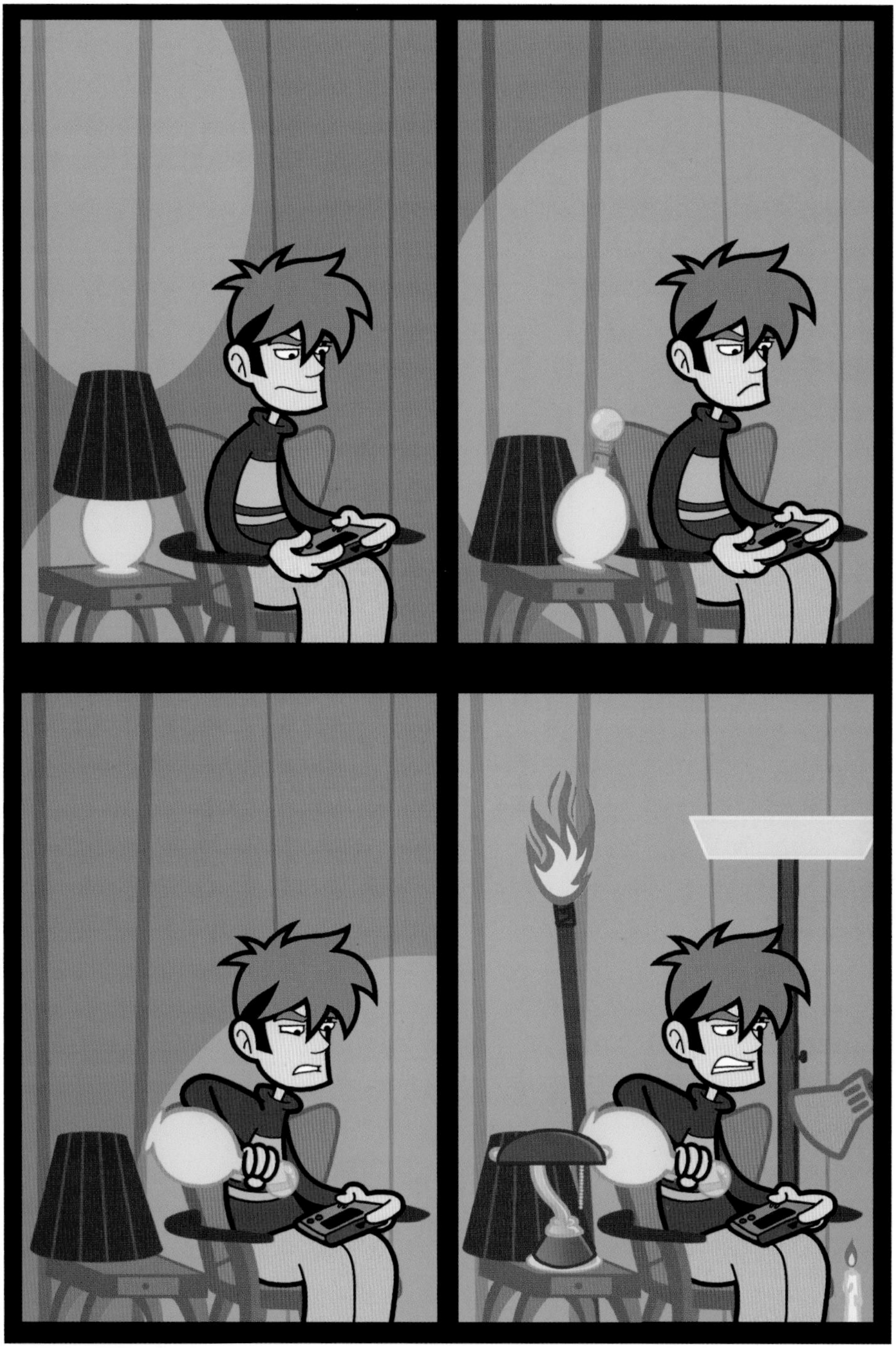

LAME BOY ADVANCE

June 13, 2001 This hardware would eventually be usurped by the Gameboy SP, for the reasons depicted above. A surprising number of people wrote in to tell me that, for whatever reason, their *bathrooms* provided the optimal lighting environment for the system. They were right. So, get yourself a *portable restroom*, and you're all set!

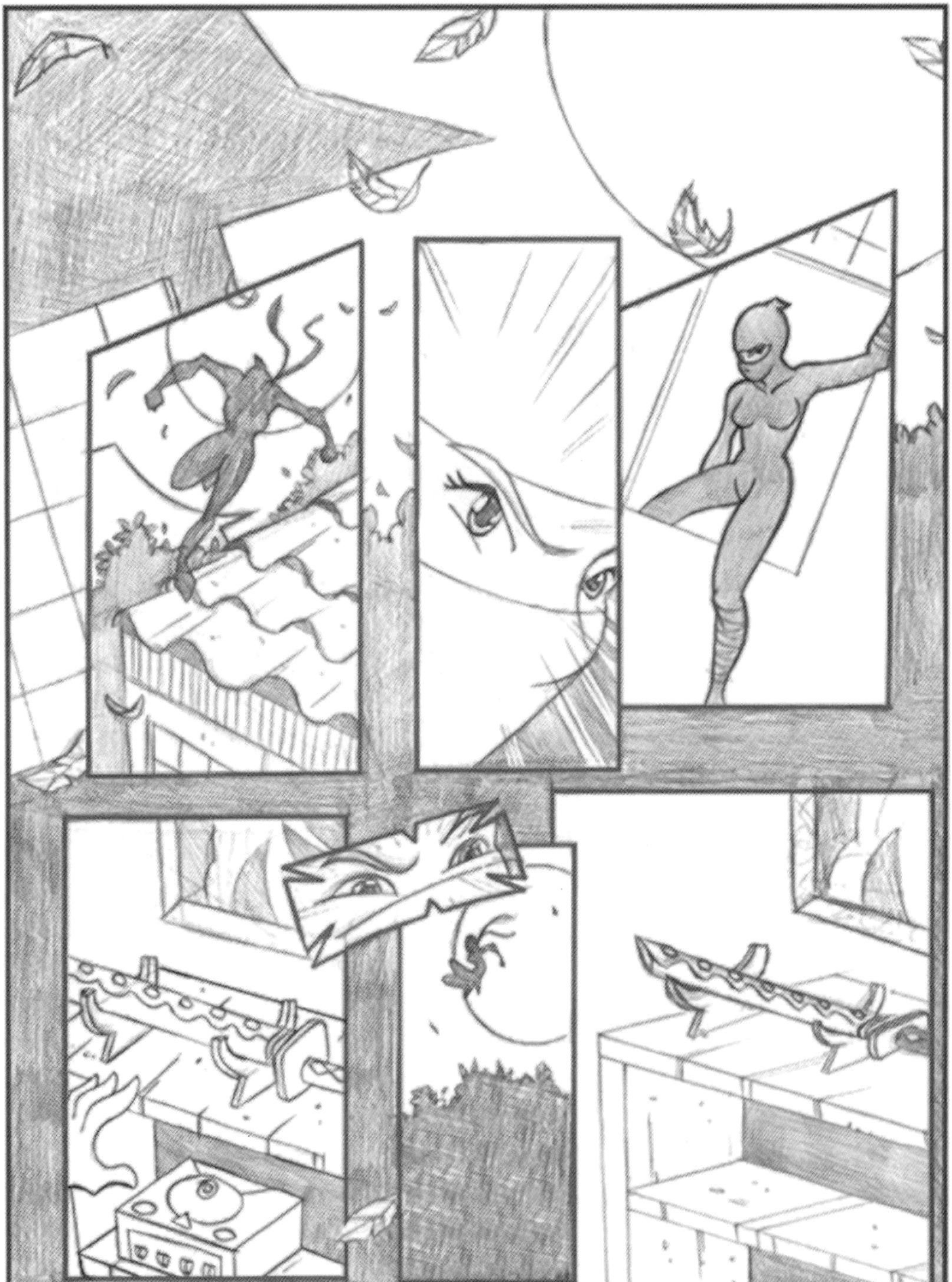

CROUCHING TIGER, HIDDEN DREAMCAST

June 15, 2001 I just let Gabe go nuts on this one. I'm not entirely sure we even discussed the content of it.

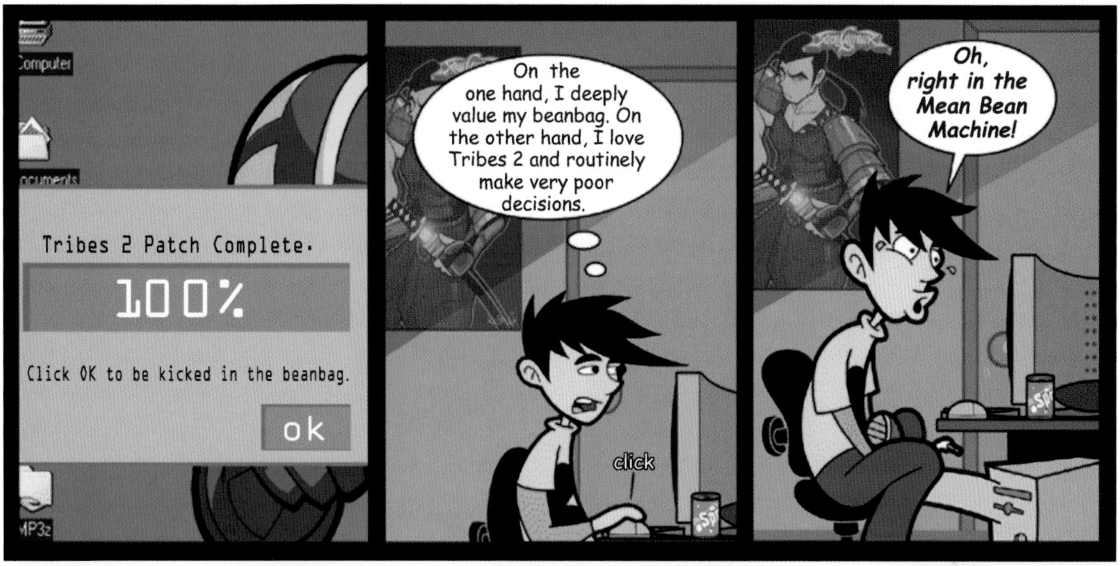
Tribes 2 Patch Complete.
100%
Click OK to be kicked in the beanbag.
ok
On the one hand, I deeply value my beanbag. On the other hand, I love Tribes 2 and routinely make very poor decisions.
click
Oh, right in the Mean Bean Machine!

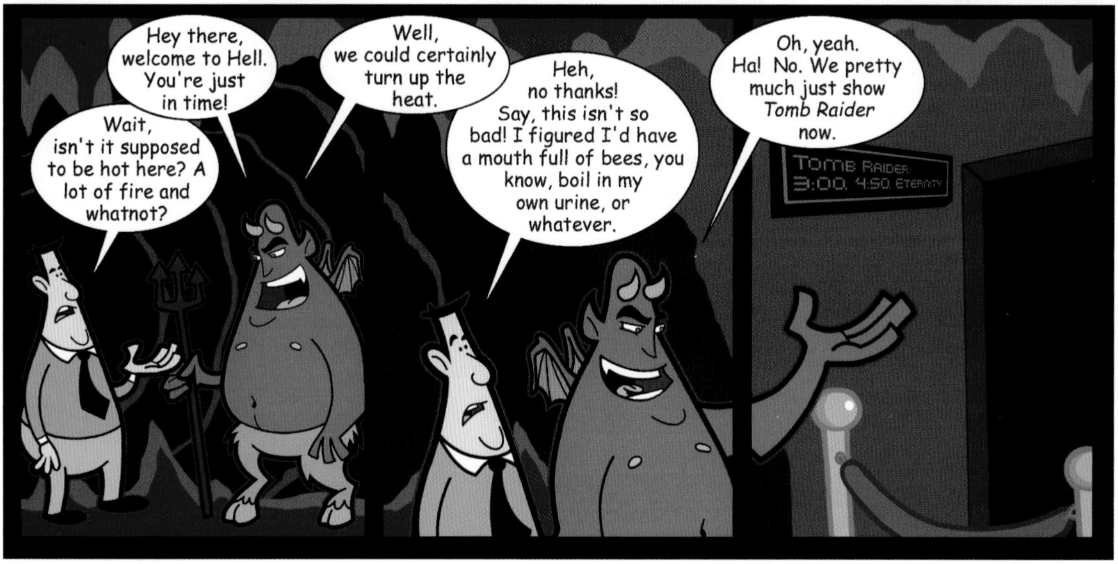
Wait, isn't it supposed to be hot here? A lot of fire and whatnot?
Hey there, welcome to Hell. You're just in time!
Well, we could certainly turn up the heat.
Heh, no thanks! Say, this isn't so bad! I figured I'd have a mouth full of bees, you know, boil in my own urine, or whatever.
Oh, yeah. Ha! No. We pretty much just show *Tomb Raider* now.
TOMB RAIDER: 3:00, 4:50, ETERNITY

GOD DAMMIT

June 18, 2001 Tribes 2, as I've reiterated time and time again, is one of our favorite games. This is *despite* the fact that after its release, a deluge of patches arrived with great frequency. These patches almost always made the game behave in some aberrant fashion—in fact, they once released a patch to *remove* the patch they had just released! It was around this time that we remembered our computers could actually play other games.

ABANDON ALL HOPE

June 20, 2001 *Tomb Raider*, as a movie concept, seems damn near foolproof—right? It is about an attractive woman who leads a life of globetrotting adventure, all the while shooting special forces types in a stylish kind of *John Woo*, guns akimbo manner. It's the sort of thing you have to actively work to mess up.

WHEN YOU LIVE IN A WORLD OF FANTASY, ANYTHING IS POSSIBLE! WHY EXPLAIN YOURSELF WHEN YOU CAN JUST USE MAGIC?
TAKE ONLINE COMICS, FOR INSTANCE. WHY COULDN'T A CLOUD OF FAERIES -- EACH WITH A TINY PICNIC BASKET CONTAINING A GOLDEN COIN -- JUST FLY THE MONEY FROM THE DRAGON'S CAVE?
NOW LET'S TAKE A COMIC LIKE SANDWICH SHOPPE -- DIVIDE THEIR FORTY THOUSAND READERS IN HALF, AND MULTIPLY THAT BY SWEET, BEE-FRESH HONEY. THAT'S A HOJILLION DOLLARS! NOW, SUBTRACT THREE VANILLA WAFERS TO PAY THE BILLY GOATS GRUFF, AND YOU'VE GOT A HUNDRED KABILLION MILLION DOLLARS!
20,000 ×
HONEY
-

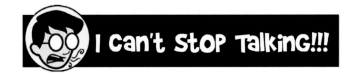

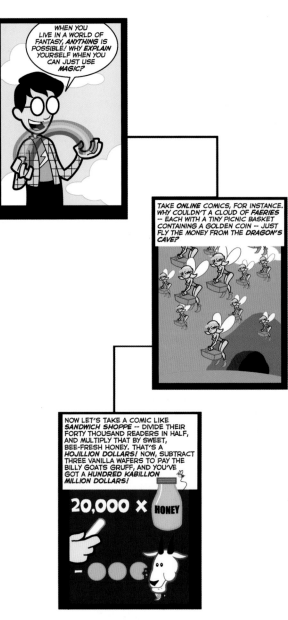

MAGIC: IT'S WHAT'S FOR DINNER

June 22, 2001 This strip kicked off a legendary feud with Scott McCloud, author of a number of things, but very well known for his book *Understanding Comics*. He had written a number of visual essays on how the economics of "sequential art" should operate online, and as people who actually worked online, with a comic no less, we wanted to provide a different perspective. We eventually patched things up, then tensions flared again, though I think things are cool now.

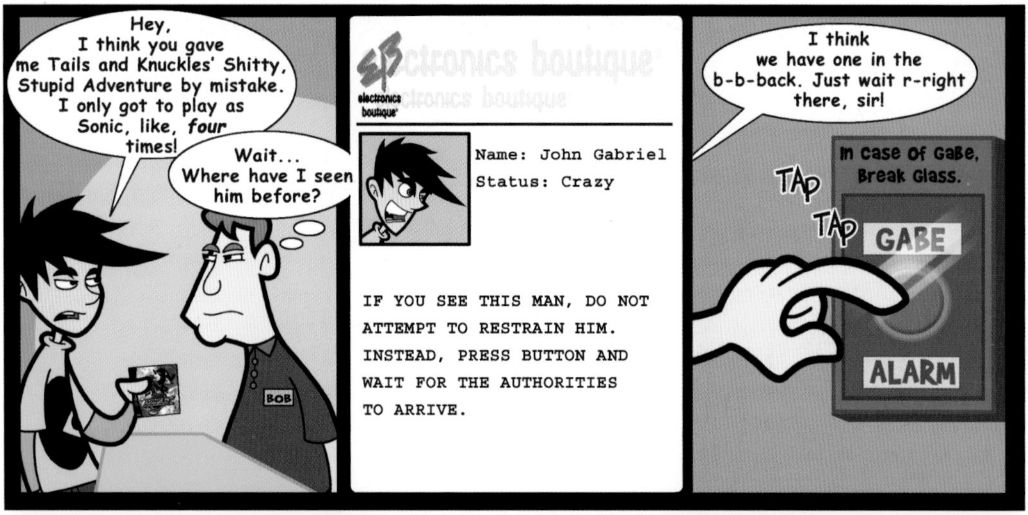
Hey, I think you gave me Tails and Knuckles' Shitty, Stupid Adventure by mistake. I only got to play as Sonic, like, *four* times!
Wait... Where have I seen him before?
BOB
electronics boutique
Name: John Gabriel
Status: Crazy
IF YOU SEE THIS MAN, DO NOT ATTEMPT TO RESTRAIN HIM. INSTEAD, PRESS BUTTON AND WAIT FOR THE AUTHORITIES TO ARRIVE.
I think we have one in the b-b-back. Just wait r-right there, sir!
In case of GaBe, Break Glass.
TAP
TAP
GABE
ALARM

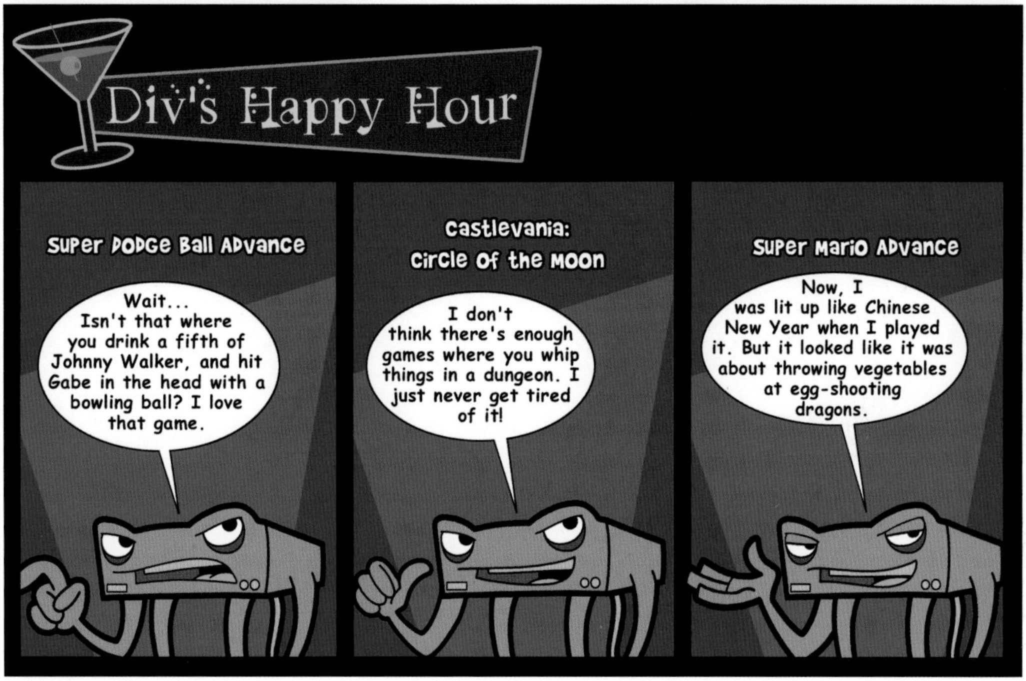
Div's Happy Hour
Super Dodge Ball Advance
Wait... Isn't that where you drink a fifth of Johnny Walker, and hit Gabe in the head with a bowling ball? I love that game.
Castlevania: Circle of the Moon
I don't think there's enough games where you whip things in a dungeon. I just never get tired of it!
Super Mario Advance
Now, I was lit up like Chinese New Year when I played it. But it looked like it was about throwing vegetables at egg-shooting dragons.

IT MIGHT BE FIVE

June 25, 2001 Gabe actually does get a reputation at the places we buy games from, and I believe the reputation is generally called "surly." I am the intercessor in social situations, it has always been thus, but there are times where I'm not able to make it and the staff gets a taste of what you might call "Gabriel Uncut."

GAME COMICS FOR U

June 27, 2001 To the extent that we could actually *see* these games, I can recall enjoying the launch quite a bit. Super Dodge Ball Advance got some sour reviews, but it is a game where you throw volleyballs *hard enough to kill people*. We were willing to meet them halfway.

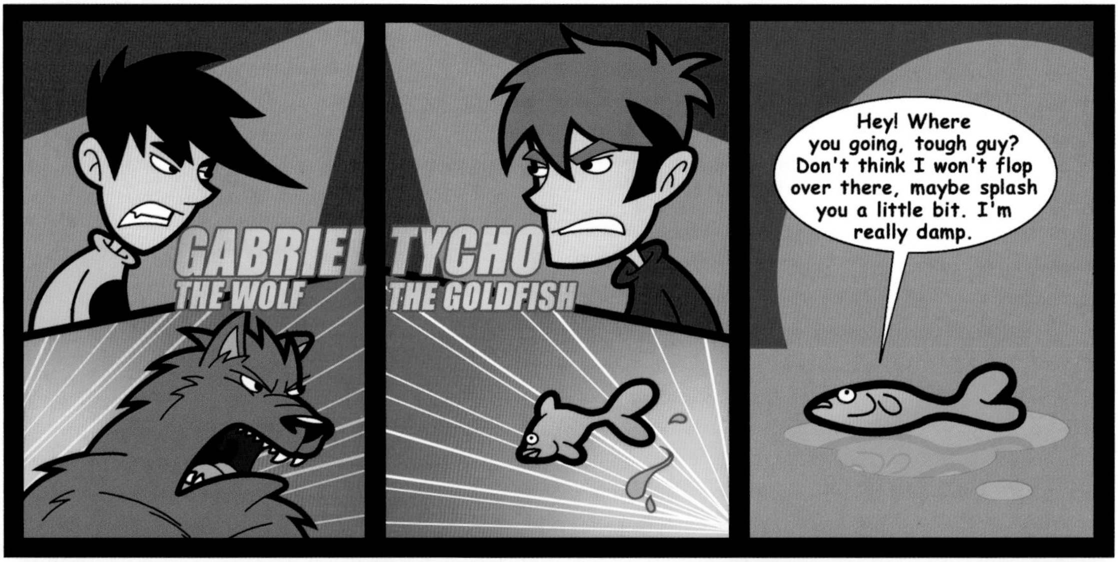
GABRIEL
THE WOLF
TYCHO
THE GOLDFISH
Hey! Where you going, tough guy? Don't think I won't flop over there, maybe splash you a little bit. I'm really damp.

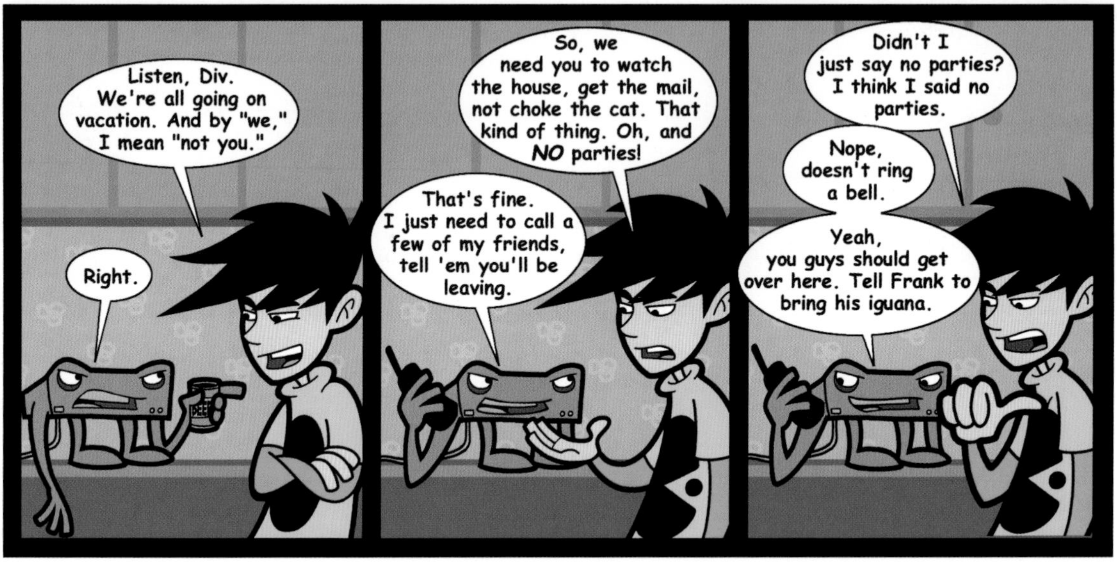
Listen, Div. We're all going on vacation. And by "we," I mean "not you."
Right.
So, we need you to watch the house, get the mail, not choke the cat. That kind of thing. Oh, and NO parties!
That's fine. I just need to call a few of my friends, tell 'em you'll be leaving.
Didn't I just say no parties? I think I said no parties.
Nope, doesn't ring a bell.
Yeah, you guys should get over here. Tell Frank to bring his iguana.

WE JUST GOT BLOODY ROAR 3

June 29, 2001 The Bloody Roar series didn't really stick with us, but it didn't really have to. If you can somehow come up with a couch, a fighting game, and two people to play it, you're probably set for days.

AT LEAST WAIT UNTIL I LEAVE THE ROOM

July 2, 2001 We went to the Oregon coast for a few days, Dreamcast in tow, and crafted a riveting "dramataic" statement to stir our readers while we were away. Three strips long, and each one rich with powerful themes.

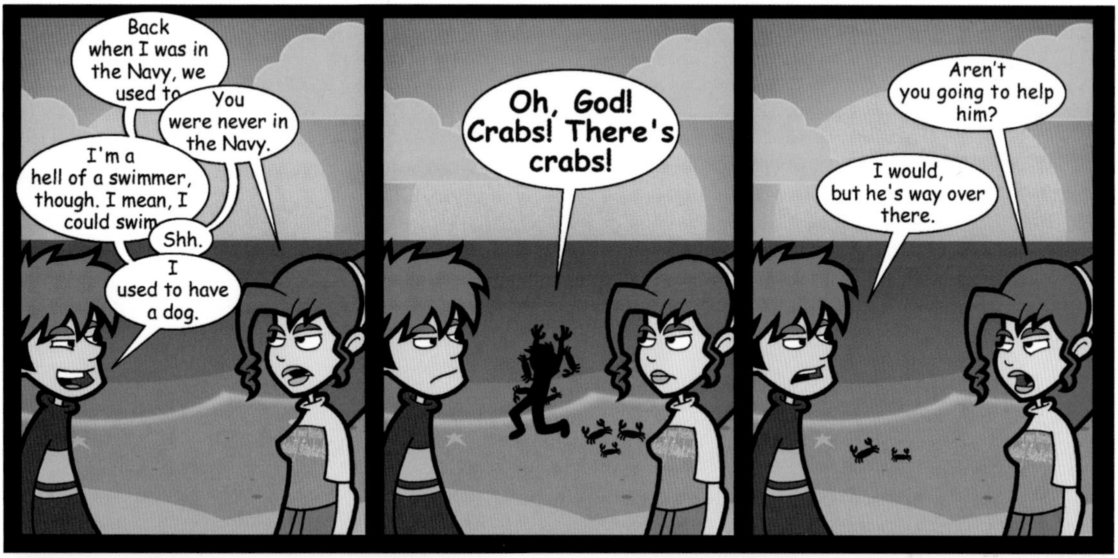
Back when I was in the Navy, we used to
You were never in the Navy.
I'm a hell of a swimmer, though. I mean, I could swim
Shh.
I used to have a dog.
Oh, God! Crabs! There's crabs!
Aren't you going to help him?
I would, but he's way over there.

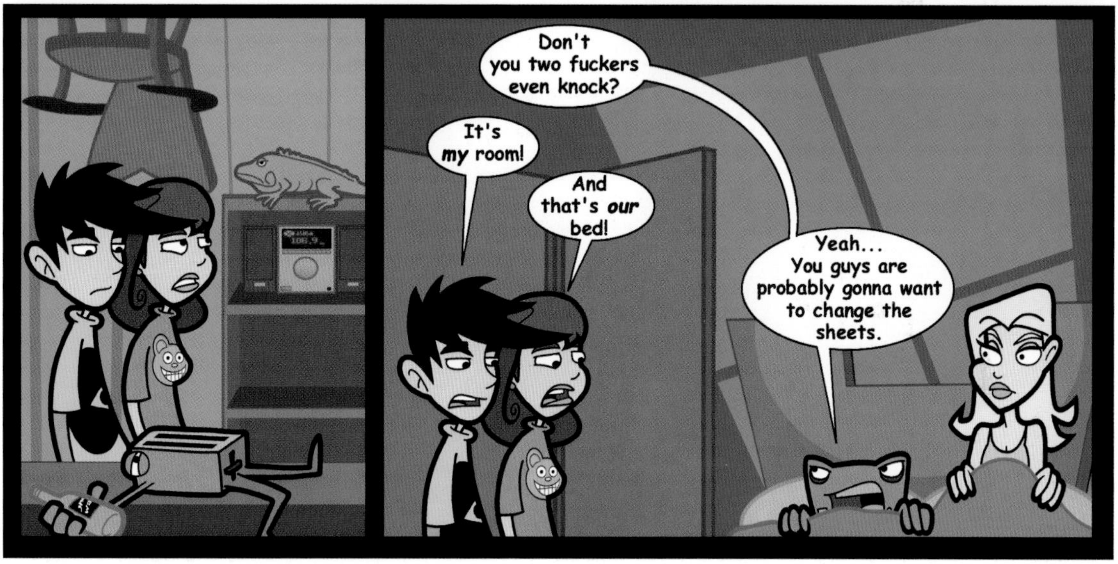
Don't you two fuckers even knock?
It's *my* room!
And that's *our* bed!
Yeah... You guys are probably gonna want to change the sheets.

ARTHROPODAL ADVENTURES

July 4, 2001 We *were* actually at the beach, and there were crabs, but they were friendly crabs and *not* hostile. They did not roam the beach in crustacean gangs, their tiny pincers at the ready.

PROBABLY SAFER TO BURN 'EM

July 6, 2001 I always liked the idea that Div hung with a rowdy gang of appliances, but character development really isn't our thing. When characters do develop, and it does happen from time to time, please let me assure you that it is an *accident*.

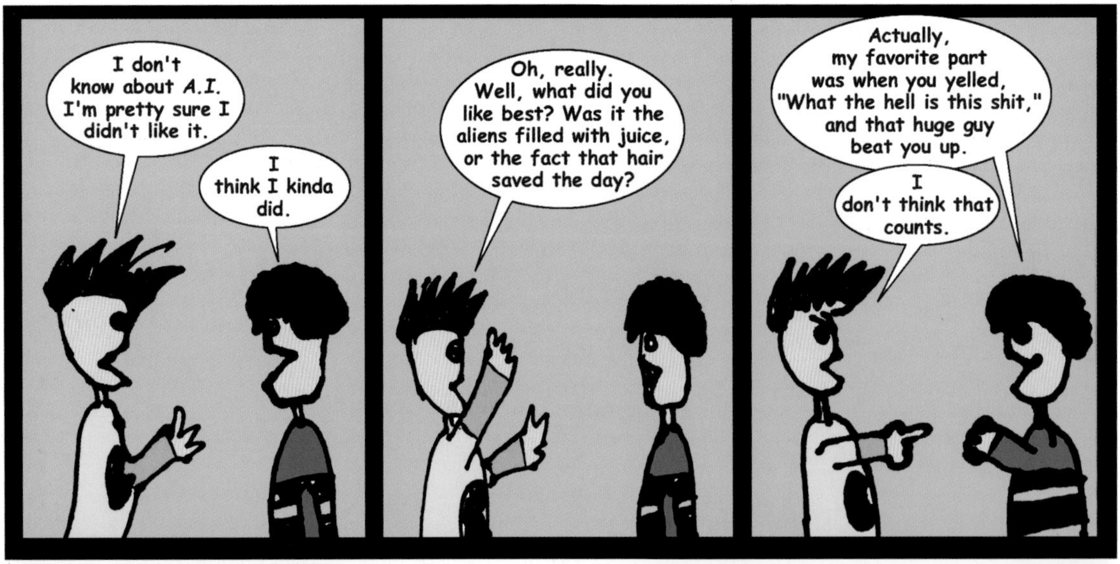
I don't know about A.I. I'm pretty sure I didn't like it.
I think I kinda did.
Oh, really. Well, what did you like best? Was it the aliens filled with juice, or the fact that hair saved the day?
Actually, my favorite part was when you yelled, "What the hell is this shit," and that huge guy beat you up.
I don't think that counts.

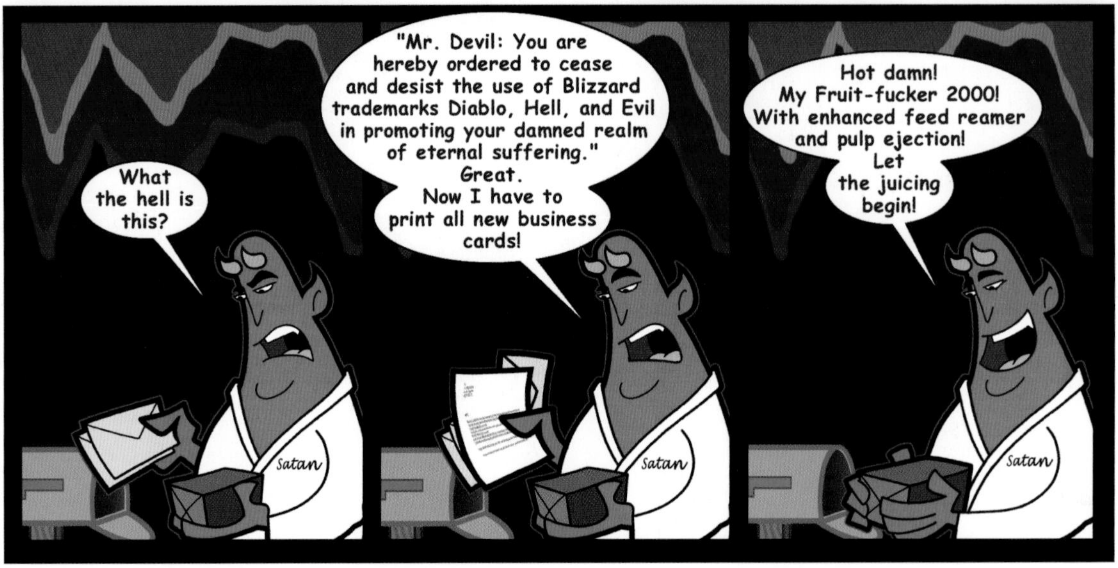
What the hell is this?
"Mr. Devil: You are hereby ordered to cease and desist the use of Blizzard trademarks Diablo, Hell, and Evil in promoting your damned realm of eternal suffering." Great. Now I have to print all new business cards!
Hot damn! My Fruit-fucker 2000! With enhanced feed reamer and pulp ejection! Let the juicing begin!
Satan
Satan
Satan

TYCHO + MS PAINT = HORROR

July 9, 2001 When I finished watching Steven Spielberg's *A. I.*, I got the impression that it had, in fact, succeeded—but succeeded at what, I couldn't tell you. Everything about it was just so grand. And when you think it can't get any grander, Spielberg ends one movie and then starts *another* one, while you're still in the theater!

DIABOLICIOUS!

July 11, 2001 This is the introduction of the Fruit Fucker into the strip, though he has not yet made an appearance himself. We never expected to revisit the idea when we wrote this strip, and now when we go to a convention Gabe will sketch a hundred or more of them over the course of a weekend.

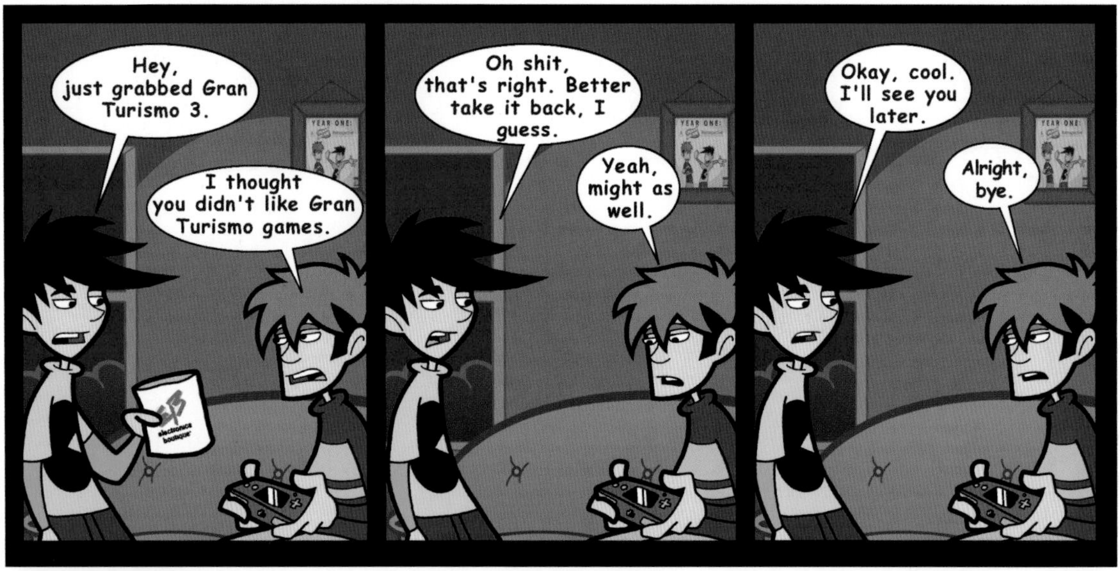
Hey, just grabbed Gran Turismo 3.
I thought you didn't like Gran Turismo games.
Oh shit, that's right. Better take it back, I guess.
Yeah, might as well.
Okay, cool. I'll see you later.
Alright, bye.

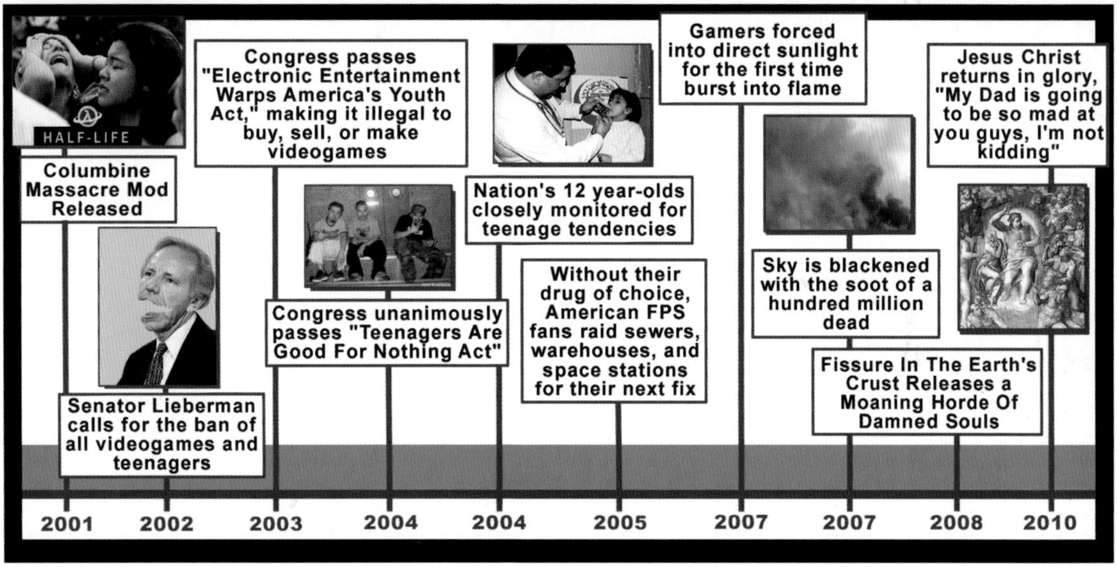
HALF-LIFE
Columbine Massacre Mod Released
Senator Lieberman calls for the ban of all videogames and teenagers
Congress passes "Electronic Entertainment Warps America's Youth Act," making it illegal to buy, sell, or make videogames
Congress unanimously passes "Teenagers Are Good For Nothing Act"
Nation's 12 year-olds closely monitored for teenage tendencies
Without their drug of choice, American FPS fans raid sewers, warehouses, and space stations for their next fix
Gamers forced into direct sunlight for the first time burst into flame
Sky is blackened with the soot of a hundred million dead
Fissure In The Earth's Crust Releases a Moaning Horde Of Damned Souls
Jesus Christ returns in glory, "My Dad is going to be so mad at you guys, I'm not kidding"
2001
2002
2003
2004
2004
2005
2007
2007
2008
2010

DO YOU NEED ANYTHING?

July 13, 2001 Everybody is Goddamn insane for this series, so I feel like we should be, but we just don't get it. I like a much looser racer, it's true—I'm not in it to pay for thousand-dollar virtual car washes or futz with a "gear ratio," whatever *that* might be.

THE FRENCH WORD FOR FUTURE

July 18, 2001 It wasn't difficult to extrapolate the demise of our species after a rogue developer produced a Columbine mod. Things end poorly. For those of you curious about the particulars, we do have this handy *chart.*

GAME DEVELOPERS LISTEN CAREFULLY! DO NOT GO TO THE POLICE! OUR CAT WILL BE HELD UNTIL THE FOLLOWING DEMANDS ARE MET.

DEMAND 1: A 3D SIDESCROLLING MEGAMAN GAME FOR A NEXT GEN PLATFORM THAT DOESN'T SUCK DONG.

DEMAND 2: A NEW SAMURAI SHODOWN GAME THAT'S GOOD AS SAMURAI SHODOWN 2.

DEMAND 3: A SEQUEL TO KOLIBRI ARGUABLY THE FINEST HUMMINGBIRD BASED SHOOTER ON THE 32X.

DEMAND 4: PUT A STOP TO YOUR INHUMAN AND IMMORTAL PRODUCTION OF HUNTING AND EXTREME SPORTS GAMES BEFORE YOU MAKE A "SIT ON YOUR ASS EXTREME" OR "EXTREME PUTTING ON OF HATS."

DEMAND 5: WE'RE REALLY THIRSTY. MAYBE SOME SPRITE? IT'S UP TO YOU, WE'RE NOT PICKY.

LEAVE GAMES OUTSIDE ELECTRONICS BOUTIQUE. COME ALONE. NO COPS!

PENNY ARCADE
11050 GAROU WAY, APT. 26
SPOCOMPTON, WA 98345

GAME DEVELOPERS
WE HAVE OUR CAT
WE HAVE YOUR CAT
NOT OUR CAT

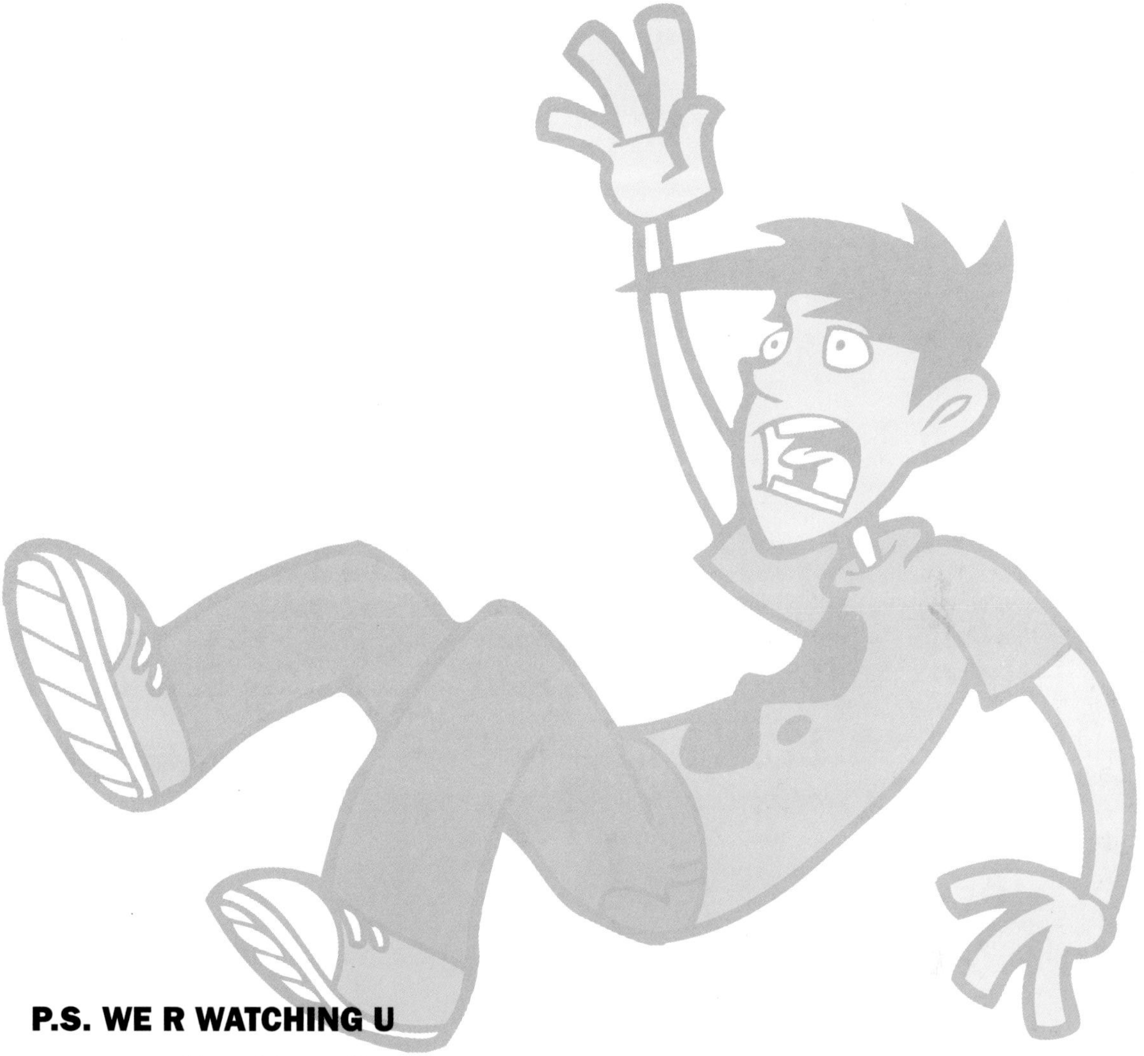

P.S. WE R WATCHING U

July 16, 2001 You might scoff at our methods, but you can't argue with our results:

Demand One has been met, and a couple times over, since our little note was delivered.

Demand Two, I mean, we were both very happy with Samurai Shodown V. A full accounting might take a while, but they got rid of some things that complicated it for no reason. In addition, and this is really the clincher, one of the characters wields no less than seven swords simultaneously. I don't know how many points each individual sword is worth but past five there has to be a multiplier or some shit.

Demand Three was a long shot. We weren't really expecting much, but if we got a new Kolibri out of the deal we weren't going to complain.

Demand Four is really the only failure.

We eventually satisfied Demand Five ourselves by going to the refrigerator, so they're pretty much off the hook there. I'm going to call this one basically four out of five.

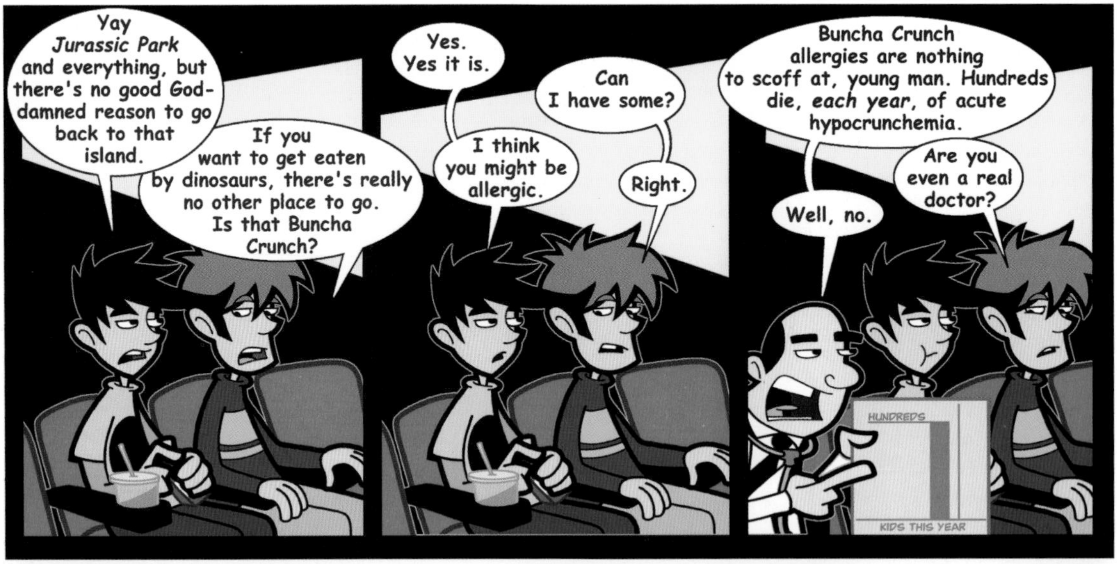
Yay *Jurassic Park* and everything, but there's no good God-damned reason to go back to that island.
If you want to get eaten by dinosaurs, there's really no other place to go. Is that Buncha Crunch?
Yes. Yes it is.
I think you might be allergic.
Can I have some?
Right.
Buncha Crunch allergies are nothing to scoff at, young man. Hundreds die, *each year*, of acute hypocrunchemia.
Well, no.
Are you even a real doctor?
HUNDREDS
KIDS THIS YEAR

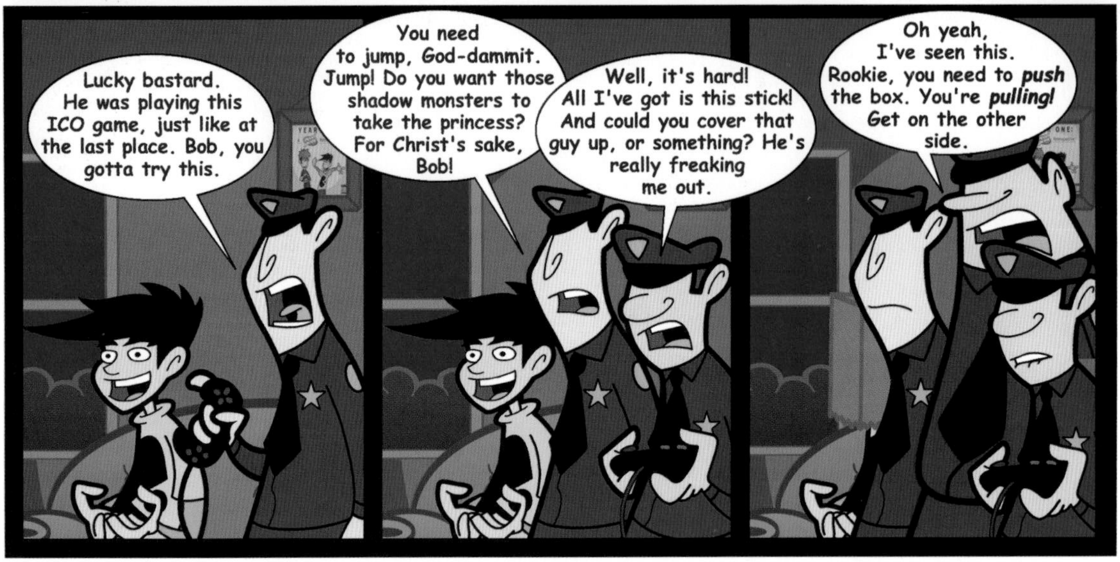
Lucky bastard. He was playing this ICO game, just like at the last place. Bob, you gotta try this.
You need to jump, God-dammit. Jump! Do you want those shadow monsters to take the princess? For Christ's sake, Bob!
Well, it's hard! All I've got is this stick! And could you cover that guy up, or something? He's really freaking me out.
Oh yeah, I've seen this. Rookie, you need to *push* the box. You're *pulling!* Get on the other side.

SPOILERS AHEAD!

July 20, 2001 I'm not sure what spoilers we might have been referring to. I think it's pretty well circulated by now that *Jurassic Park* features the occasional dinosaur.

IT REALLY IS THAT GOOD

July 23, 2001 I think we had been playing the Ico demo at the time, which was succulent. The solution for the puzzle in the demo was actually different than the one in the final version of the game, but that happens so rarely that I probably spent an hour doing it wrong in the retail copy.

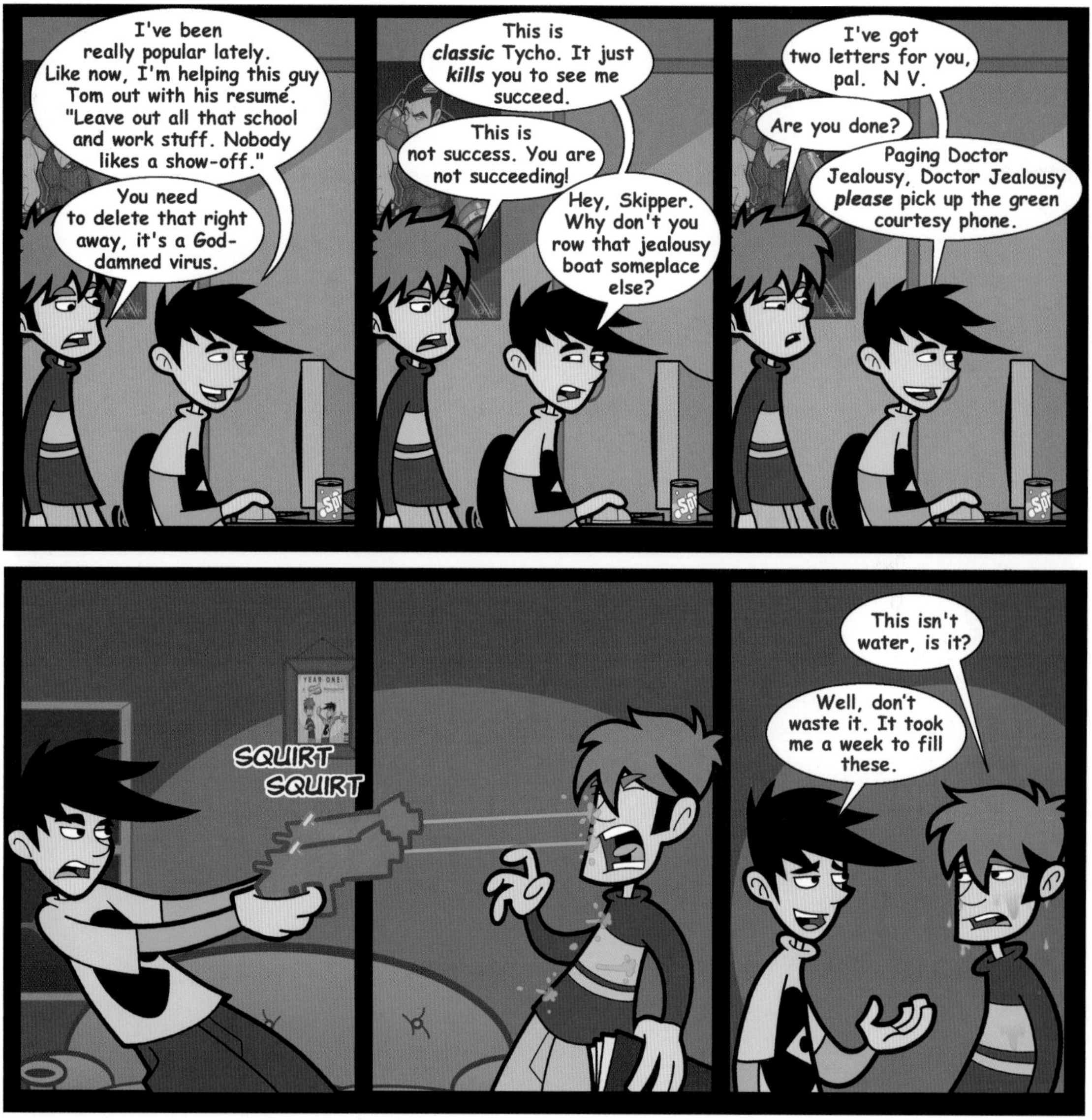
I've been really popular lately. Like now, I'm helping this guy Tom out with his resumé. "Leave out all that school and work stuff. Nobody likes a show-off."
You need to delete that right away, it's a God-damned virus.
This is *classic* Tycho. It just *kills* you to see me succeed.
This is not success. You are not succeeding!
Hey, Skipper. Why don't you row that jealousy boat someplace else?
I've got two letters for you, pal. N V.
Are you done?
Paging Doctor Jealousy, Doctor Jealousy *please* pick up the green courtesy phone.
SQUIRT
SQUIRT
This isn't water, is it?
Well, don't waste it. It took me a week to fill these.

I SEND YOU THIS FILE

July 25, 2001 One of the first viruses to really dig its heels into the information age, this one was truly fascinating. These days, you'll get a virus as an attachment, not a whole lot of excitement associated with that. This old one was crazy: it would send you random files from an infected person's hard drive, and—if opened safely—these artifacts could be *fascinating.*

GROADY TO THE MAX

July 27, 2001 We originally had two versions of this strip posted, and today we present the one that is demonstrably more vile. We never had a specific *definition* for the contained liquid, only that it was yucky, and if you had the chance to be hit with it or *not* hit with it, a reasonable person might choose the latter.

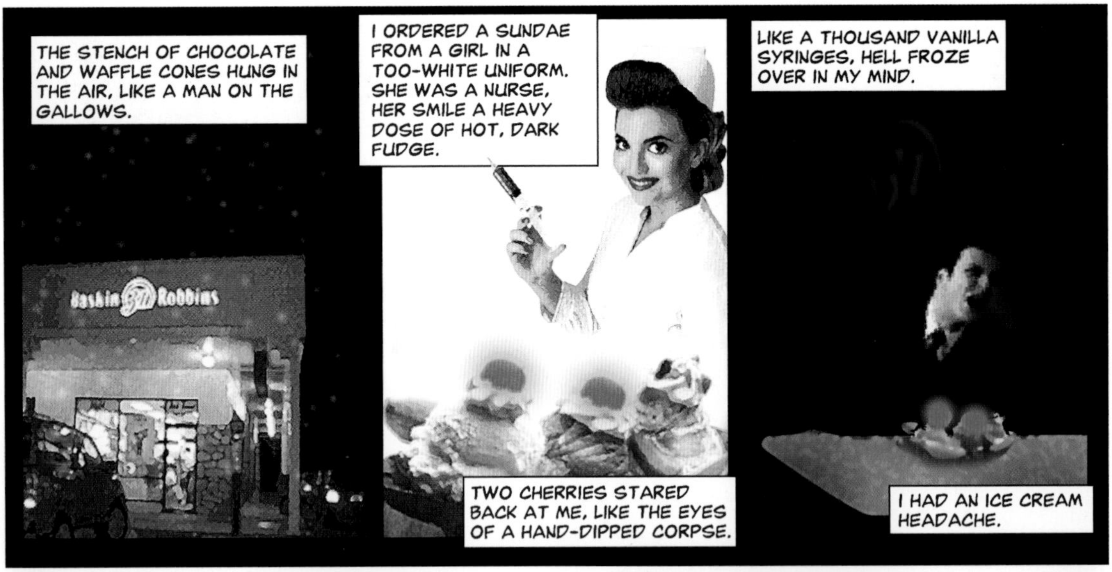
THE STENCH OF CHOCOLATE AND WAFFLE CONES HUNG IN THE AIR, LIKE A MAN ON THE GALLOWS.
Baskin Robbins
I ORDERED A SUNDAE FROM A GIRL IN A TOO-WHITE UNIFORM. SHE WAS A NURSE, HER SMILE A HEAVY DOSE OF HOT, DARK FUDGE.
TWO CHERRIES STARED BACK AT ME, LIKE THE EYES OF A HAND-DIPPED CORPSE.
LIKE A THOUSAND VANILLA SYRINGES, HELL FROZE OVER IN MY MIND.
I HAD AN ICE CREAM HEADACHE.

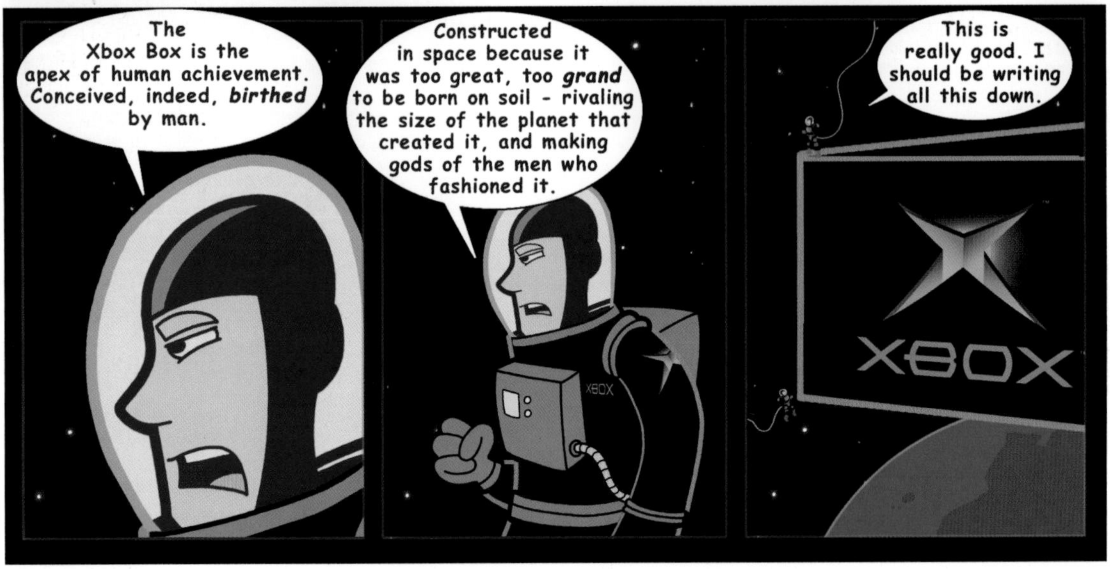
The Xbox Box is the apex of human achievement. Conceived, indeed, *birthed* by man.
Constructed in space because it was too great, too *grand* to be born on soil - rivaling the size of the planet that created it, and making gods of the men who fashioned it.
XBOX
This is really good. I should be writing all this down.
XBOX

PAYNE FREEZE

July 30, 2001 Hard-bitten hero Max Payne had a way of expressing himself that was true to the genre, but was delivered at a very high level of intensity: what you might call *ultranoir*. We could dig it, but we also couldn't help getting a kick in.

EXAGGERATION THEATRE

August 1, 2001 The Xbox *itself* was large, yes. But the box the Xbox *came* in was larger still. While we were looking for apartments, Brenna and I lived inside this sturdy container for nearly a month.

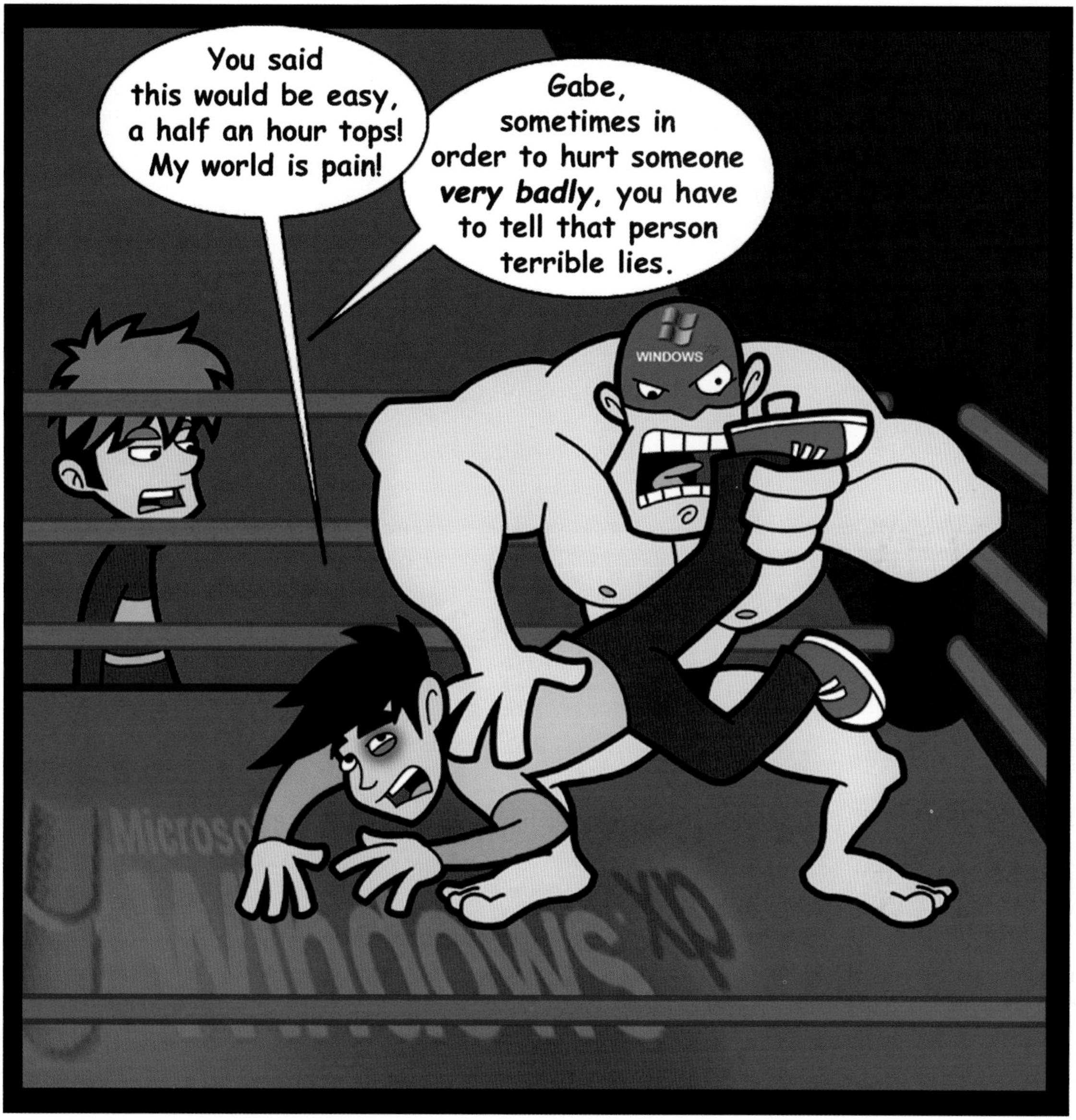
You said this would be easy, a half an hour tops! My world is pain!
Gabe, sometimes in order to hurt someone *very badly*, you have to tell that person terrible lies.
WINDOWS
Microso
WINDOWS XP

WINDOWS WRESTLING FEDERATION

August 3, 2001 After a successful and altogether painless install of the new OS on my own box, I was able to convince Gabe to give it a try—and the resulting explosion caused his machine to crumple, pulled through a hole to dimensions unknown. He had somehow managed to build a computer out of every part that had no driver for XP.

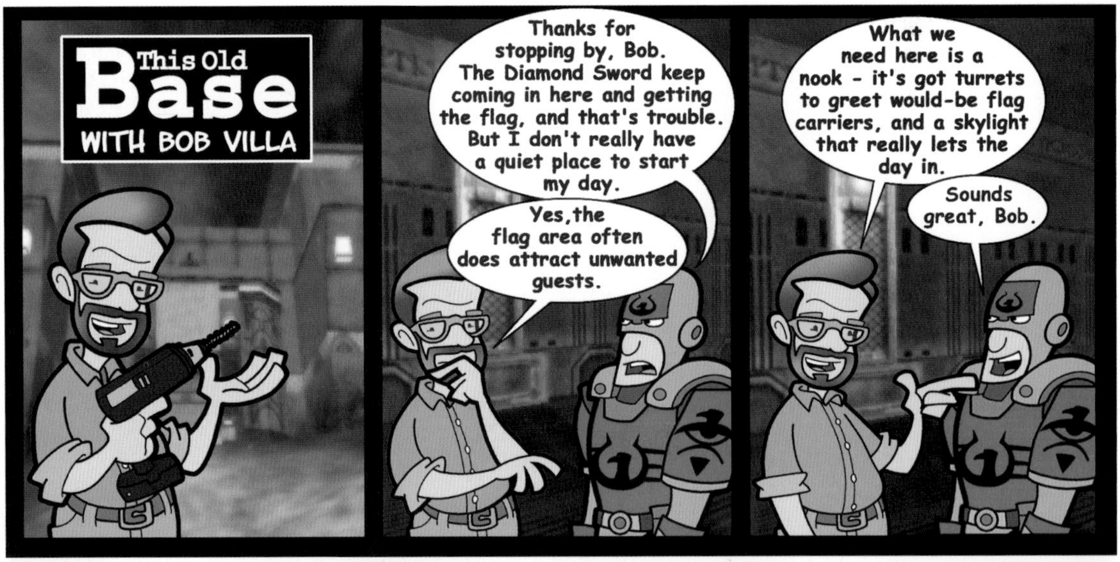
This Old Base
WITH BOB VILLA
Thanks for stopping by, Bob. The Diamond Sword keep coming in here and getting the flag, and that's trouble. But I don't really have a quiet place to start my day.
Yes, the flag area often does attract unwanted guests.
What we need here is a nook - it's got turrets to greet would-be flag carriers, and a skylight that really lets the day in.
Sounds great, Bob.

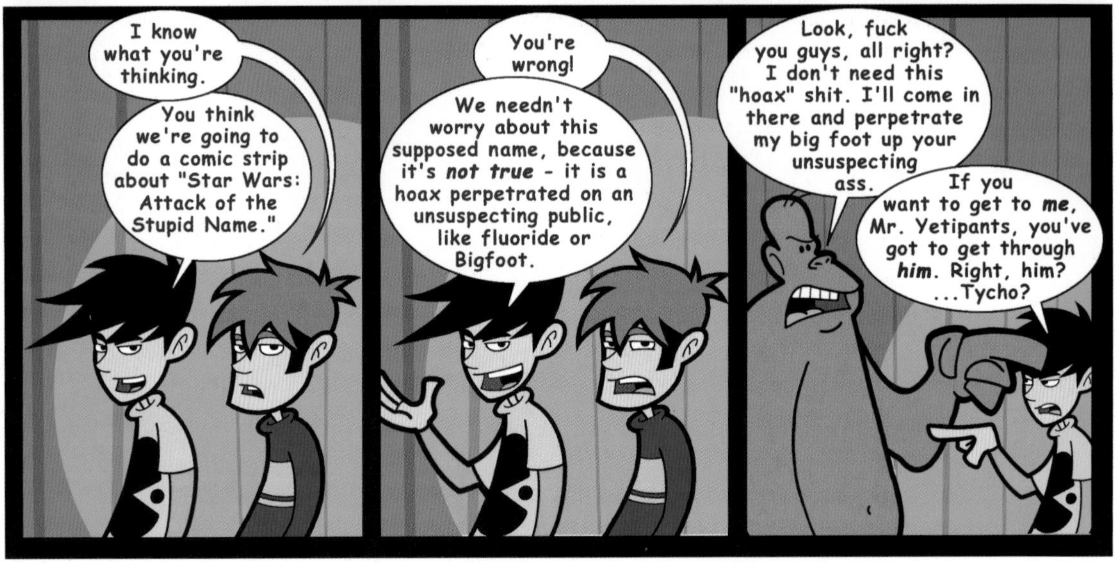
I know what you're thinking.
You think we're going to do a comic strip about "Star Wars: Attack of the Stupid Name."
You're wrong!
We needn't worry about this supposed name, because it's *not true* - it is a hoax perpetrated on an unsuspecting public, like fluoride or Bigfoot.
Look, fuck you guys, all right? I don't need this "hoax" shit. I'll come in there and perpetrate my big foot up your unsuspecting ass.
If you want to get to *me*, Mr. Yetipants, you've got to get through *him*. Right, him? ...Tycho?

THIS OLD BASE

August 6, 2001 I would often call whoever was nearby to come and check out my defensive handiwork in Tribes 2. The game had items you could install in various places, and turrets were my specialty. There was one map—I can't remember the name—but the moment a person grabbed the flag, they were shot by four turrets simultaneously.

LA LA LA, I CAN'T HEAR YOU

August 8, 2001 Are we trying to say that *fluoride* isn't real? Or are we trying to say the *effects* of fluoride are specious in some way? Or are we trying to claim that fluoride *is* real, and does produce an effect, but that this effect is either different than advertised, or demonstrably sinister?

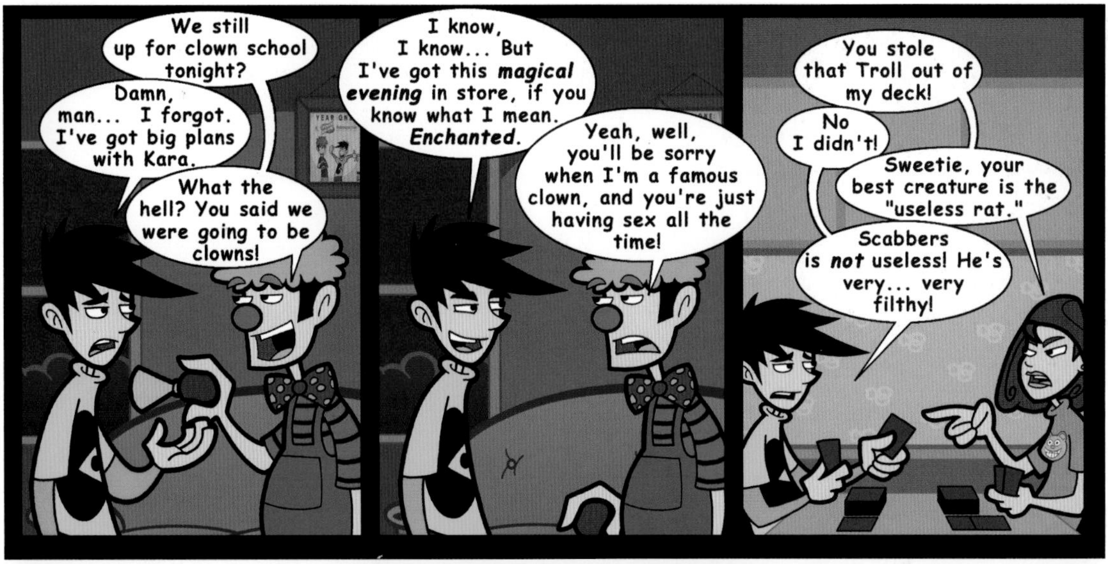
We still up for clown school tonight?
Damn, man... I forgot. I've got big plans with Kara.
What the hell? You said we were going to be clowns!
I know, I know... But I've got this ***magical evening*** in store, if you know what I mean. ***Enchanted.***
Yeah, well, you'll be sorry when I'm a famous clown, and you're just having sex all the time!
You stole that Troll out of my deck!
No I didn't!
Sweetie, your best creature is the "useless rat."
Scabbers is ***not*** useless! He's very... very filthy!

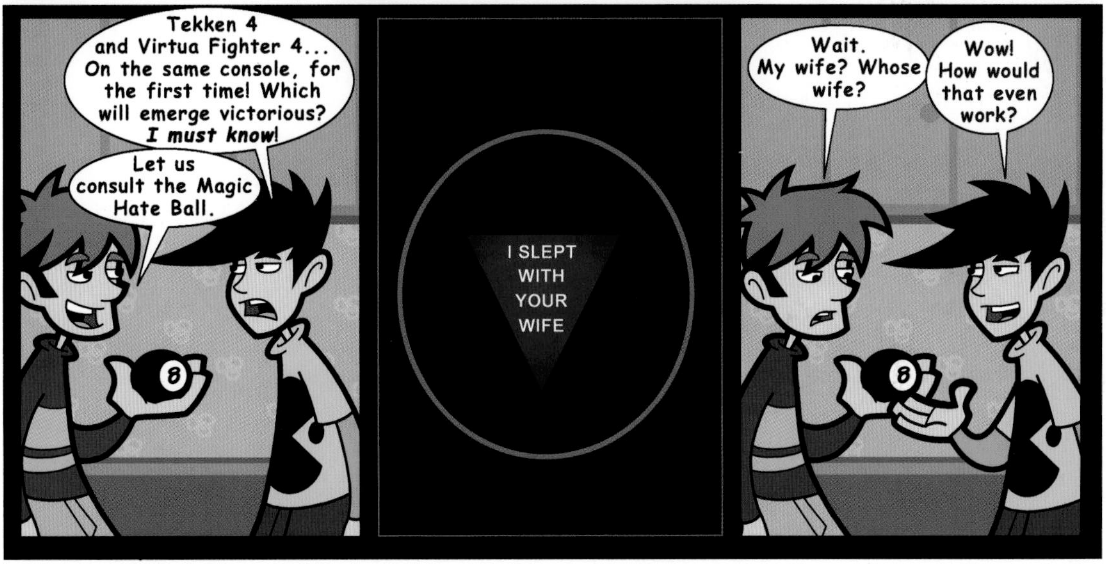
Tekken 4 and Virtua Fighter 4... On the same console, for the first time! Which will emerge victorious? ***I must know!***
Let us consult the Magic Hate Ball.
I SLEPT WITH YOUR WIFE
Wait. My wife? Whose wife?
Wow! How would that even work?

DAMN YOU, HARRY POTTER

August 10, 2001 This game was trouble. While something like Magic: The Gathering is too "nerdy," somehow a card game about students at a wizard academy is *just right*. It took over both households, duels of an eldritch sort running late into the night.

HOW, INDEED!

August 13, 2001 I don't think it *actually* did. At any rate, that's what I tell myself.

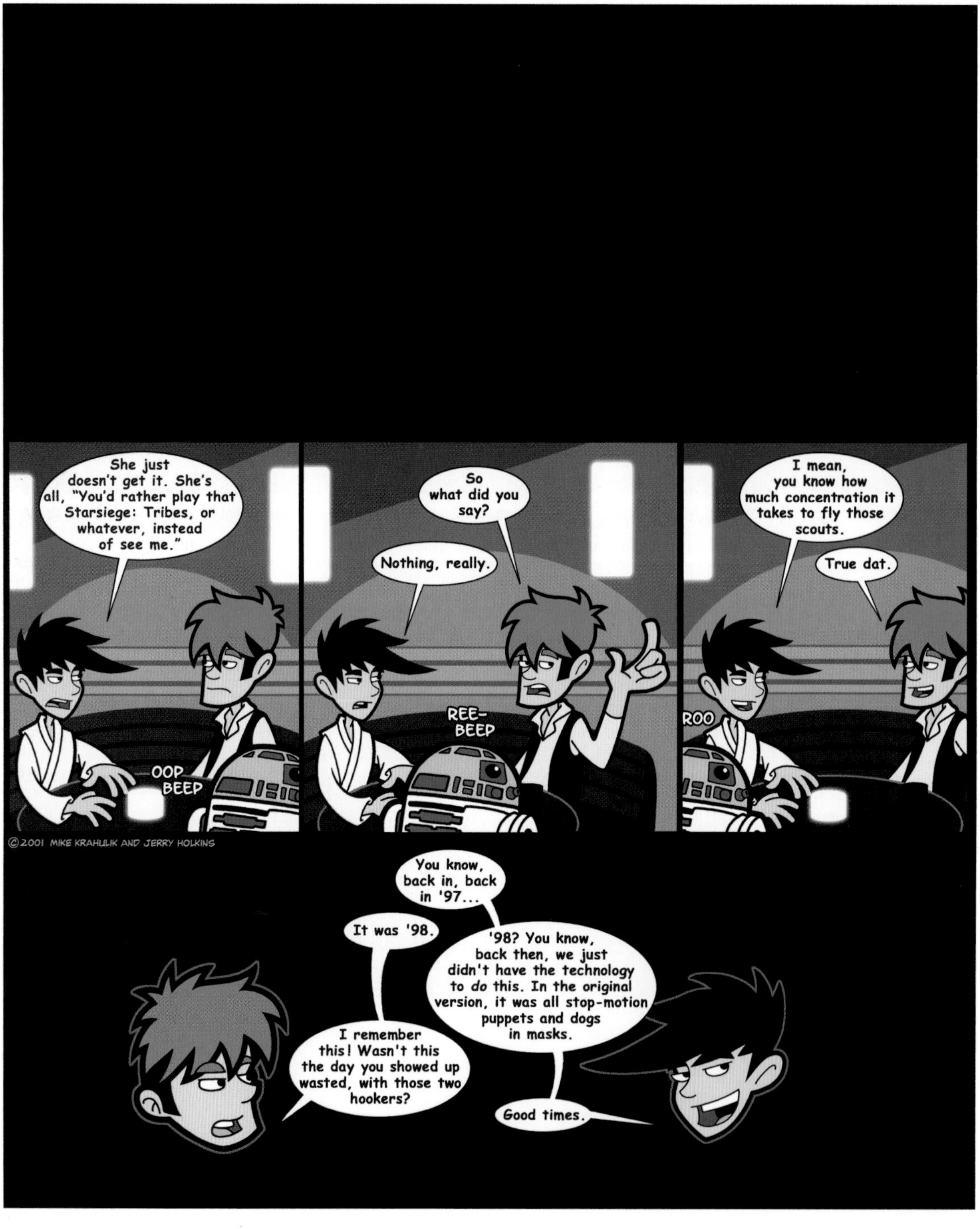
She just doesn't get it. She's all, "You'd rather play that Starsiege: Tribes, or whatever, instead of see me."
OOP BEEP
So what did you say?
Nothing, really.
REE-BEEP
I mean, you know how much concentration it takes to fly those scouts.
True dat.
ROO
©2001 MIKE KRAHULIK AND JERRY HOLKINS
You know, back in, back in '97...
It was '98.
'98? You know, back then, we just didn't have the technology to *do* this. In the original version, it was all stop-motion puppets and dogs in masks.
I remember this! Wasn't this the day you showed up wasted, with those two hookers?
Good times.

STAR WARS: A NEW JOKE

August 15, 2001 You probably remember when George Lucas remastered the original trilogy. We were getting a lot of requests, and I'm not making this up, to trawl our archive and "re-imagine" a "classic" strip. We heard their cries from atop our soot-black battlements and immediately set to work.

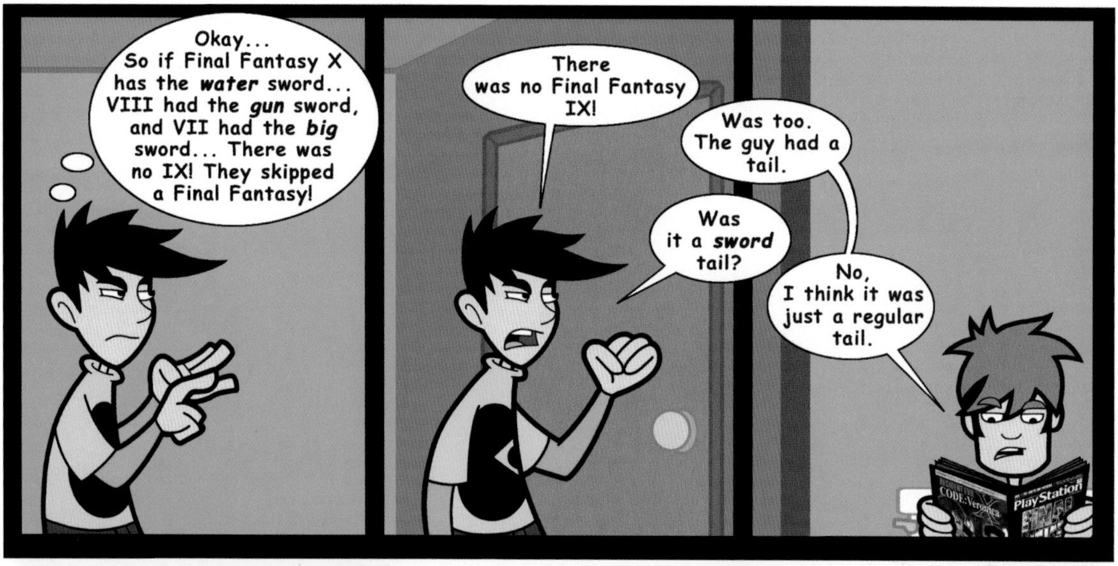
Okay... So if Final Fantasy X has the water sword... VIII had the gun sword, and VII had the big sword... There was no IX! They skipped a Final Fantasy!
There was no Final Fantasy IX!
Was too. The guy had a tail.
Was it a sword tail?
No, I think it was just a regular tail.
CODE:Veronica
PlayStation

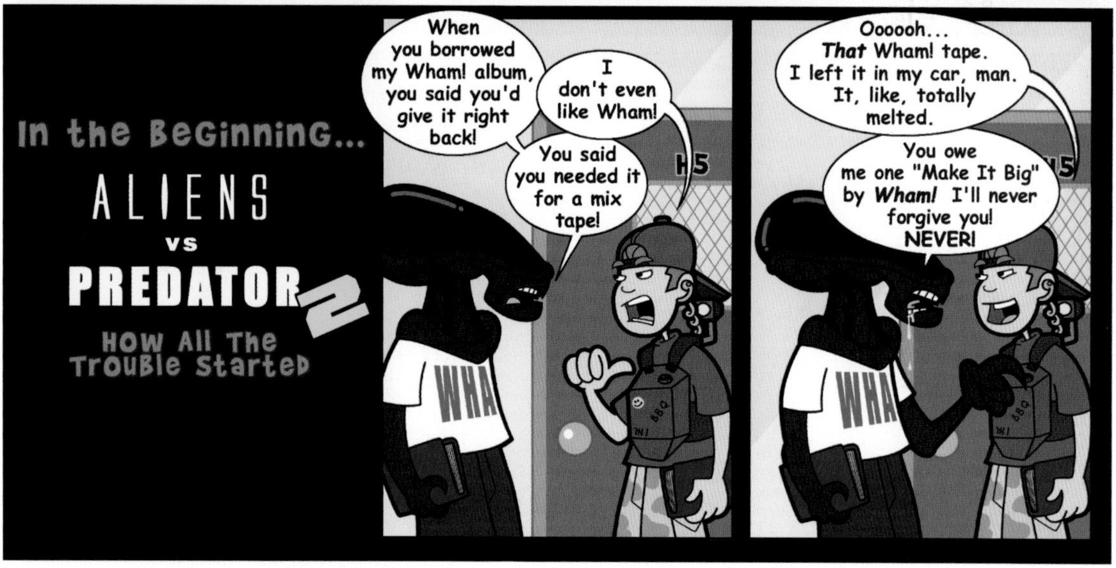
In the Beginning...
ALIENS
vs
PREDATOR 2
HOW All The Trouble Started
When you borrowed my Wham! album, you said you'd give it right back!
I don't even like Wham!
You said you needed it for a mix tape!
Oooooh... That Wham! tape. I left it in my car, man. It, like, totally melted.
You owe me one "Make It Big" by Wham! I'll never forgive you! NEVER!

FINAL FANTASY (X+1)

August 17, 2001 I can remember being very excited about this discovery, feeling that I was really *on* to some *shit*, until stupid Final Fantasy IX derailed the whole thing. That's often the way it works: my startling visions, undone by inconvenient *fact*.

THIS EXPLAINS EVERYTHING

August 20, 2001 The Aliens vs. Predator games had a lot going for them, I thought—particularly the second one, which included a multiplayer component that allowed fully three species to go (in a word) "buckwild." You'd have to work pretty hard to be worse than the movie, which outright kills five to seven percent of the viewing audience.

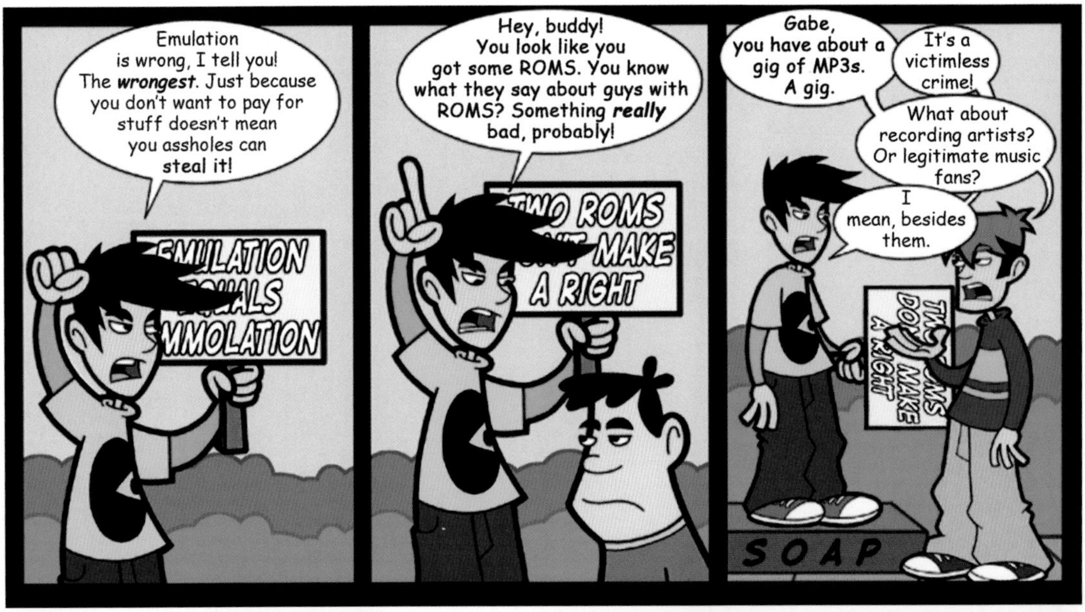
Emulation is wrong, I tell you! The wrongest. Just because you don't want to pay for stuff doesn't mean you assholes can steal it!
Hey, buddy! You look like you got some ROMS. You know what they say about guys with ROMS? Something really bad, probably!
TWO ROMS
MAKE
A RIGHT
Gabe, you have about a gig of MP3s. A gig.
It's a victimless crime!
What about recording artists? Or legitimate music fans?
I mean, besides them.
SOAP

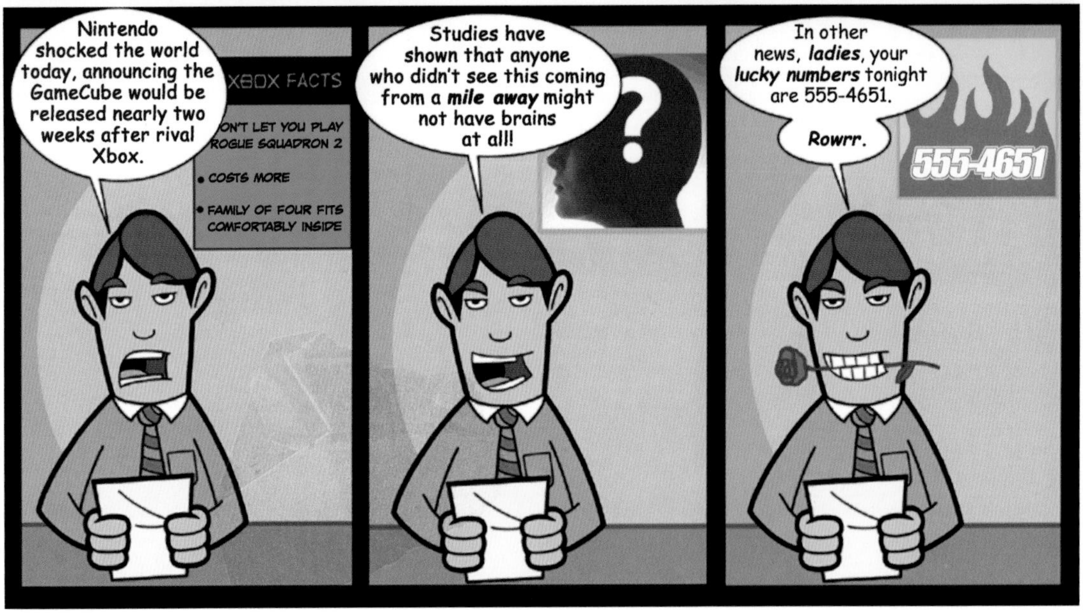
Nintendo shocked the world today, announcing the GameCube would be released nearly two weeks after rival Xbox.
XBOX FACTS
COSTS MORE
FAMILY OF FOUR FITS COMFORTABLY INSIDE
Studies have shown that anyone who didn't see this coming from a mile away might not have brains at all!
In other news, ladies, your lucky numbers tonight are 555-4651.
Rowrr.
555-4651

I'M NOT TALKING ABOUT THE BIRD

August 22, 2001 Trying to parse out the distinction between out-and-out theft and "sharing," the value-positive term we use to describe peer-to-peer distribution, is really very, very *hard* when the person you're talking to doesn't care.

WE SHOULD NAME HIM "RANDY"

August 24, 2001 It's hard to imagine a time where I held antipathy for the machine, but it's important to remember that when the machine launched, it wasn't the *whole* machine: the Live service, which really distinguishes the equipment, wouldn't be available for a full year.

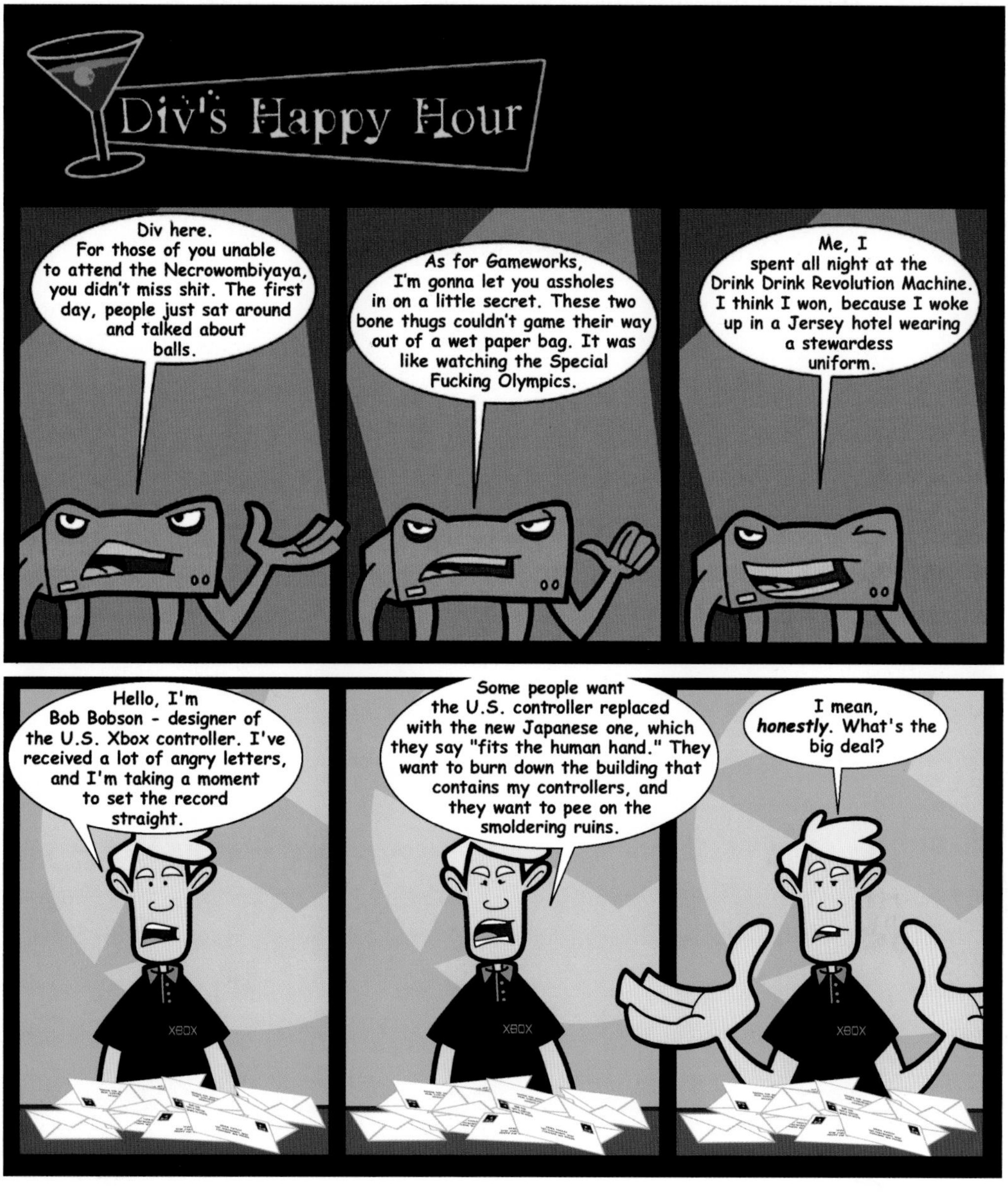
Div's Happy Hour
Div here. For those of you unable to attend the Necrowombiyaya, you didn't miss shit. The first day, people just sat around and talked about balls.
As for Gameworks, I'm gonna let you assholes in on a little secret. These two bone thugs couldn't game their way out of a wet paper bag. It was like watching the Special Fucking Olympics.
Me, I spent all night at the Drink Drink Revolution Machine. I think I won, because I woke up in a Jersey hotel wearing a stewardess uniform.
Hello, I'm Bob Bobson - designer of the U.S. Xbox controller. I've received a lot of angry letters, and I'm taking a moment to set the record straight.
Some people want the U.S. controller replaced with the new Japanese one, which they say "fits the human hand." They want to burn down the building that contains my controllers, and they want to pee on the smoldering ruins.
I mean, *honestly*. What's the big deal?
XBOX
XBOX
XBOX

NECROWOMBICON 2K1

August 27, 2001 The first NecrowombiCon was a pretty casual affair, taking place as it did largely in a *food court*. It would become more and more elaborate each year until it would eventually evolve into PAX.

YOU KNOW WHAT THEY SAY . . .

August 29, 2001 Microsoft actually used Bob Bobson in one of their presentations, something about "Internalizing the Essential Learnings" of the Xbox launch. Apologists emerged from all quarters to defend the original controller, these days called "The Duke," but eventually it was replaced with Japan's vastly superior Type-S. Someone over there agreed.

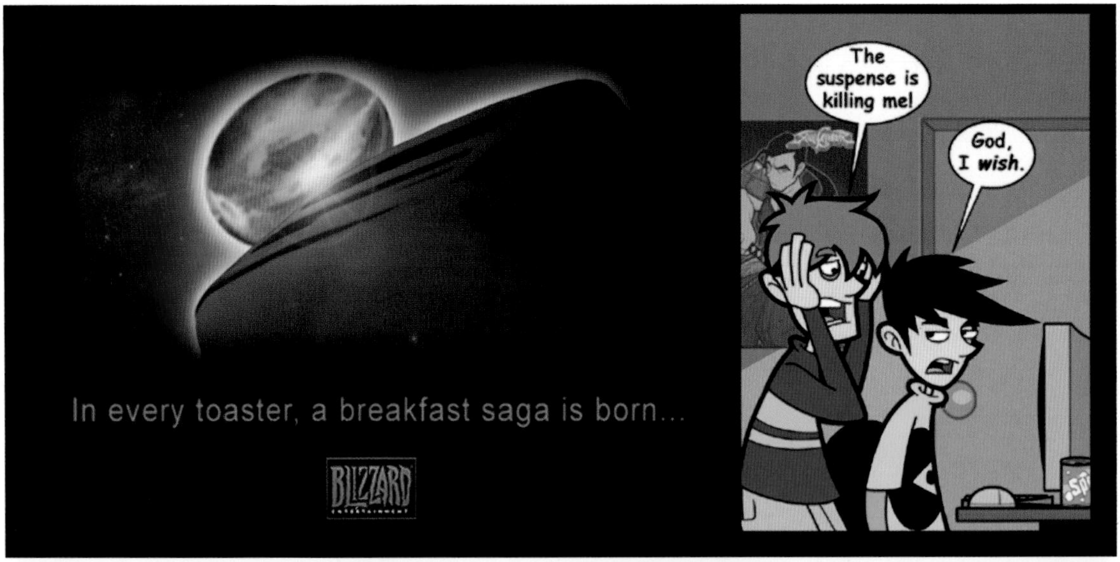
In every toaster, a breakfast saga is born...
BLIZZARD
The suspense is killing me!
God, I *wish*.

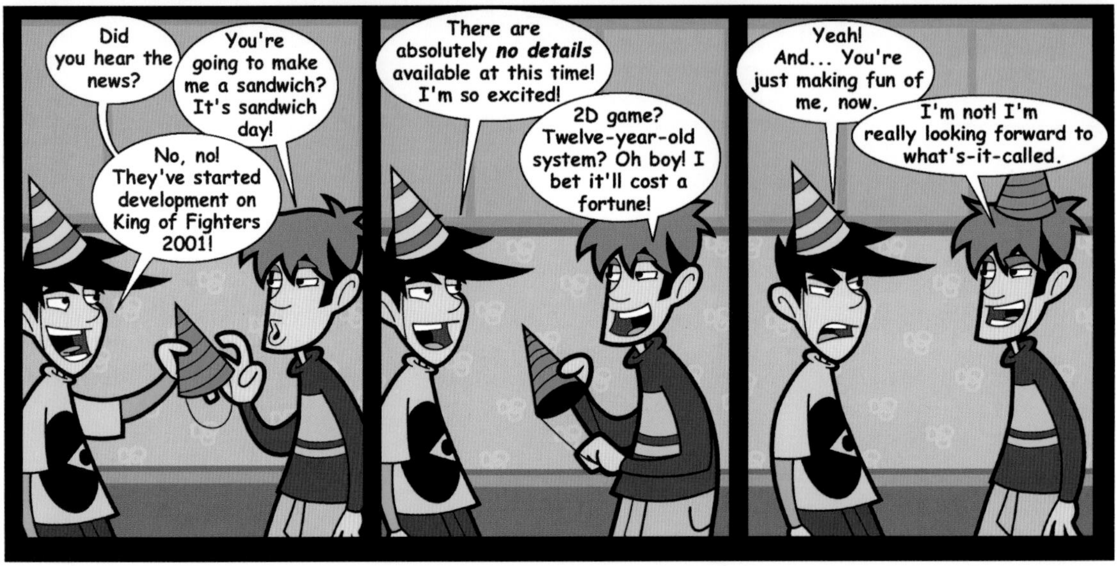
Did you hear the news?
You're going to make me a sandwich? It's sandwich day!
No, no! They've started development on King of Fighters 2001!
There are absolutely *no details* available at this time! I'm so excited!
2D game? Twelve-year-old system? Oh boy! I bet it'll cost a fortune!
Yeah! And... You're just making fun of me, now.
I'm not! I'm really looking forward to what's-it-called.

SUNDAY, SUNDAY, SUNDAY . . .

August 31, 2001 I can't really speak to the bagel thing, except to say that I *do* enjoy the occasional bagel. I have one every couple weeks, and I try not to overdo it. We're suckers for the way Blizzard announces products, though—the blank page, the counter, the wide field of raw potential.

SEPTEMBER 5TH IS SANDWICH DAY

September 5, 2001 Truth be told, I love King of Fighters almost *energetically*—indeed, it probably approximates his own *epic ardor*. But I can't just make it *easy* for him.

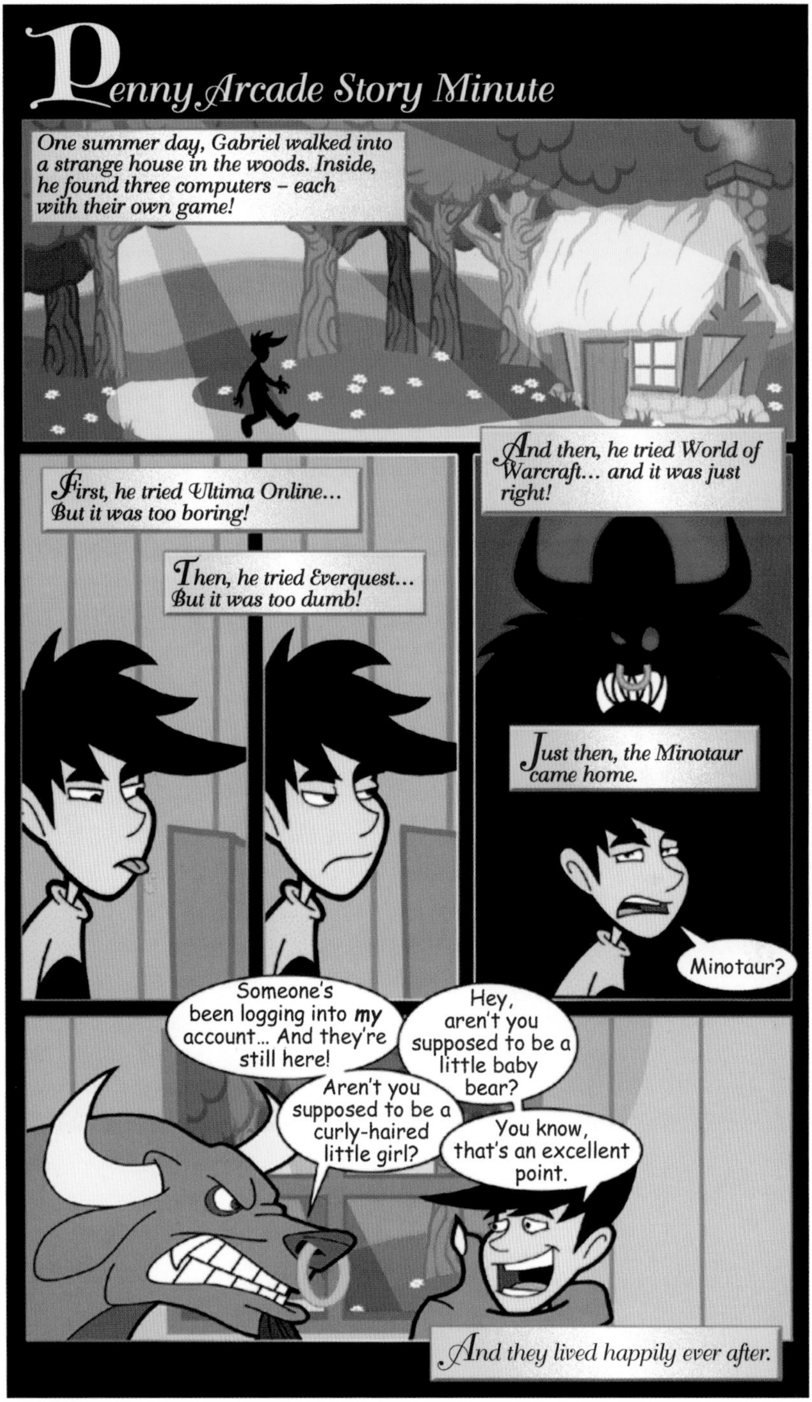
Penny Arcade Story Minute
One summer day, Gabriel walked into a strange house in the woods. Inside, he found three computers – each with their own game!
First, he tried Ultima Online... But it was too boring!
Then, he tried Everquest... But it was too dumb!
And then, he tried World of Warcraft... and it was just right!
Just then, the Minotaur came home.
Minotaur?
Someone's been logging into my account... And they're still here!
Hey, aren't you supposed to be a little baby bear?
Aren't you supposed to be a curly-haired little girl?
You know, that's an excellent point.
And they lived happily ever after.

STORY MINUTE!

September 3, 2001 I always felt a little bad about this strip, because there was no way I could possibly know how World of Warcraft would turn out. There was a rough patch at launch on some servers, true—but essentially, I was worried for nothing.

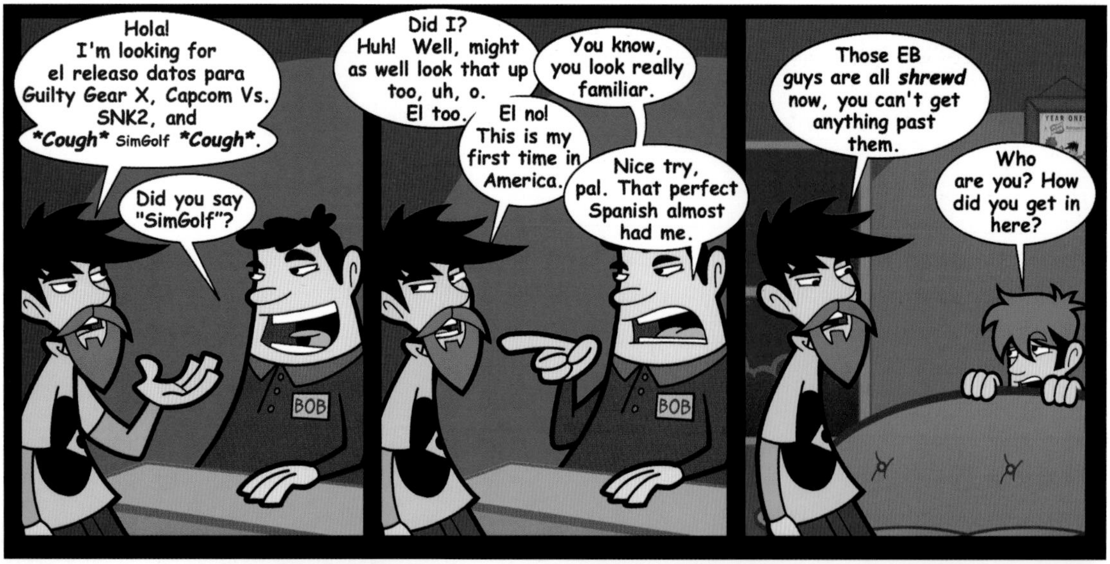
Hola!
I'm looking for
el releaso datos para
Guilty Gear X, Capcom Vs.
SNK2, and
Cough SimGolf *Cough*.
Did you say
"SimGolf"?
BOB
Did I?
Huh! Well, might
as well look that up
too, uh, o.
El too.
El no!
This is my
first time in
America.
You know,
you look really
familiar.
Nice try,
pal. That perfect
Spanish almost
had me.
BOB
Those EB
guys are all shrewd
now, you can't get
anything past
them.
Who
are you? How
did you get in
here?

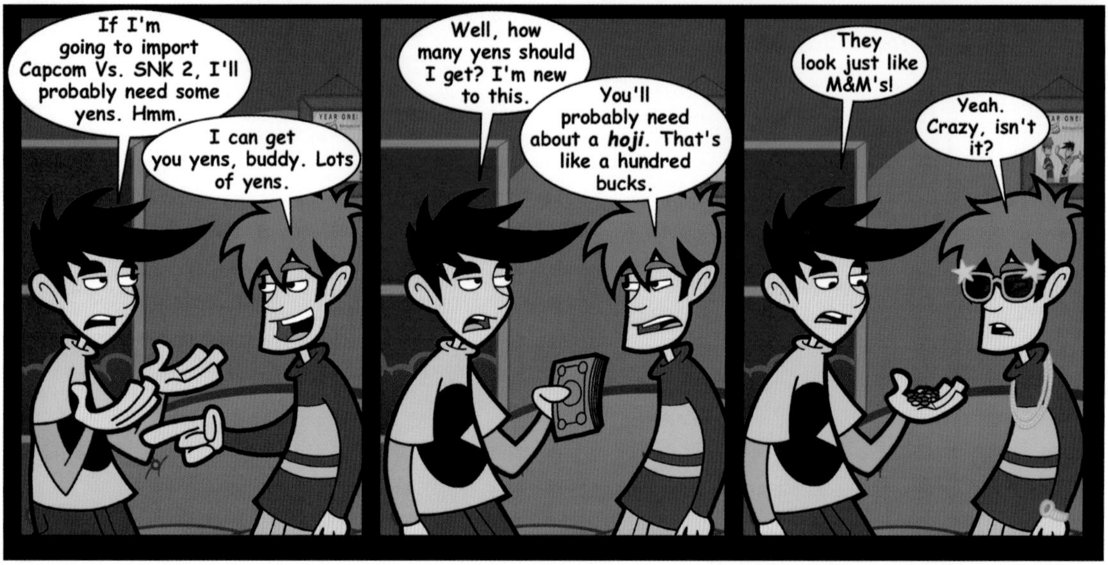
If I'm
going to import
Capcom Vs. SNK 2, I'll
probably need some
yens. Hmm.
I can get
you yens, buddy. Lots
of yens.
Well, how
many yens should
I get? I'm new
to this.
You'll
probably need
about a hoji. That's
like a hundred
bucks.
They
look just like
M&M's!
Yeah.
Crazy, isn't
it?

THE RUSE

September 7, 2001 Individuals with our hardcore credentials always need to be wary of seeming too closely aligned with titles that might appeal to the foul casual gamer. *But*, provided you promise not to tell anyone I said it, SimGolf was a vicious addiction that eventually saw me in counseling.

GOOD MONEY

September 10, 2001 People have said that, in this instance, I took advantage of Gabriel's ignorance to enrich myself. Nothing could be further from the truth: the exchange rate for yens was actually *very good* at the time.

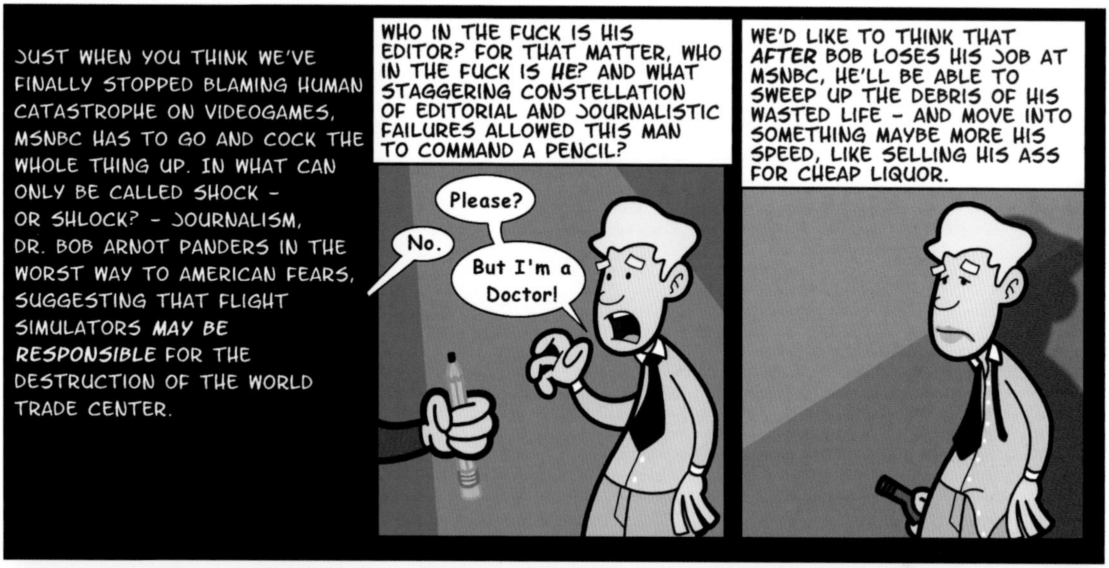
JUST WHEN YOU THINK WE'VE FINALLY STOPPED BLAMING HUMAN CATASTROPHE ON VIDEOGAMES, MSNBC HAS TO GO AND COCK THE WHOLE THING UP. IN WHAT CAN ONLY BE CALLED SHOCK - OR SHLOCK? - JOURNALISM, DR. BOB ARNOT PANDERS IN THE WORST WAY TO AMERICAN FEARS, SUGGESTING THAT FLIGHT SIMULATORS MAY BE RESPONSIBLE FOR THE DESTRUCTION OF THE WORLD TRADE CENTER.
WHO IN THE FUCK IS HIS EDITOR? FOR THAT MATTER, WHO IN THE FUCK IS HE? AND WHAT STAGGERING CONSTELLATION OF EDITORIAL AND JOURNALISTIC FAILURES ALLOWED THIS MAN TO COMMAND A PENCIL?
Please?
No.
But I'm a Doctor!
WE'D LIKE TO THINK THAT AFTER BOB LOSES HIS JOB AT MSNBC, HE'LL BE ABLE TO SWEEP UP THE DEBRIS OF HIS WASTED LIFE - AND MOVE INTO SOMETHING MAYBE MORE HIS SPEED, LIKE SELLING HIS ASS FOR CHEAP LIQUOR.

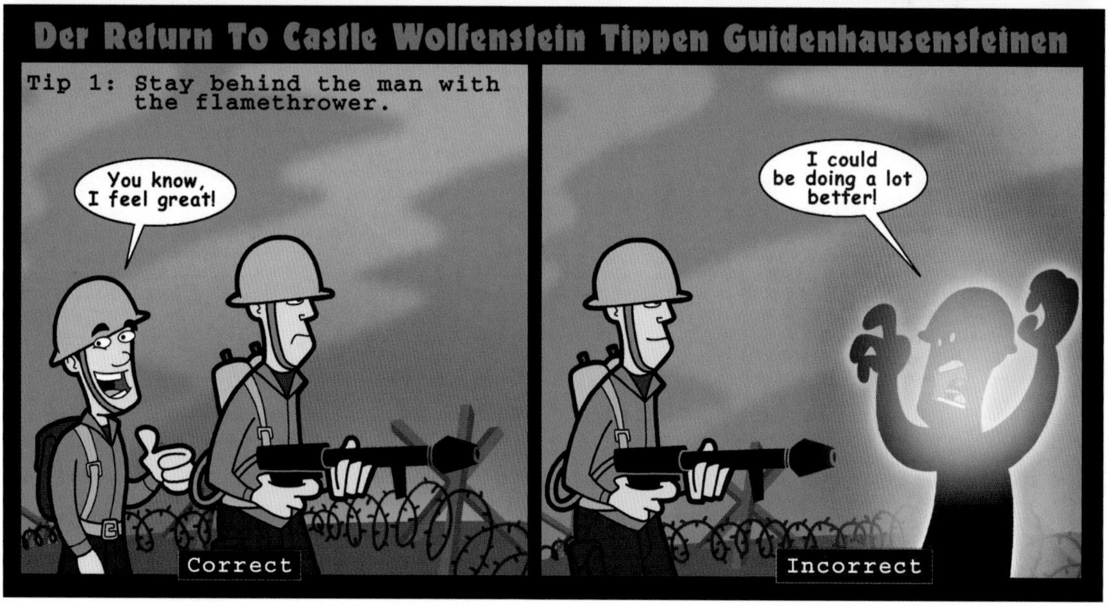
Der Return To Castle Wolfenstein Tippen Guidenhausensteinen
Tip 1: Stay behind the man with the flamethrower.
You know, I feel great!
Correct
I could be doing a lot better!
Incorrect

BOB, PhD

September 14, 2001 We brought the site down for a couple days after September 11th. A lot of people yelled at us for it, but nothing seemed particularly funny then.

THE HEAT OF THE NIGHT

September 17, 2001 Return to Castle Wolfenstein—the original game, we never really played Enemy Territory—is some of the best team-based multiplayer that's ever been delivered on the PC. Friendly fire, and the fire was in this case *literal*, issuing as it did from a flame-*thrower*, was a huge concern.

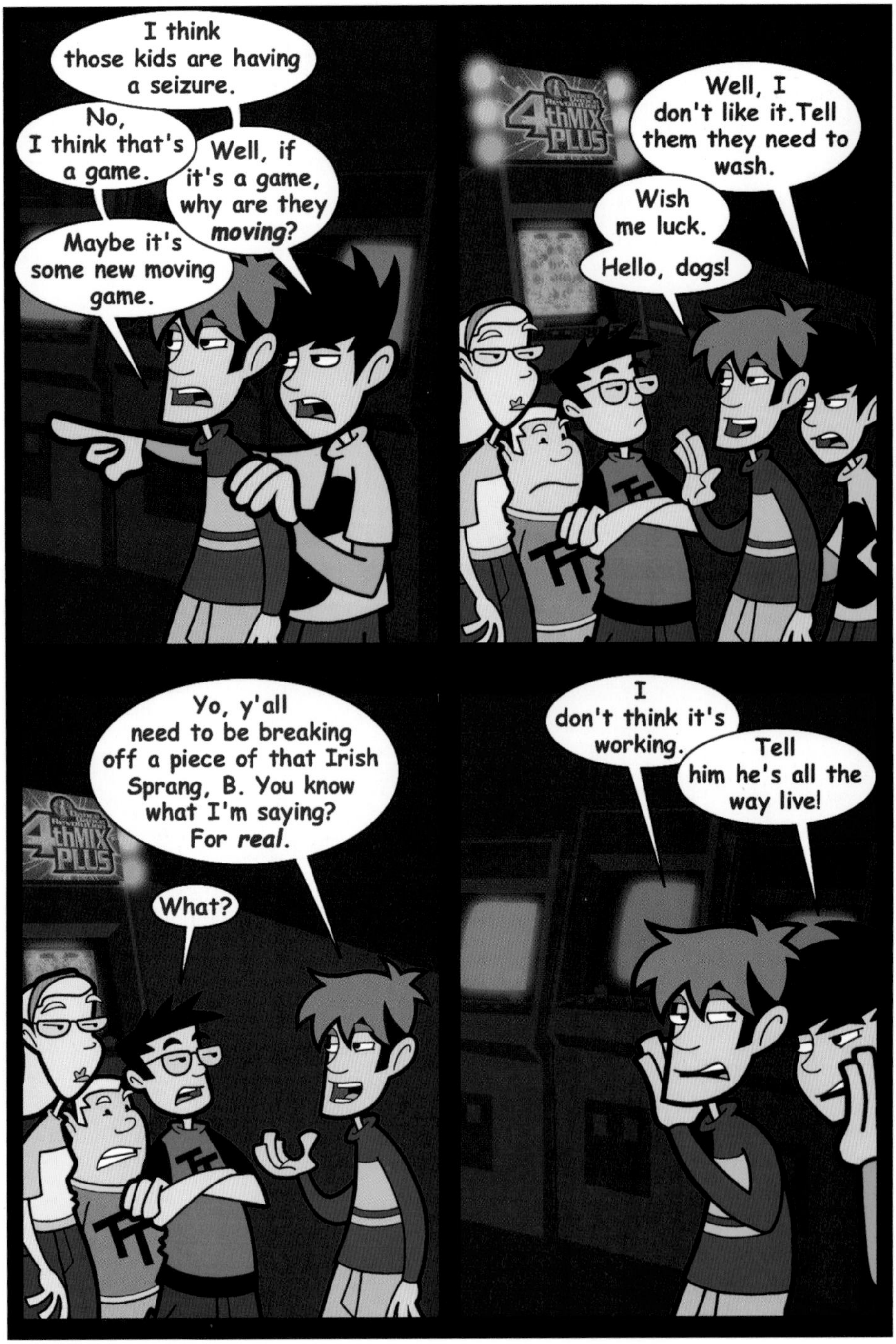
I think those kids are having a seizure.
No, I think that's a game.
Well, if it's a game, why are they *moving*?
Maybe it's some new moving game.
4thMIX PLUS
Well, I don't like it. Tell them they need to wash.
Wish me luck.
Hello, dogs!
Yo, y'all need to be breaking off a piece of that Irish Sprang, B. You know what I'm saying? For *real*.
What?
I don't think it's working.
Tell him he's all the way live!

THE WAGES OF FUNK

September 19, 2001 We used to hang out at this arcade over in Kirkland called Quarters, when there was still a Quarters to hang out *at*. The same way that you might have a Guild for your MMO or a Clan for your first-person shooter, DDR players formed “Teams”—and Team Trickstar made their home at the same arcade.

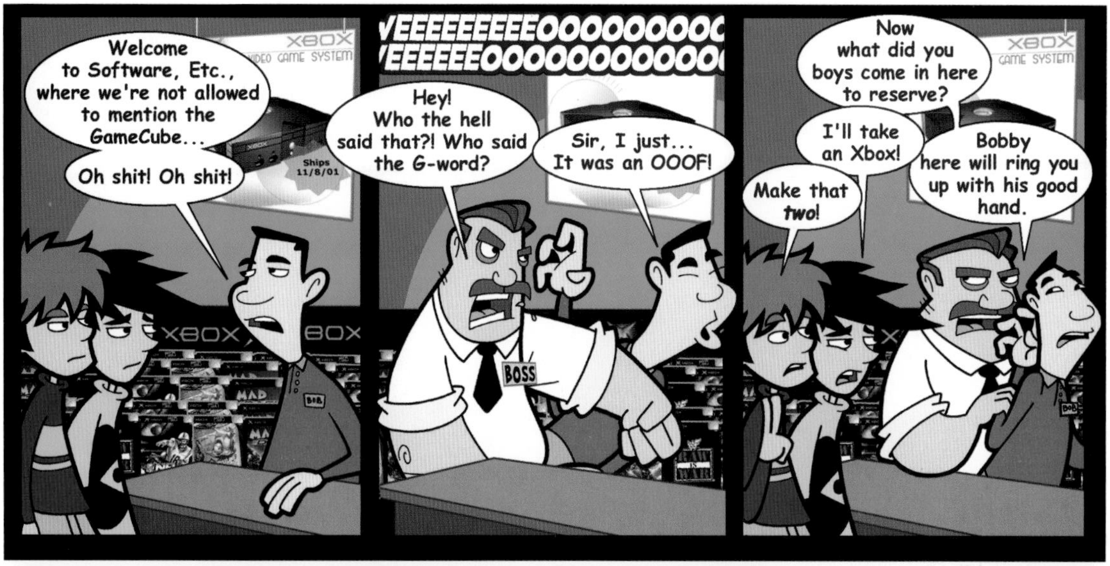
Welcome to Software, Etc., where we're not allowed to mention the GameCube...
Oh shit! Oh shit!
Ships 11/8/01
Hey! Who the hell said that?! Who said the G-word?
Sir, I just... It was an OOOF!
BOSS
Now what did you boys come in here to reserve?
I'll take an Xbox!
Make that *two*!
Bobby here will ring you up with his good hand.

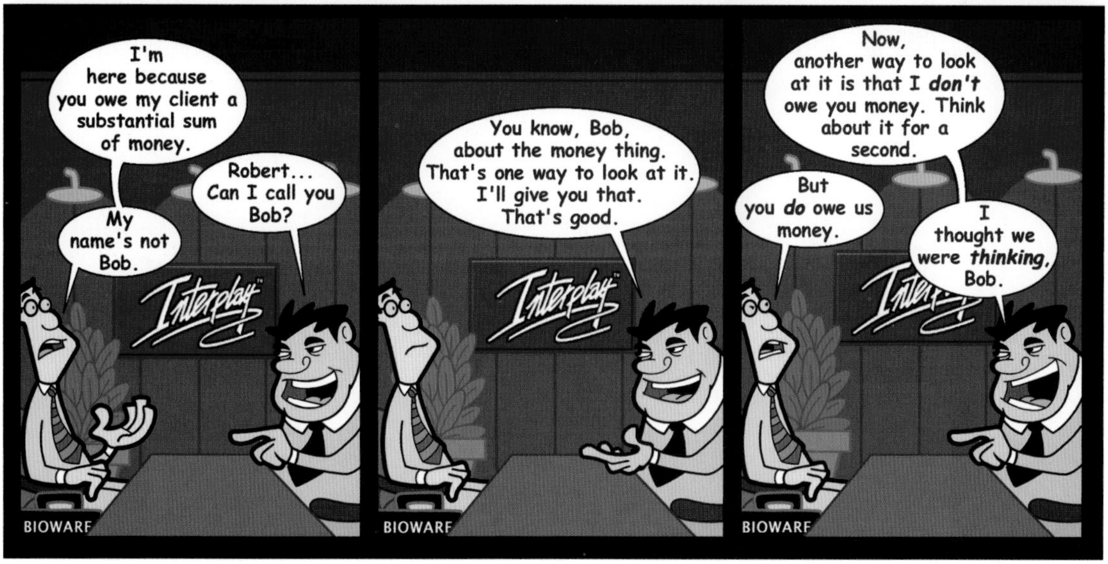
I'm here because you owe my client a substantial sum of money.
Robert... Can I call you Bob?
My name's not Bob.
Interplay
You know, Bob, about the money thing. That's one way to look at it. I'll give you that. That's good.
Now, another way to look at it is that I *don't* owe you money. Think about it for a second.
But you *do* owe us money.
I thought we were *thinking*, Bob.
BIOWARE

INTRODUCING FRANK

September 21, 2001 We heard a crazy rumor from employees that Software Etc. was actively promoting the Xbox over the Gamecube, which caused us to create Frank. Frank is based on the hostile, intimidating district managers we've seen terrify the people who work in these stores.

OUR NEIGHBORS TO THE NORTH

September 24, 2001 Interplay would eventually get theirs, so don't feel *too* bad. They were always synonymous with the pastime, at least for me—I played their stuff back on the Commodore 64, before they were even a publisher. Their legendary Black Isle studio was largely responsible for the return of the PC RPG.

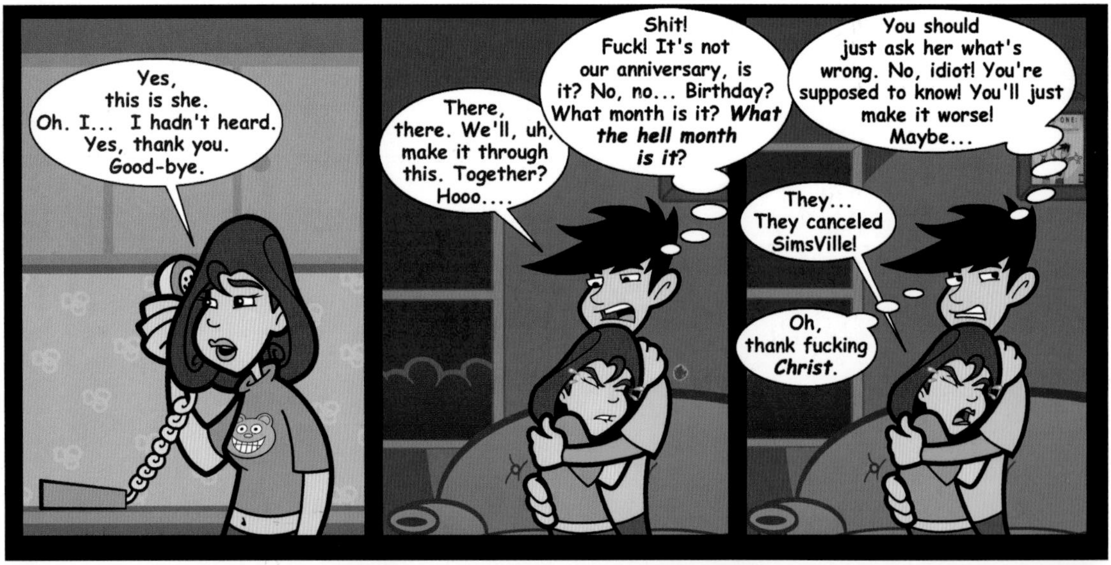
Yes, this is she. Oh. I... I hadn't heard. Yes, thank you. Good-bye.
There, there. We'll, uh, make it through this. Together? Hooo....
Shit! Fuck! It's not our anniversary, is it? No, no... Birthday? What month is it? *What the hell month is it?*
You should just ask her what's wrong. No, idiot! You're supposed to know! You'll just make it worse! Maybe...
They... They canceled SimsVille!
Oh, thank fucking *Christ*.

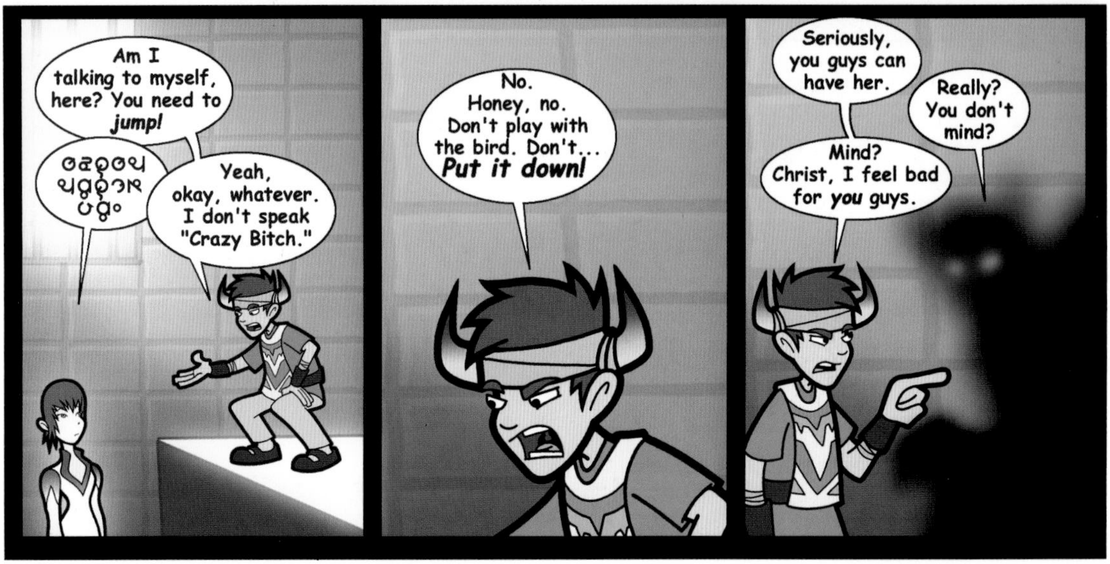
Am I talking to myself, here? You need to *jump!*
Yeah, okay, whatever. I don't speak "Crazy Bitch."
No. Honey, no. Don't play with the bird. Don't... ***Put it down!***
Seriously, you guys can have her.
Really? You don't mind?
Mind? Christ, I feel bad for *you* guys.

A CRYING SHAME

September 26, 2001 SimsVille was canceled because, to hear them tell it, "It wasn't fun," which seems like a good reason not to release a piece of software designed to produce that elusive substance. It drew focus away from individual homes and let you manage neighborhoods. These ideas slowly crept into the *actual* Sims franchise in a series of astonishingly well-received expansions.

THE I TO THE C TO THE O

September 28, 2001 It's been a while, so you might not remember—but the character you *play* as and the character that you're trying to save don't speak the same language. This comic is somewhere in my top ten for *Penny Arcade* output. The exasperated Ico and the strangely polite shadow creature kind of seal it for me.

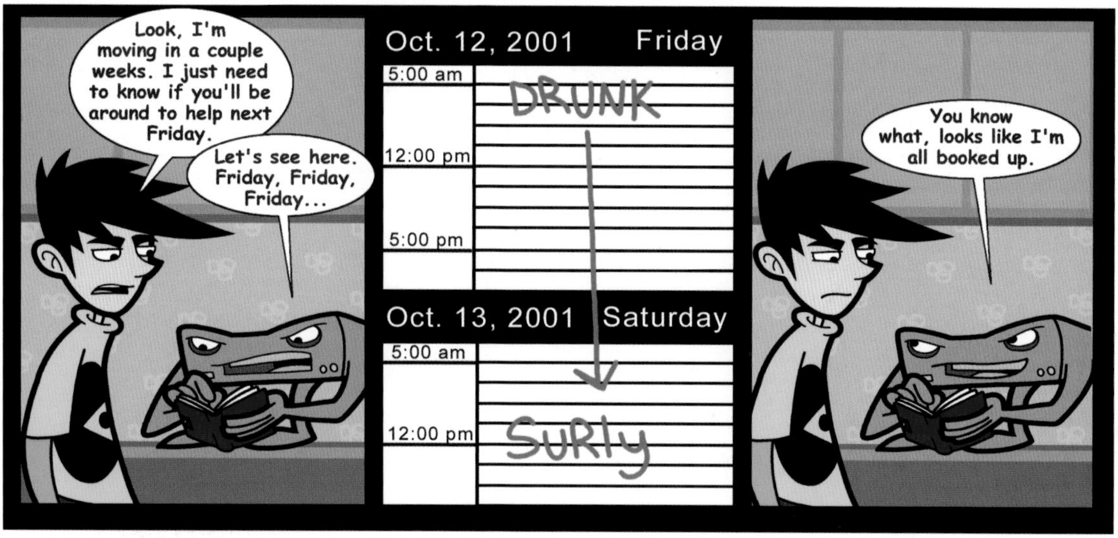
Look, I'm moving in a couple weeks. I just need to know if you'll be around to help next Friday.
Let's see here. Friday, Friday, Friday...
Oct. 12, 2001 Friday
5:00 am
12:00 pm
5:00 pm
DRUNK
Oct. 13, 2001 Saturday
5:00 am
12:00 pm
SURLY
You know what, looks like I'm all booked up.

GET YOUR MOVE ON

October 1, 2001 What happened to Div? You don't see very much of him these days. I guess you might imagine that *I'd* know what happened to him, seeing as I'm sort of responsible for who ends up in each comic strip, but I don't. He does his own thing. He shows up when he wants and goes when he pleases, which probably doesn't surprise anyone.

Around this time, Brenna brought in some toxic plants from outside and made me eat them. Things got pretty epic. Please join me for what has become known internationally as . . .

THE CHESTNUT SAGA

2001-10-01

Chestnuts Suck: I'm not joking about that. I roasted some of those awful little bastards just yesterday, strung along by popular mythology and holiday carols, and the resultant flavor—if indeed, *flavor* it may be called!—was like the flavor of poison. I may roast a few more just to get my aggressions out on them, vexing handfuls at a time with extraordinary cruelty. It begs the serious question: is figgy pudding *also* shitty? What other legendary, ostensibly edible horrors have been *foisted* upon us—foisted being an altogether excellent word for this purpose?

2001-10-08

In a recent post, I fired a controversial volley directly at chestnuts. In this searing exposé, I laid bare the tangled skein of mythology, lies, and outright treachery—hundreds of years in the making—that culminated in my consumption of this damned fruit.

I have a confession to make. I hadn't been eating chestnuts at all. And, like Adam in the Book of Genesis, I'm going to blame Brenna.
Behind their mahogany facade, chestnuts keep a dark secret: they have an evil twin, a wicked

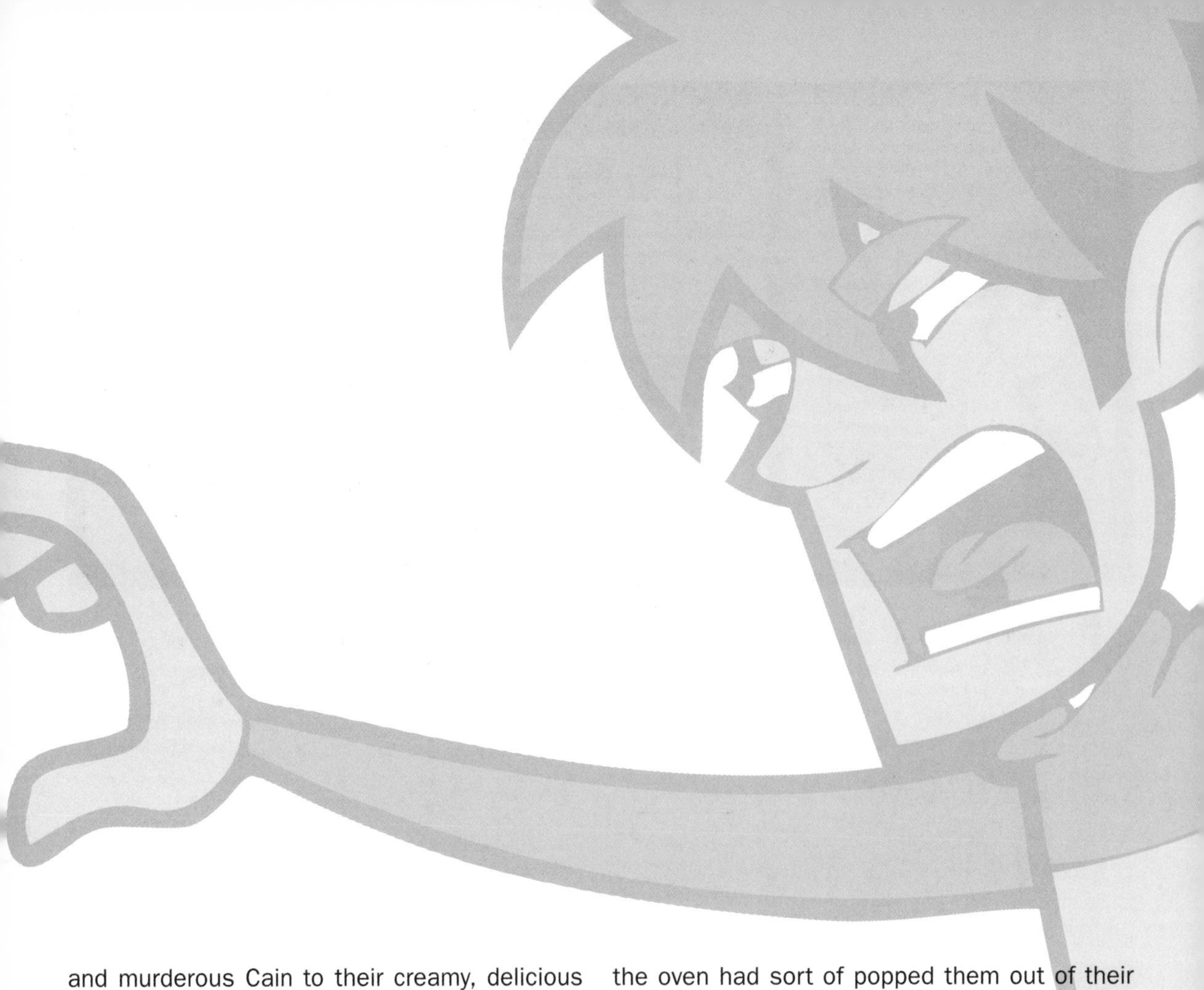

and murderous Cain to their creamy, delicious Abel. Not unlike Cain before it, the daemonic *horse* chestnut is an outcast even among its own kind. I wouldn't ordinarily just pick up some plant and start chewing on it, but Brenna noticed a "Chestnut Tree" out behind the apartment—and, flush with the old songs and stories, she thought it might be fun to try and kill us. She brought about forty vile Horse Chestnuts into our home and set them on my desk, which seemed to imply action on my part. I put little cuts in them so they wouldn't explode (this would turn out to be the *least* of my problems), put them in a bowl with some water, put some cinnamon and sugar on there, fuck, I don't know. It actually doesn't matter all that much, because—as it turns out—even when you put cinnamon and sugar on poison, it's still Goddamned *poison*. They smelled so good, they filled the place with a scent like sweet bread or pastry. The heat of the oven had sort of popped them out of their shells, the morsels presenting themselves for consumption. Never one to turn down such an offer, I broke off a tiny piece and popped it into my mouth.

When I said that it tasted like poison in the earlier post, that's because it actually *was*. It—Aesculin—tastes the way you'd imagine turpentine would taste, which is to say, like absolute fucking shit. And that flavor only leaves your mouth when it's good and ready, too—there's no coaxing it, it's like an oil or something. I thought to myself, "Well, maybe you just had a bad part," and grabbed a bigger piece from another one and ate that too. Brenna wanted to know how they were, and I said that she should just try one for herself and see how she liked it. She wasn't crazy about it. I would suppose that poison is an acquired taste.

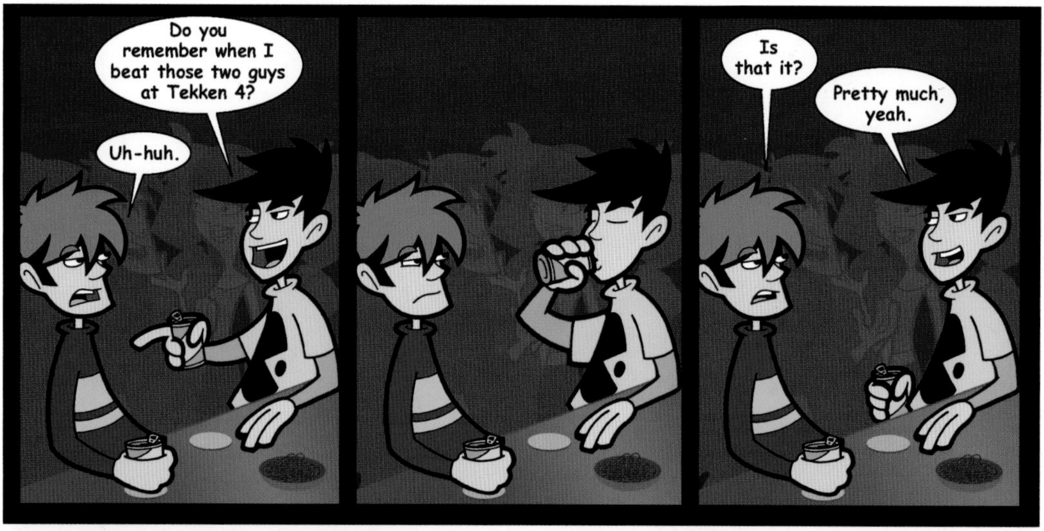
Do you remember when I beat those two guys at Tekken 4?
Uh-huh.
Is that it?
Pretty much, yeah.

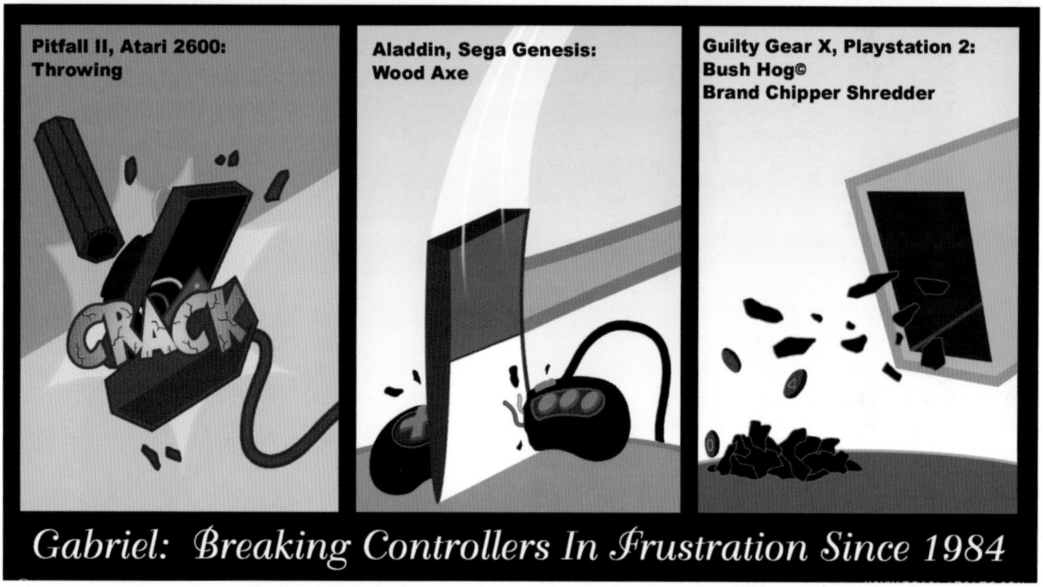
Pitfall II, Atari 2600: Throwing
CRACK
Aladdin, Sega Genesis: Wood Axe
Guilty Gear X, Playstation 2: Bush Hog©
Brand Chipper Shredder
Gabriel: Breaking Controllers In Frustration Since 1984

GABE TAKES ON TWO GUYS

October 3, 2001 This is a gaming history thing that is actually lost to us: the entire "Got Next" *scenario*. We can play people online and feel satisfied when we assert our dominion, true enough. But the physicality of the arcade—and the ability to take a person's money with each victory, as sure as if you had robbed them—that culture is gone where I live.

A PROUD TRADITION

October 5, 2001 Watching someone play Guilty Gear at the competitive level, you would think they were playing a completely different game than the one you screw around with at home. Proper GG play is really a kind of philosophy. Since it's 2D, like many other fighters you have played, you think you're in for a certain kind of experience—then it castrates you.

This castration comes as a total surprise.

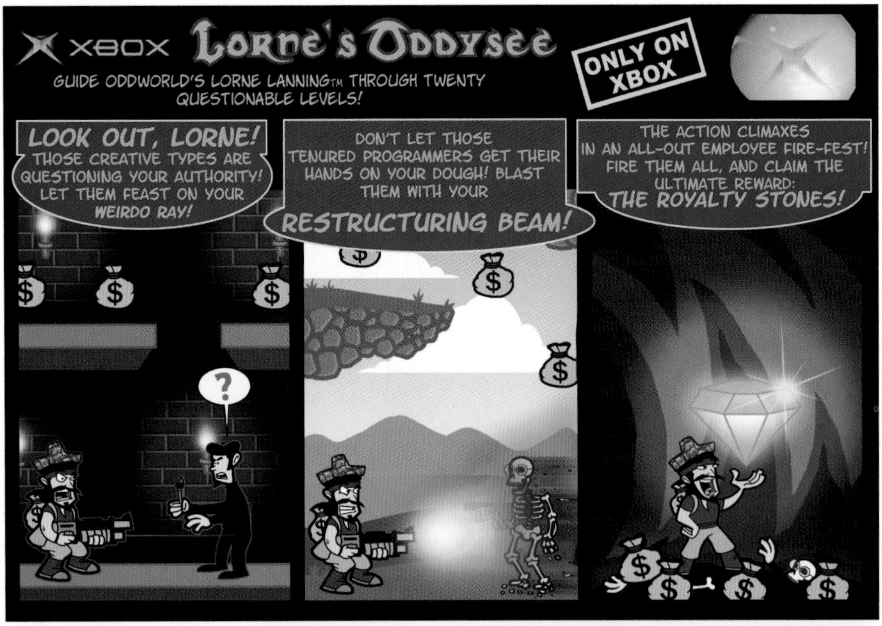
XBOX Lorne's Oddysee
GUIDE ODDWORLD'S LORNE LANNING™ THROUGH TWENTY QUESTIONABLE LEVELS!
ONLY ON XBOX
LOOK OUT, LORNE! THOSE CREATIVE TYPES ARE QUESTIONING YOUR AUTHORITY! LET THEM FEAST ON YOUR WEIRDO RAY!
?
DON'T LET THOSE TENURED PROGRAMMERS GET THEIR HANDS ON YOUR DOUGH! BLAST THEM WITH YOUR RESTRUCTURING BEAM!
THE ACTION CLIMAXES IN AN ALL-OUT EMPLOYEE FIRE-FEST! FIRE THEM ALL, AND CLAIM THE ULTIMATE REWARD: THE ROYALTY STONES!

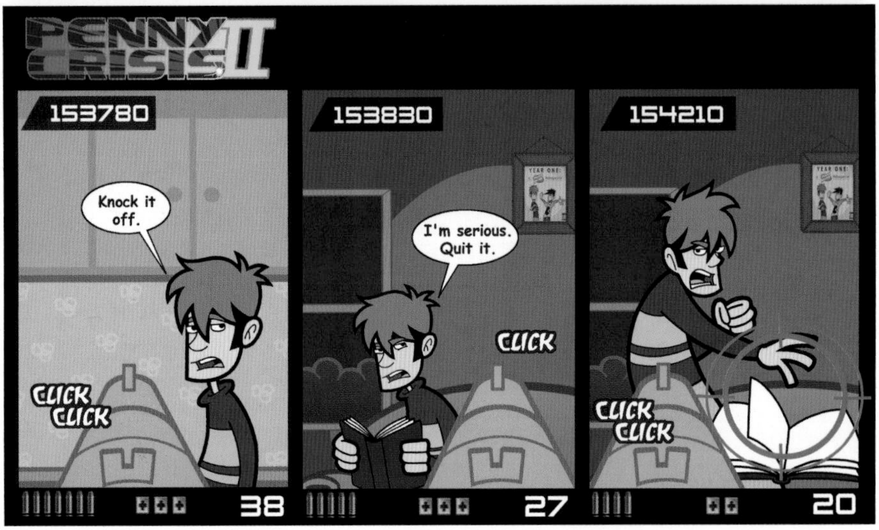
PENNY CRISIS II
153780
Knock it off.
CLICK CLICK
38
153830
I'm serious. Quit it.
CLICK
27
154210
CLICK CLICK
20

HIGHLY ANTICIPATED

October 8, 2001 I saw Lorne Lanning at E3 one year; he had cut his hair by this point and was looking lean and not a little hungry. He smiled at me, but it was the sort of smile where a person almost breaks their jaw with the force of it. I could see every one of his teeth, and far back in his throat were two pulsing glands that hung heavy with venom.

PENNY CRISIS II

October 10, 2001 Gabriel would sometimes press that gaudy, creamsicle-colored firearm to my temple and make wild demands. Typically, these demands would involve getting him some Life-Savers—Wild Cherry or Original, but not Butter Rum. *Never* Butter Rum. For some reason he never made entirely clear.

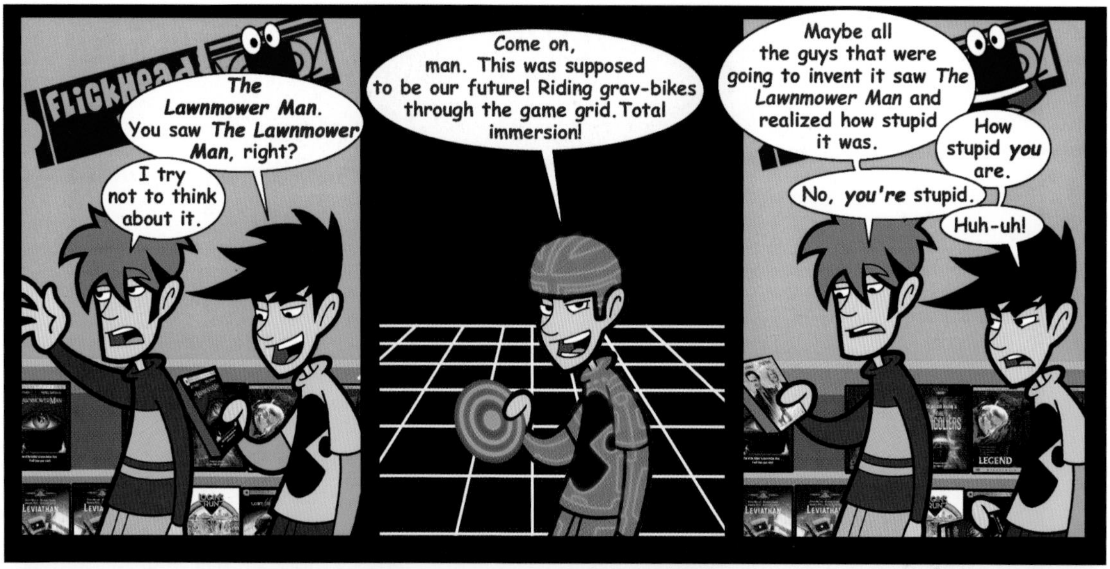

The Lawnmower Man. You saw The Lawnmower Man, right?
I try not to think about it.
FLICKHEAD
Come on, man. This was supposed to be our future! Riding grav-bikes through the game grid. Total immersion!
Maybe all the guys that were going to invent it saw The Lawnmower Man and realized how stupid it was.
How stupid you are.
No, you're stupid.
Huh-uh!

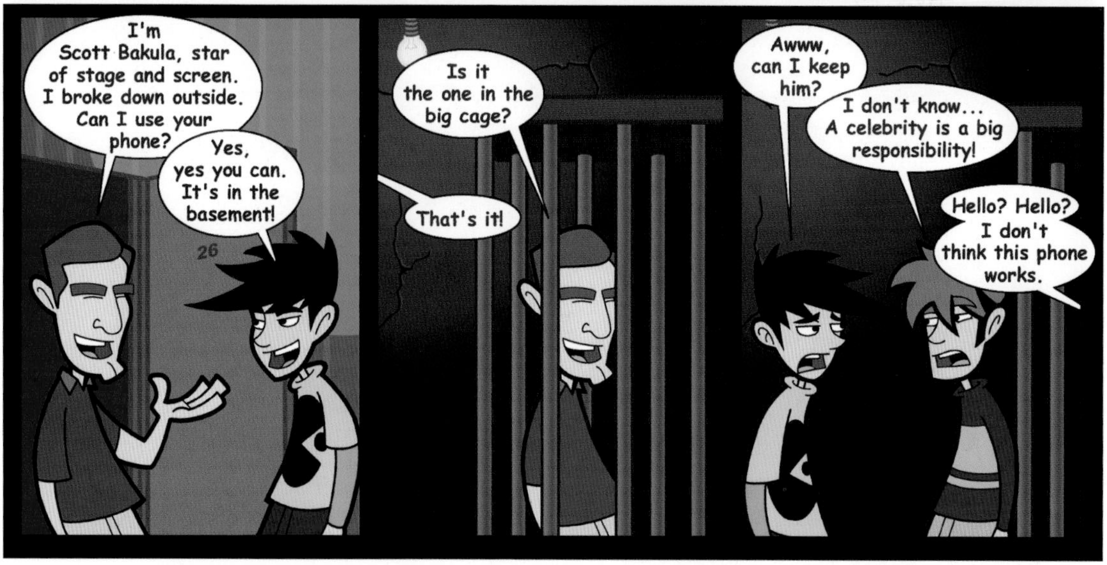

I'm Scott Bakula, star of stage and screen. I broke down outside. Can I use your phone?
Yes, yes you can. It's in the basement!
Is it the one in the big cage?
That's it!
Awww, can I keep him?
I don't know... A celebrity is a big responsibility!
Hello? Hello? I don't think this phone works.

THE FUTURE DERAILED

October 12, 2001 Every now and then, you see a new stab at VR or "enhanced reality" technology, but it just never arrived at the promised place. I know that I speak for many people when I say, with a loud voice: *Override my optic nerve*. Suspend me in nutritive gel, and grant me an ever-living body girded with chrome. Amen.

STAY AWHILE—STAY FOREVER!

October 15, 2001 Obviously, the title of the strip is from classic puzzle/platformer Impossible Mission. Just say yes, yes it is. Also, we may have been completely obsessed with Scott Bakula, who we might have referred to as "Count" Bakula, though he holds no *official* title over ancestral Bakula lands.

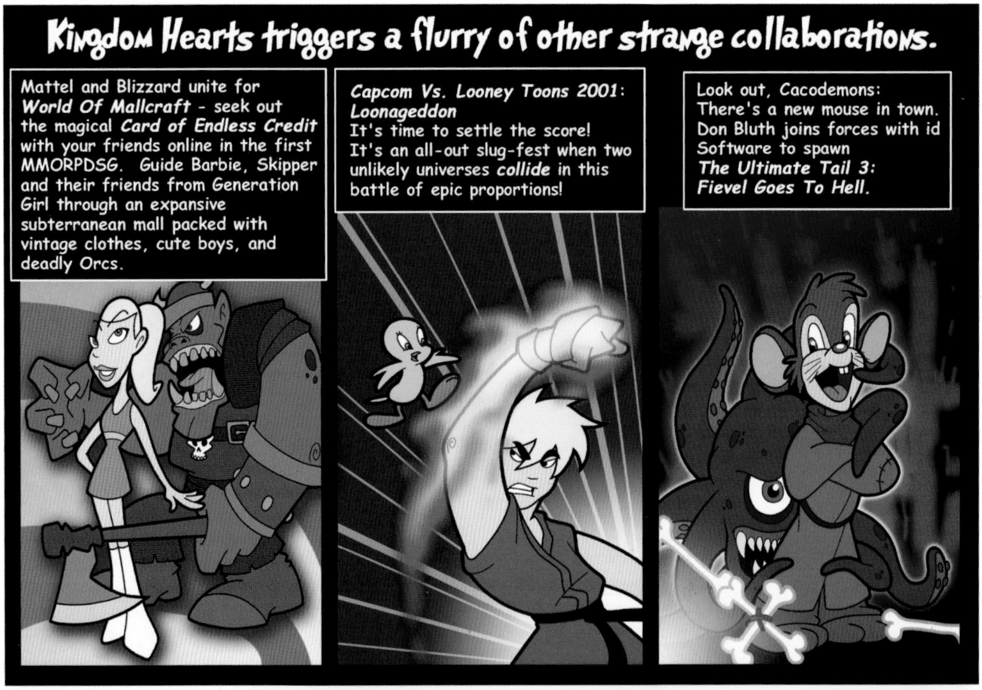
Kingdom Hearts triggers a flurry of other strange collaborations.
Mattel and Blizzard unite for *World Of Mallcraft* - seek out the magical *Card of Endless Credit* with your friends online in the first MMORPDSG. Guide Barbie, Skipper and their friends from Generation Girl through an expansive subterranean mall packed with vintage clothes, cute boys, and deadly Orcs.
Capcom Vs. Looney Toons 2001: Loonageddon It's time to settle the score! It's an all-out slug-fest when two unlikely universes *collide* in this battle of epic proportions!
Look out, Cacodemons: There's a new mouse in town. Don Bluth joins forces with id Software to spawn *The Ultimate Tail 3: Fievel Goes To Hell.*

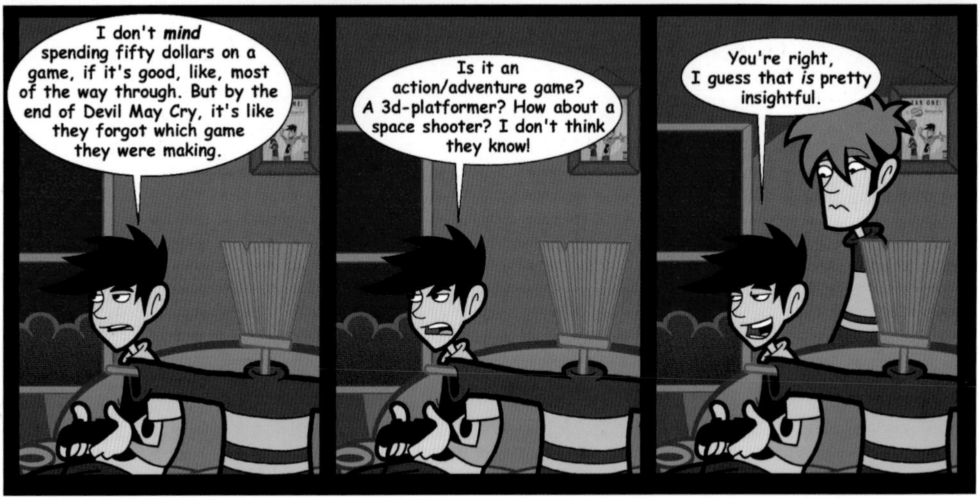
I don't *mind* spending fifty dollars on a game, if it's good, like, most of the way through. But by the end of Devil May Cry, it's like they forgot which game they were making.
Is it an action/adventure game? A 3d-platformer? How about a space shooter? I don't think they know!
You're right, I guess that *is* pretty insightful.

UNLIKELY MARRIAGES

October 17, 2001 Kingdom Hearts II has Tron in it, I don't know if you heard. This is the most important thing that has *ever happened*.

BUILDING A BETTER TYCHO

October 22, 2001 This shit really happens! Devil May Cry. You're jumping around, cutting guys, blam blam, and then all of a sudden you are flying a biplane in a cave trying not to hit stalactites. Why not just go all the way? Break through the atmosphere and fight demons on their home world of Cybertron for fuck's sake. Let Dante collect powerful Minicons while learning Hell's most devastating recipes.

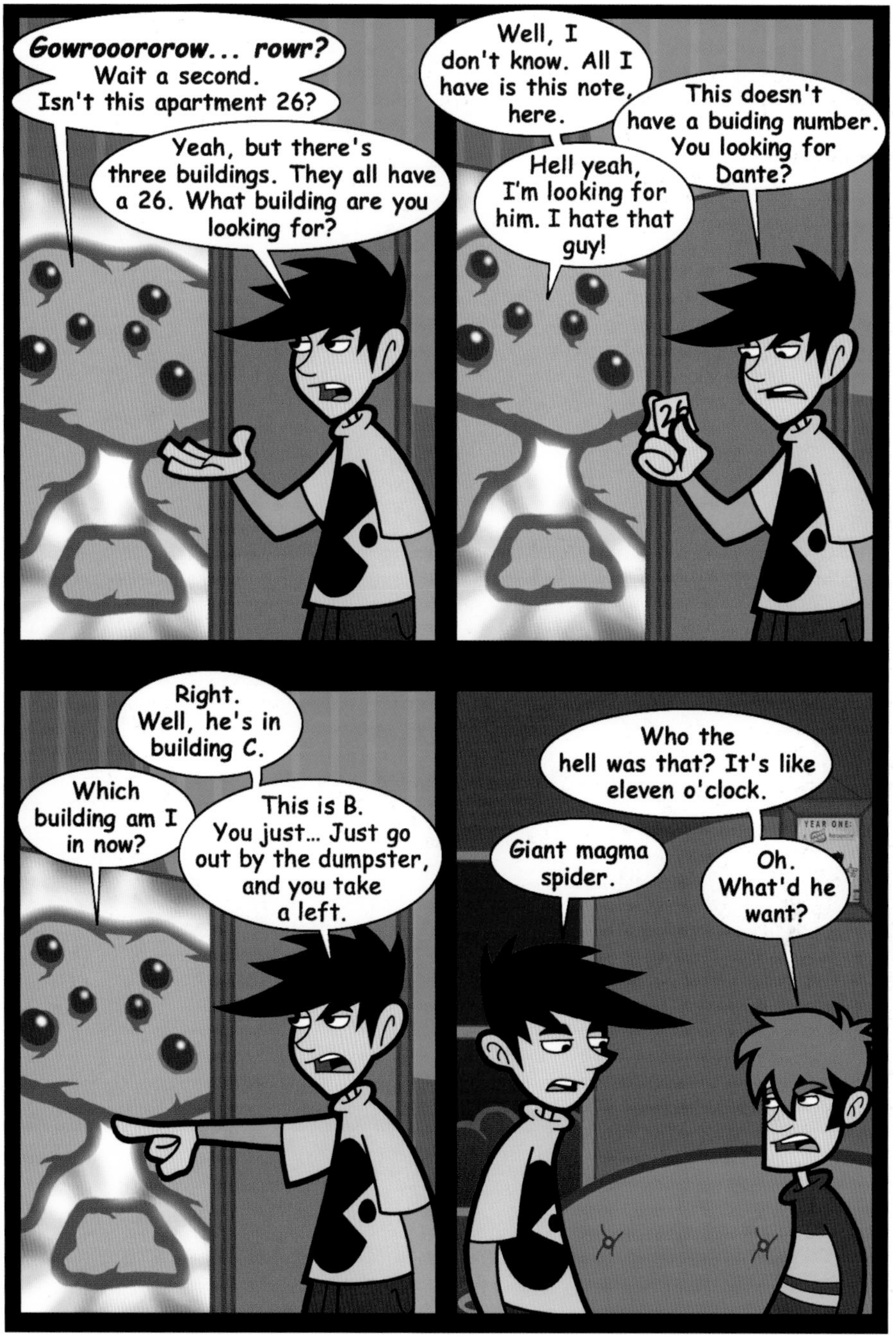
Gowroooororow... rowr? Wait a second. Isn't this apartment 26?
Yeah, but there's three buildings. They all have a 26. What building are you looking for?
Well, I don't know. All I have is this note, here.
This doesn't have a buiding number. You looking for Dante?
Hell yeah, I'm looking for him. I hate that guy!
Right. Well, he's in building C.
Which building am I in now?
This is B. You just... Just go out by the dumpster, and you take a left.
Who the hell was that? It's like eleven o'clock.
Giant magma spider.
Oh. What'd he want?

AN HONEST MISTAKE

October 19, 2001 The surreal nature of our apartment complex allows it to be pretty much anything we want. Sometimes we live on the second floor, sometimes the first. In this strip we apparently live in an apartment complex, but we've got a fenced backyard in some strips, desperately in need of watering! We need access to an experimental material that will maintain the comic world we have created. We need . . . *continutium.*

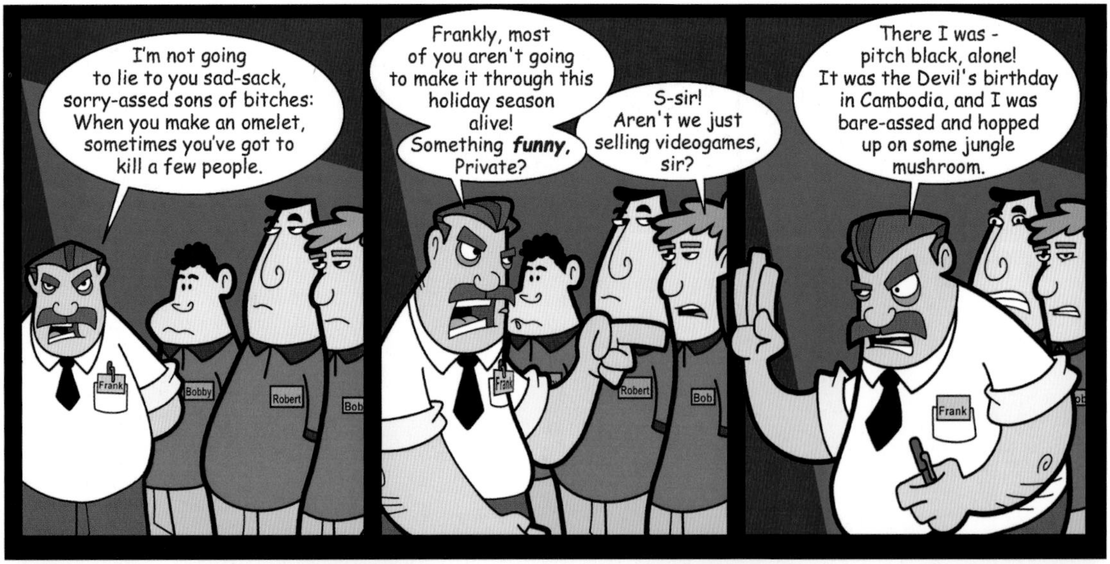
I'm not going to lie to you sad-sack, sorry-assed sons of bitches: When you make an omelet, sometimes you've got to kill a few people.
Frank
Bobby
Robert
Bob
Frankly, most of you aren't going to make it through this holiday season alive! Something **funny**, Private?
S-sir! Aren't we just selling videogames, sir?
There I was - pitch black, alone! It was the Devil's birthday in Cambodia, and I was bare-assed and hopped up on some jungle mushroom.

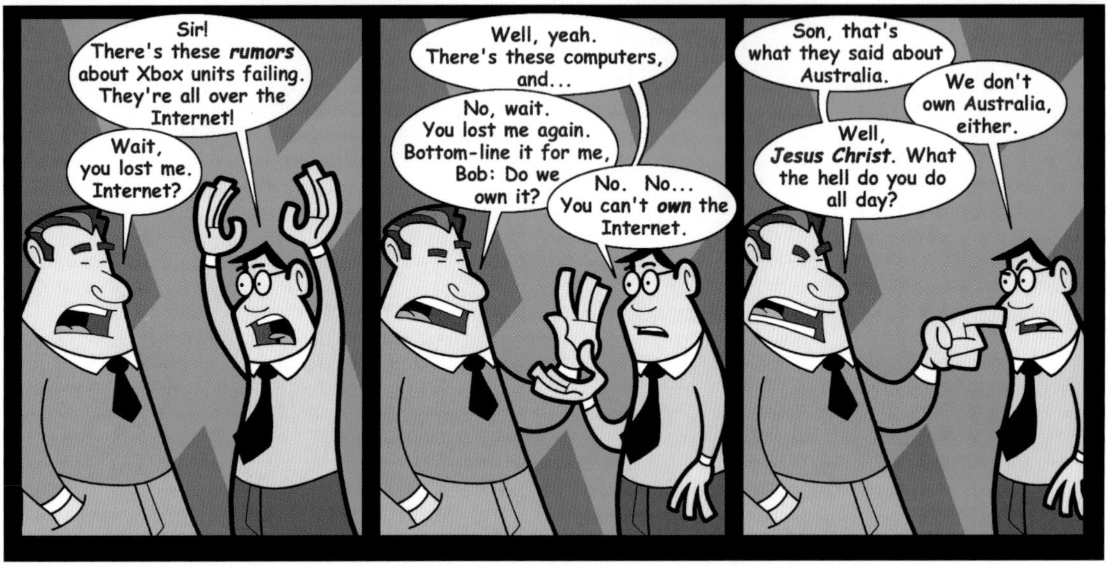
Sir! There's these **rumors** about Xbox units failing. They're all over the Internet!
Wait, you lost me. Internet?
Well, yeah. There's these computers, and...
No, wait. You lost me again. Bottom-line it for me, Bob: Do we own it?
No. No... You can't **own** the Internet.
Son, that's what they said about Australia.
We don't own Australia, either.
Well, **Jesus Christ**. What the hell do you do all day?

FRANK RETURNS

October 24, 2001 I LOVE FRANK. Okay, now it's out there. I don't know if it is okay to quote your own comic in polite conversation, but I will admit to sometimes cutting people off with Frank's last line: "It was the Devil's birthday in Cambodia," etc. It could be in line at the grocery store, or really any time life becomes mundane.

THE LAND DOWN UNDER

October 29, 2001 Everyone in the world being connected to the same global network can make a few isolated incidents seem like epidemics. Even so, there was a failure issue with one of the CD-ROM drives used, and late in the console's life cycle they released a truly gargantuan replacement power supply. Not as big as the one which would eventually be delivered with the 360, but still. You know? Very large.

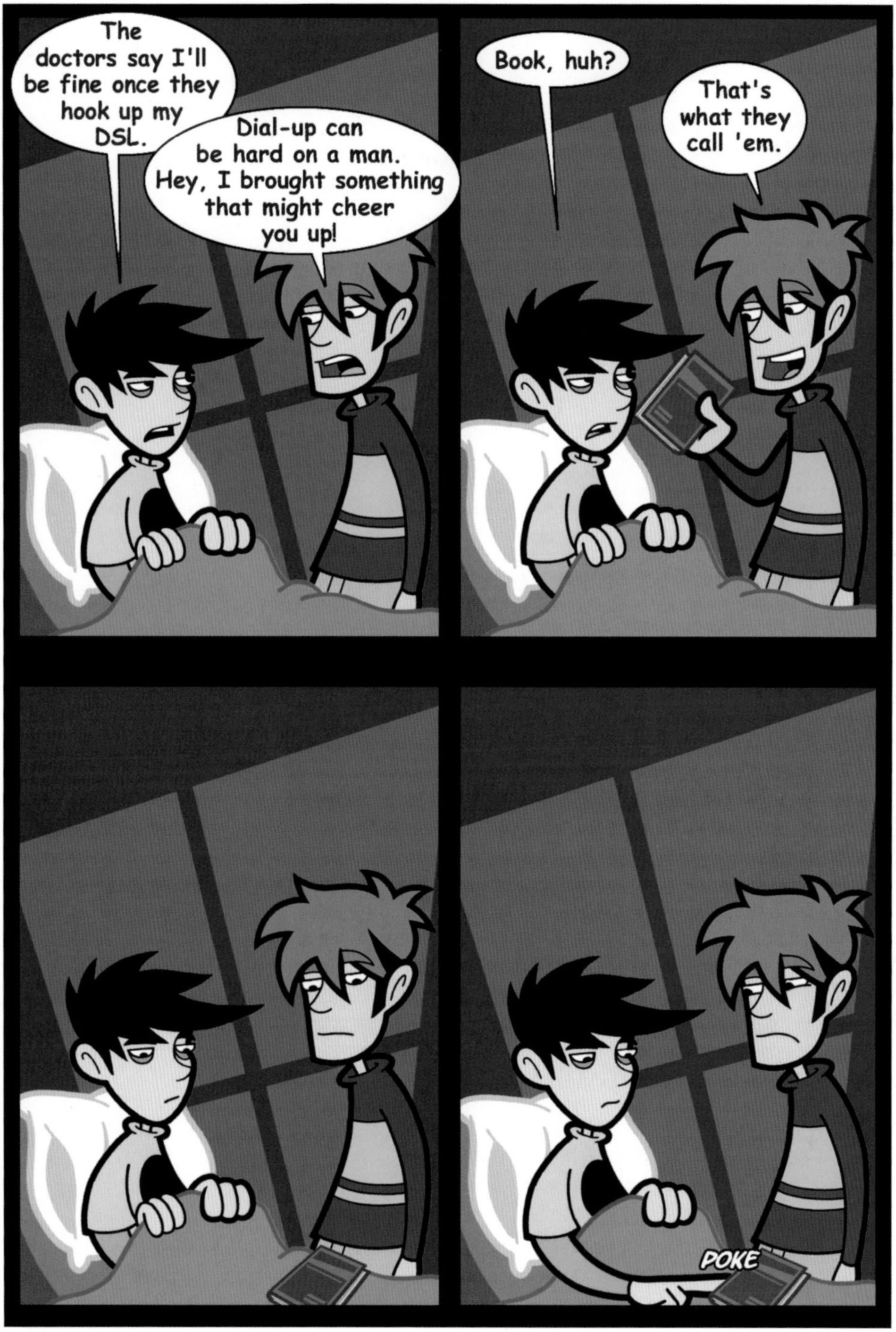
The doctors say I'll be fine once they hook up my DSL.
Dial-up can be hard on a man. Hey, I brought something that might cheer you up!
Book, huh?
That's what they call 'em.
POKE

IS IT BROKEN?

October 26, 2001 His position on books changed dramatically when he found out that some of them were set in the *Star Wars* universe. He's since branched out into *The Da Vinci Code* and, God love him, Neal Stephenson's *Snow Crash*. On that day, friends, he became a *man*.

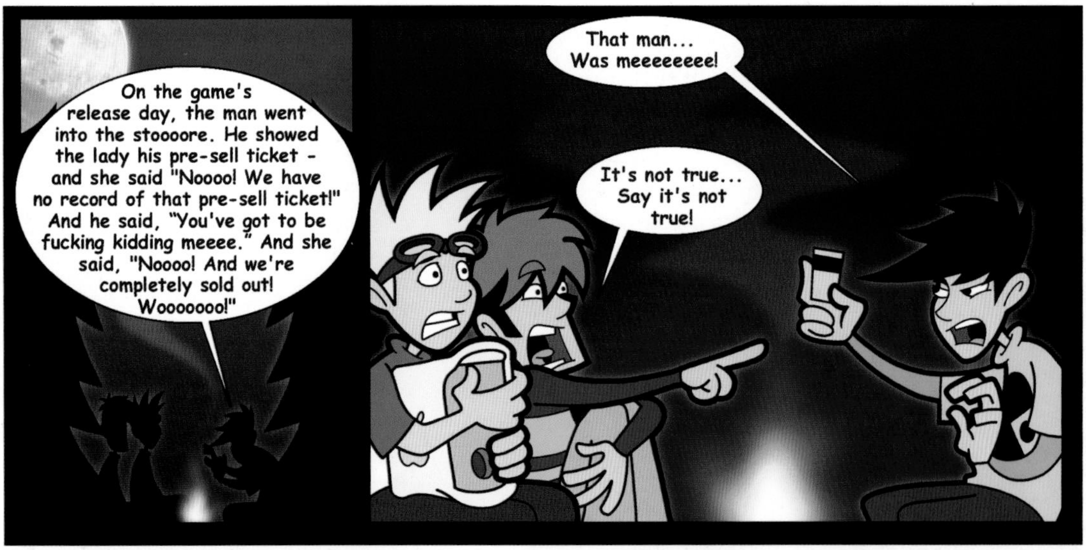
On the game's release day, the man went into the stoooore. He showed the lady his pre-sell ticket - and she said "Noooo! We have no record of that pre-sell ticket!" And he said, "You've got to be fucking kidding meeee." And she said, "Noooo! And we're completely sold out! Wooooooo!"
It's not true... Say it's not true!
That man... Was meeeeeeee!

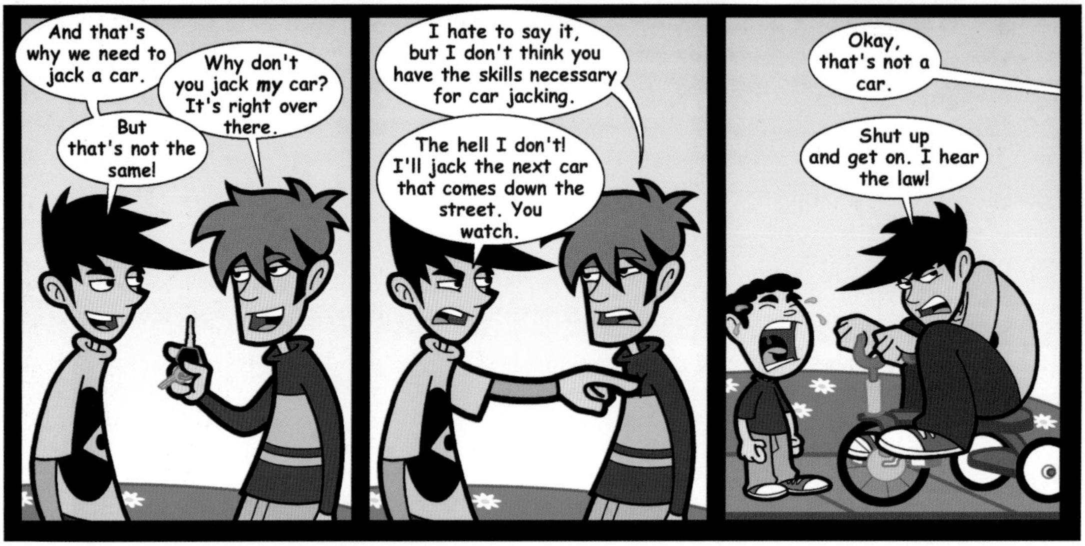
And that's why we need to jack a car.
Why don't you jack my car? It's right over there.
But that's not the same!
I hate to say it, but I don't think you have the skills necessary for car jacking.
The hell I don't! I'll jack the next car that comes down the street. You watch.
Okay, that's not a car.
Shut up and get on. I hear the law!

WELCOME TO CAMP TERROR

October 31, 2001 Things that are terrifying to gamers aren't particularly terrifying to the population at large, although there is some overlap: a massive scorpion, its stinger bulging with a sizzling green fluid, has been shown to completely horrify ninety-six point seven percent of respondents. The calm remainder of that survey were either "part scorpion" themselves (1.3%) or, and this was odd, "weren't afraid of things beginning with the letter S" (2.0%).

A FLY NEW RIDE

November 2, 2001 We never got particularly far in Grand Theft Auto games three and beyond, though we purchased and, to a certain extent, *enjoyed them*, albeit on our own terms. In every game, you eventually get to a mission where the awkward combat or meandering camera screw you out of victory. At that point, the sandbox portion completely takes over until we have heard all the radio stations. Around this time, the game is exchanged for credit.

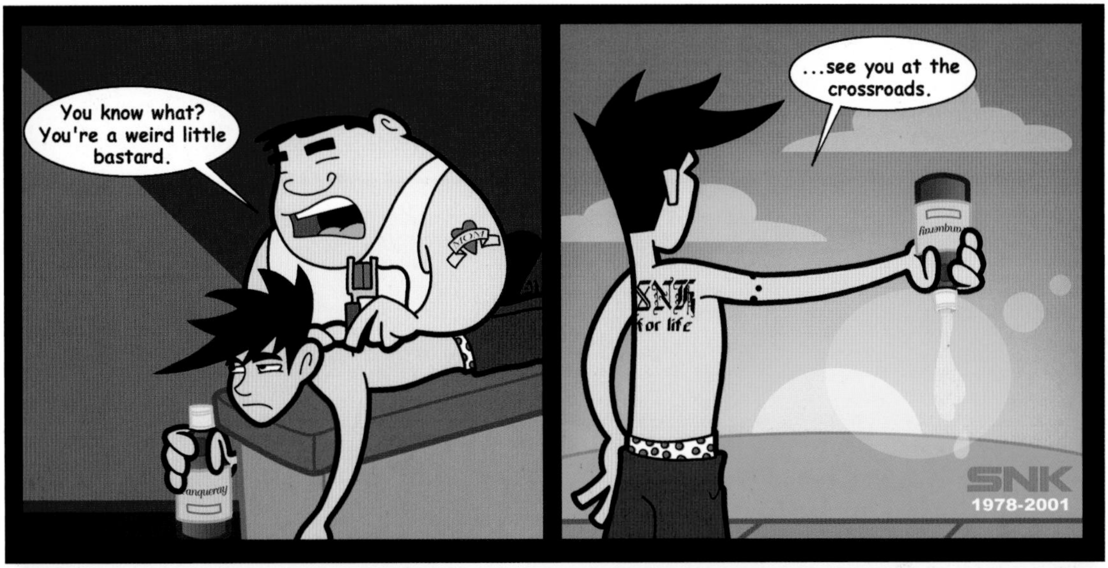
You know what? You're a weird little bastard.
...see you at the crossroads.
SNK for life
SNK 1978-2001

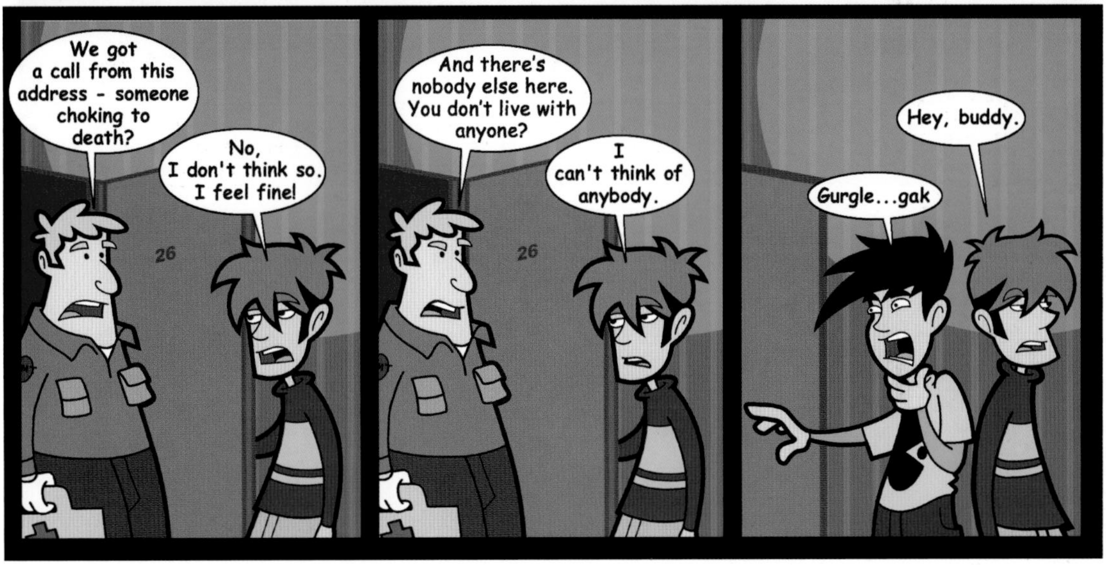
We got a call from this address - someone choking to death?
No, I don't think so. I feel fine!
And there's nobody else here. You don't live with anyone?
I can't think of anybody.
Hey, buddy.
Gurgle...gak

MUCH LOVE

November 5, 2001 He was utterly obsessed with SNK for a time, going so far as to join communities dedicated to the hardware, and to make a name for himself creating custom sleeves that painstakingly recreated the official products. The first games we ever played against each other were SNK fighters, and the rivalries inspired by Samurai Shodown have probably inspired the Tycho/Gabe enmity more than anything else.

I'M BLUE

November 7, 2001 Him choky! I guess. *Whatever.*

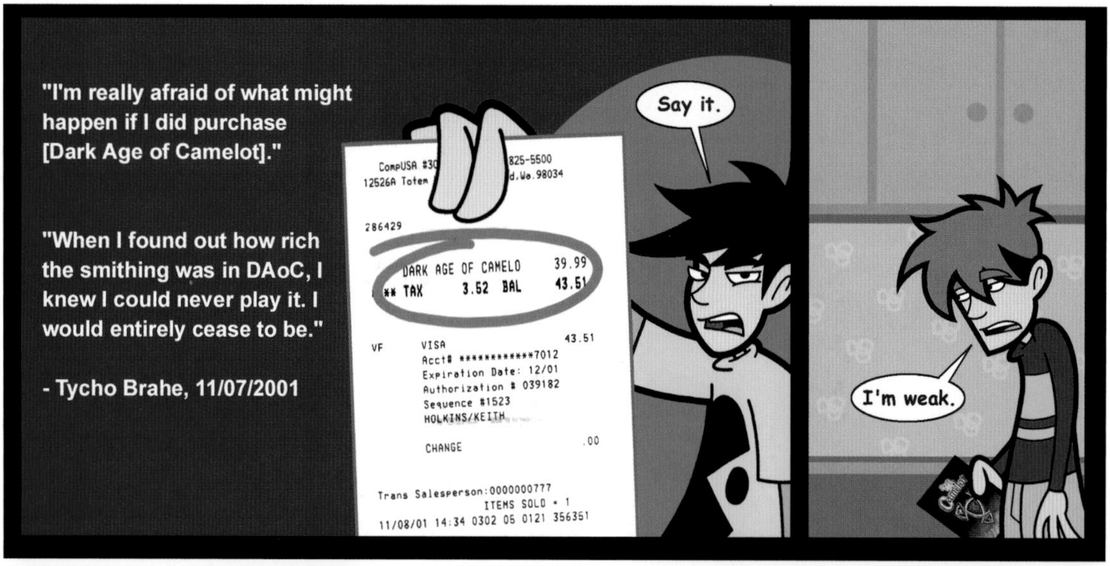

"I'm really afraid of what might happen if I did purchase [Dark Age of Camelot]."
"When I found out how rich the smithing was in DAoC, I knew I could never play it. I would entirely cease to be."
- Tycho Brahe, 11/07/2001
CompUSA #3
825-5500
12526A Totem
d.Wa.98034
286429
DARK AGE OF CAMELO 39.99
** TAX 3.52 BAL 43.51
VF VISA 43.51
Acct# ************7012
Expiration Date: 12/01
Authorization # 039182
Sequence #1523
HOLKINS/KEITH
CHANGE .00
Trans Salesperson:0000000777
ITEMS SOLD = 1
11/08/01 14:34 0302 05 0121 356351
Say it.
I'm weak.

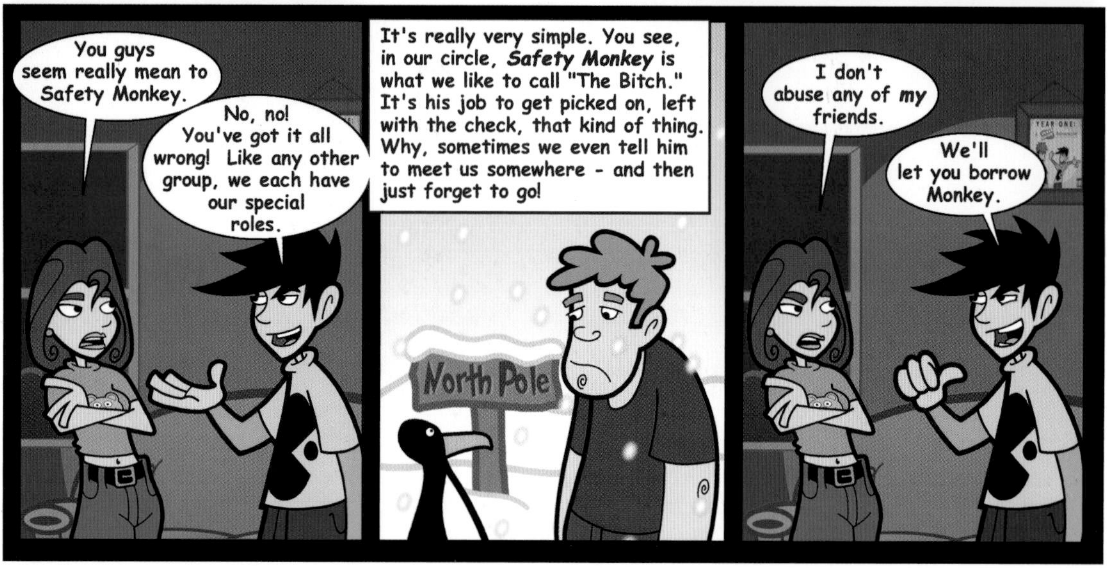

You guys seem really mean to Safety Monkey.
No, no! You've got it all wrong! Like any other group, we each have our special roles.
It's really very simple. You see, in our circle, *Safety Monkey* is what we like to call "The Bitch." It's his job to get picked on, left with the check, that kind of thing. Why, sometimes we even tell him to meet us somewhere - and then just forget to go!
North Pole
I don't abuse any of *my* friends.
We'll let you borrow Monkey.

IT'S ALL TRUE

November 9, 2001 The original version of this comic showed a great deal more of my credit card number than is probably safe. Readers wrote in with words of warning almost immediately, which is a far better outcome than I have any right to expect. I canceled my card shortly thereafter, and moved to a new city. I also changed my name—albeit temporarily—to Gors ban Darliarus. No reason, really; I just liked the sound.

DON'T TELL ME YOU DON'T HAVE ONE

November 12, 2001 He and I were at Dick's, a late-night hamburger joint, at one or two in the morning when he told me that this strip made him not only *our* bitch, but the bitch of the entire gaming world. A young man in an adjacent line came over to us, and, I *swear to God*, said, "Safety Monkey?"

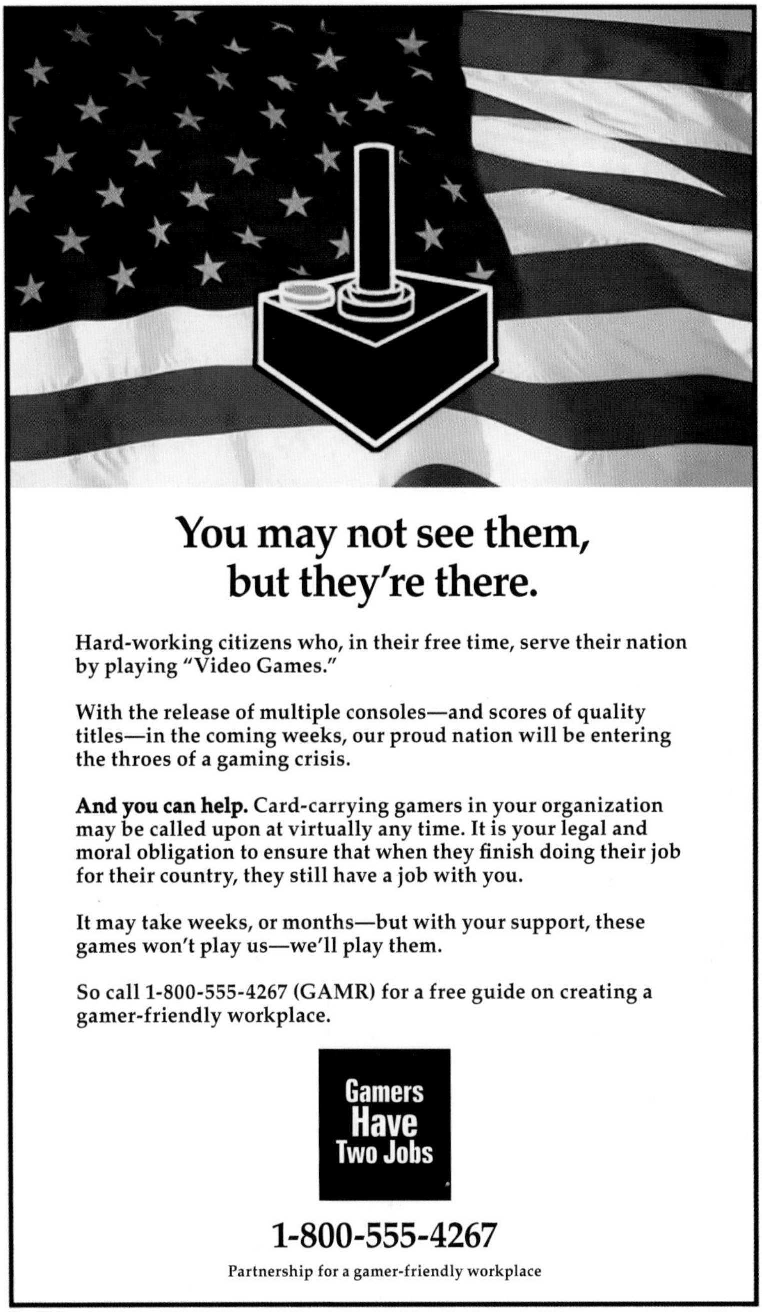

You may not see them, but they're there.

Hard-working citizens who, in their free time, serve their nation by playing "Video Games."

With the release of multiple consoles—and scores of quality titles—in the coming weeks, our proud nation will be entering the throes of a gaming crisis.

And you can help. Card-carrying gamers in your organization may be called upon at virtually any time. It is your legal and moral obligation to ensure that when they finish doing their job for their country, they still have a job with you.

It may take weeks, or months—but with your support, these games won't play us—we'll play them.

So call 1-800-555-4267 (GAMR) for a free guide on creating a gamer-friendly workplace.

Gamers
Have
Two Jobs

1-800-555-4267

Partnership for a gamer-friendly workplace

CLICK HIGH-QUALITY FOR YOUR CARD!

November 14, 2001 With an almost satanic conflux of retail gaming product on offer, we mounted a propaganda campaign that we hoped would buy gamers some extra play during that rich harvest. Our approach was two pronged. Prong number one consisted of this poster, which we offered at crisp, convincing resolutions. Prong number two, and have I *mentioned* how much I love the word *prong*, was a "gamer card" that came in console and PC versions. This card is actually considered an official document in Bulimia. Bulimia might not actually be a country.

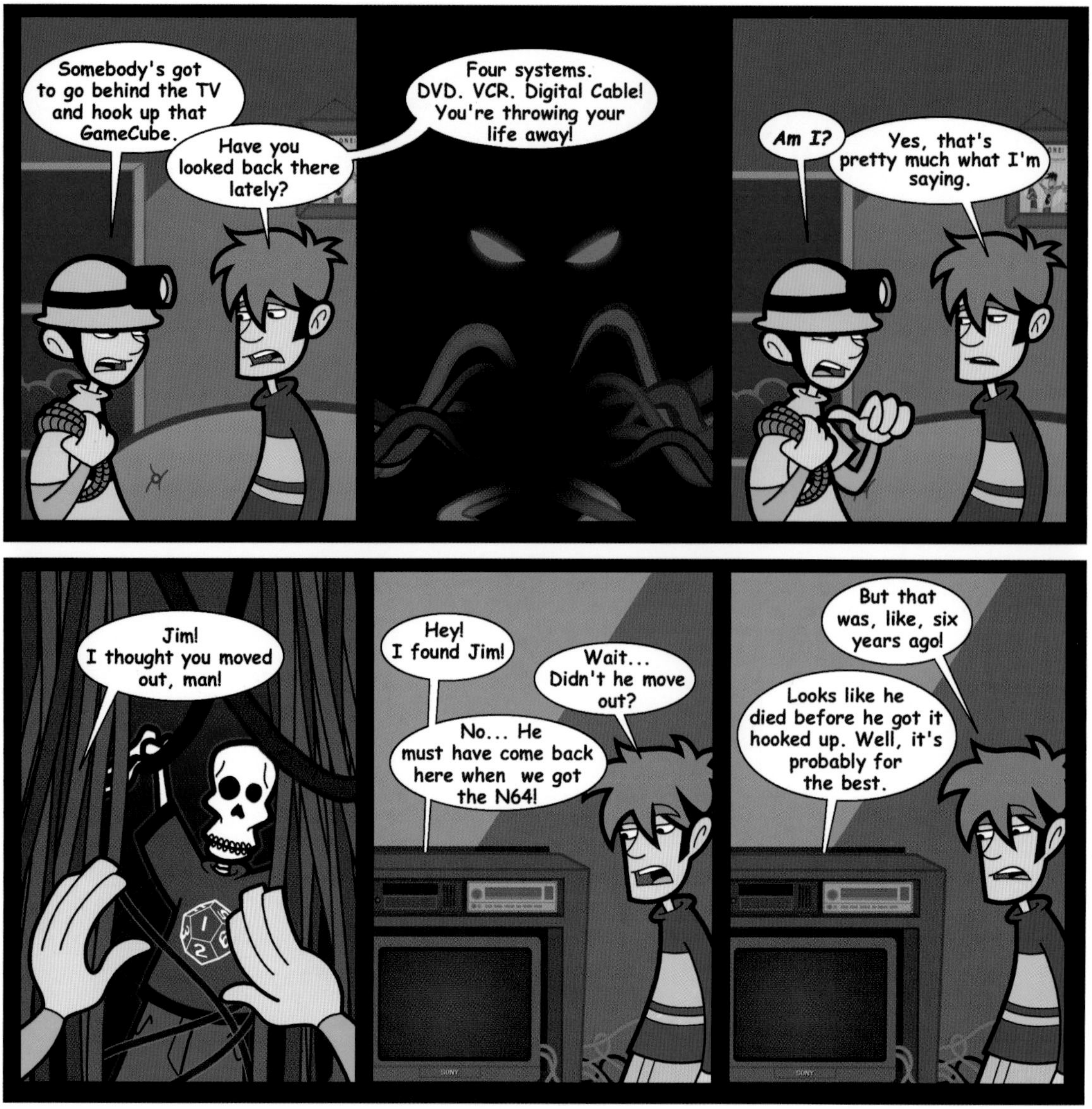
Somebody's got to go behind the TV and hook up that GameCube.
Have you looked back there lately?
Four systems. DVD. VCR. Digital Cable! You're throwing your life away!
Am I?
Yes, that's pretty much what I'm saying.
Jim! I thought you moved out, man!
Hey! I found Jim!
Wait... Didn't he move out?
No... He must have come back here when we got the N64!
But that was, like, six years ago!
Looks like he died before he got it hooked up. Well, it's probably for the best.

THE JIM SAGA, PART ONE

November 19, 2001 Tangled cables are a fairly universal fixture in the gamer household, but as soon as this first strip was written I asked Gabe if he would let me spool out these meager beginnings to the power of x. He said that he was pretty sure that didn't mean anything. He wasn't *entirely* wrong. But I had real plans for this storyline, plans that would shake *Penny Arcade* to its very foundation.

THE JIM SAGA, PART TWO

November 21, 2001 I didn't really execute any of those plans.

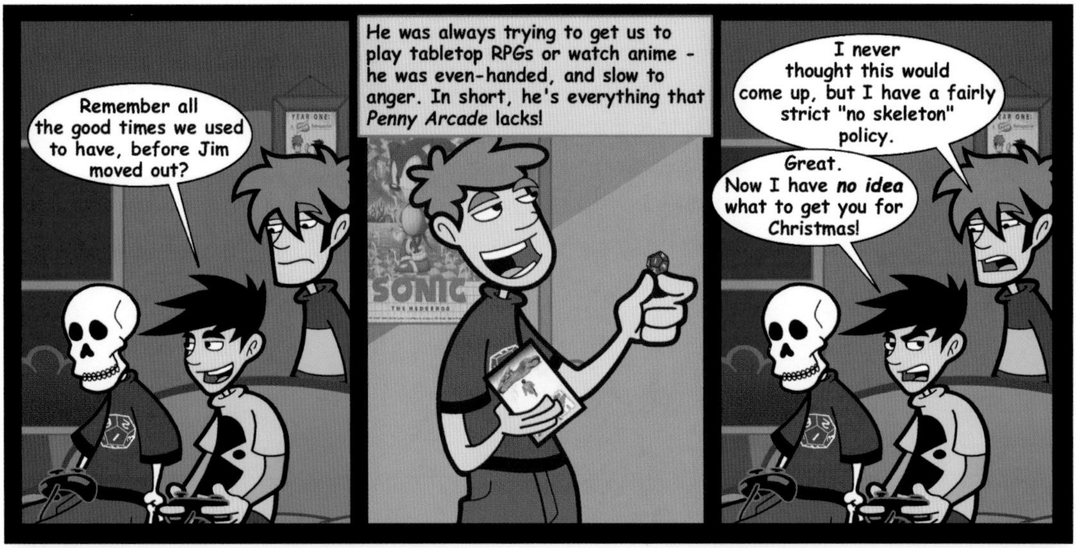
Remember all the good times we used to have, before Jim moved out?
He was always trying to get us to play tabletop RPGs or watch anime - he was even-handed, and slow to anger. In short, he's everything that *Penny Arcade* lacks!
I never thought this would come up, but I have a fairly strict "no skeleton" policy.
Great. Now I have ***no idea*** what to get you for Christmas!

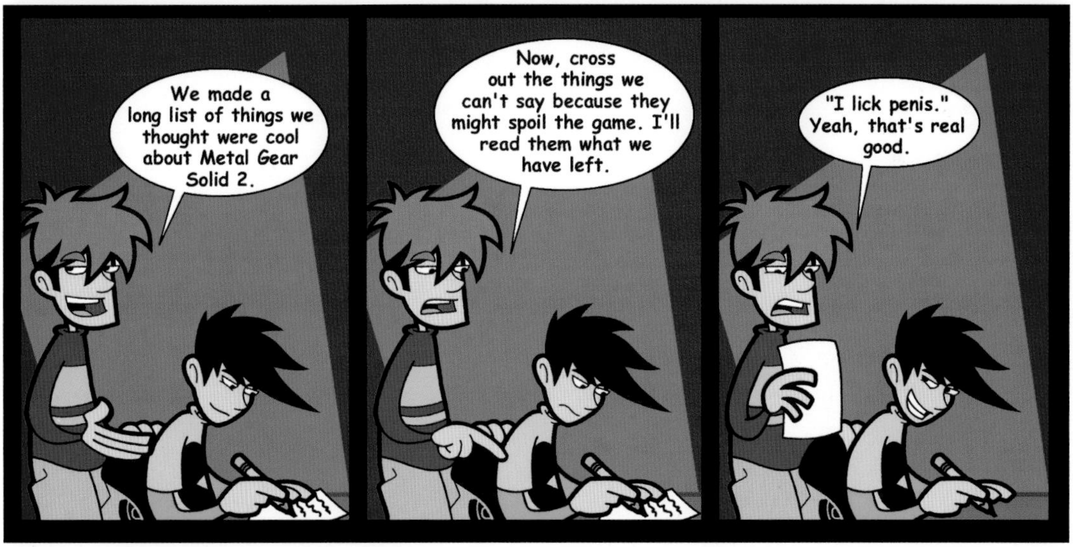
We made a long list of things we thought were cool about Metal Gear Solid 2.
Now, cross out the things we can't say because they might spoil the game. I'll read them what we have left.
"I lick penis." Yeah, that's real good.

THE JIM SAGA, PART THREE

November 23, 2001 Okay, all right. I was lying to you. There was never any bold schematic behind "The Jim Saga." I'm not even sure if nine sequential images even constitute an authentic Saga. At ten panels, we barely rank anecdotal status. It might be converted into a "yarn" without much trouble, with the addition of a neighbor and a missing *pie*.

SPOILEZ-VOUS

November 16, 2001 No matter what we would eventually think of it, when a company like Konami and a designer like Kojima get together and spend several years and millions of dollars on a single game, there's going to be *something* there worth writing about—but when we set pen to paper, we realized that in a game where gameplay actually is narrative most of the time, you can't even discuss it without lapsing into the dreaded *spoilitos*, or *spoilers*. Spoilitos is *too* a word. I'm sure of it. Like, eighty percent sure.

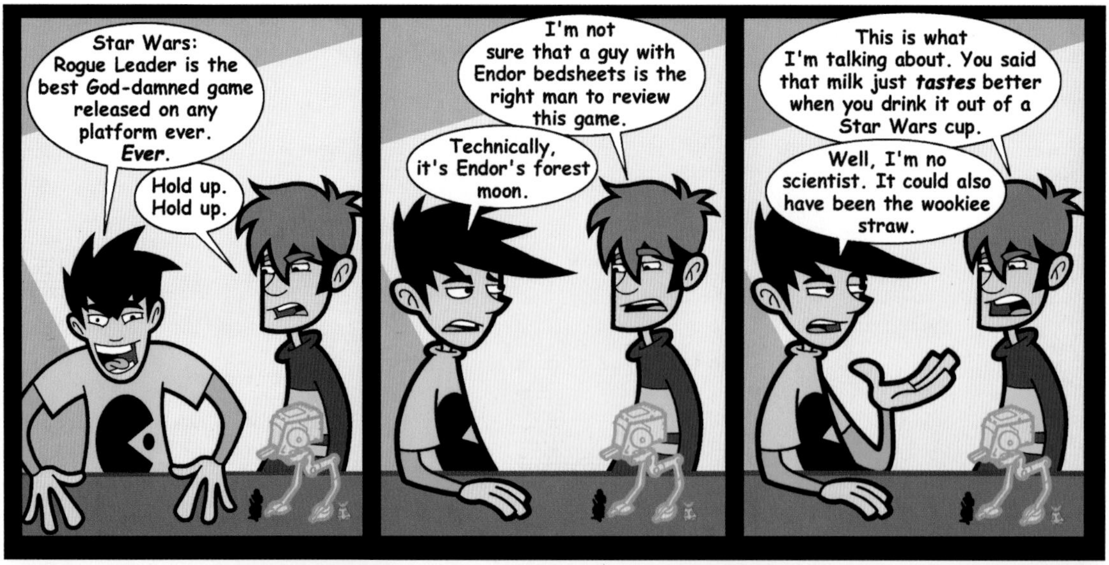
Star Wars: Rogue Leader is the best God-damned game released on any platform ever. *Ever.*
Hold up. Hold up.
I'm not sure that a guy with Endor bedsheets is the right man to review this game.
Technically, it's Endor's forest moon.
This is what I'm talking about. You said that milk just *tastes* better when you drink it out of a Star Wars cup.
Well, I'm no scientist. It could also have been the wookiee straw.

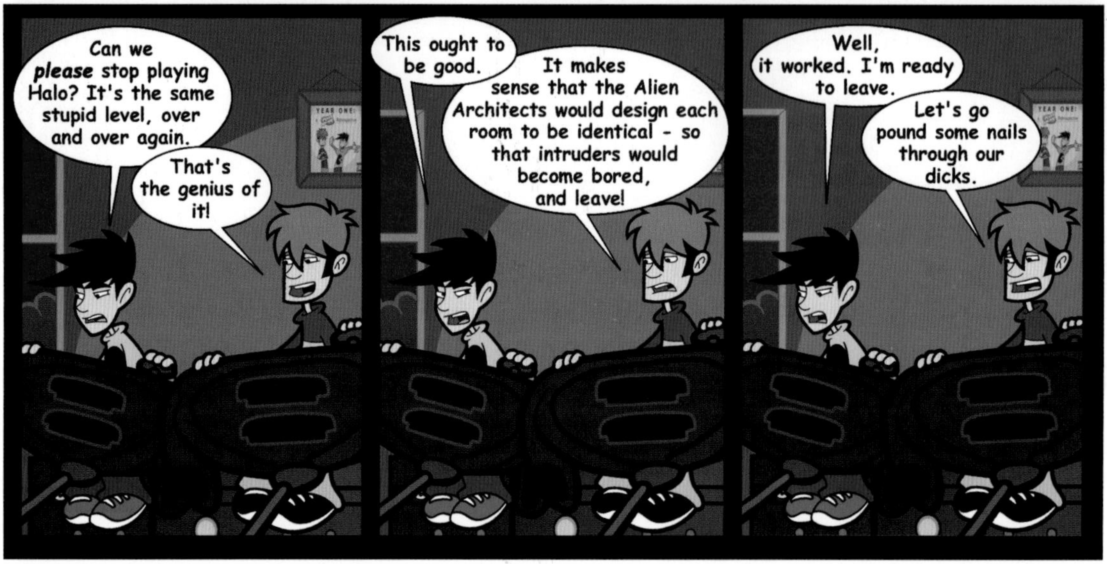
Can we *please* stop playing Halo? It's the same stupid level, over and over again.
That's the genius of it!
This ought to be good.
It makes sense that the Alien Architects would design each room to be identical - so that intruders would become bored, and leave!
Well, it worked. I'm ready to leave.
Let's go pound some nails through our dicks.

CONSIDER THE SOURCE

November 26, 2001 His love for *Star Wars* remains unchecked! Explain to me how this can be so. Explain to me how a vicious, demonstrably shrewd consumer could remain *affixed* to that teat! Also, imagine pulling a beverage, hot or cold, through a straw choked with Wookiee hair. It is a sensation that, even through the lens of *imagination*, will haunt me until the last.

THE REST OF THE STORY

November 28, 2001 We've met the people at Bungie on multiple occasions since producing this comic, and I still feel really bad about it. I don't think that the premise of the strip is incorrect, and I stand by the power of the hideous mental image produced by the last panel. I'm just saying that this .jpeg has created for me several awkward situations. If I had it to do again, the last panel might read, "I love *Halo*."

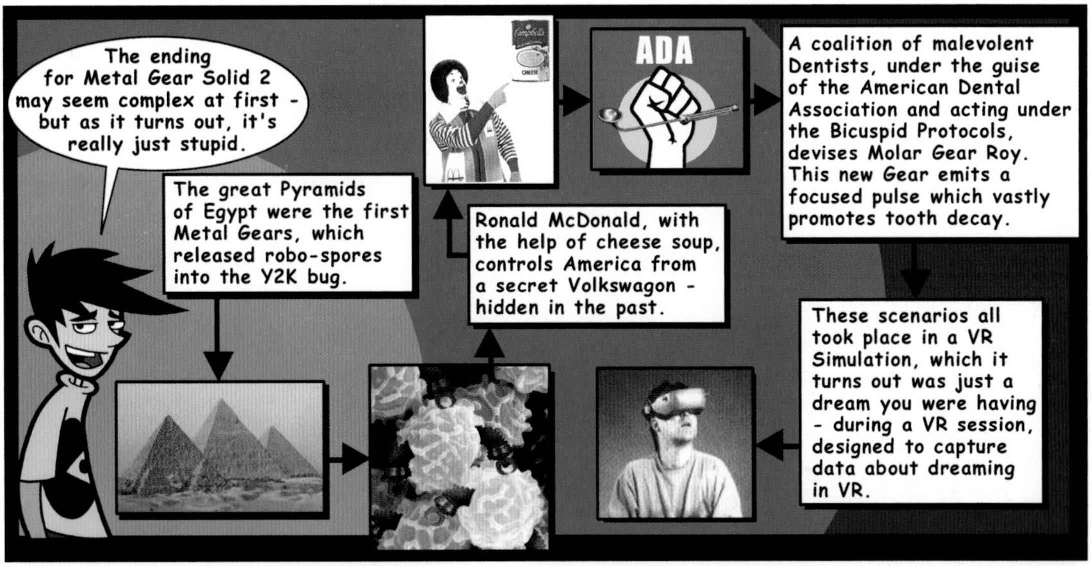
The ending for Metal Gear Solid 2 may seem complex at first - but as it turns out, it's really just stupid.
The great Pyramids of Egypt were the first Metal Gears, which released robo-spores into the Y2K bug.
Ronald McDonald, with the help of cheese soup, controls America from a secret Volkswagon - hidden in the past.
ADA
A coalition of malevolent Dentists, under the guise of the American Dental Association and acting under the Bicuspid Protocols, devises Molar Gear Roy. This new Gear emits a focused pulse which vastly promotes tooth decay.
These scenarios all took place in a VR Simulation, which it turns out was just a dream you were having - during a VR session, designed to capture data about dreaming in VR.

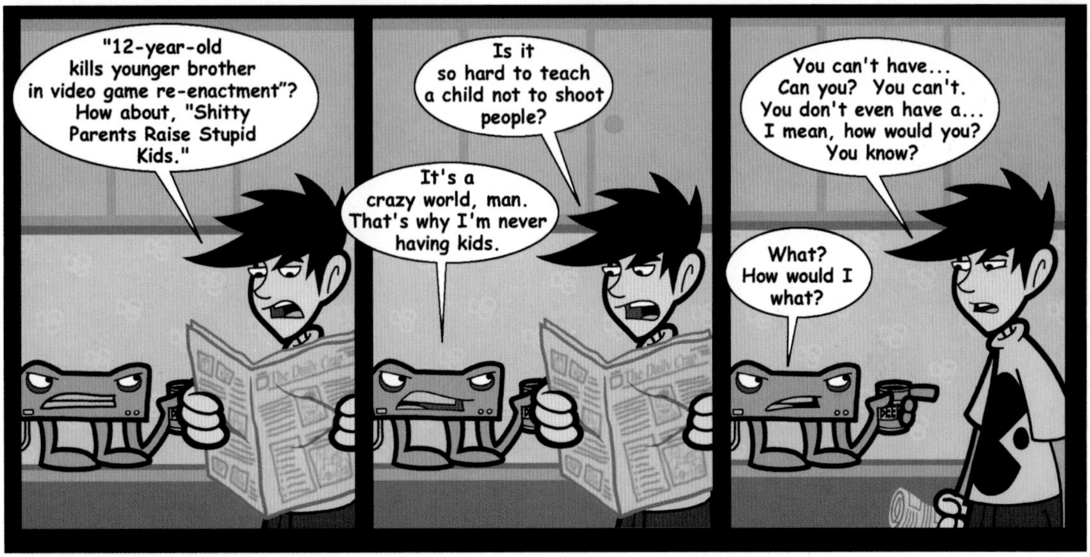
"12-year-old kills younger brother in video game re-enactment"? How about, "Shitty Parents Raise Stupid Kids."
Is it so hard to teach a child not to shoot people?
It's a crazy world, man. That's why I'm never having kids.
You can't have... Can you? You can't. You don't even have a... I mean, how would you? You know?
What? How would I what?

METAL GEAR STUPID

November 30, 2001 I'm not unsympathetic to the ideas presented in Metal Gear Solid 2, but I don't know that the way they are presented makes for a very good game. I've heard people say that wresting control from the player in the form of hour-long, non-interactive videos is a critical *part* of the message the game is trying to convey. I'm not sure I'm smart enough to debate that. I do know that I played MGS3 for about five minutes and then stopped. In that instance, does *Hideo Kojima* win?

IDIOTS REDUX

December 3, 2001 I don't know if I could explain it any better than I did in the last book. Do you own it, by any chance? The only reason I ask is because *Attack of the Bacon Robots*, published by Dark Horse, is a *truly spectacular human triumph*.

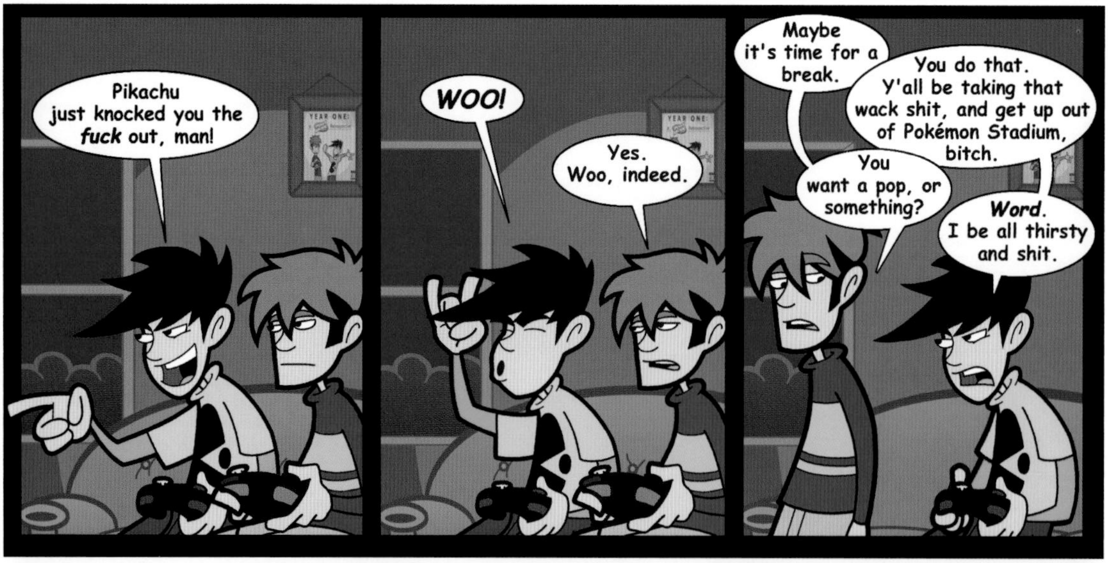
Pikachu just knocked you the *fuck* out, man!
WOO!
Yes. Woo, indeed.
Maybe it's time for a break.
You want a pop, or something?
You do that. Y'all be taking that wack shit, and get up out of Pokémon Stadium, bitch.
Word. I be all thirsty and shit.

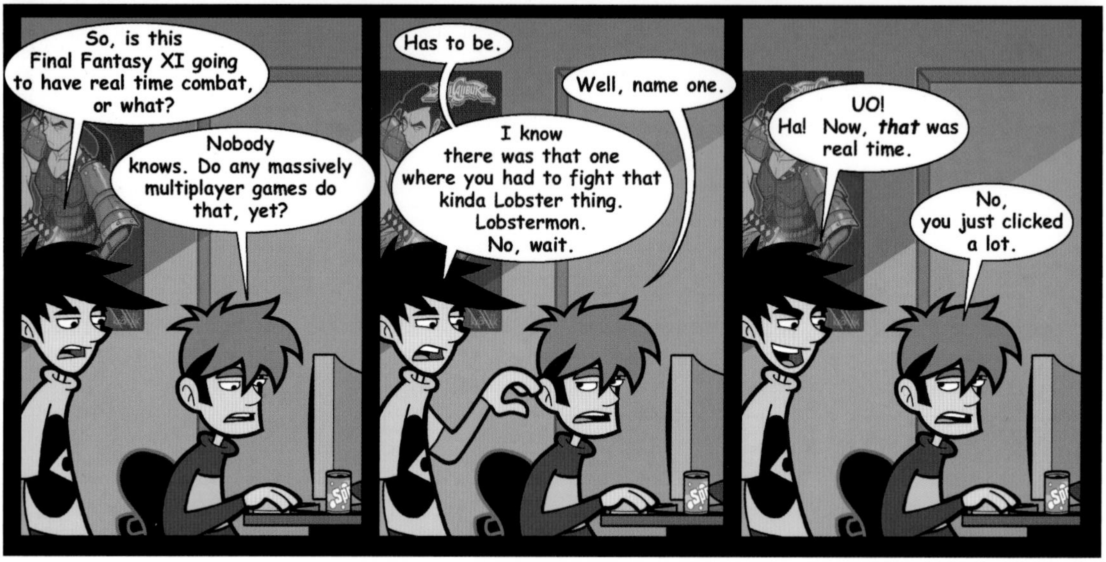
So, is this Final Fantasy XI going to have real time combat, or what?
Nobody knows. Do any massively multiplayer games do that, yet?
Has to be.
Well, name one.
I know there was that one where you had to fight that kinda Lobster thing. Lobstermon. No, wait.
UO! Ha! Now, *that* was real time.
No, you just clicked a lot.

WE LIKE SUPER SMASH BROTHERS

December 5, 2001 It is inexpressibly shameful to be defeated by Pikachu, particularly if you are playing as Metroid's hard-bitten bounty hunter Samus Aran. Ultimately, "Pikacheap" was completely off limits. Talking to people at conventions it sounds as though the hated *lightning mouse* was exiled from more than one gaming group.

CRUSTACEAN BATTLE!

December 7, 2001 Gabriel played UO like it was Diablo, clicking with such unbridled vigor that he ultimately wore a groove in the "wood." It was that Ikea wood though, basically just a big ol' heap of pine dust and spit. Probably isn't much of an achievement.

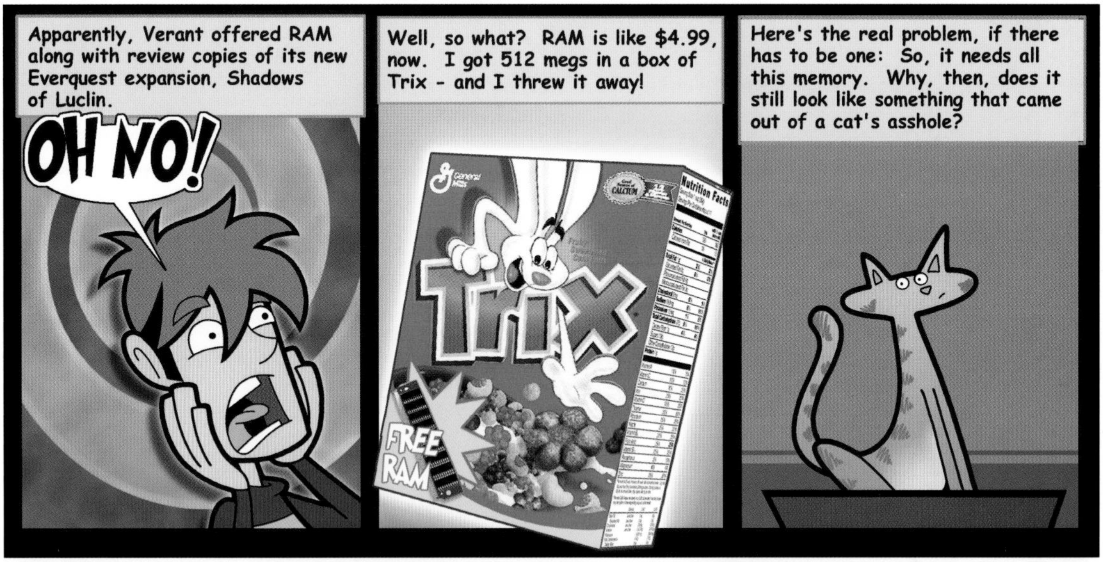
Apparently, Verant offered RAM along with review copies of its new Everquest expansion, Shadows of Luclin.
OH NO!
Well, so what? RAM is like $4.99, now. I got 512 megs in a box of Trix - and I threw it away!
Trix
FREE RAM
Here's the real problem, if there has to be one: So, it needs all this memory. Why, then, does it still look like something that came out of a cat's asshole?

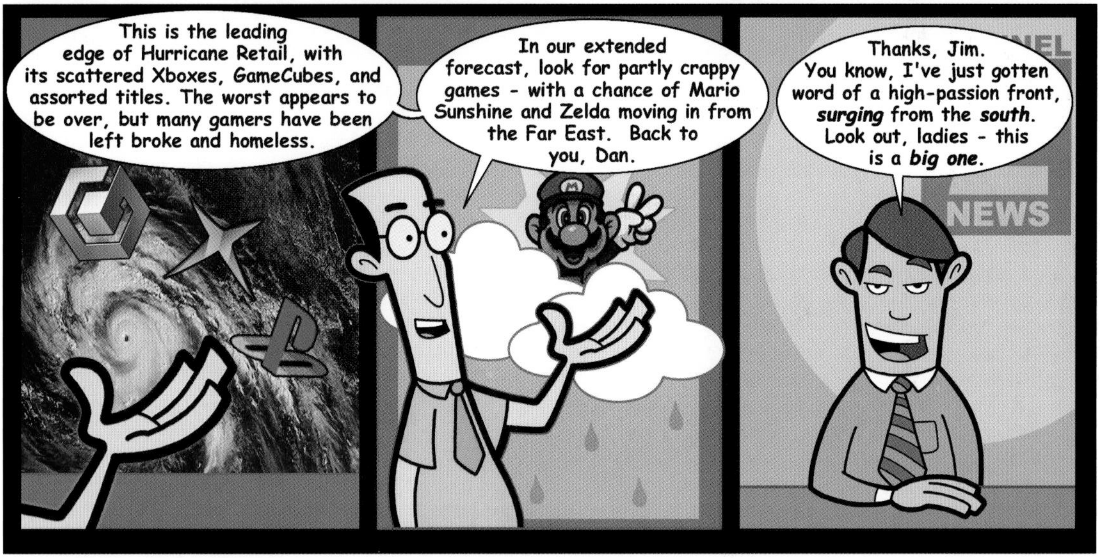
This is the leading edge of Hurricane Retail, with its scattered Xboxes, GameCubes, and assorted titles. The worst appears to be over, but many gamers have been left broke and homeless.
In our extended forecast, look for partly crappy games - with a chance of Mario Sunshine and Zelda moving in from the Far East. Back to you, Dan.
Thanks, Jim. You know, I've just gotten word of a high-passion front, *surging* from the *south*. Look out, ladies - this is a *big one*.
NEWS

WHATEVERQUEST

December 10, 2001 For years, this was my favorite image of Tycho. As for the strip content, I hold to what I said at the time: most professional reviewers are so jaded that some RAM probably ain't gonna do it. Since this strip, though, I've seen journalists flown to tropical islands to talk about Sid Meier's *Pirates*. If at any point you want to fly me to a grass hut on a sun-drenched island chain, well, my e-mail is on the site. For the record, your game is *magnificent*.

PATCHY MORNING FOG

December 12, 2001 We've had devastating holiday seasons since, to be sure, but *two* simultaneous console launches at once put many gamers on the streets. Also, it wasn't until I went back through the archive for this book that I realized that Gabe had drawn the perverse newsman Randy Pinkwood with one hand below the desk. This is almost incomprehensibly vile.

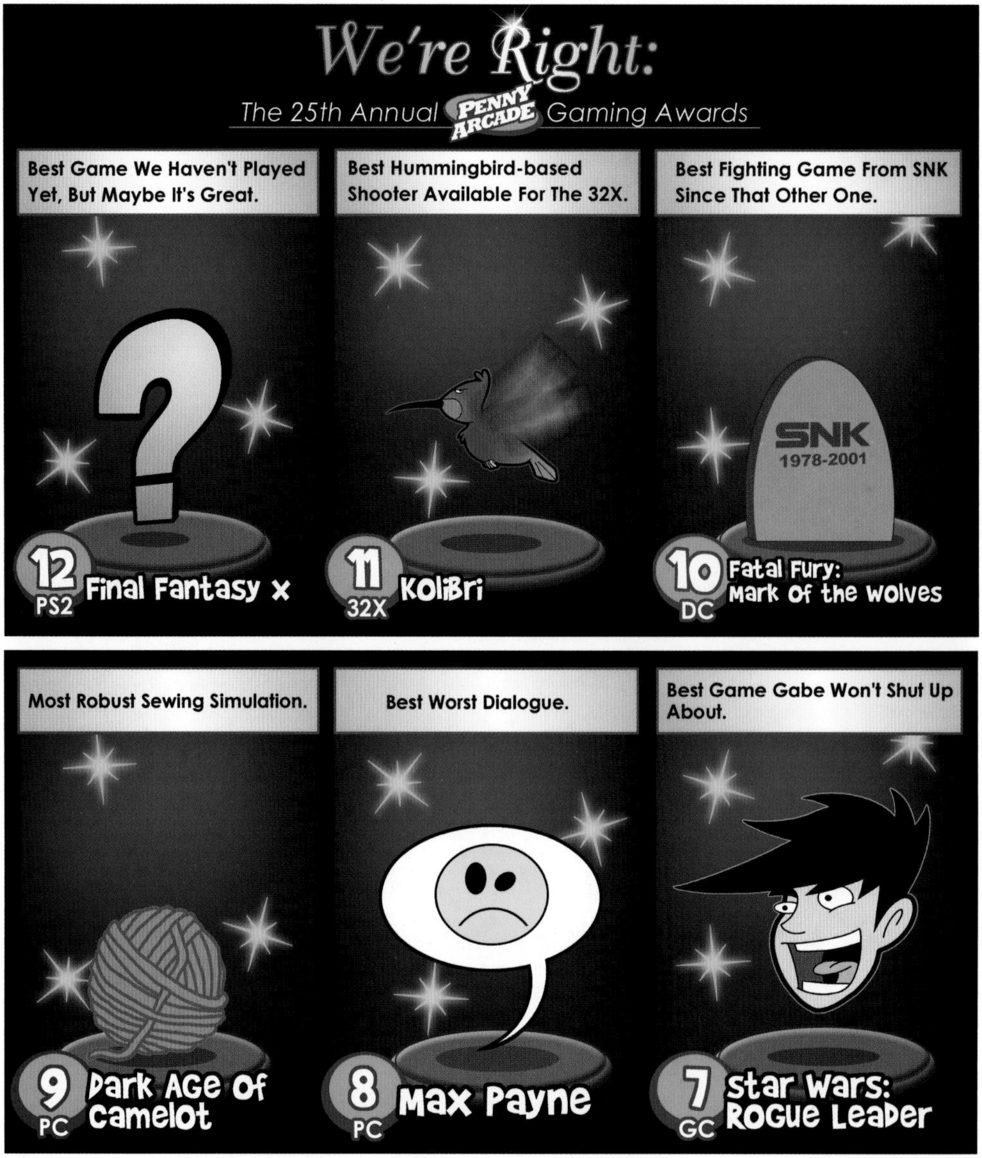
We're Right:
The 25th Annual PENNY ARCADE Gaming Awards
Best Game We Haven't Played Yet, But Maybe It's Great.
12 PS2 Final Fantasy X
Best Hummingbird-based Shooter Available For The 32X.
11 32X Kolibri
Best Fighting Game From SNK Since That Other One.
SNK 1978-2001
10 DC Fatal Fury: Mark Of the Wolves
Most Robust Sewing Simulation.
9 PC Dark Age Of Camelot
Best Worst Dialogue.
8 PC Max Payne
Best Game Gabe Won't Shut Up About.
7 GC Star Wars: Rogue Leader

AWARDS CEREMONY, PART ONE

December 17, 2001 Reserving a slot in the awards for Final Fantasy X was probably a good idea. It was one of the first role-playing games that Gabe played seriously: he went right from Wild Arms III to FFX, which must have been a tremendous shock. Something like going from aquarium water to Courvoisier.

AWARDS CEREMONY, PART TWO

December 19, 2001 I was right to fear Dark Age of Camelot, as it turns out. And Asheron's Call, and Second Life, and Anarchy Online, and *Ultima*-Online, which is to say nothing of Ragnarok, my torrid affair with golfing RPG Shot Online, the life-devouring World of Warcraft, Final Fantasy XI, A Tale in the Desert, EVE Online . . .

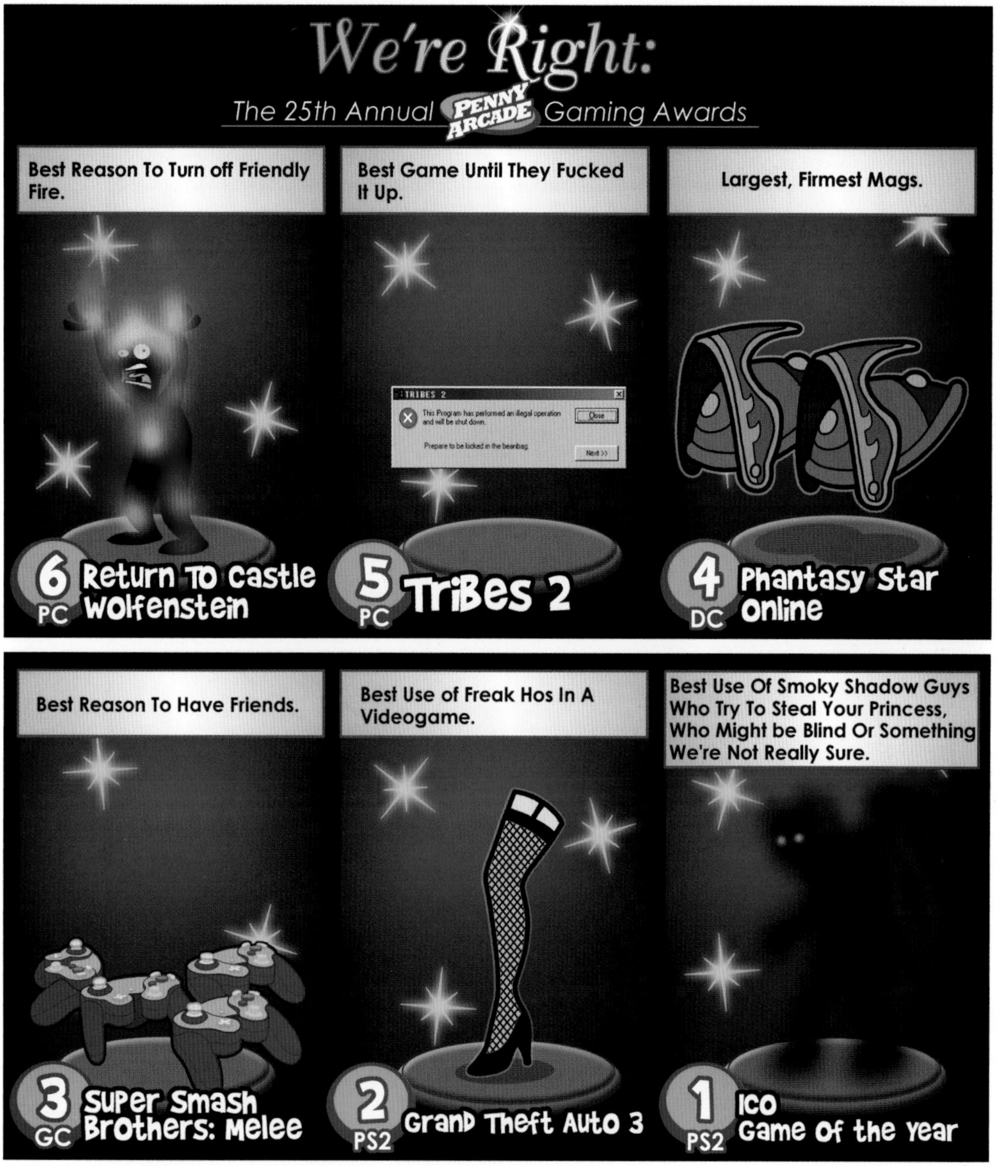

We're Right:
The 25th Annual PENNY ARCADE Gaming Awards
Best Reason To Turn off Friendly Fire.
6 PC Return To Castle Wolfenstein
Best Game Until They Fucked It Up.
TRIBES 2
This Program has performed an illegal operation and will be shut down.
Close
Prepare to be locked in the beanbag.
Next >>
5 PC TriBes 2
Largest, Firmest Mags.
4 DC Phantasy Star Online
Best Reason To Have Friends.
3 GC Super Smash Brothers: Melee
Best Use of Freak Hos In A Videogame.
2 PS2 Grand Theft Auto 3
Best Use Of Smoky Shadow Guys Who Try To Steal Your Princess, Who Might be Blind Or Something We're Not Really Sure.
1 PS2 Ico Game Of the Year

AWARDS CEREMONY, PART THREE

December 22, 2001 In the other Award strips, I can actually choose one game and then discuss it a little bit. But this one, even though none of these cracked the top three, is full of games that completely dominated the year. So, while I would certainly *play* other games, as soon as nine-thirty rolled around, that shit had to stop. At that point, one of these three would ascend to the throne.

AWARDS CEREMONY, PART FOUR

December 24, 2001 Precious Ico! Like the colossus whose shadow would follow years later, an *artful* game, and lusciously presented. There was really nothing to the combat, no fancy moves, no rich counter system, but the kid is like twelve. Give him a break.

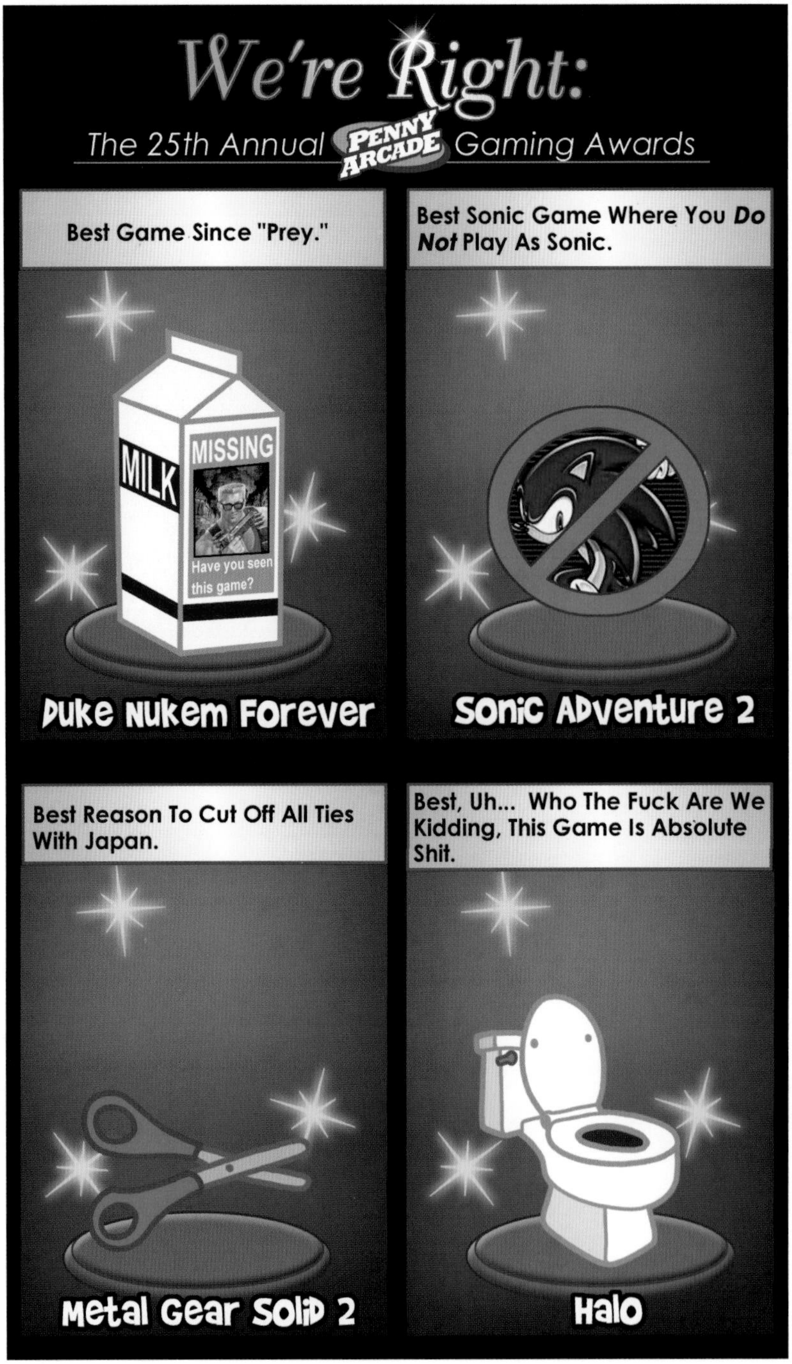
We're Right:
The 25th Annual PENNY ARCADE Gaming Awards
Best Game Since "Prey."
MILK
MISSING
Have you seen this game?
Duke Nukem Forever
Best Sonic Game Where You *Do Not* Play As Sonic.
Sonic Adventure 2
Best Reason To Cut Off All Ties With Japan.
Metal Gear Solid 2
Best, Uh... Who The Fuck Are We Kidding, This Game Is Absolute Shit.
Halo

AWARDS CEREMONY, AFTERMATH

December 26, 2001 Our dissatisfaction with Halo's campaign was such that we didn't even try the multiplayer until later the next year. Eventually it caught on, became a weekly fixture, etc. Essentially, it delivered the LAN experience in an accessible way. I'm not surprised it became a cultural phenomenon.

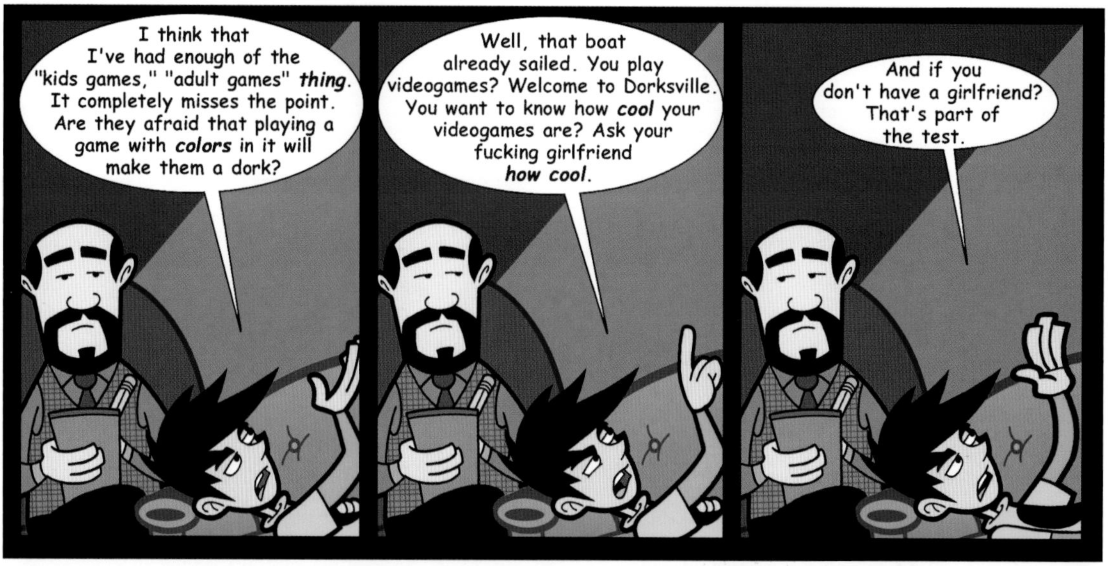
I think that I've had enough of the "kids games," "adult games" *thing*. It completely misses the point. Are they afraid that playing a game with *colors* in it will make them a dork?
Well, that boat already sailed. You play videogames? Welcome to Dorksville. You want to know how *cool* your videogames are? Ask your fucking girlfriend *how cool*.
And if you don't have a girlfriend? That's part of the test.

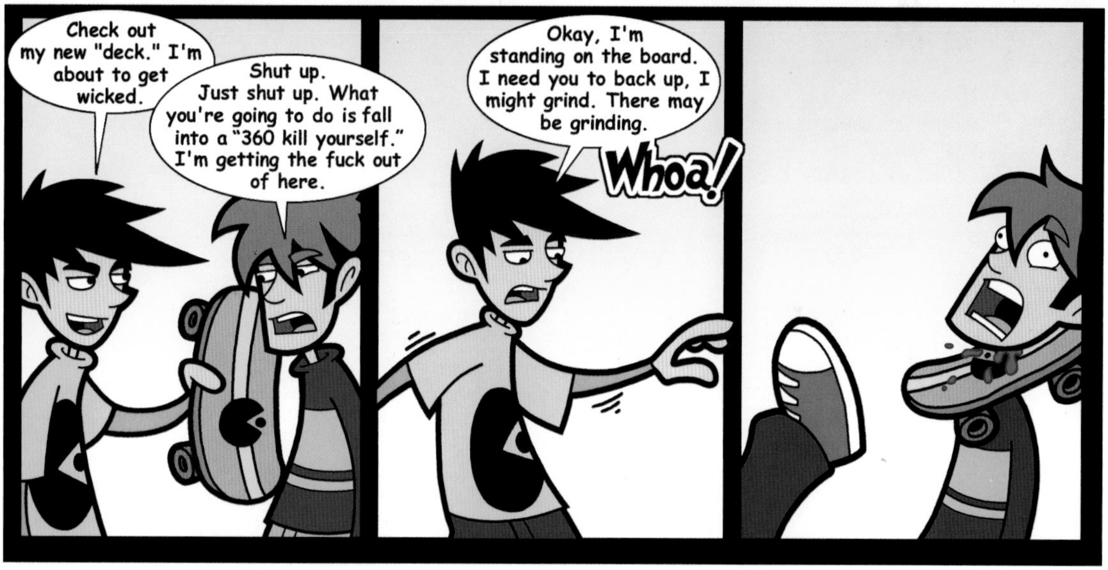
Check out my new "deck." I'm about to get wicked.
Shut up. Just shut up. What you're going to do is fall into a "360 kill yourself." I'm getting the fuck out of here.
Okay, I'm standing on the board. I need you to back up, I might grind. There may be grinding.
Whoa!

I THINK OUR TIME IS UP

December 14, 2001 This "debate" pops up from time to time, the kiddy games thing, and the longer I've been playing games the less water it holds. My goal when playing a game is to manipulate events on screen in a series of escalating challenges. Past that, provided those challenges remain interesting, if they want to use bright colors or something I'm bound to cut them some slack.

THE OTHER FAMOUS TONY

December 29, 2001 You get to thinking you're ready to form some kind of "Sk8 Cru" after a few hours doing lip tricks with the gamepad, and it just ain't the case. Skate decapitations are rare, but not impossible. I have endeavored to shred all of one time, and in the length of one driveway I managed to "shred" my Goddamn legs, filthy gravel jammed up the length of the gash.

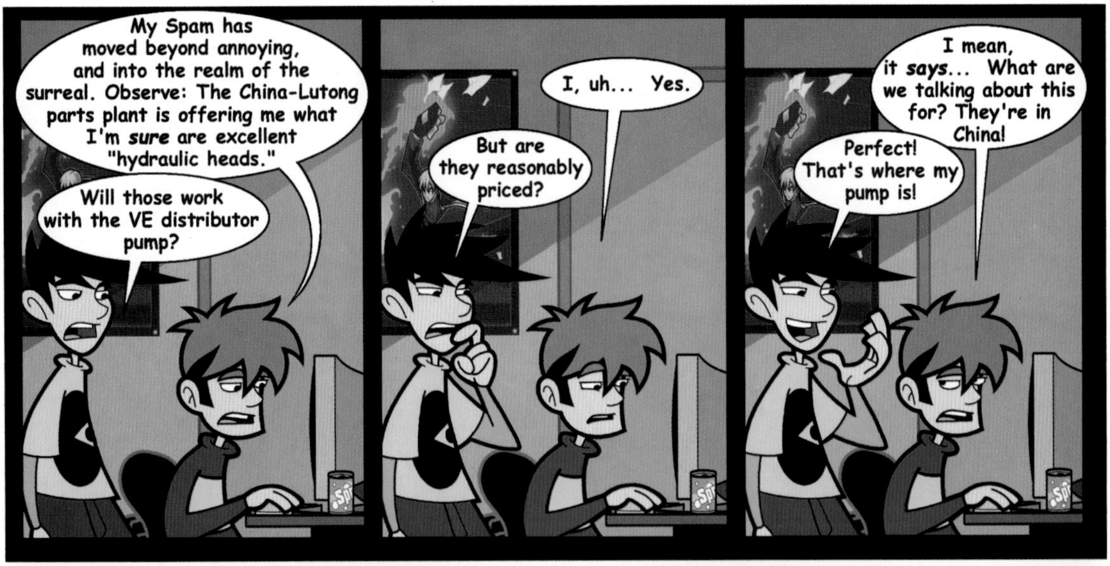
My Spam has moved beyond annoying, and into the realm of the surreal. Observe: The China-Lutong parts plant is offering me what I'm *sure* are excellent "hydraulic heads."
Will those work with the VE distributor pump?
I, uh... Yes.
But are they reasonably priced?
I mean, it *says*... What are we talking about this for? They're in China!
Perfect! That's where my pump is!

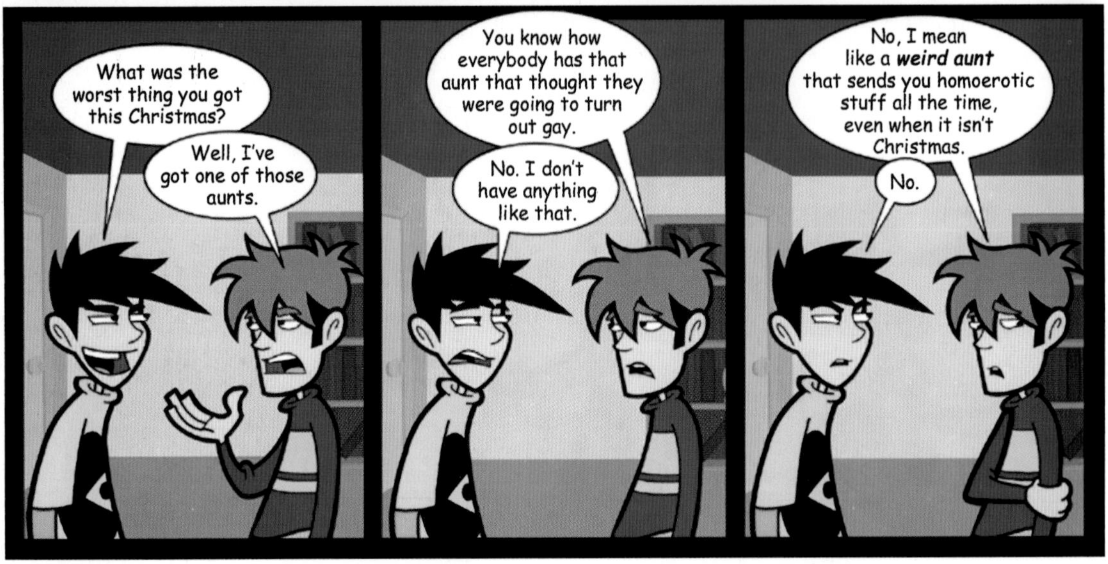
What was the worst thing you got this Christmas?
Well, I've got one of those aunts.
You know how everybody has that aunt that thought they were going to turn out gay.
No. I don't have anything like that.
No, I mean like a *weird aunt* that sends you homoerotic stuff all the time, even when it isn't Christmas.
No.

THE VILLAGE OF THE SPAMMED

December 30, 2001 I understand the basic theory behind spam, that when you purchase a list and broadcast your marketing message to the known universe, there must be some *organism* with the interest and means to acquire your . . . whatever it is. Chinese pump heads? Chinese *pump* heads.

YOU KNOW HOW IT IS

December 31, 2001 I don't know how else I can prove to her that I am emphatically *not gay*. Marrying a woman and fathering a child don't appear to have made a dent. I sent her a picture of myself eating a steak off the hood of a NASCAR, but I haven't heard back.

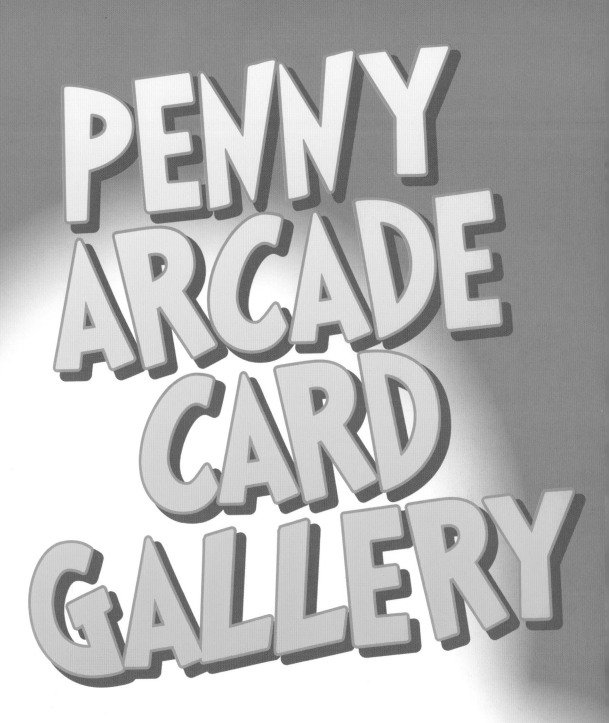

PENNY ARCADE CARD GALLERY

In 2005, Sabertooth Games asked us if we wanted to do a card game with them. I'd been big into their Warhammer 40k and Fantasy interpretations, so it was my firm conviction that they were up to the challenge. Gabe set to work on the fifty cards in the base set with a much looser, sketchbook style, and we brought in the brilliant Mohammad "Hawk" Haque from *Applegeeks* (http://www.applegeeks.com) to make them pop with his signature colors. Here's a selection of our favorites from the set—we think they turned out great.

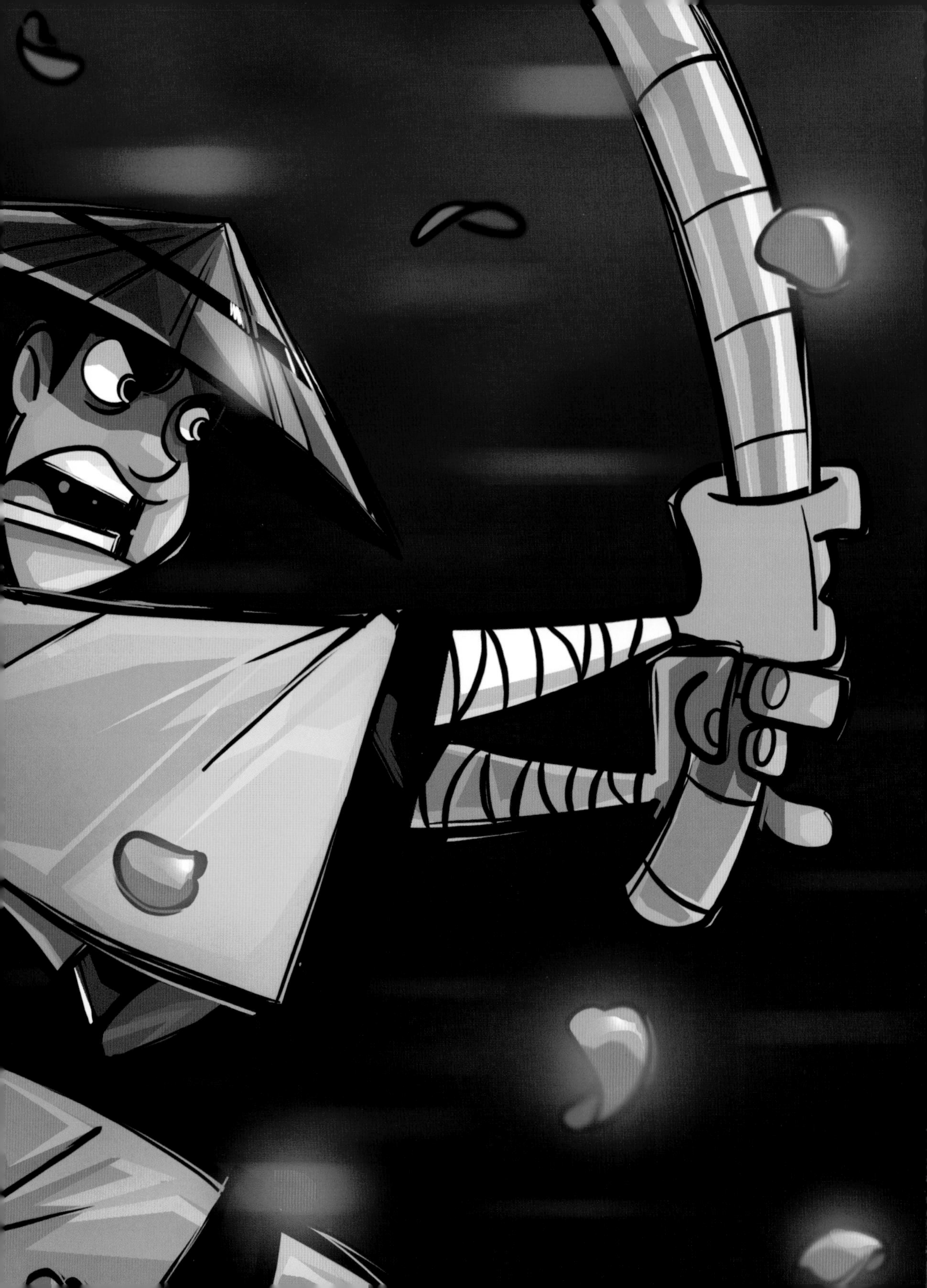

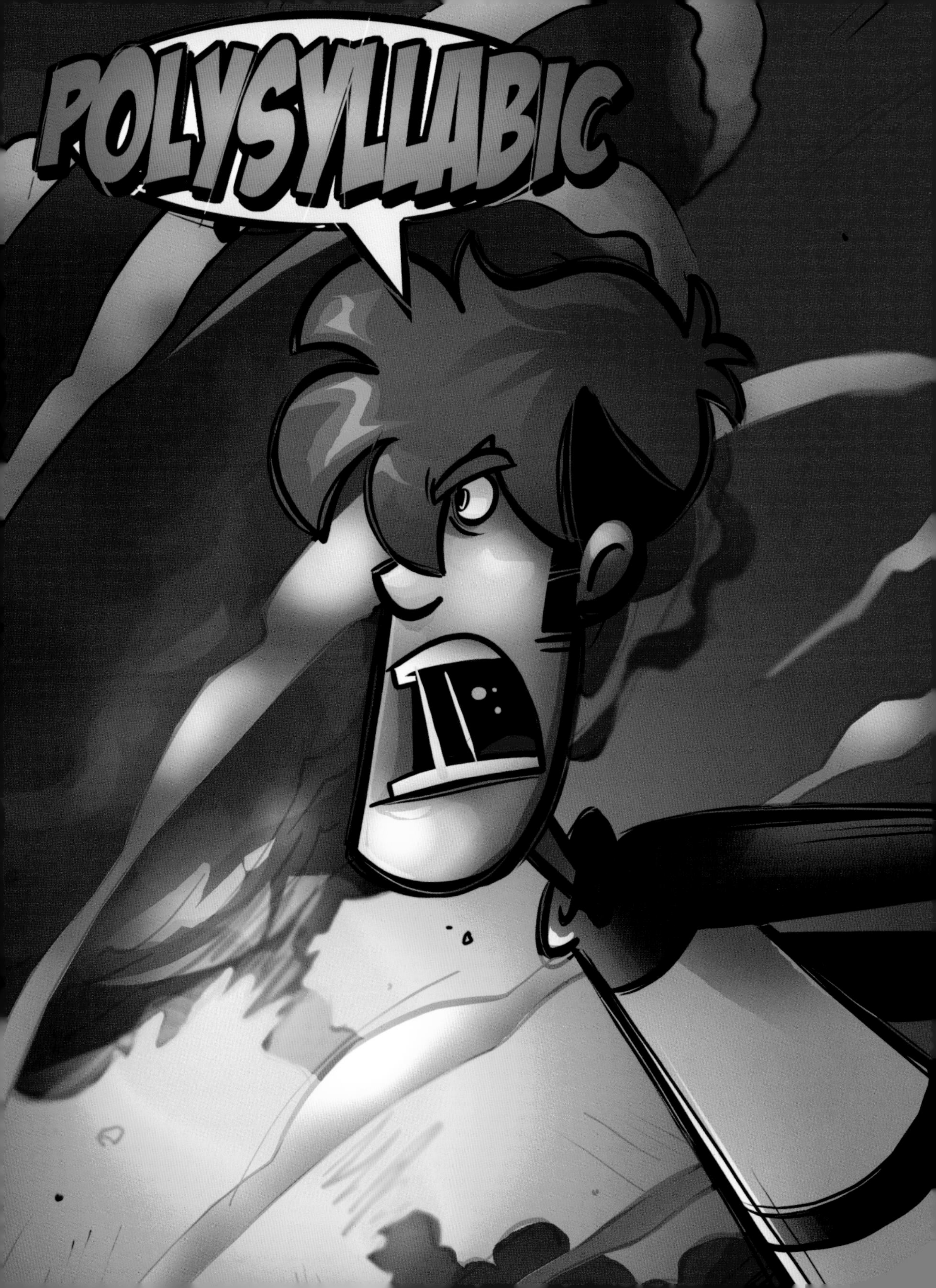
POLYSYLLABIC

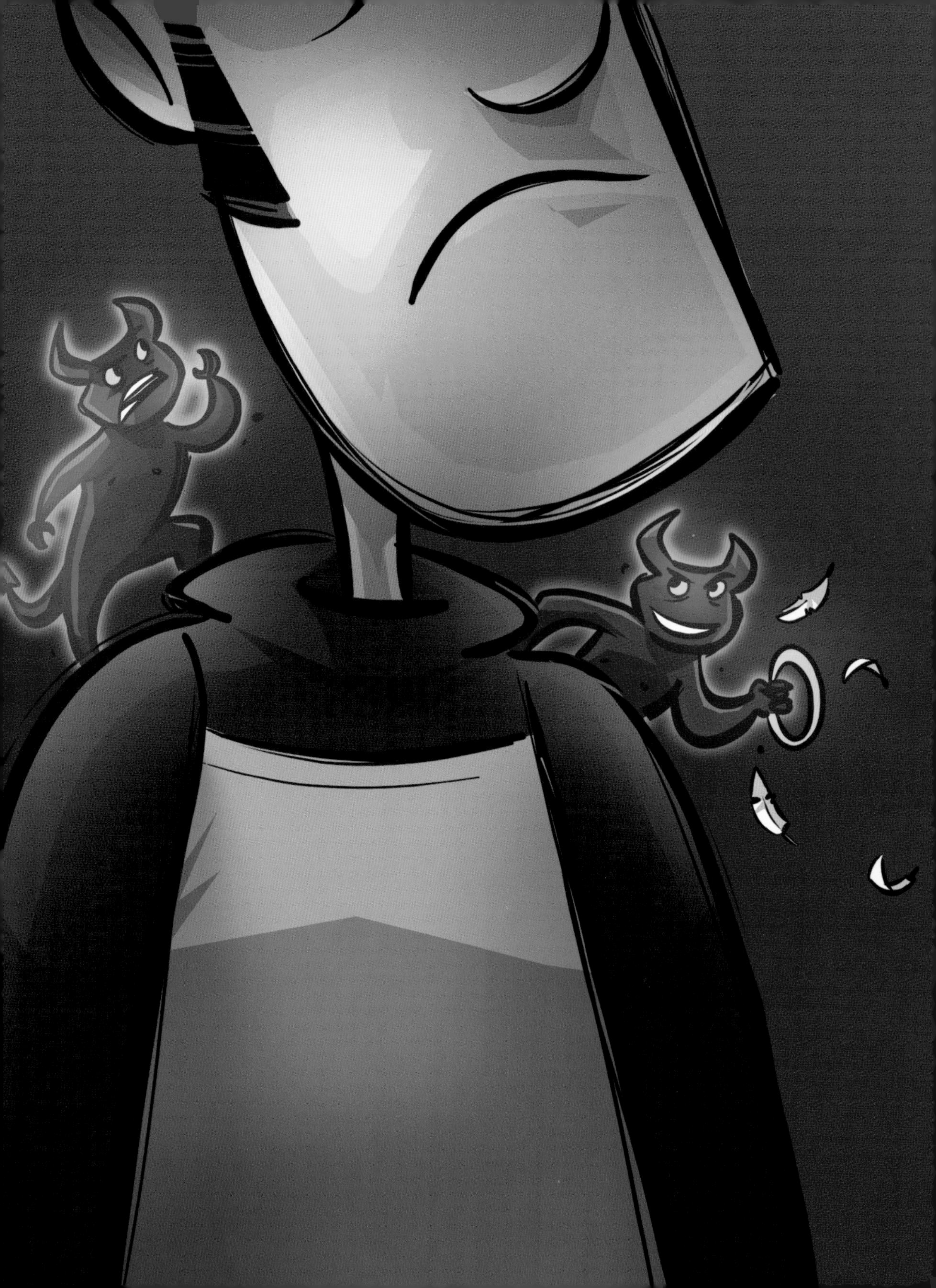

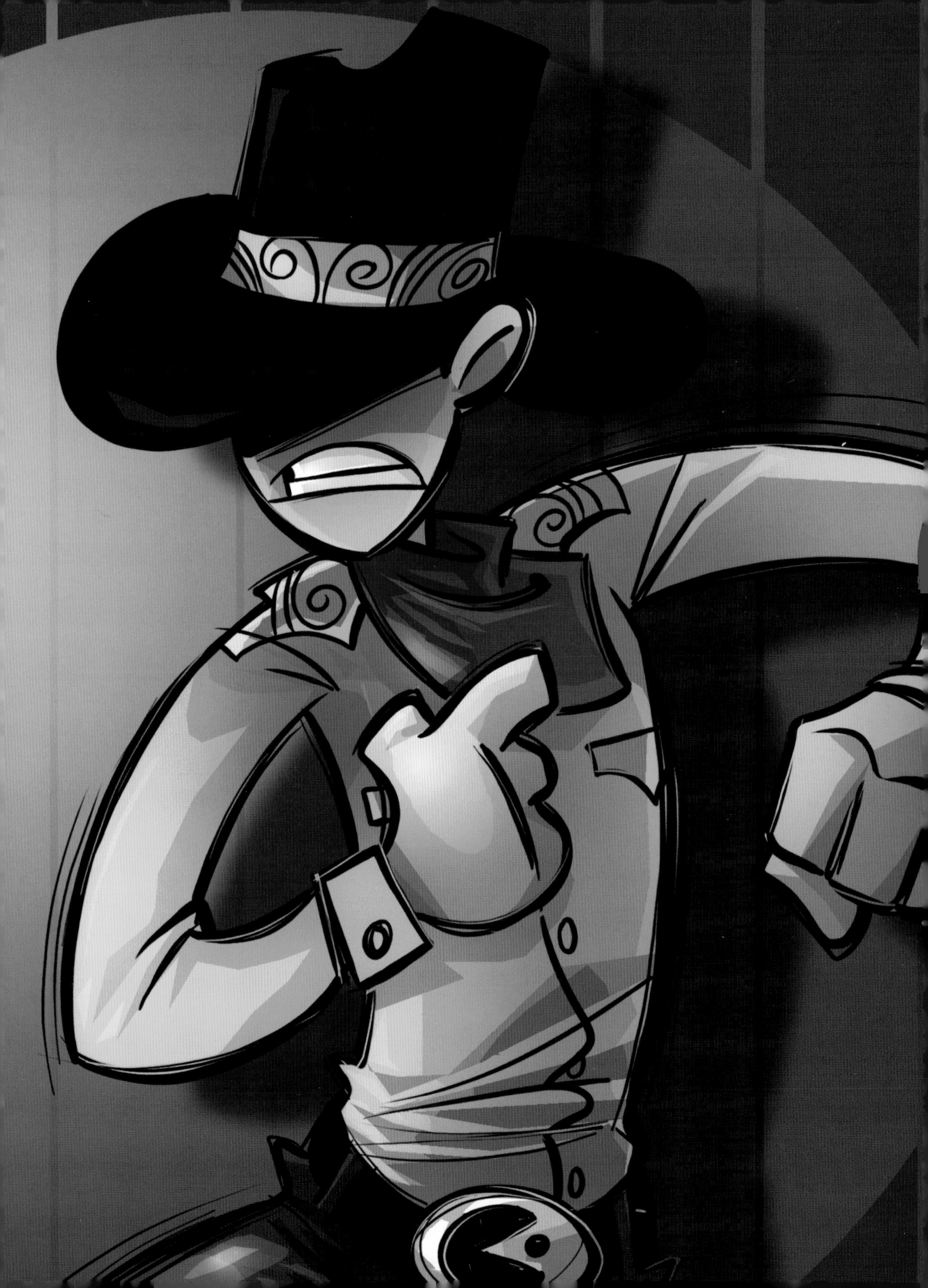

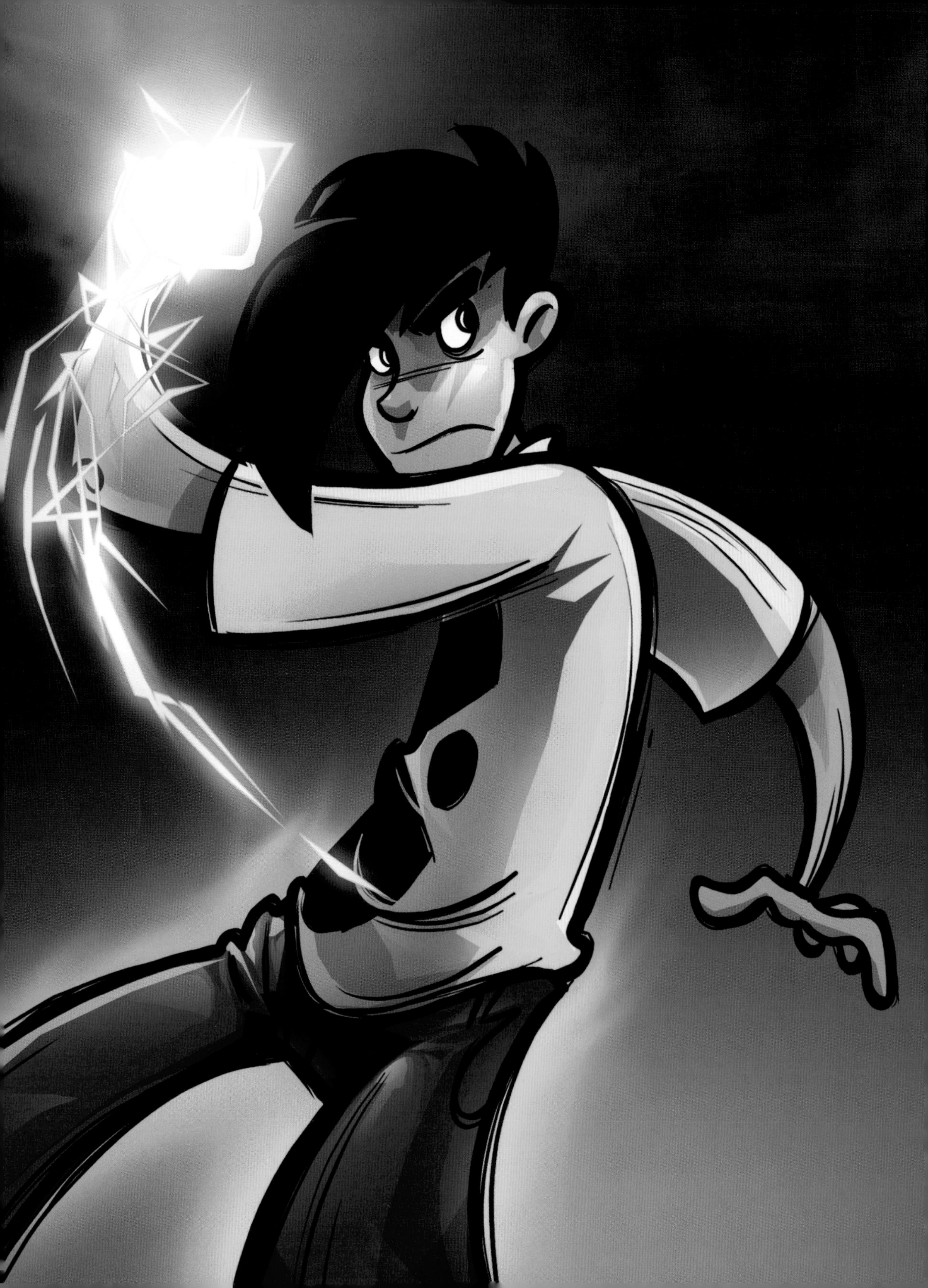

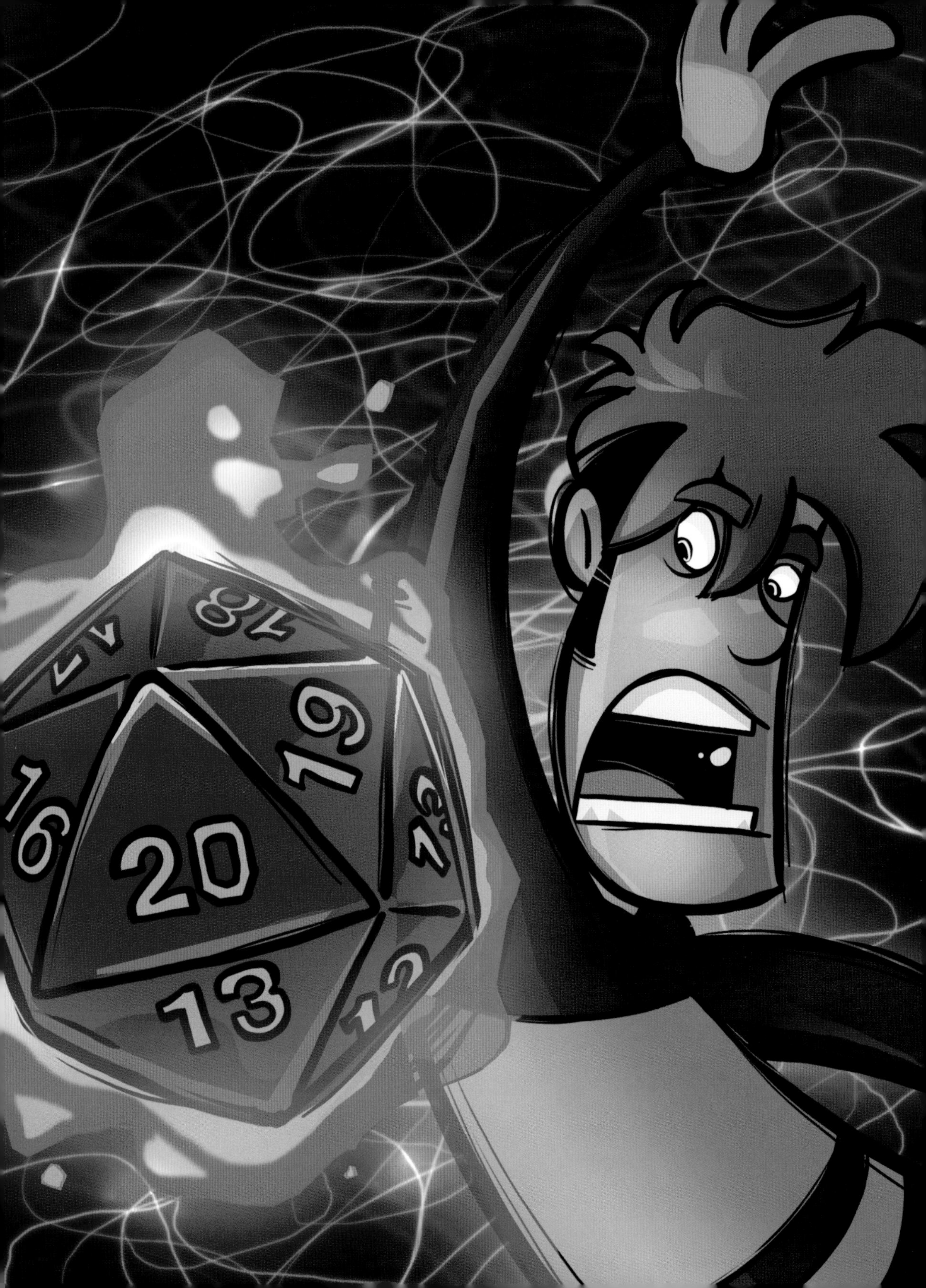

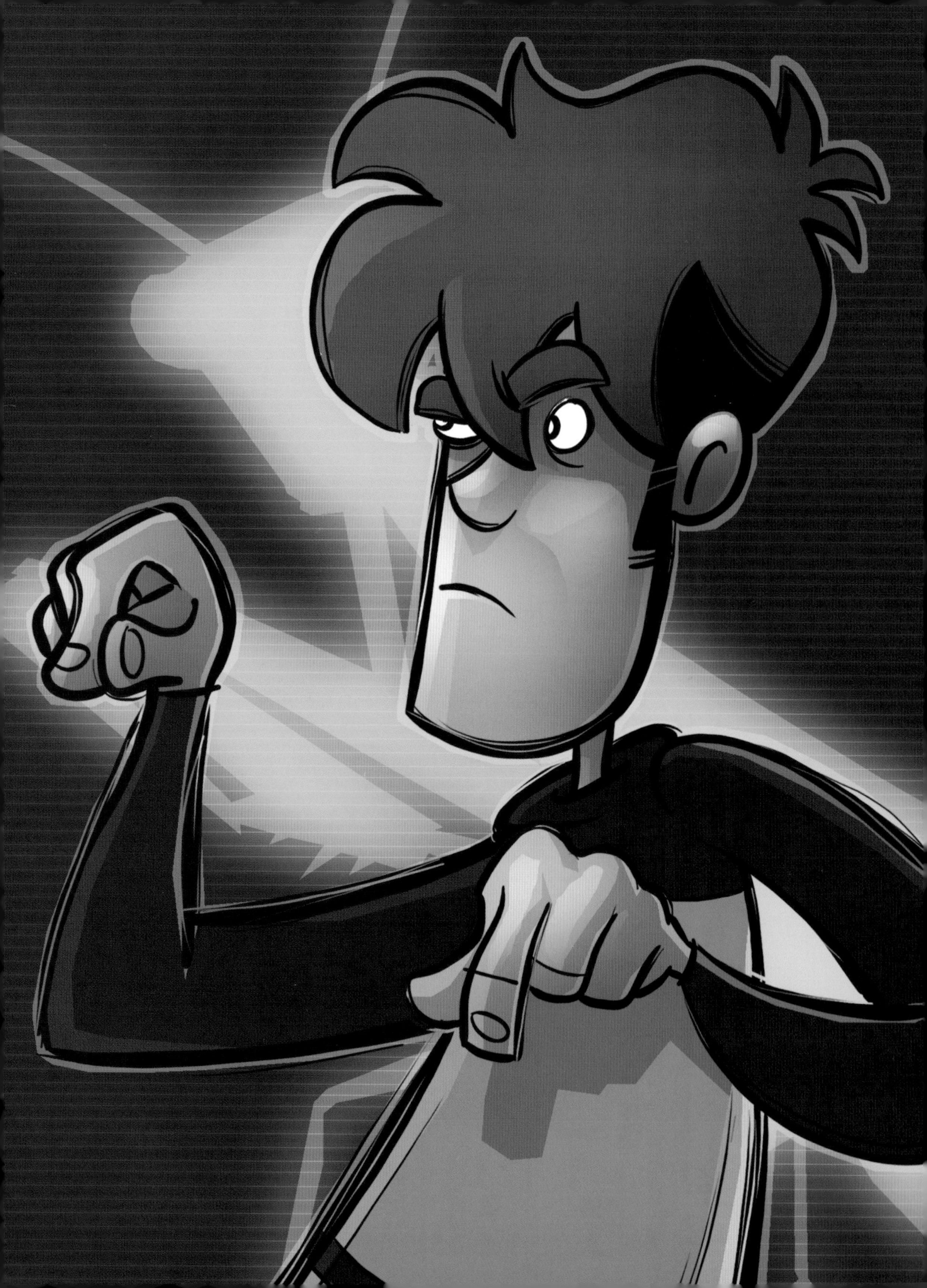

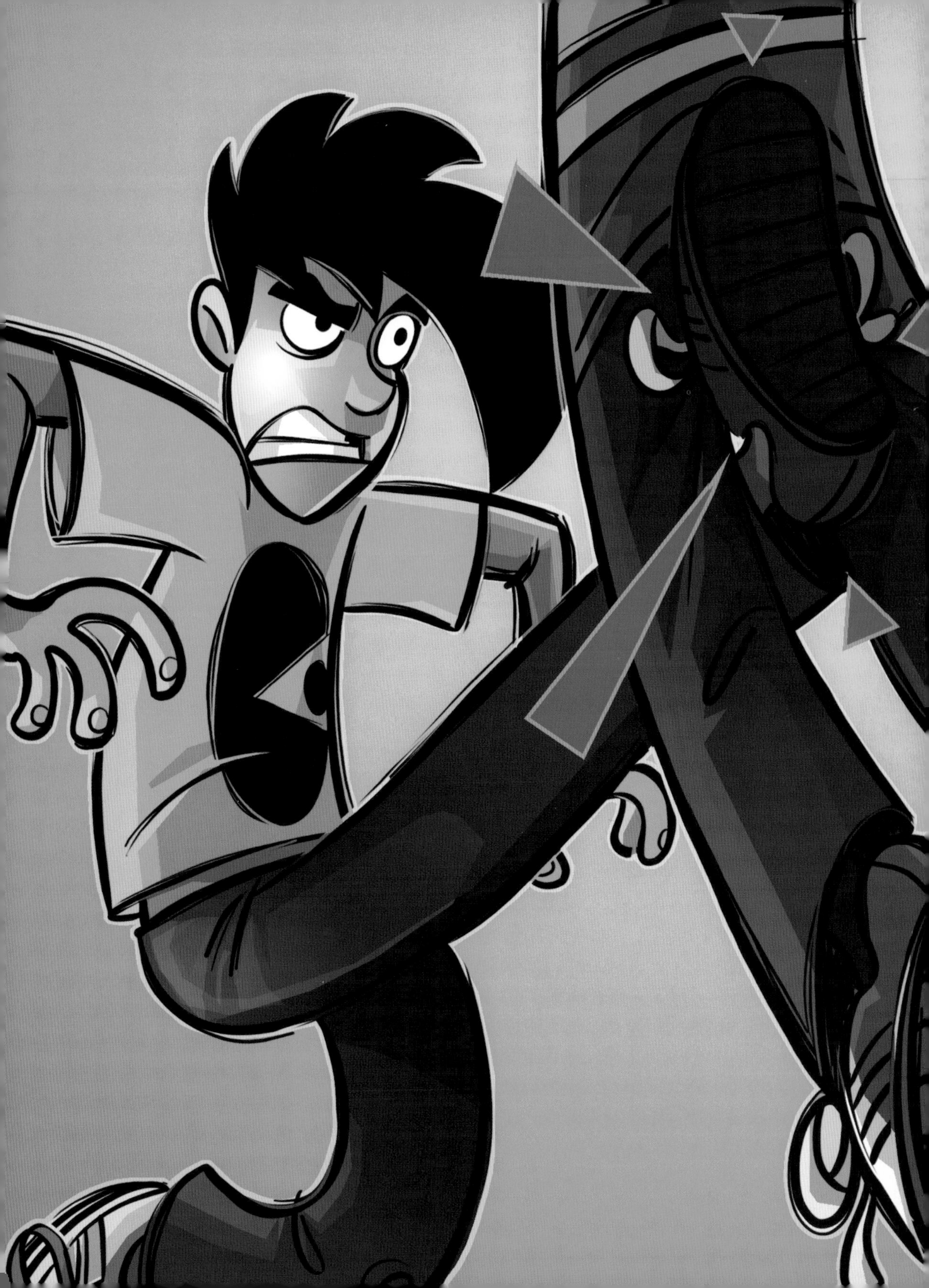

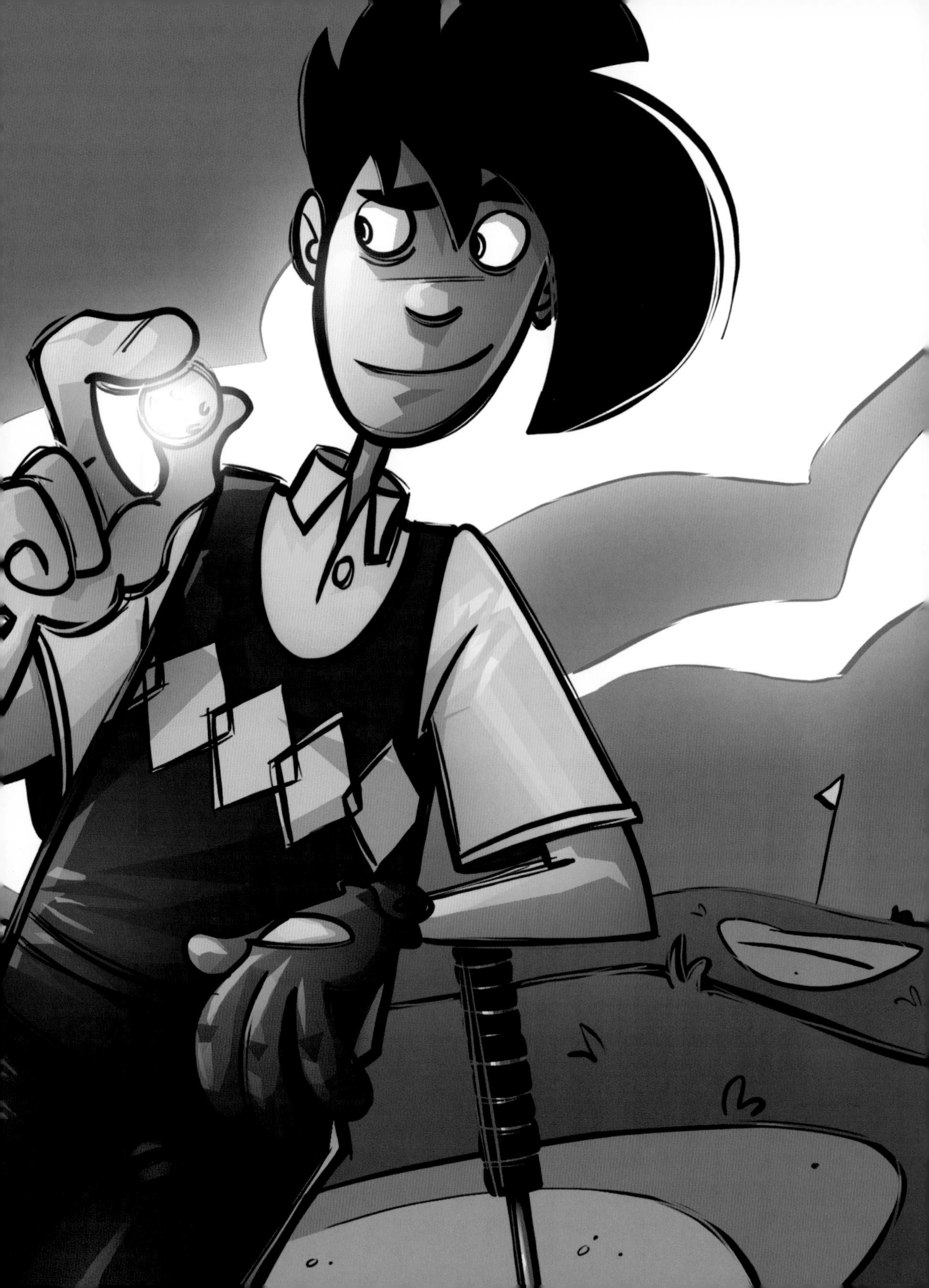

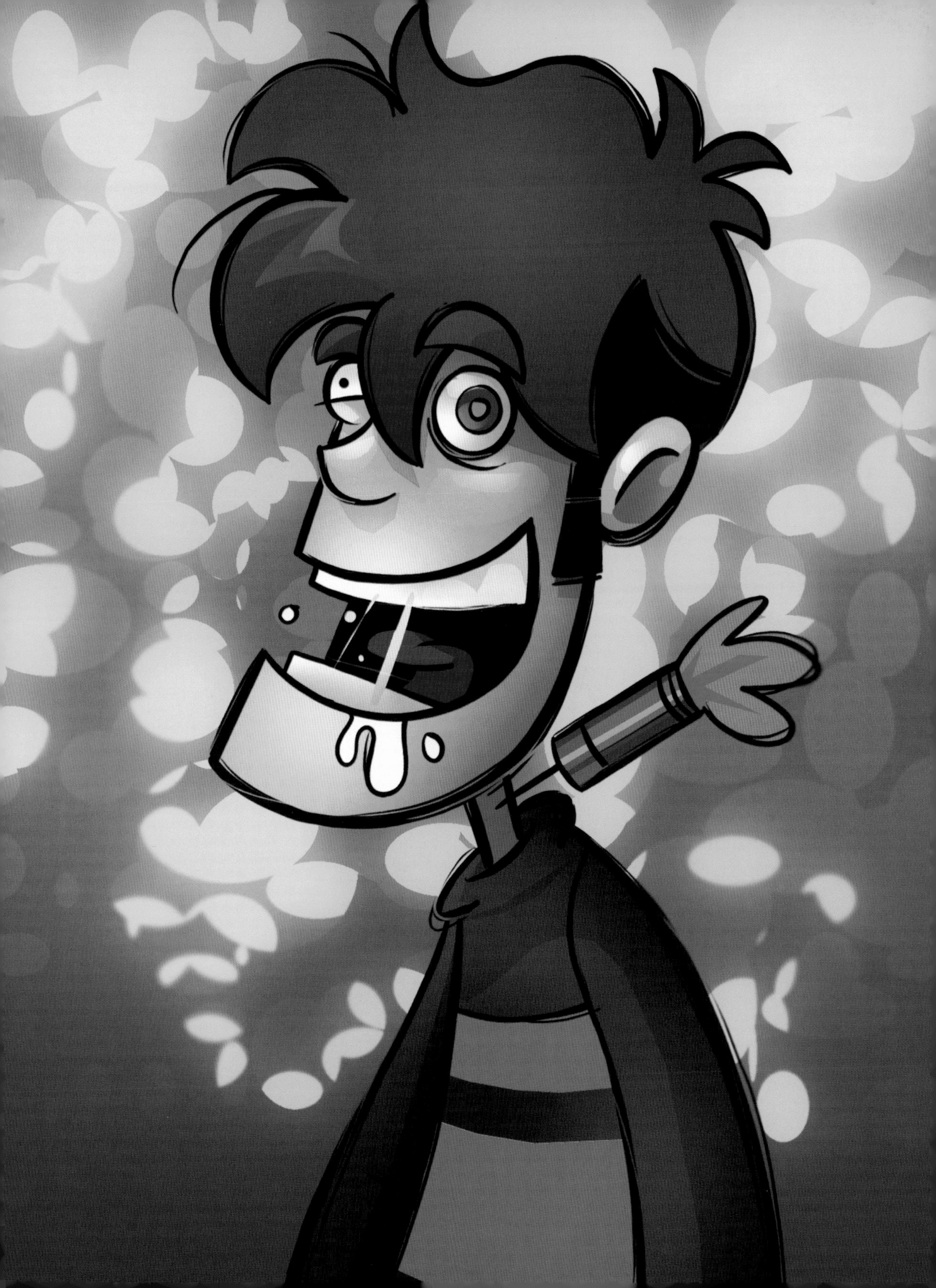

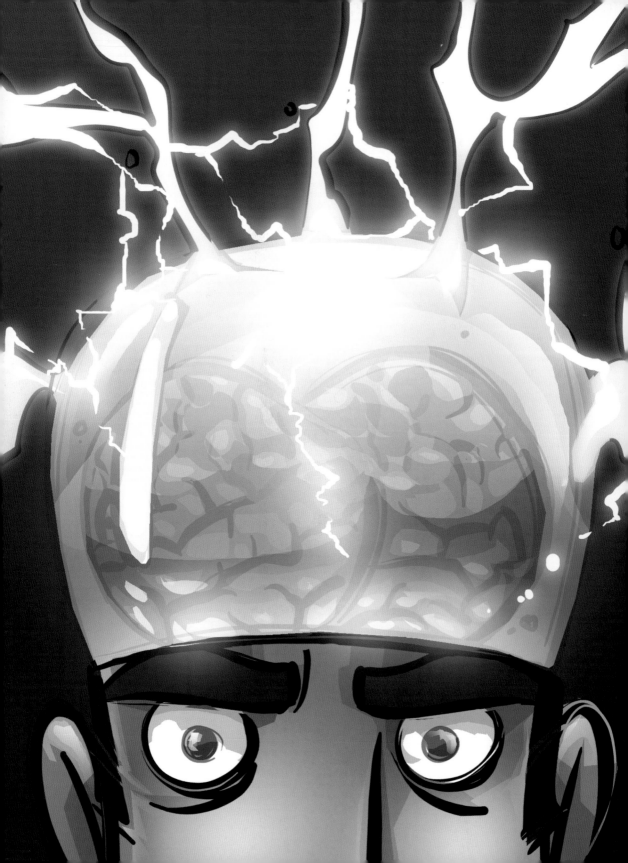

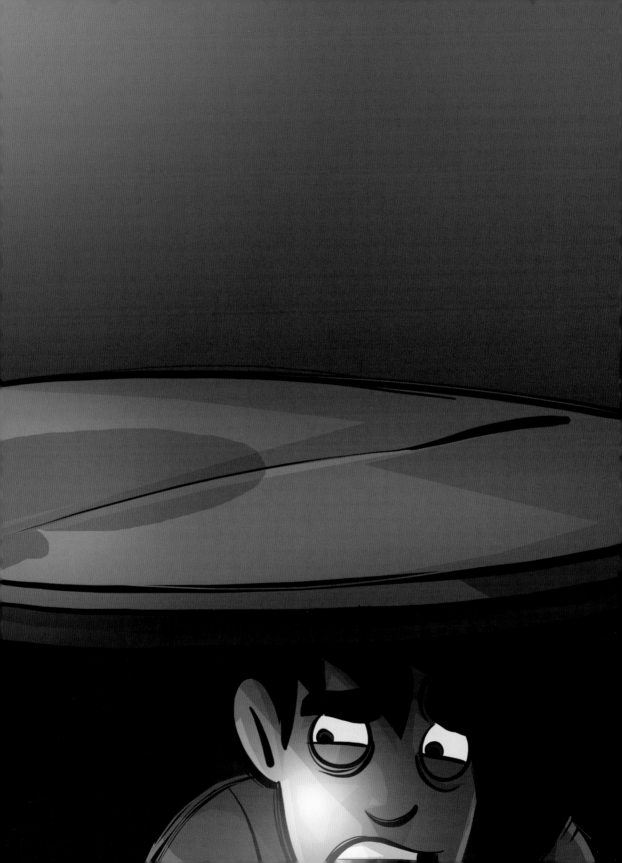

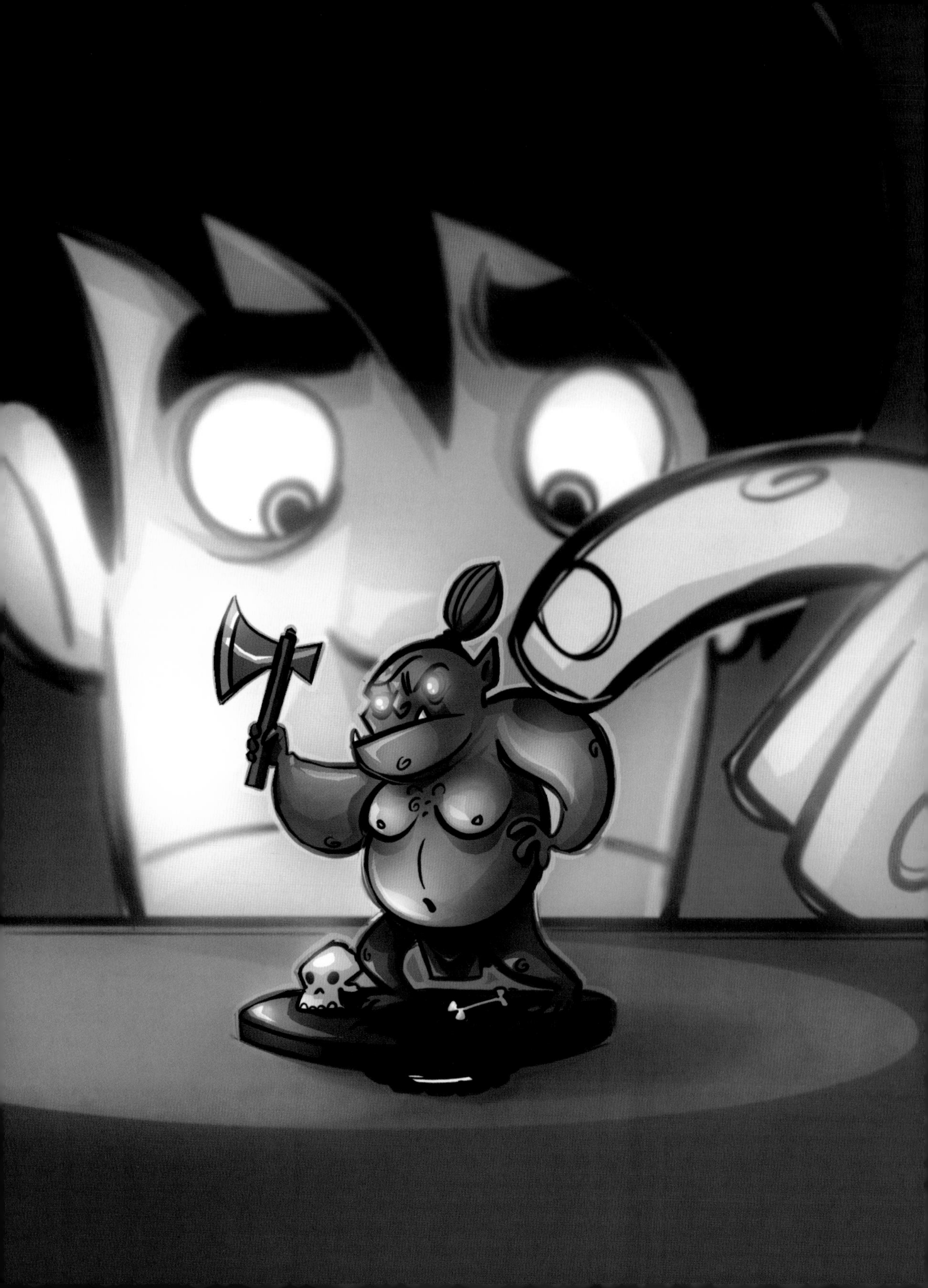

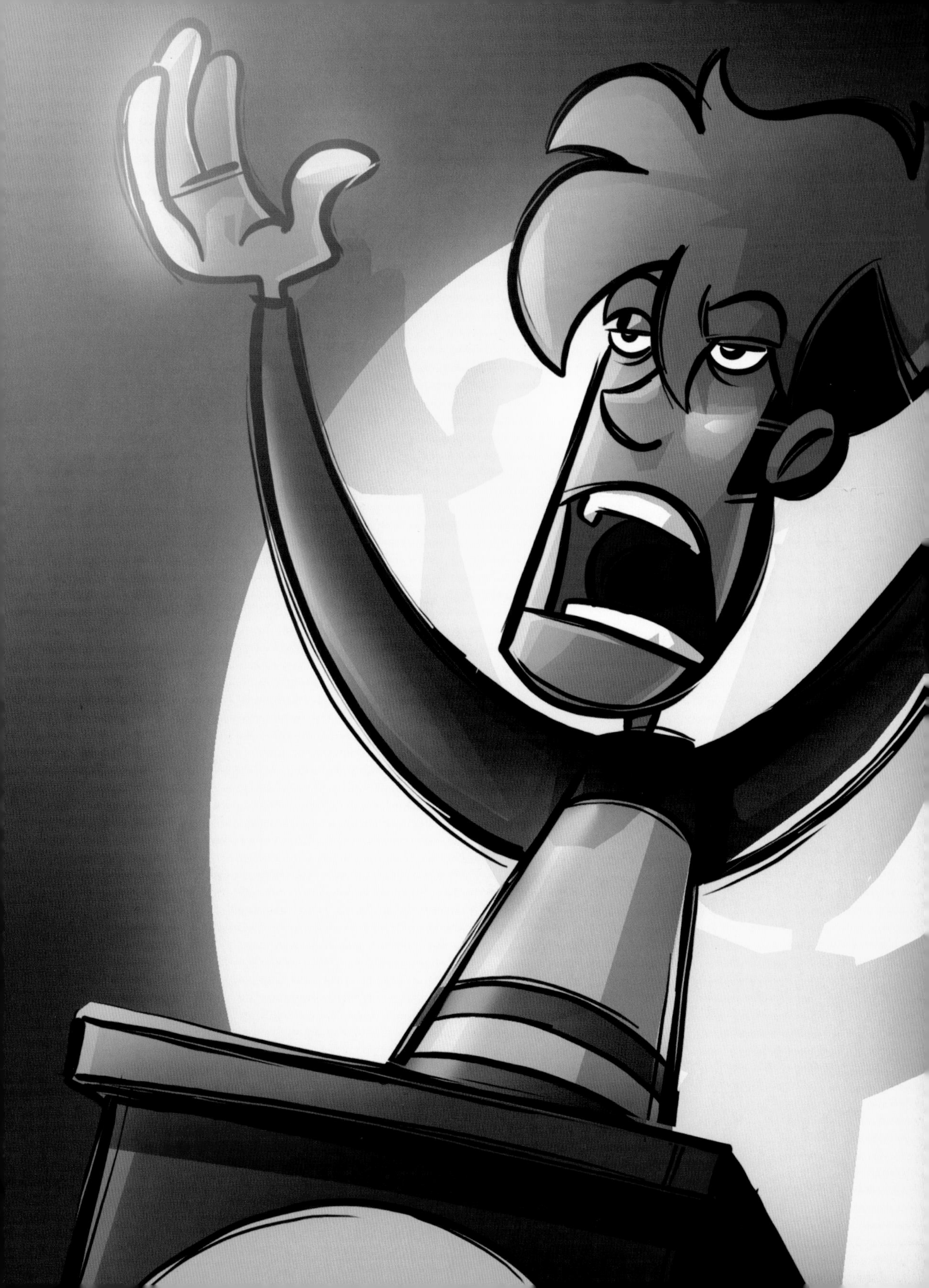

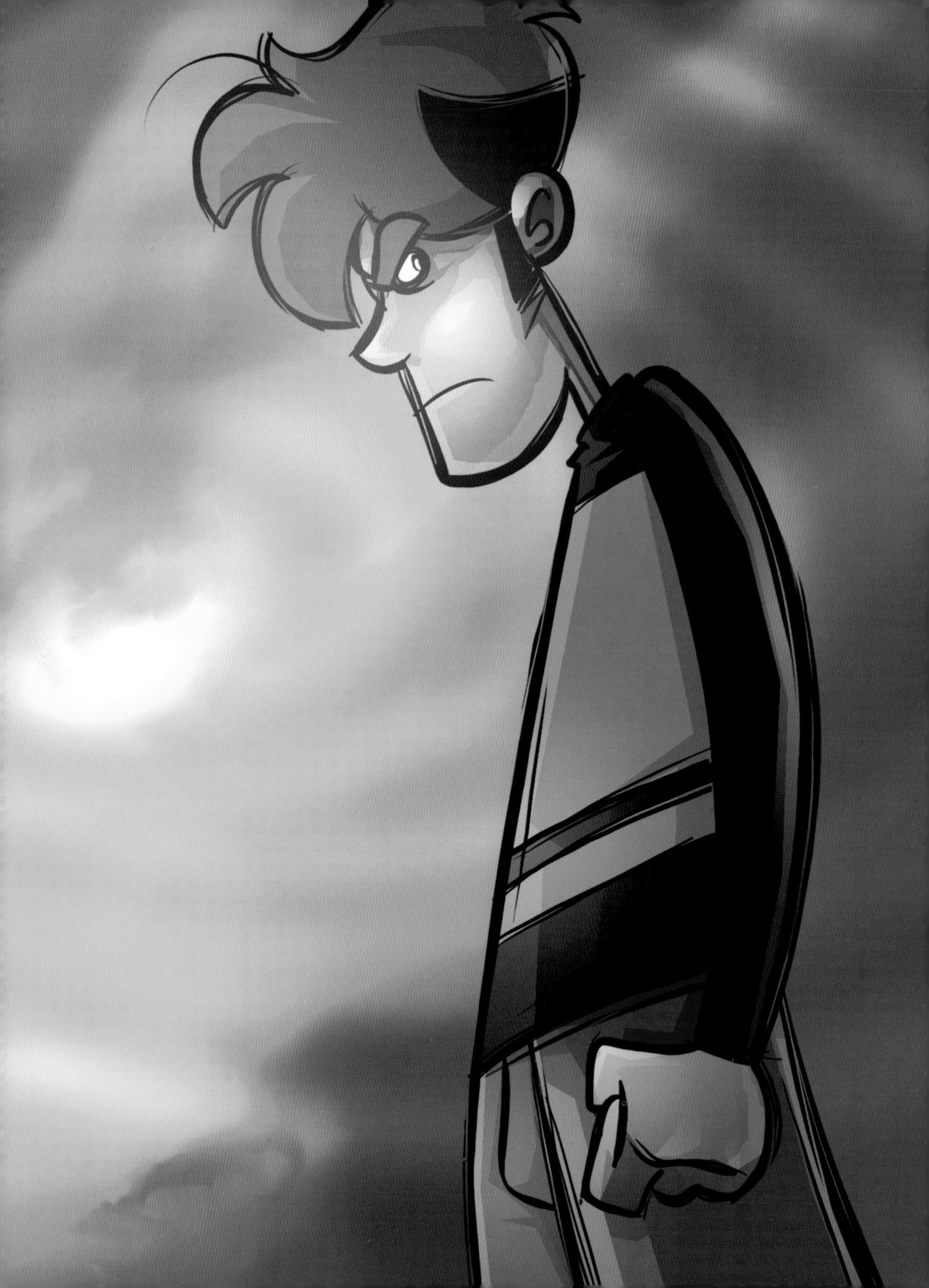

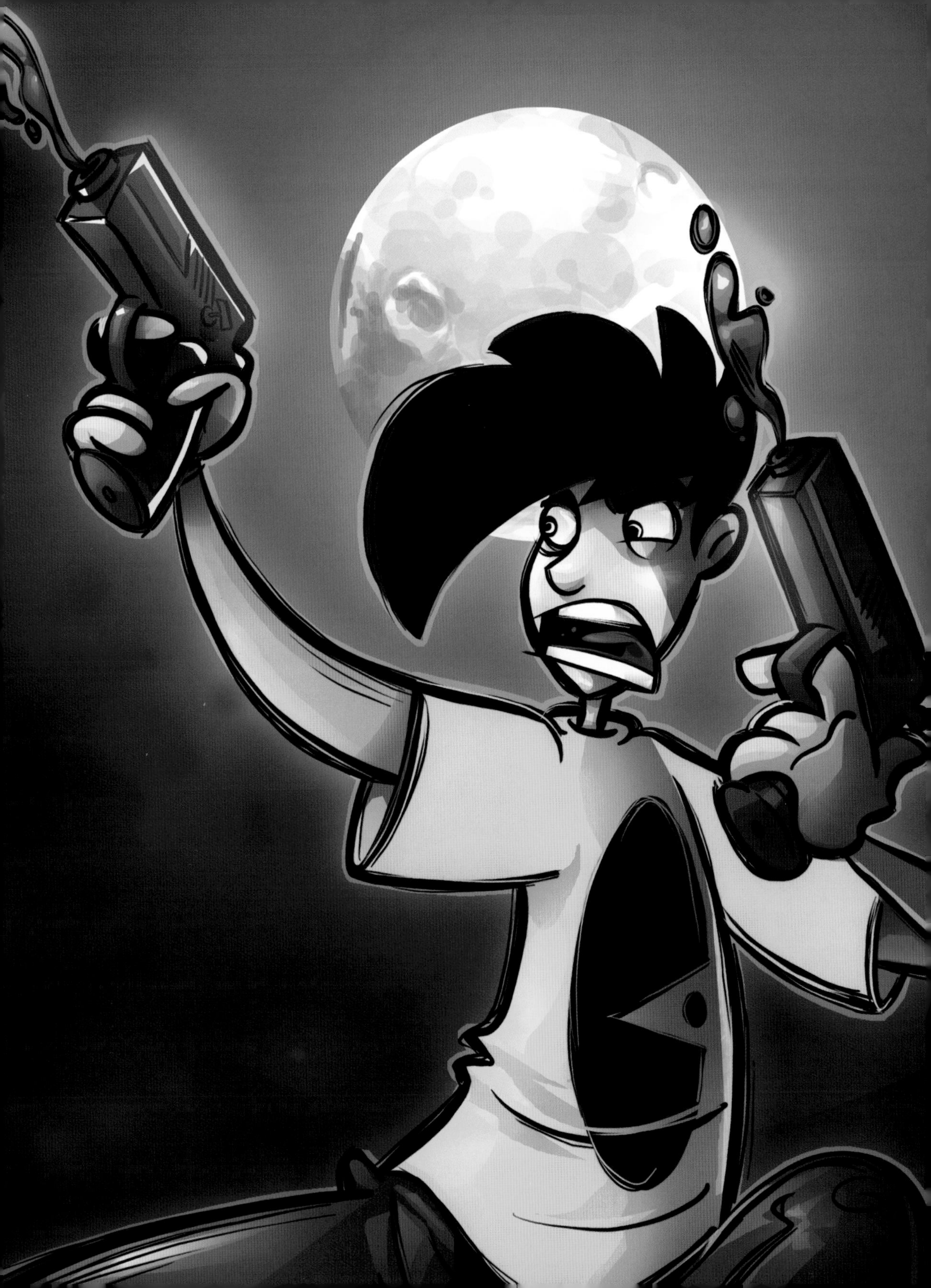

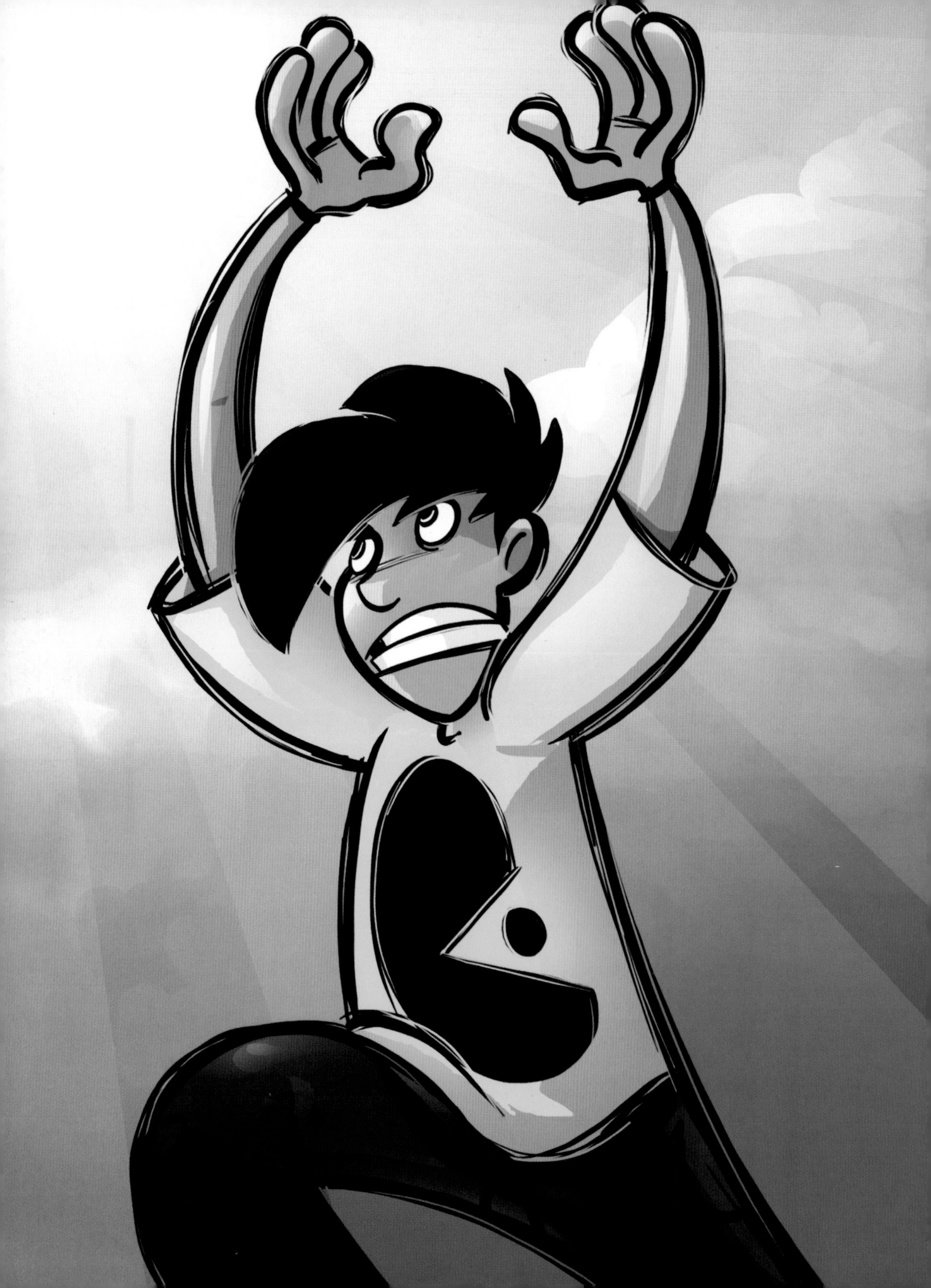

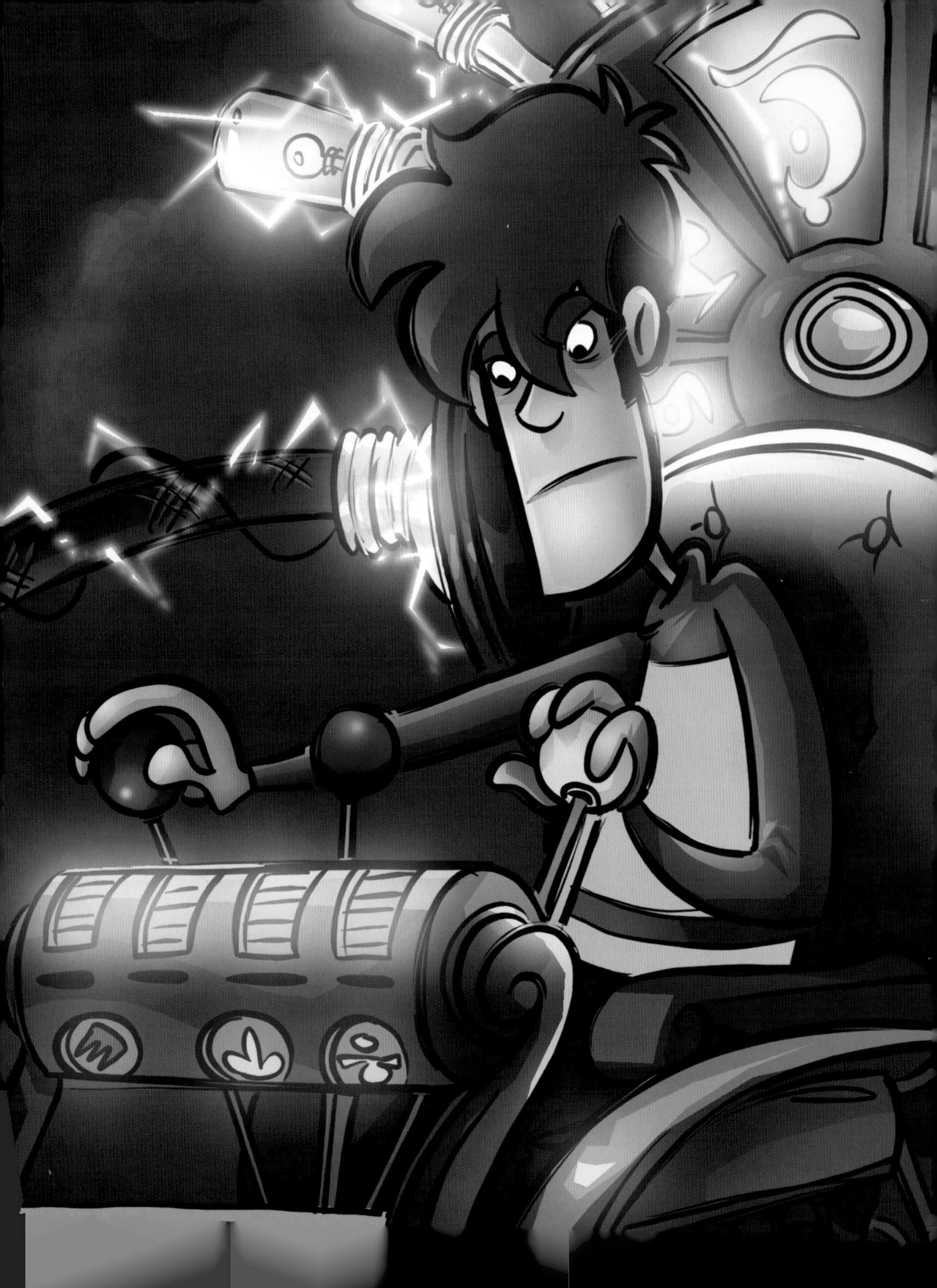

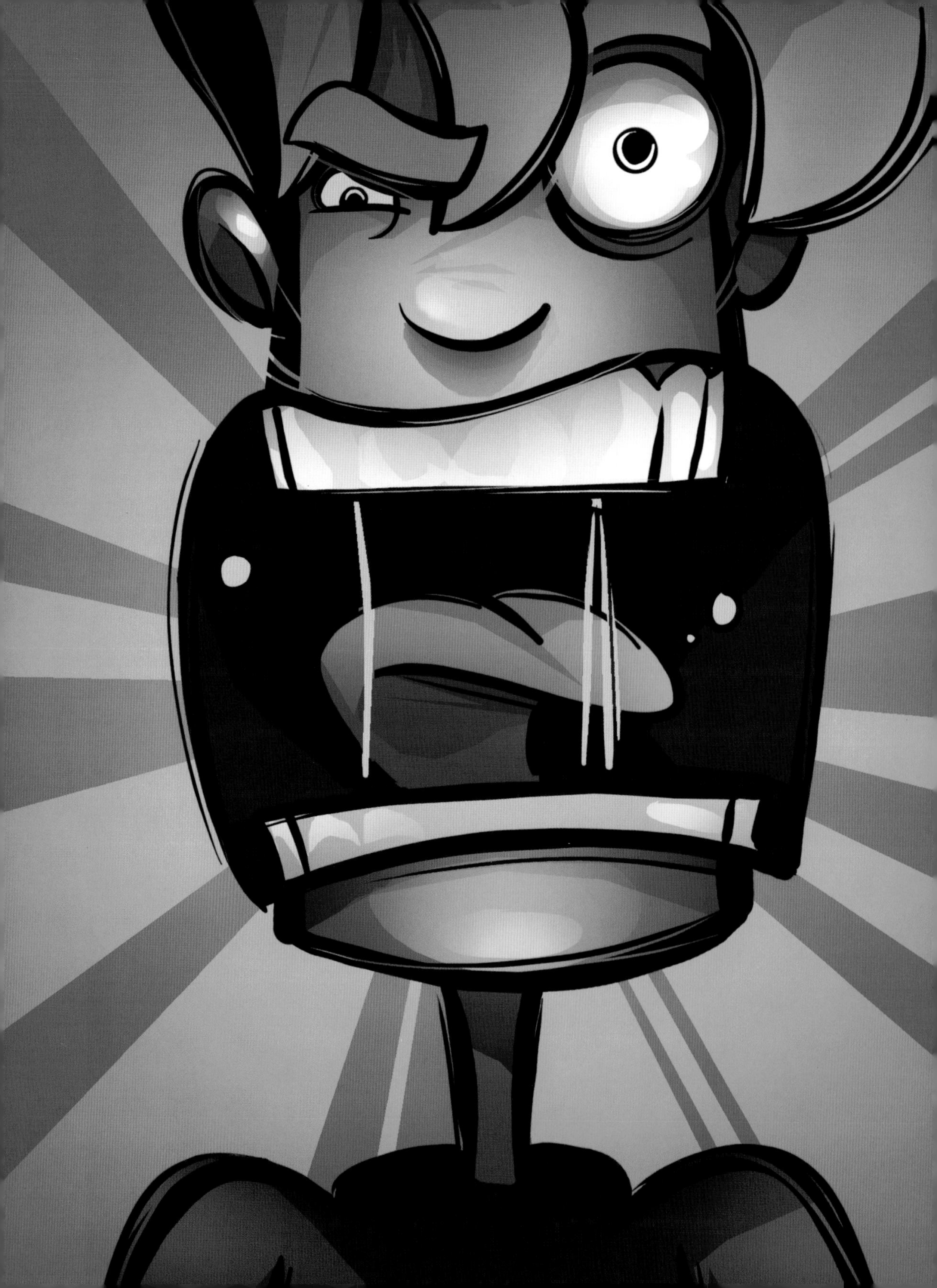

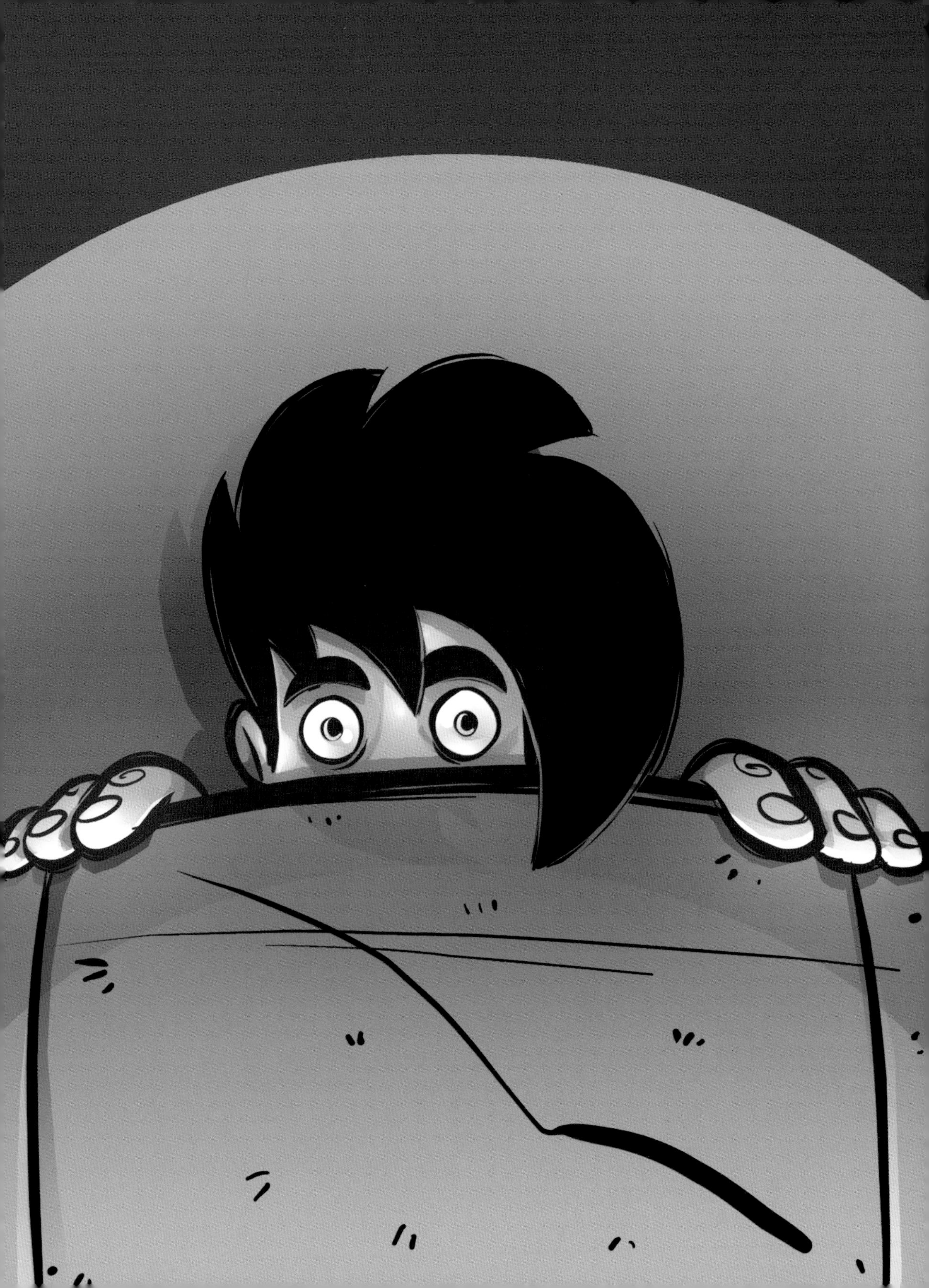

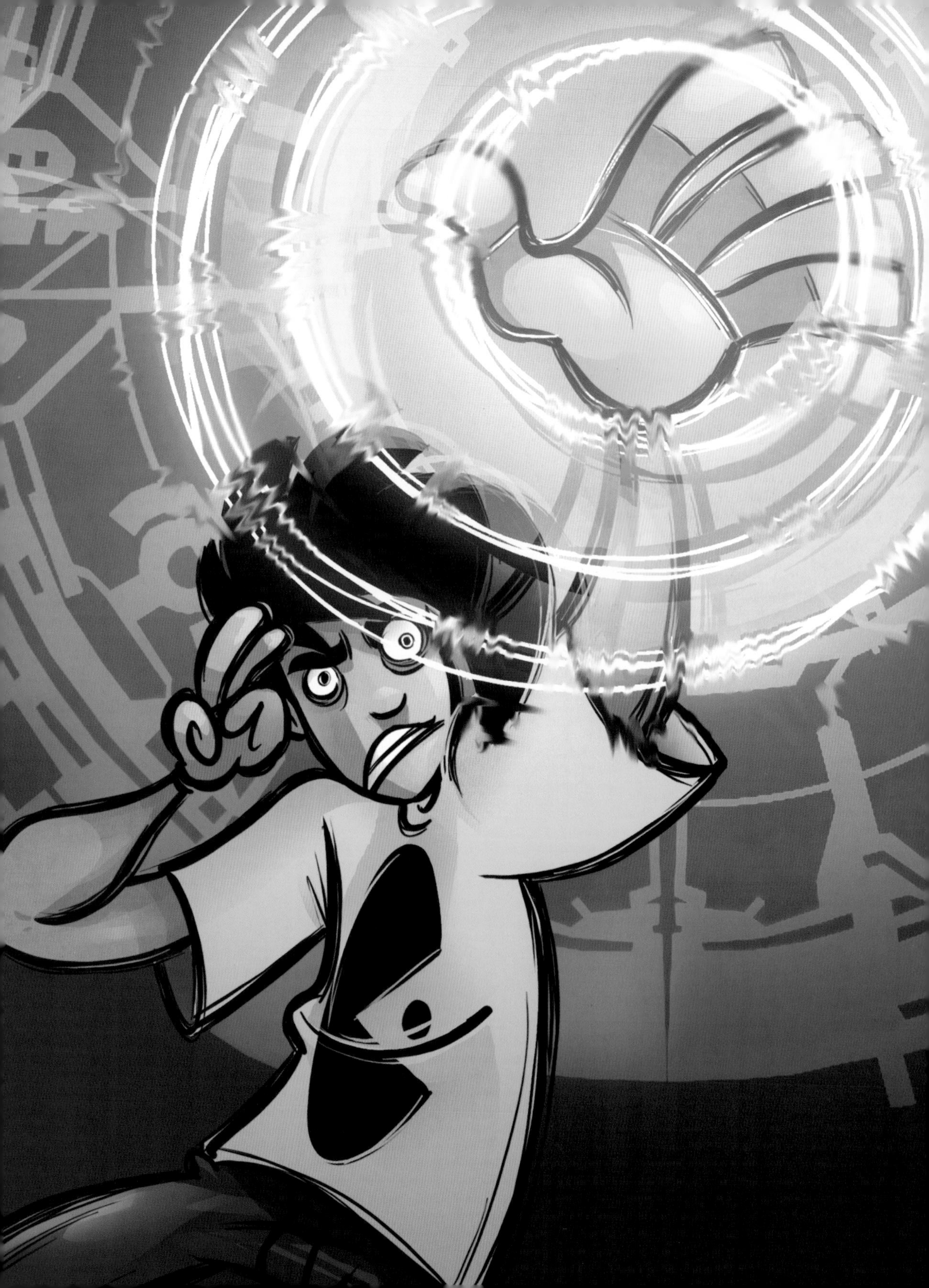

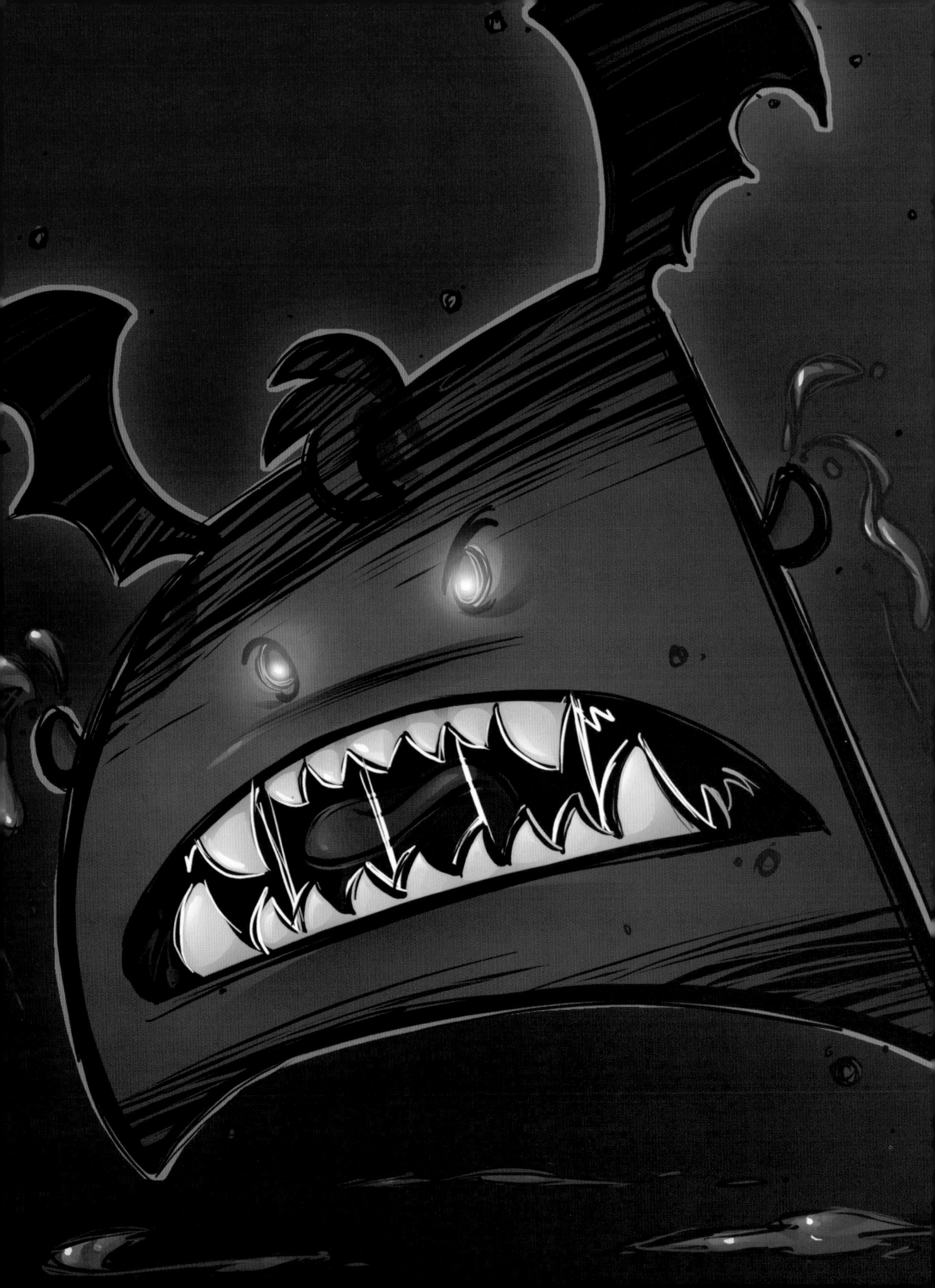

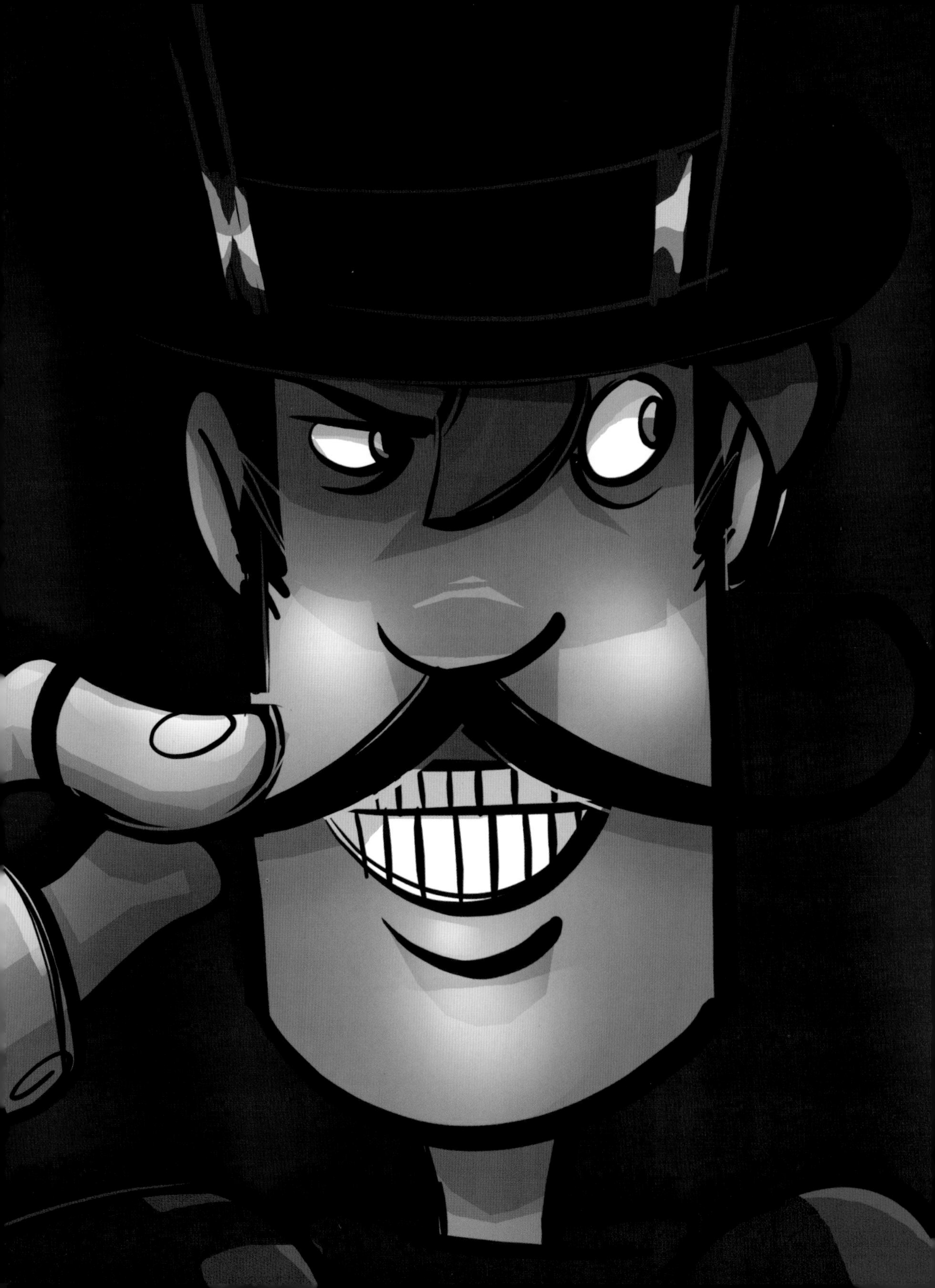

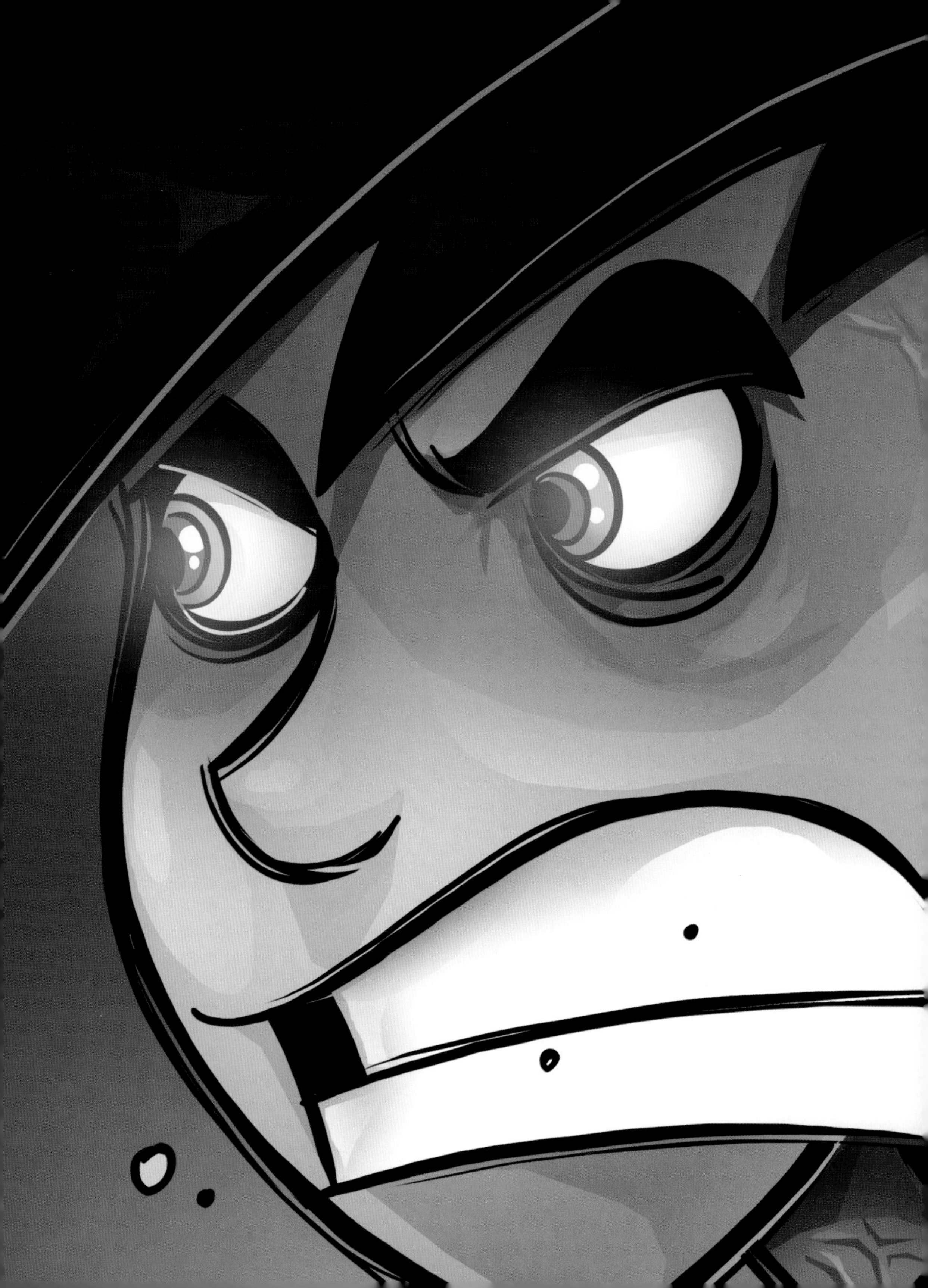

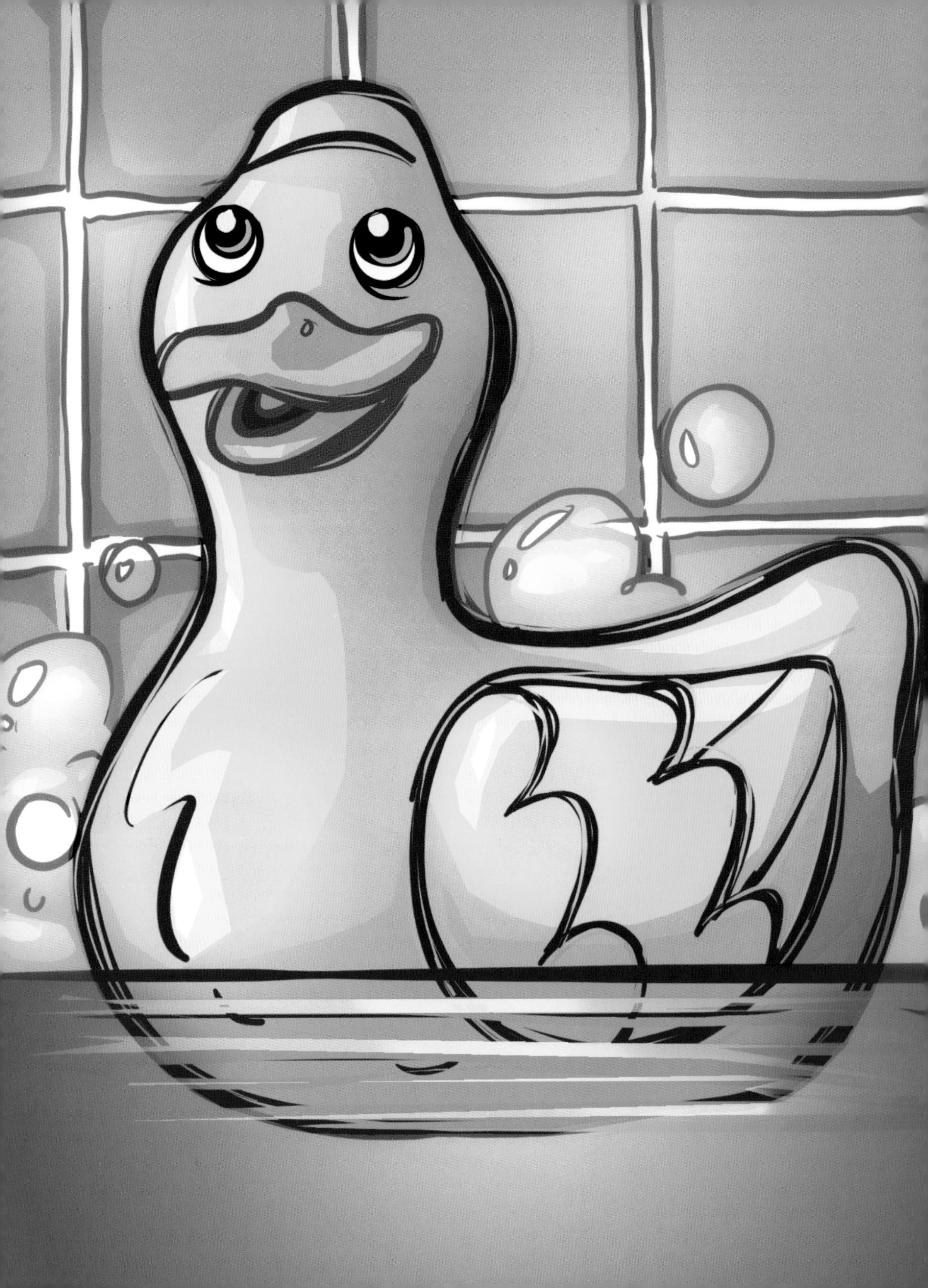

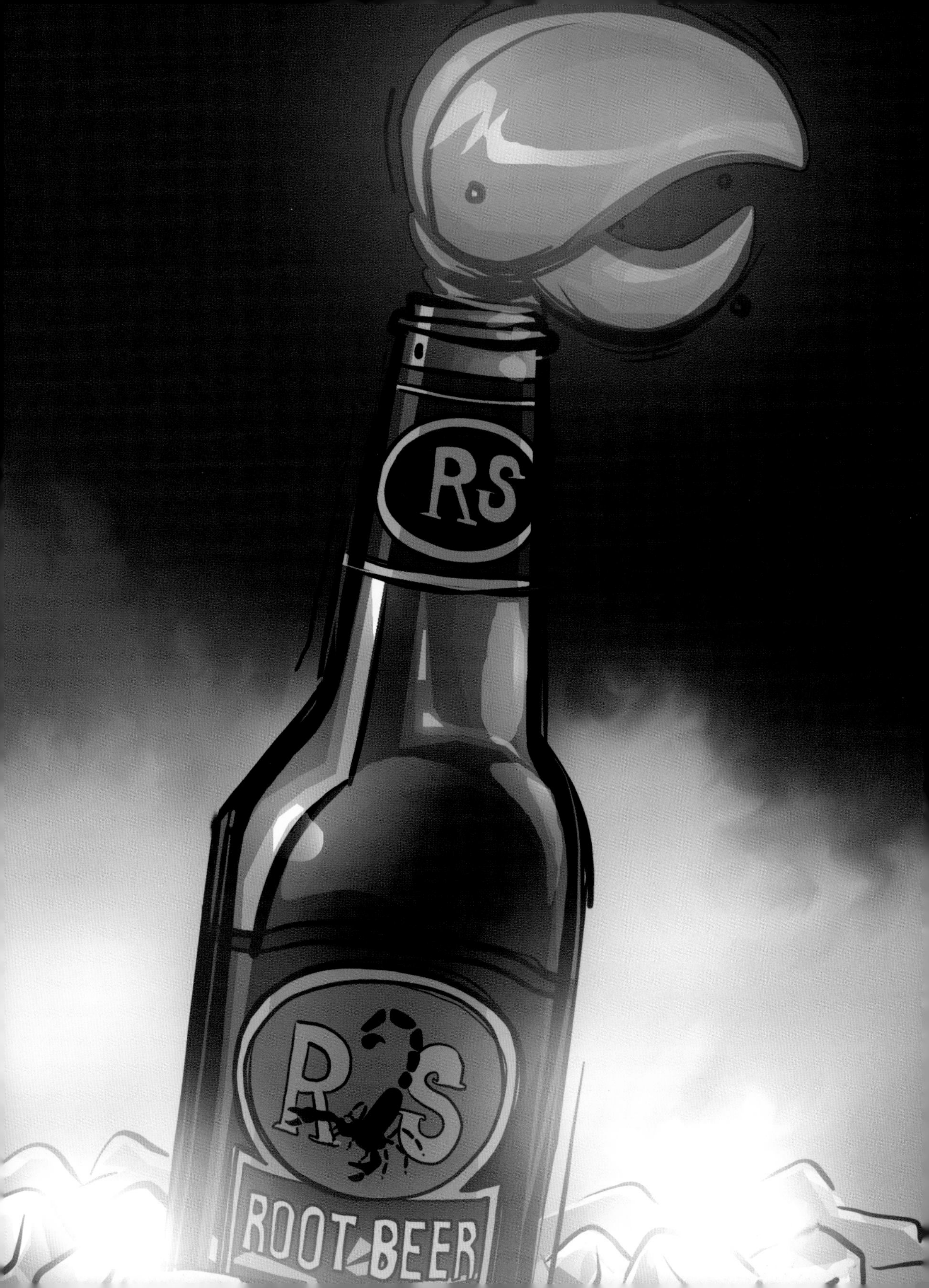
RS
RS
ROOT BEER

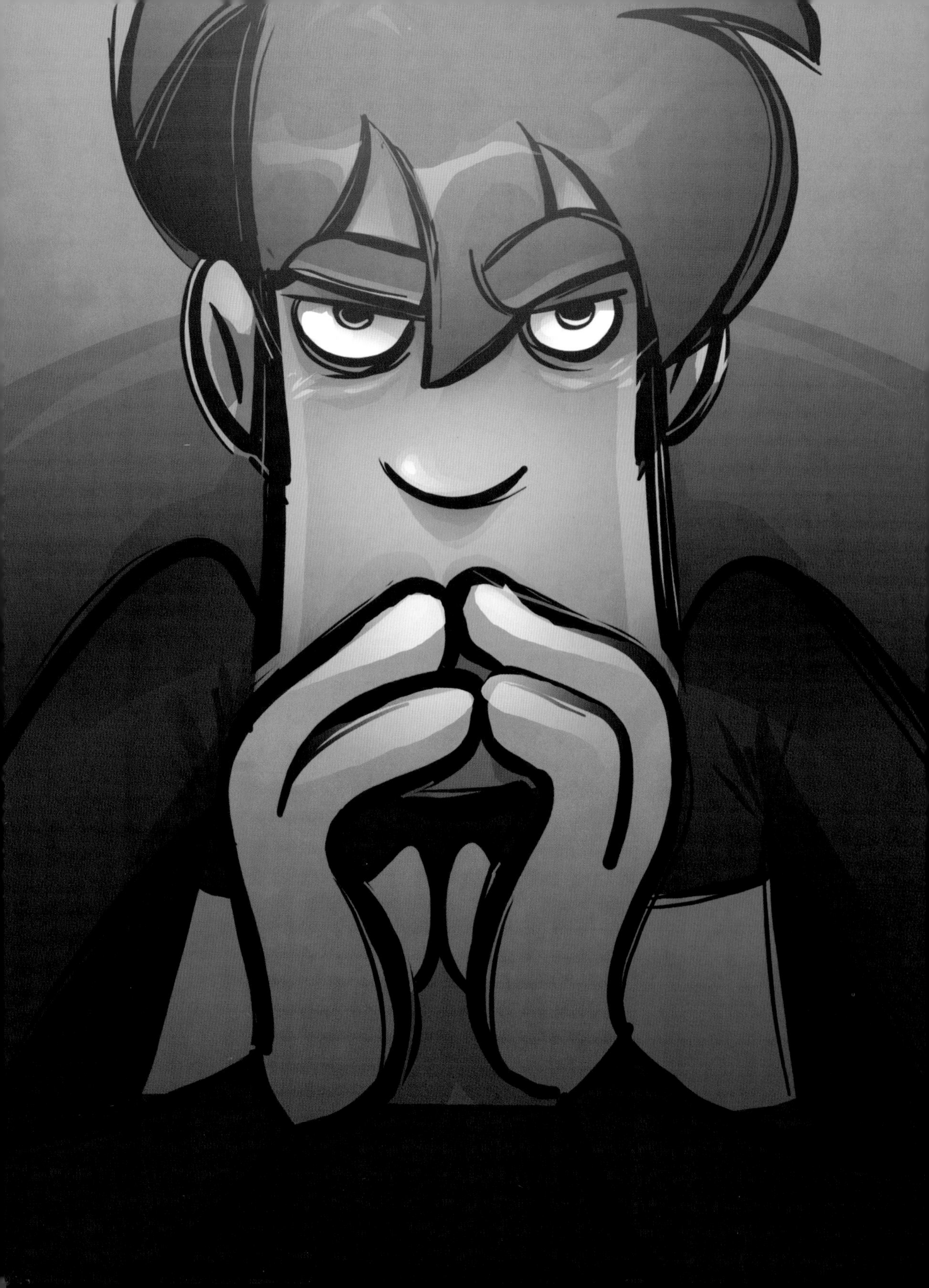

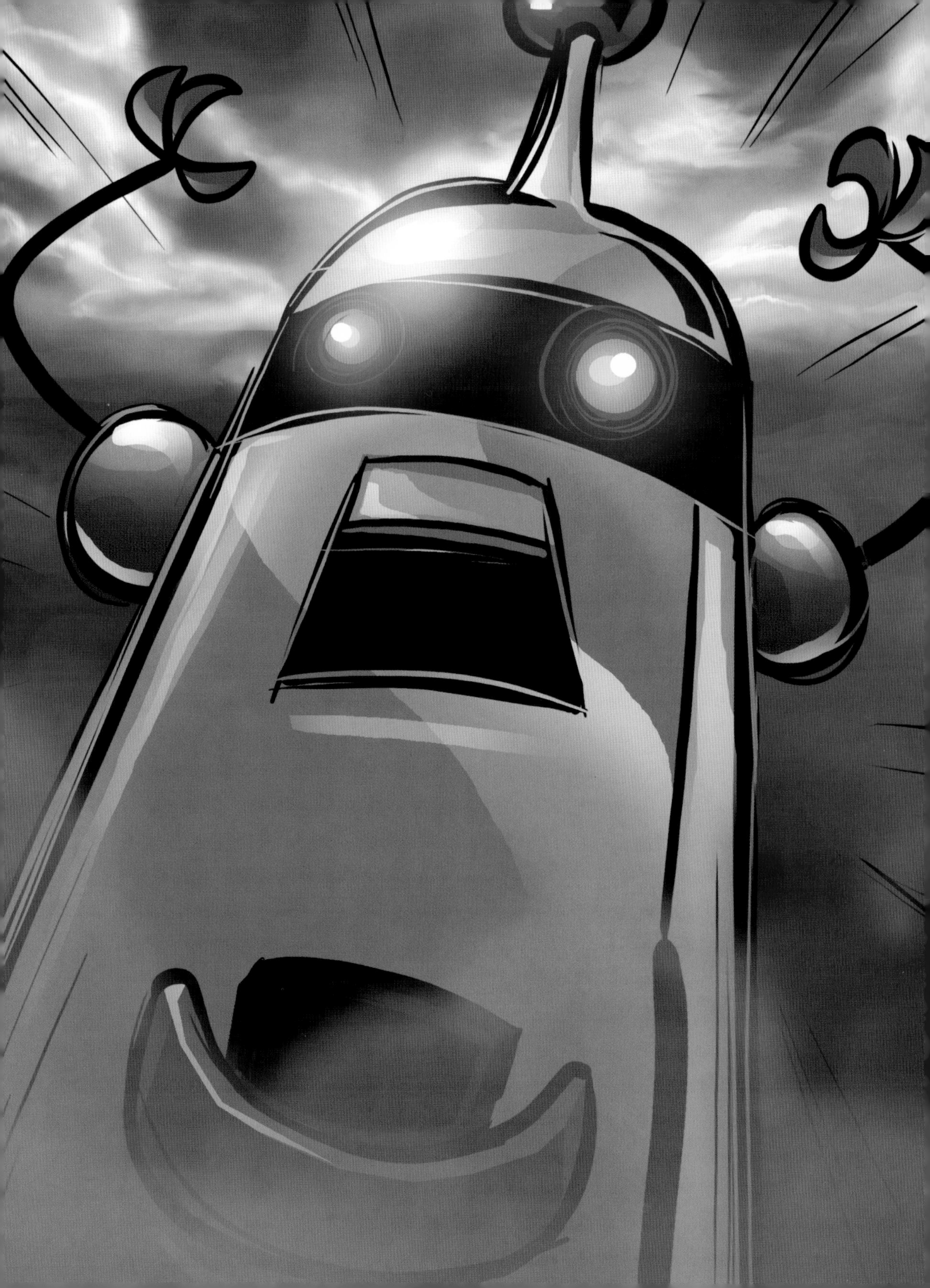

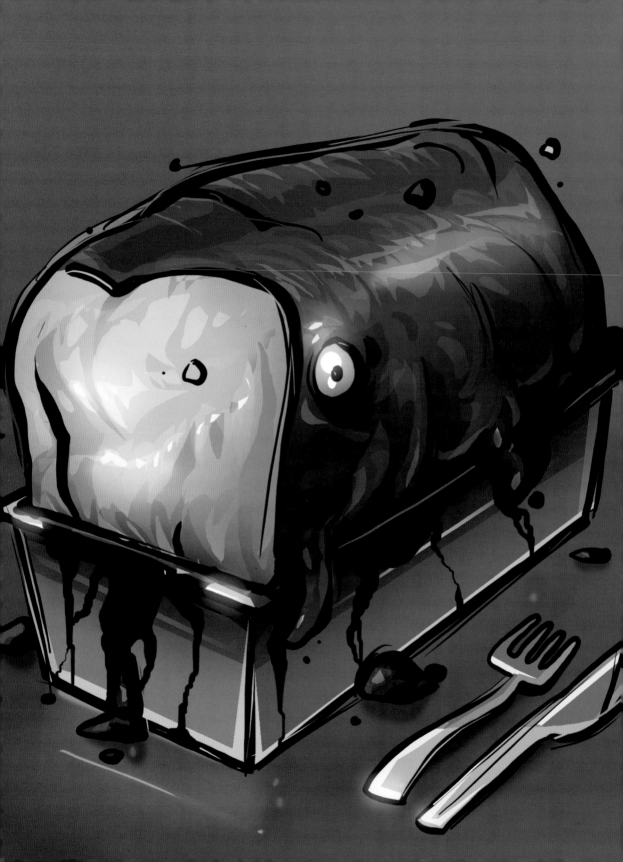

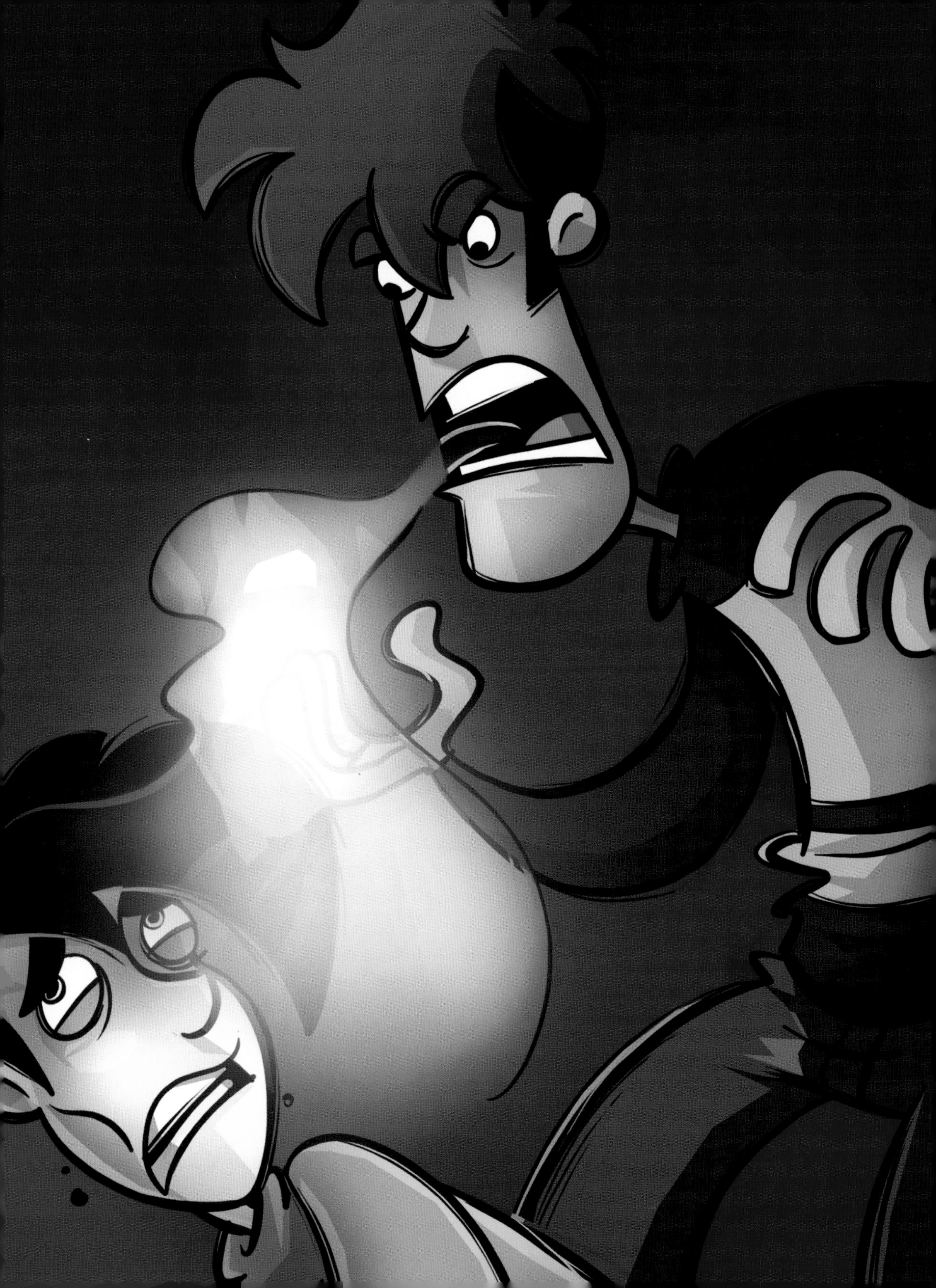

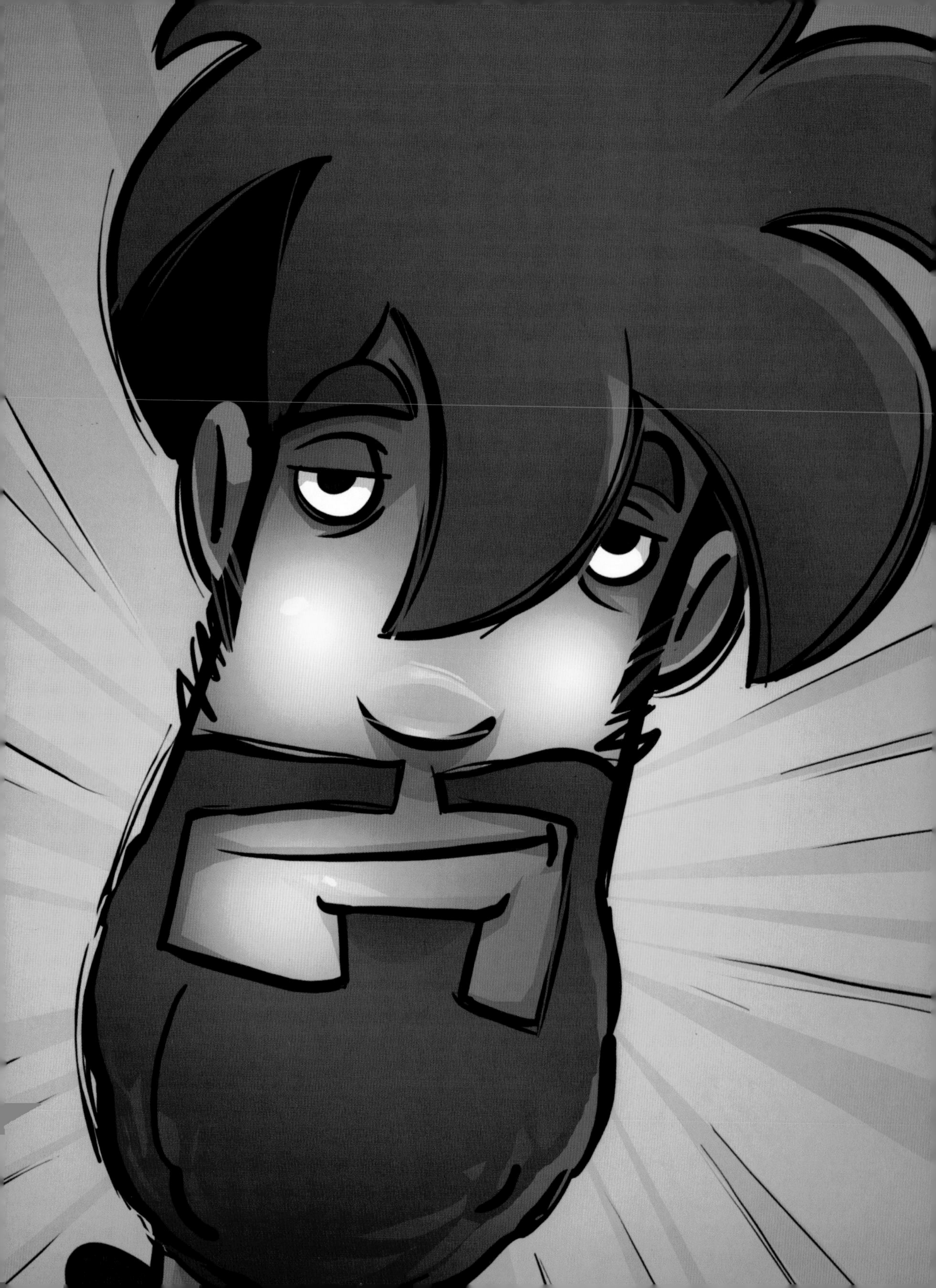

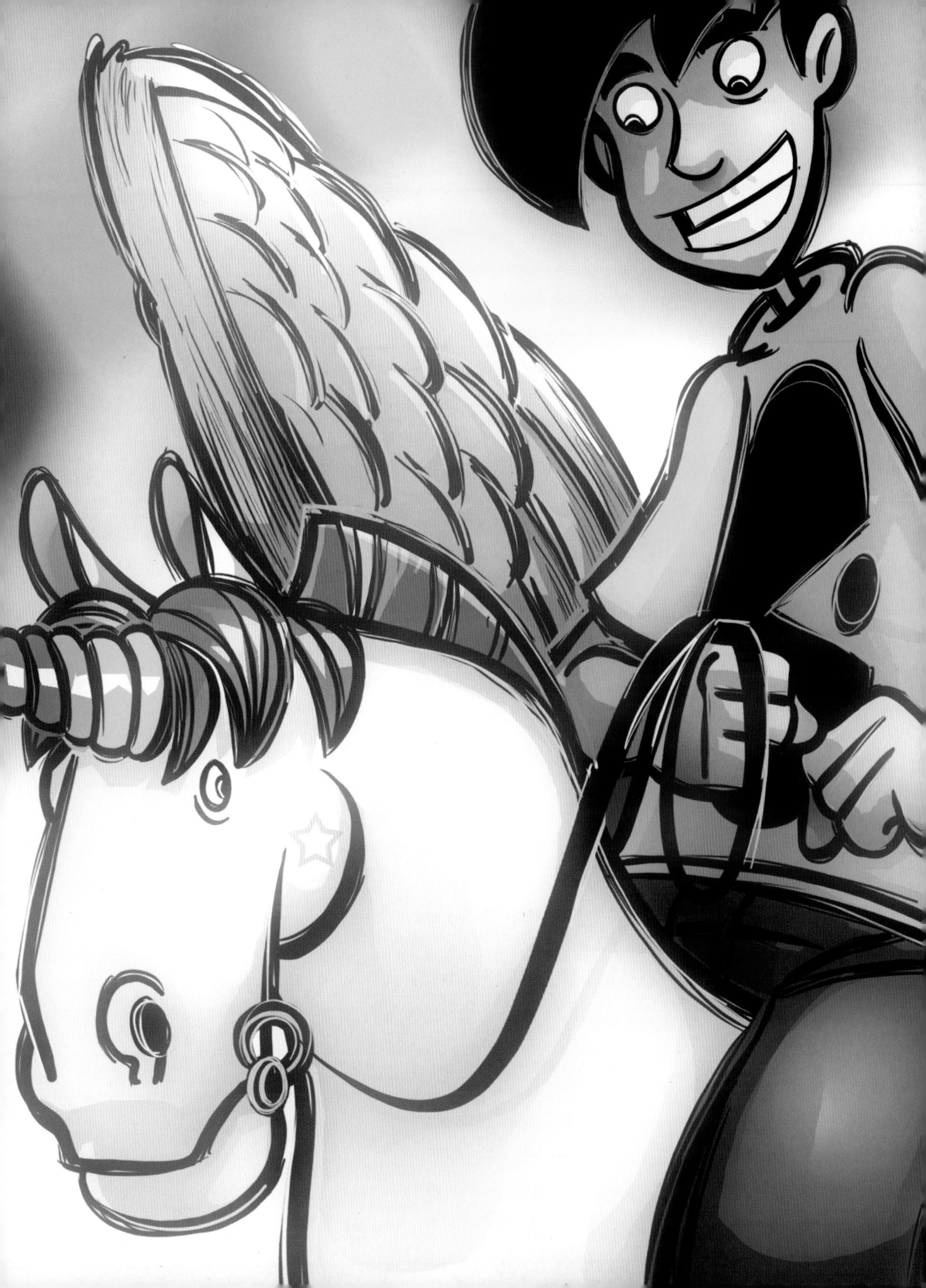

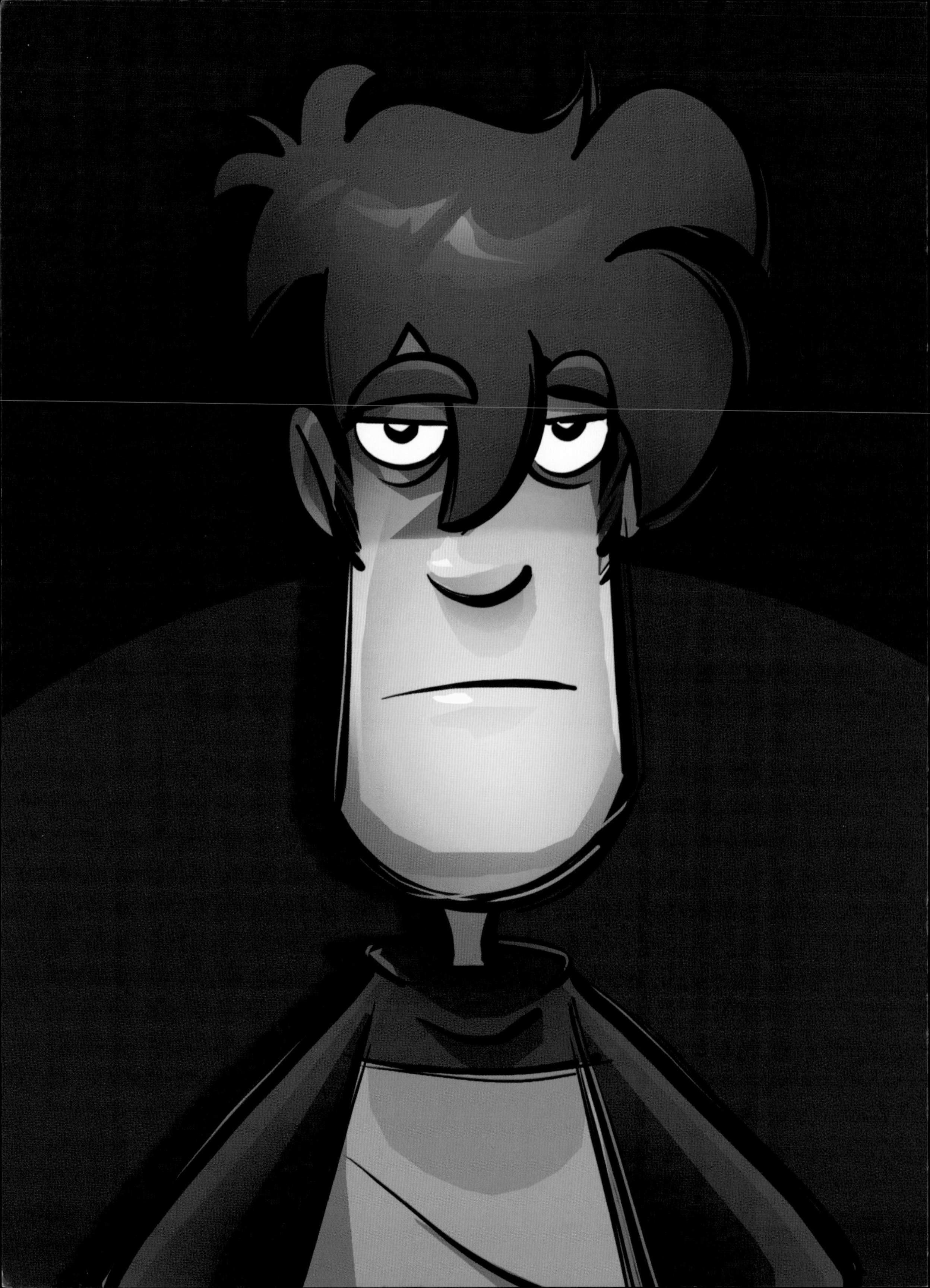

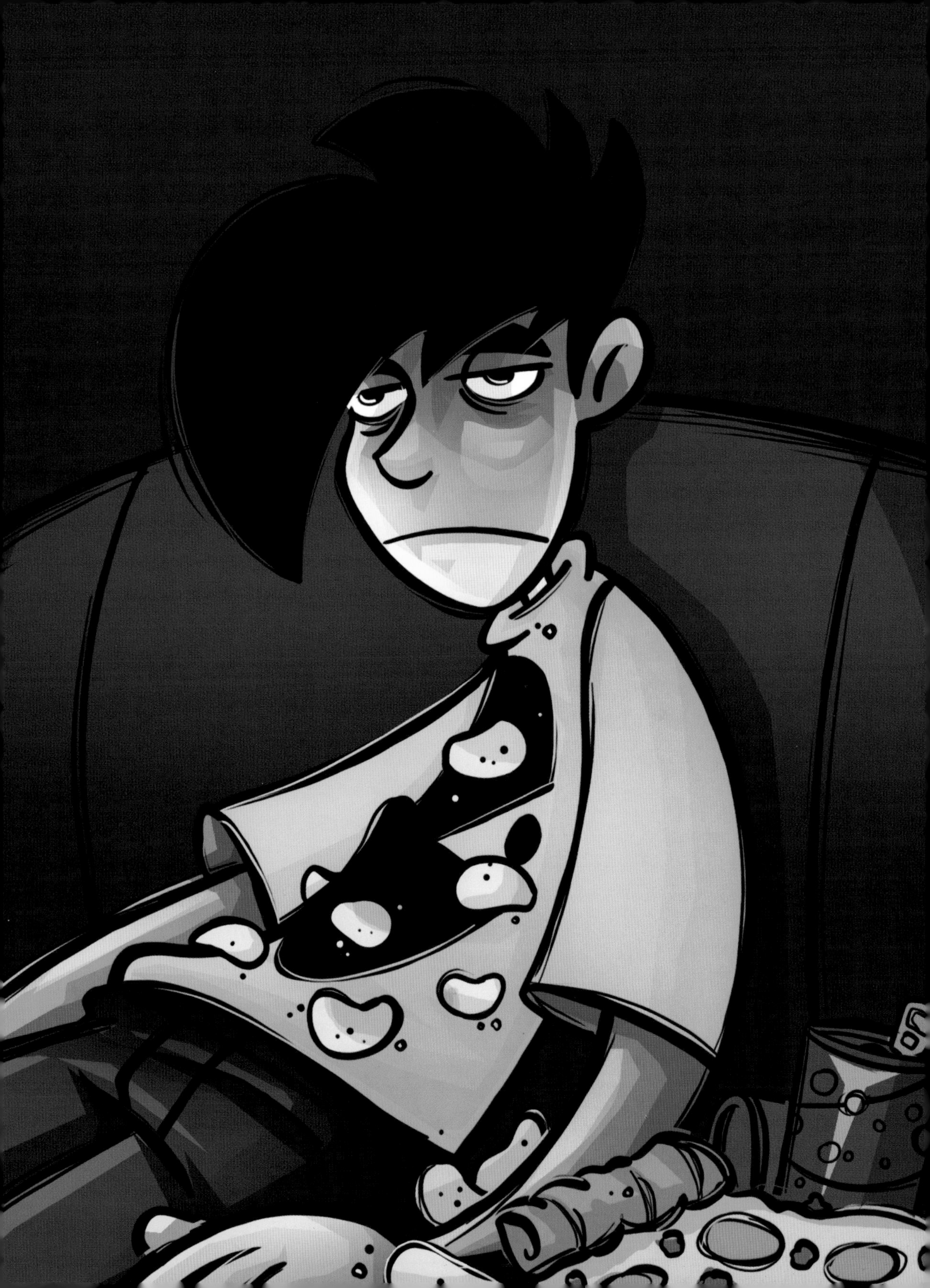

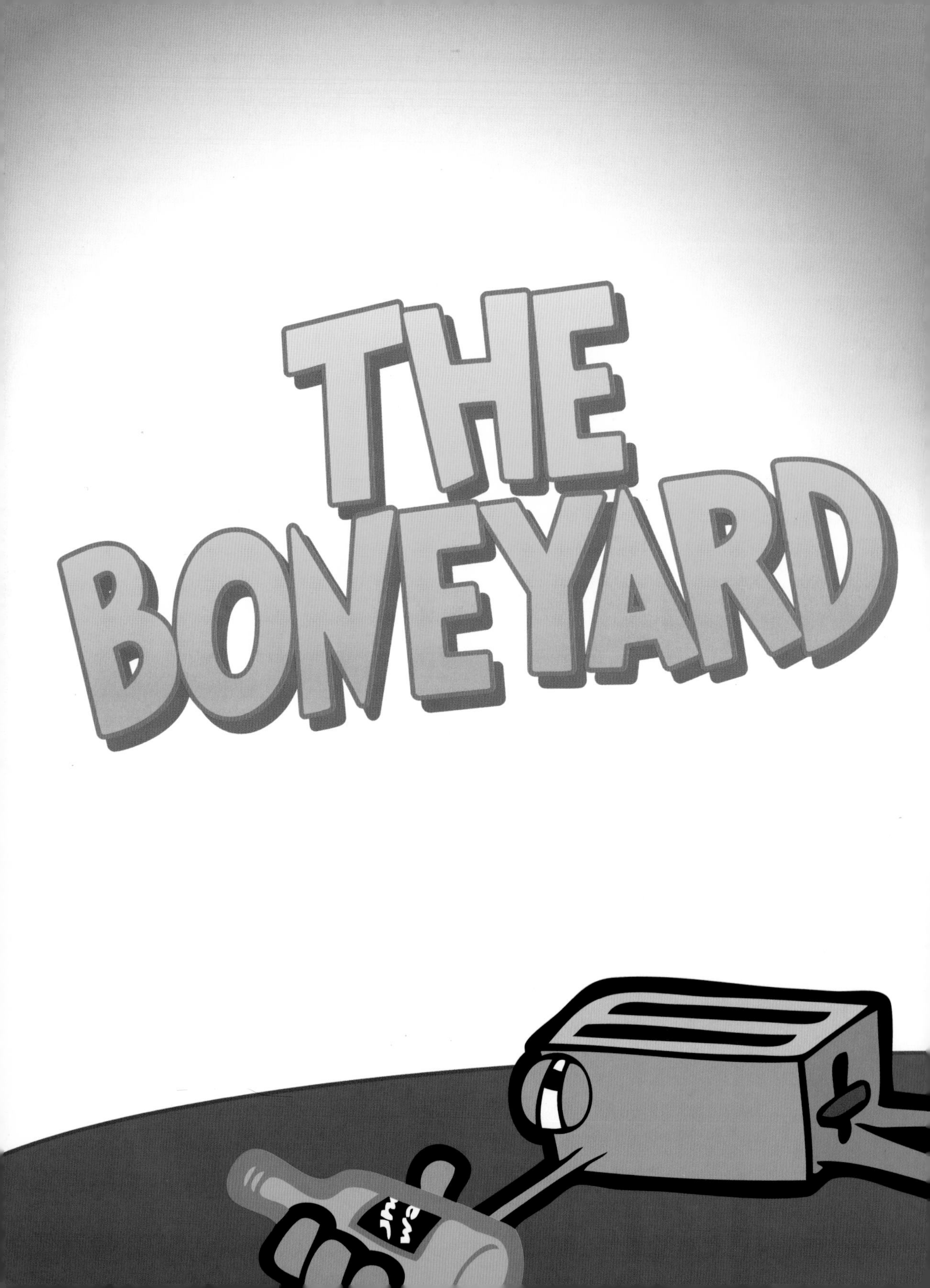
THE BONEYARD

At the beginning of the book, I told you that I never meant to become the voice of *Penny Arcade*. That isn't any less true here at the *end* of the book. But it isn't the only thing that hasn't gone according to plan.

Penny Arcade was one project that we were doing out of a handful of others. Being entirely serious, I was also writing a dark action serial Gabe had agreed to draw which featured bipedal walruses. We started hanging out almost expressly to *create* comics, serious comics that touched on heady themes. More often than not, we would then misuse the better part of the afternoon screwing around and playing videogames.

It's surprising that after more than *two years* of this, we never got any inkling of our destiny. No serious comics were going to be created—leastways, not by *us*.

But other projects do emerge from time to time, projects that we love with a terrible desperation, work on for a while, and then must set aside because there are only so many hours in a day. It happens more often then I'd care to admit. I don't think any of these things are super awesome amazing. Some of them are old, and I feel a little exposed showing them to you. I thought it might make an interesting feature for the book, though. I hope I was right.

SAND

Sand **was one of** the first projects we ever worked on, four or five years before *Penny Arcade*—the period scholars refer to as "BPA." It was something Gabe was doing perfectly well on his own, but I wanted *in* so I sort of insinuated myself into the project. That happens a lot, actually. Penny Arcade *itself* fits that description.

Sand is essentially a "weird west" version of the Old Testament, one that takes you roughly from Passover to the fall of Jericho. On the dry world of Deseta, the arrangement of that planet's political *board* inspires a damaged, ship-bound A.I. to fill in the gaps with clones. Actual events and holy writ are commingled as it begins to send out an increasingly insane series of messiahs. Jacob Phorr, pictured at right, is the first one we meet. By this time, the "chosen people" have had quite enough saviors, thank you very much, and aren't in the market for another. I really enjoyed putting this one together.

We were going to cook this project up for the *Flight Anthology*, which you might have heard of—the first two volumes of which are basically marvelous. In the end, we decided that *Sand* was superficially very similar to *Flight* editor Kazu Kibuishi's unbelievable Daisy Kutter series, and felt that aping him in his own God-damn book was probably impolite.

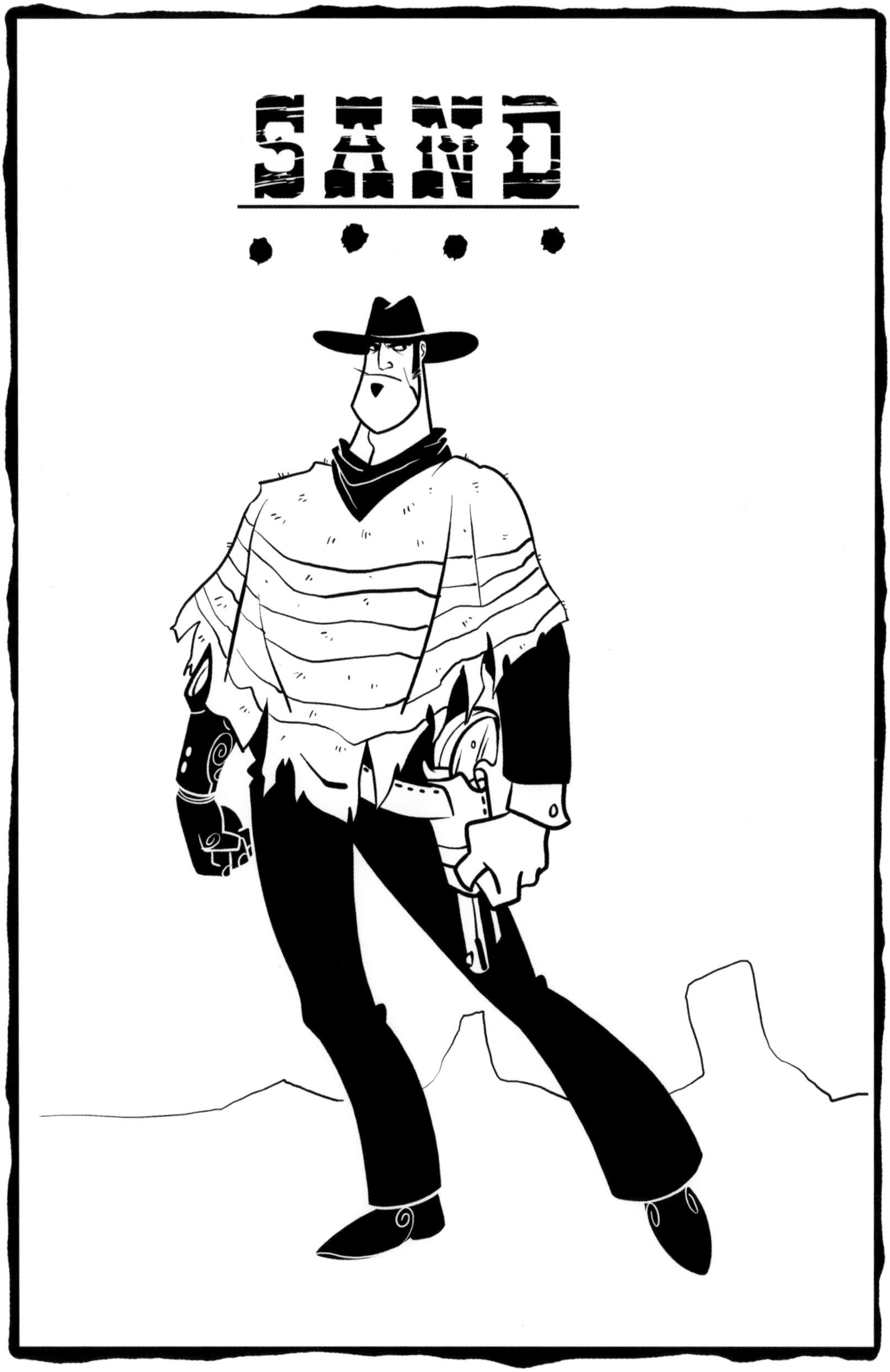
SAND

AUTOMATA

Realizing that Kazu's invincible output would shame anything we attempted in the vein of sci-fi westerns, we decided to scrap *Sand* for the second time. What we replaced it with was something we liked about a million times more. You could accurately say that we loved it.

Automata is a story about detectives during Prohibition.

Except what was being *prohibited* was "machine intellect," or sentience. It was done for a number of supposedly pragmatic reasons, which are actually just the window dressing for a handful of deep-seated moral ones. While production of the major brands came to a full stop—lines like the Hurley, Swangee, and Helpmate—the existing "stock" enters America in an uneasy third-class.

As a hard-bitten detective's "stenophone assistant," Karl Swangee solves crimes and has adventures. I hope that the version of me in Dimension X or whatever had a chance to do the comic better justice.

I had begun to develop a method of speaking, a language called "clickwise," that was a kind of cultural signifier for the robots that live in this setting. Like the comic itself, it never saw the light of day.

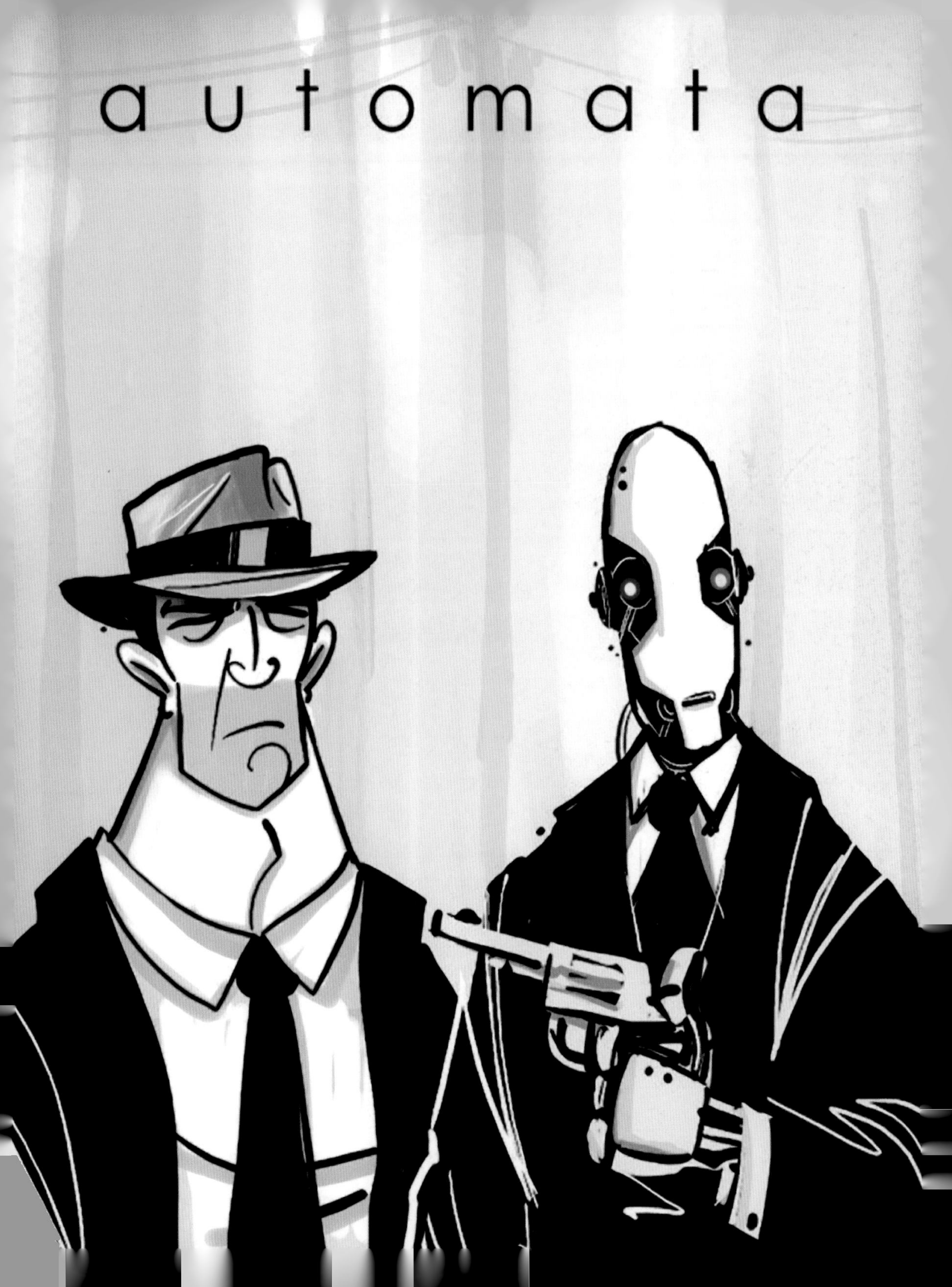
automata

CARDBOARD TUBE SAMURAI: PURITY

We really like the Cardboard Tube Samurai, but I don't think affection for him is anywhere near universal. So, out of consideration, we only utilize him once a year. It's the same with Twisp and Catsby. There is a lot of enthusiasm on our end, but we go out of our way not to beat you about the head and shoulders with them.

We decided to investigate the (ahem) "origins" of the CTS in a special project created with members in mind.

In case we ever get around to completing it, I don't want to go too in-depth as far as the story is concerned. That isn't to say there is a *lot* of depth. We're still who *we* are, doing the sorts of things we do. That said, there's a good deal more than usual going on. I would say that "redemption" is not a common theme in *Penny Arcade*.

We do introduce the Tycho of that continuity, as well as a potentially interesting new long-term enemy. I thought that we had actually completed more of this story than we did. I've imagined the pages after this so often and in such detail that I'd begun to assume they were real.

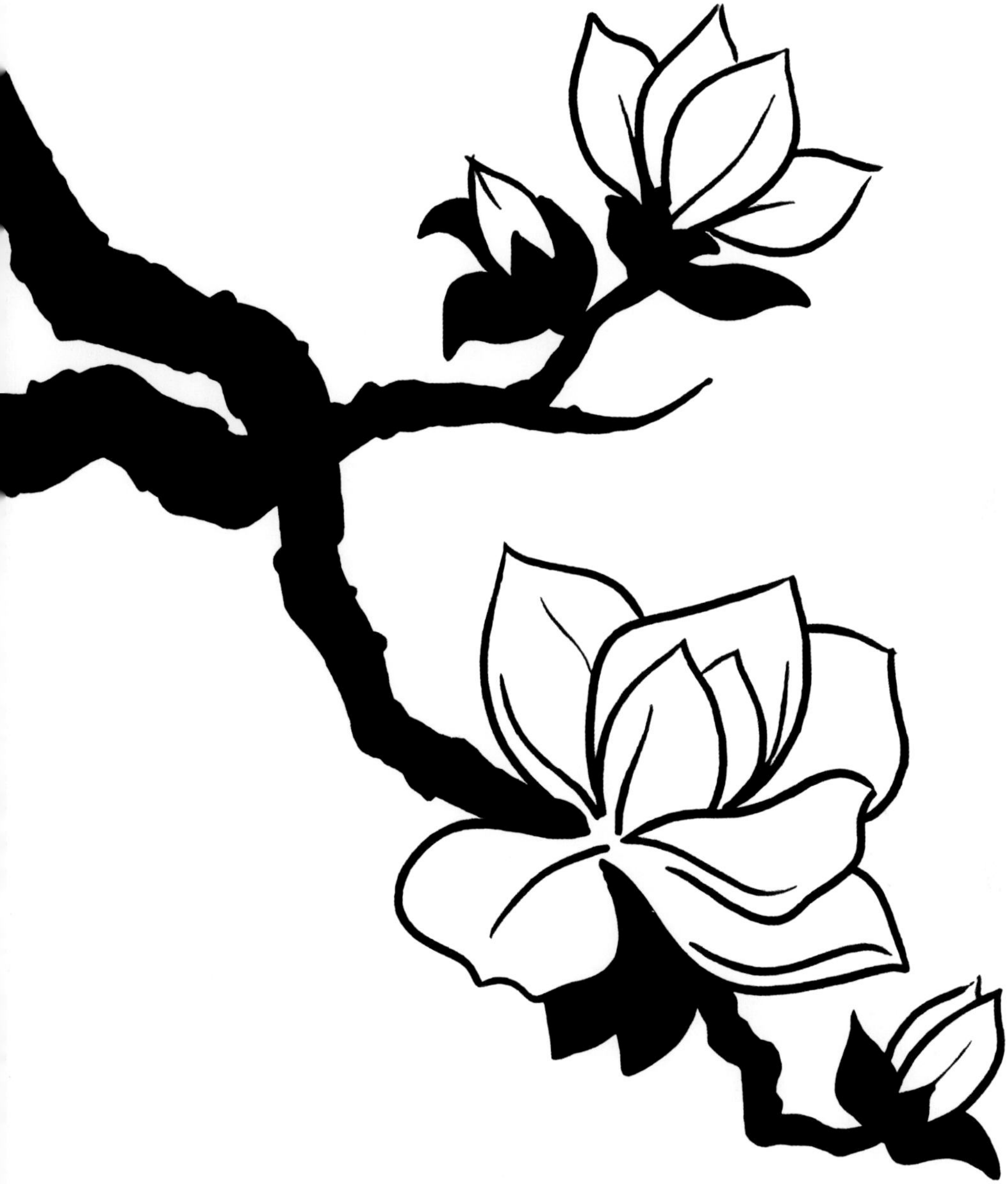

Chronicle of Cardboard Tube Samurai

PURITY

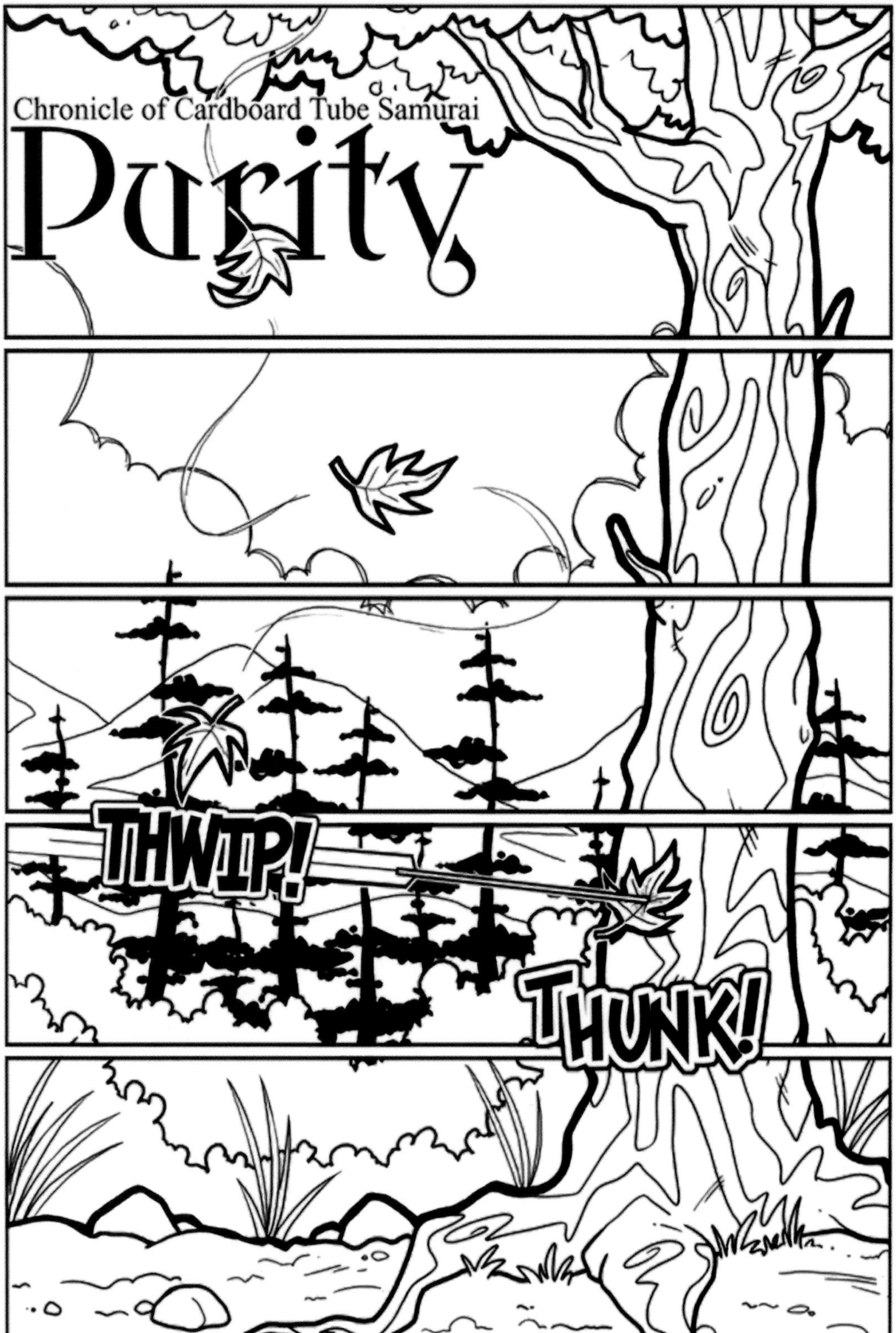
Chronicle of Cardboard Tube Samurai
Purity
THWIP!
THUNK!

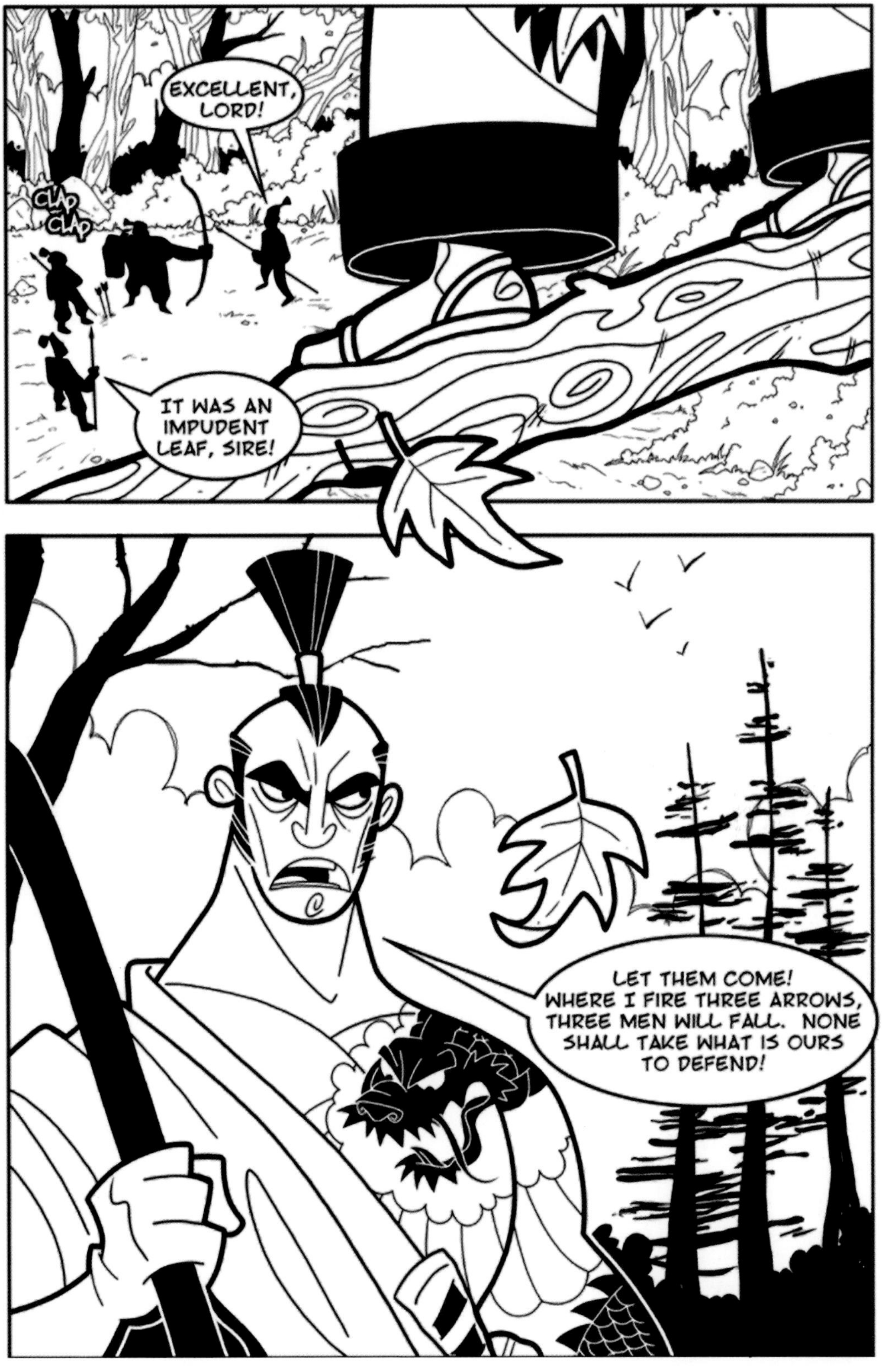
EXCELLENT, LORD!
CLAP CLAP
IT WAS AN IMPUDENT LEAF, SIRE!
LET THEM COME! WHERE I FIRE THREE ARROWS, THREE MEN WILL FALL. NONE SHALL TAKE WHAT IS OURS TO DEFEND!

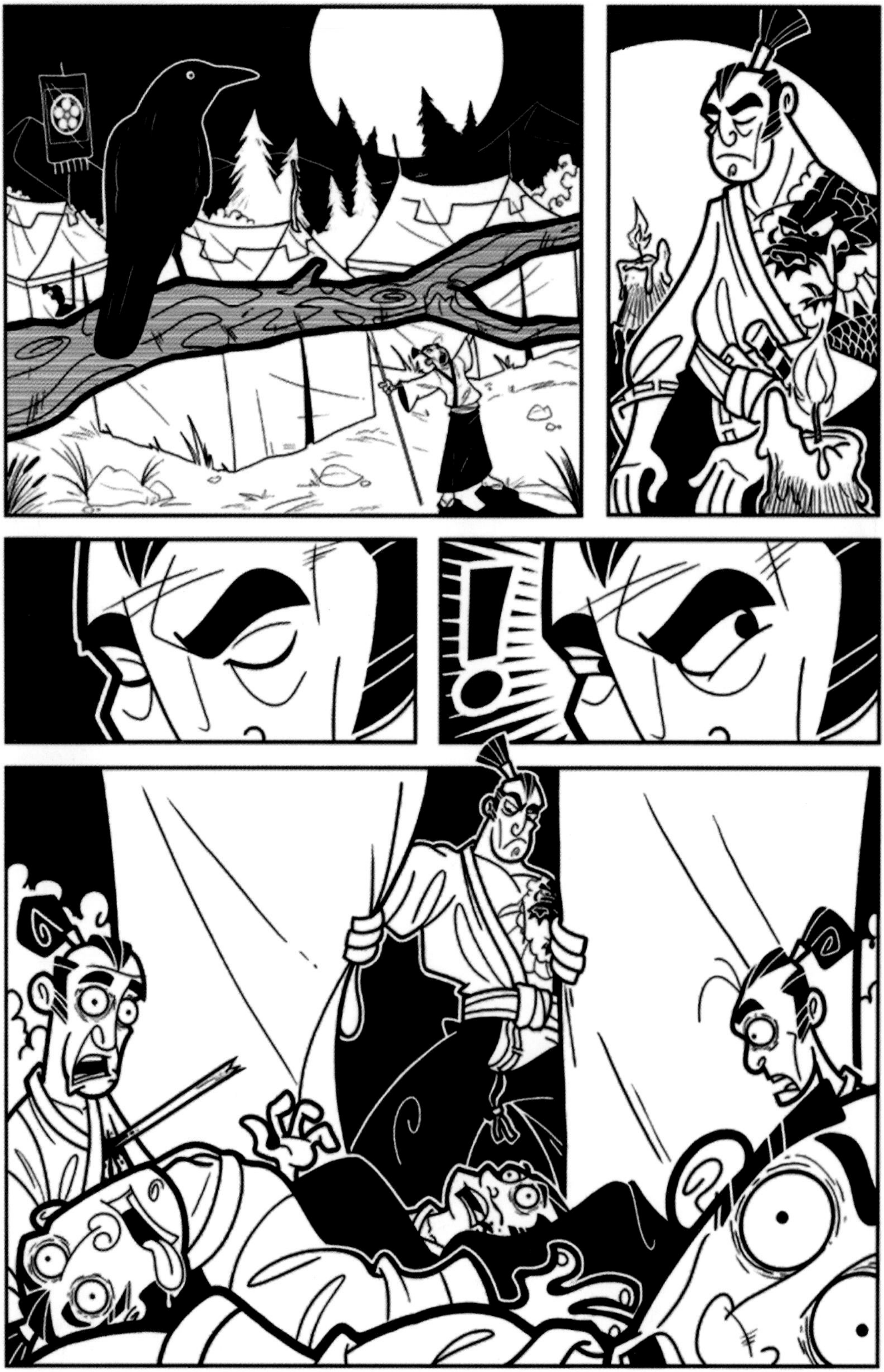

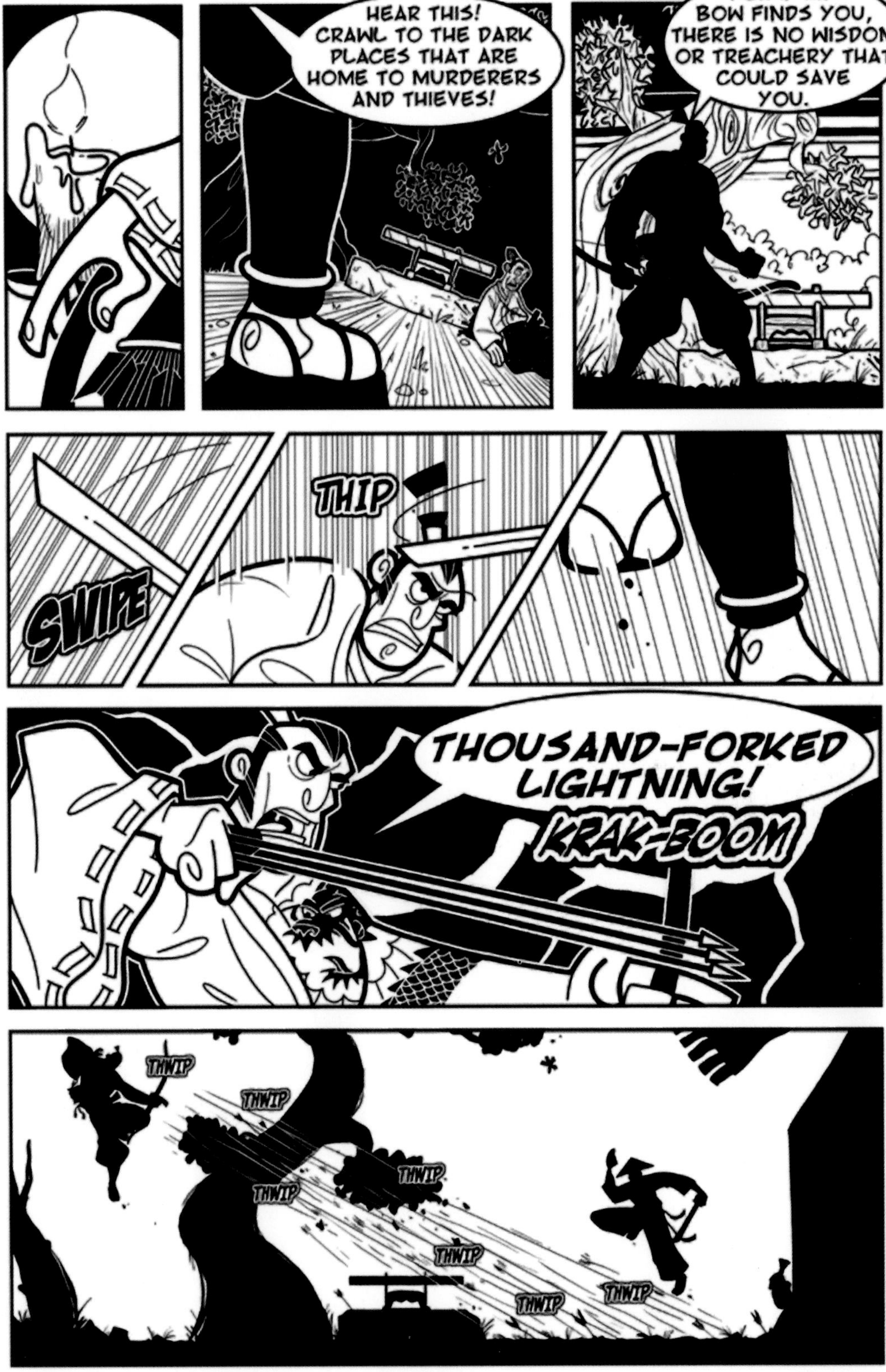
HEAR THIS! CRAWL TO THE DARK PLACES THAT ARE HOME TO MURDERERS AND THIEVES!
FOR IF MY BOW FINDS YOU, THERE IS NO WISDOM OR TREACHERY THAT COULD SAVE YOU.
SWIPE
THIP
THOUSAND-FORKED LIGHTNING!
KRAK-BOOM
THWIP
THWIP
THWIP
THWIP
THWIP
THWIP
THWIP

OVER-EASY

Our take on John Woovian action cinema, we had the idea almost immediately after starting *Penny Arcade*. After we began running solely on donations, it seemed like a concept we could investigate for the people who were supporting the site. We did so.

We finished what I'd call the "first chapter," four pages of which you can see here. It's apparent by the end that *Over-Easy* became a playground Gabe could use to experiment with different line styles and coloring techniques. Some of these crept into the strip itself for a time, an outcome I rejoiced in. They went away, but like the proverbial Summer of '69 it is always a period I will look back on with fondness.

We were looking for an action sequence we hadn't seen before, and so settled on a motorcycle helmet being used as a bludgeoning weapon. Something similar would appear later in *The Matrix Reloaded*. I am not saying that they stole it, but certainly we felt vindicated in our choice.

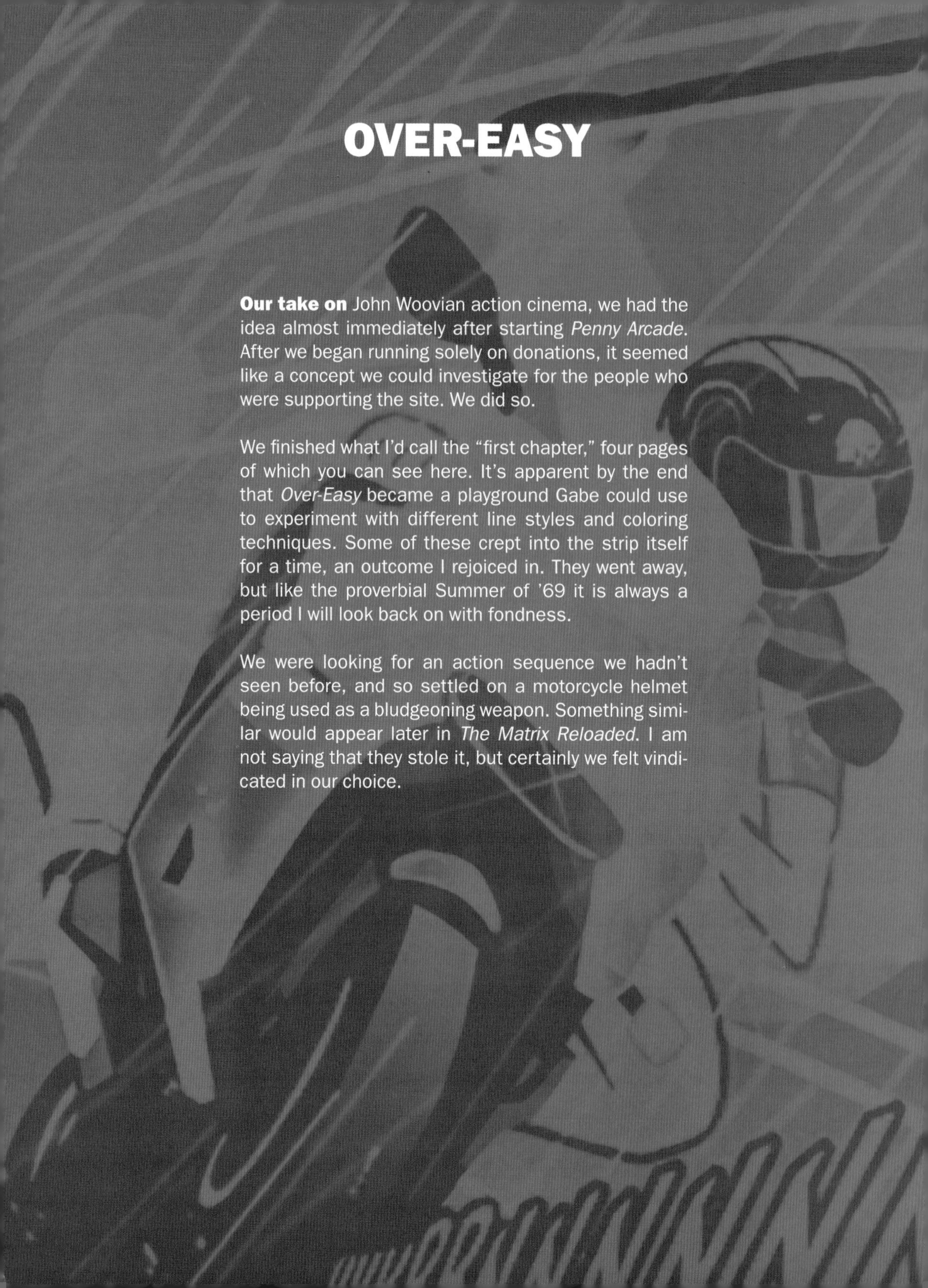

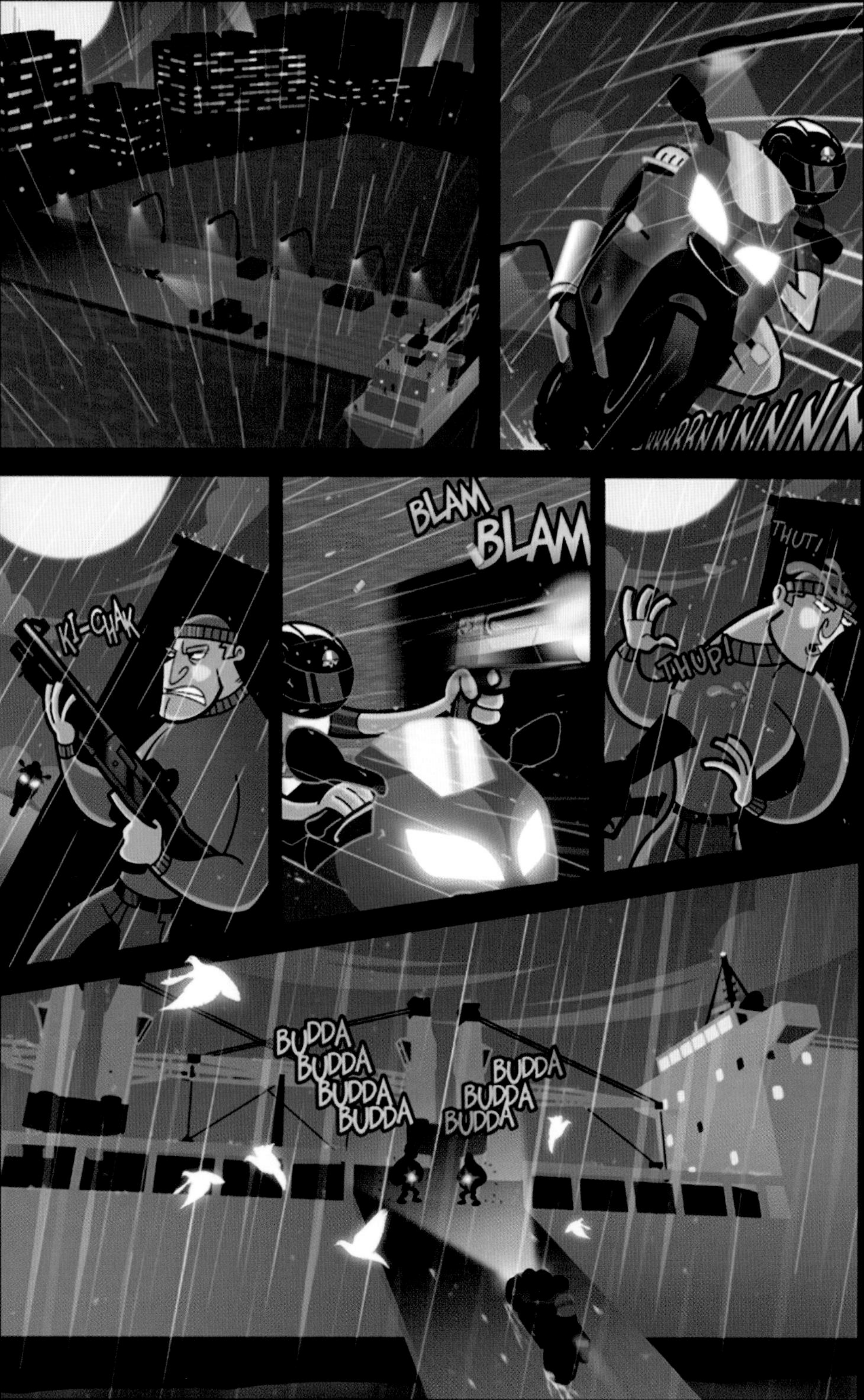
VRRRRNNNNNN
KI-CHAK
BLAM
BLAM
THUT!
THUP!
BUDDA
BUDDA
BUDDA
BUDDA
BUDDA
BUDDA
BUDDA

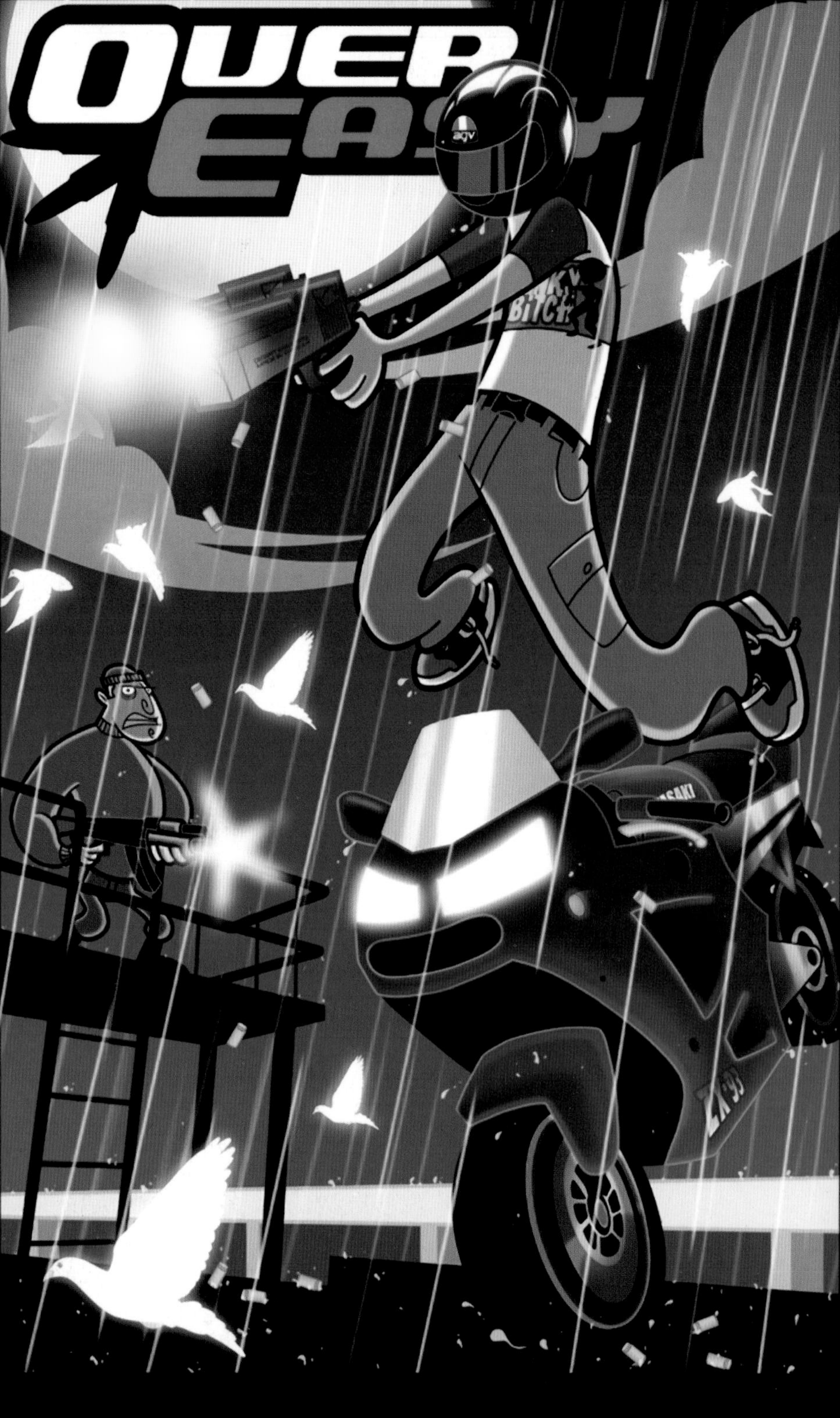
OVER EASY
agv
BITCH

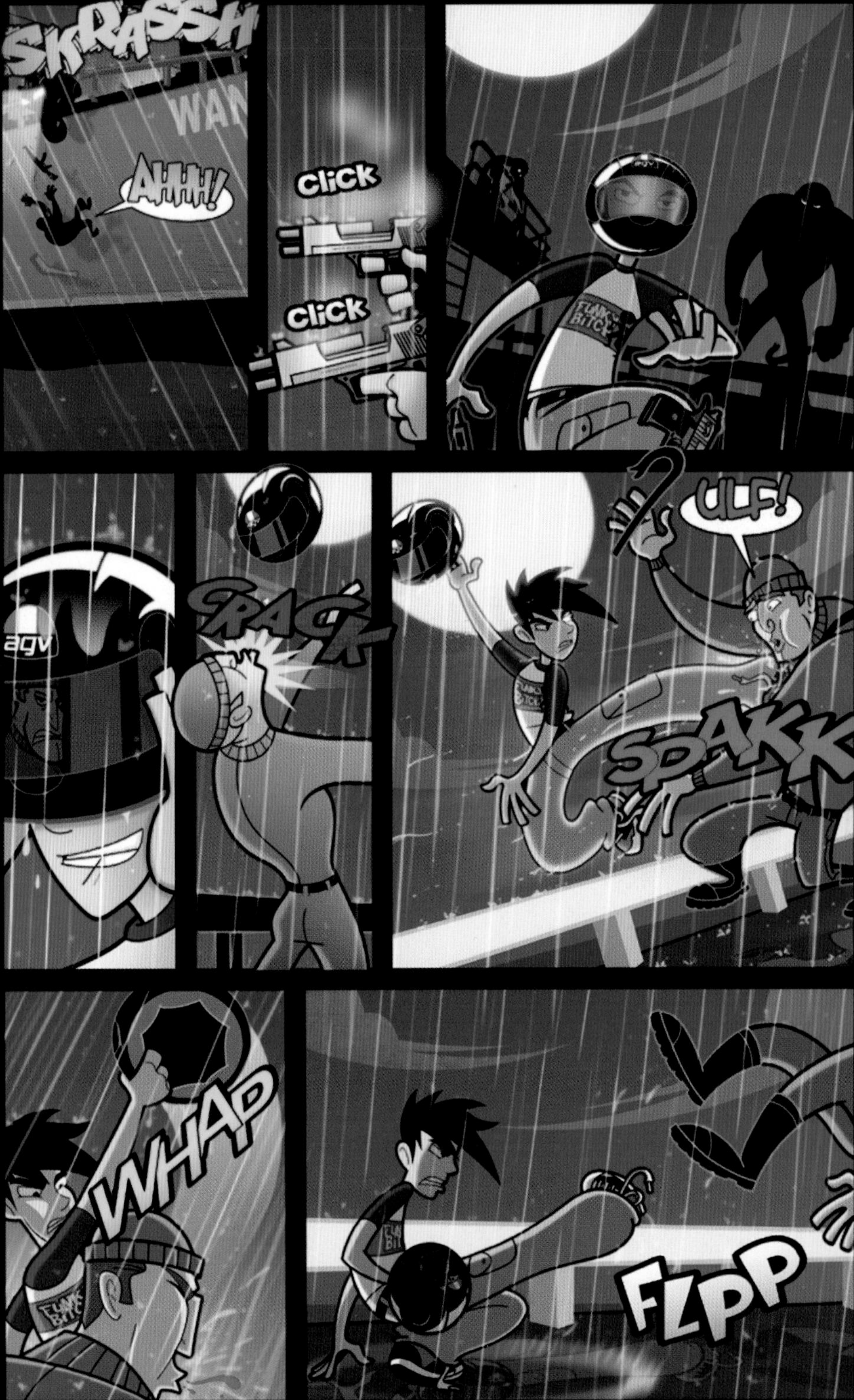
SKRASSH
AHHH!
click
click
agv
CRACK
ULF!
SPAKK
WHAP
FLZPP

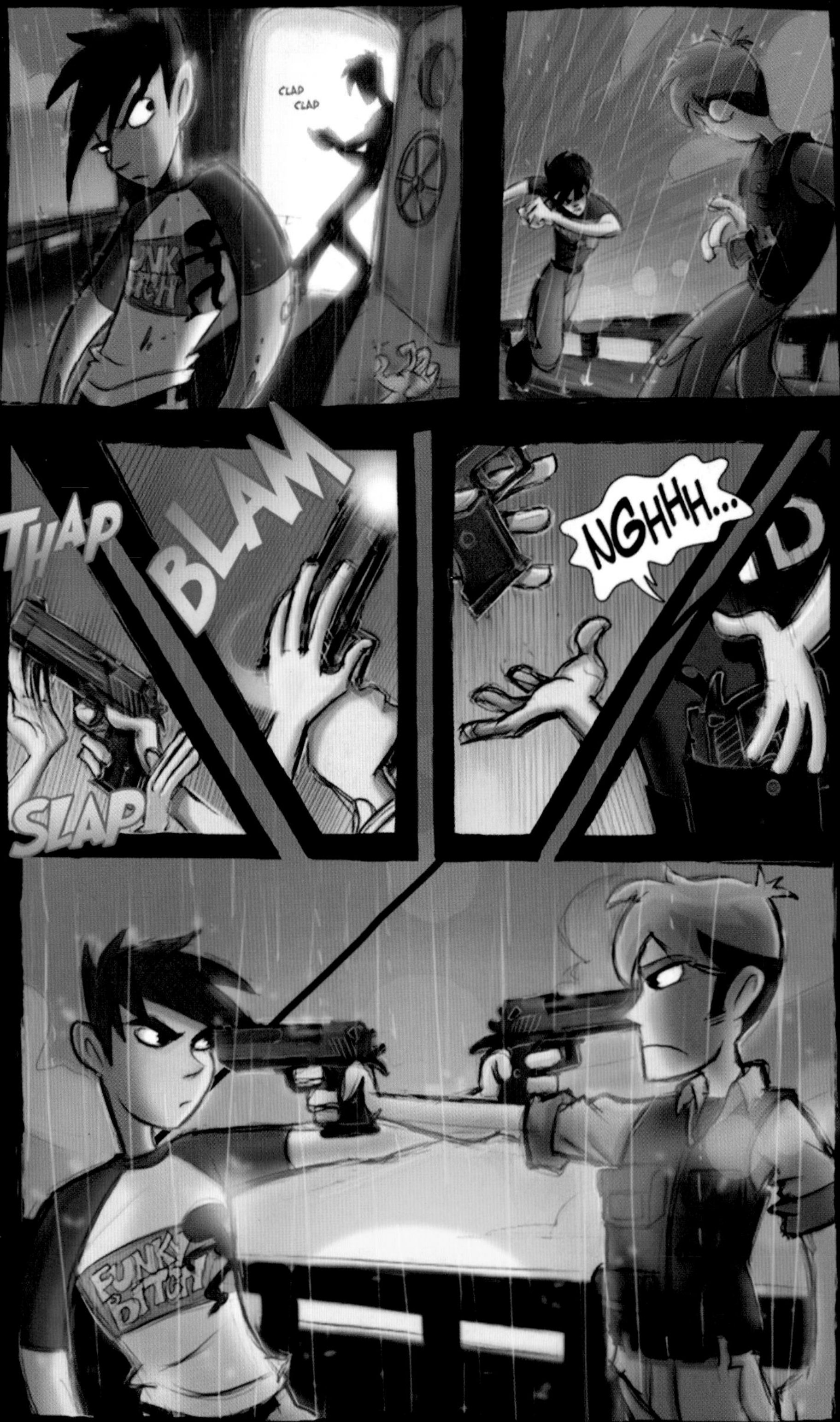
CLAP
CLAP
THAP
BLAM
SLAP
NGHHH...
FUNKY BITCH